Table of

Introduction..v

**Part I: Welcome to Our World—Parenting with
a Difference**..1
   1. Getting the Most Out of Life / 5

Part II: Taking Care of Yourself 15
   2. Put Yourself on the To-Do List / 19
   3. Ya Gotta Have Friends / 39
   4. Get Through the Day—Fuel Up with Food / 49
   5. Stay Strong and Healthy—Get Physical / 67
   6. Desperately Seeking Sleep / 81
   7. Fighting Your Inner Darkness—Anger, Anxiety,
      and Depression / 97

Part III: Daily Life—Reality Check 123
   8. The Time Crunch / 127
   9. Find the Help You Need / 151
   10. Advocacy 101—Speaking Up for Your Child / 169
   11. Taking Charge of Your Finances / 189
   12. Create a Positive Future / 205
   13. Legal and Financial Steps to Planning Ahead / 221

Part IV: Family Ties..**231**

   14. Who's Minding the Marriage? / 235
   15. Just the Two of Us—Finding Time and Energy to
       Nurture Romance / 247
   16. The Joy of Siblings / 255
   17. Grandparents and Extended Family—Getting Them
       on Board / 265

**Part V: Overcoming Barriers to Quality Care—Childhood
through Adulthood**..**273**

   18. Figure Out What Type of Care You Need / 277
   19. When Regular Care Options Don't Work—
       Custom Care Ideas / 301
   20. The Hunt for Care / 307
   21. After the Hunt—Keeping the Care, Once
       You've Found It / 319
   22. Paying the Price for Quality Care / 327

Part VI: Career and Home—The Ultimate Juggling Act....**335**

   23. Know Your Legal Rights at Work / 339
   24. Build Workplace Support / 347
   25. Explore Flexible Work Options / 355
   26. Cut Back, Take Off, or Call It Quits / 367

Part VII: Redefining Your Work Life......................................**381**

   27. Get Ready—Establishing Goals / 387
   28. Get Set—Changing Your Work Situation / 399
   29. Go! Finding and Landing the Perfect Job / 411
   30. Be Your Own Boss—Starting a Home-Based Business / 423

Part VIII: Transformations—From Struggle to Strength ... **435**

   Appendix 1. State Leave Policies / 447
   Appendix 2: Provincial (Canadian) Leave Policies / 451
   Appendix 3: Sample Flexibility Proposal Memo / 455
   Appendix 4: Checklist for Child Care Re: Special Needs / 457
   Appendix 5: Sample Caregiver Interview Questions / 459

Resources...**461**
Related Reading **472**
Research References **474**
Index **481**
Acknowledgements **487**

Introduction

How It All Began

Amy's Story

It all began with my daughter, Talia, now age thirteen. At three, she was diagnosed with autism. I spent my days researching cures on the Internet, phoning agencies for help, meeting with therapists, reading autism books, and taking my daughter for outings (while she cried and had tantrums). I had little time to spend with my older daughter, Leah. On "dates" with my husband, Jack, we'd talk endlessly about what we should do. For several years, I felt like my own life was slipping away. I even lost my name. Everyone referred to me as "Mom"— except my younger daughter, of course.

Managing Talia's days became my full-time job. Jack took over at night and on weekends, so I could squeeze part-time teaching and writing into the corners of my life. I began writing about my own mothering experience.

Eventually, I started noticing other moms of kids with special needs. Many, like me, worked sporadically or were at home full-time. Appropriate child care that would enable them to work didn't seem to exist. Some said they had lost the skills and the confidence to ever return to the workforce.

Like me, these moms presented competent images to the outside world. We all smiled, advocated for our kids, and attended meetings and appointments. But seldom did we admit our exhaustion, depression, or lack of time to ourselves. I wondered why these issues were never talked about.

Heather's Story

Robyn, who's now fifteen, was three when she suffered a startling setback. Our girl with the golden curls woke up one day changed. Normally happy to play on her own for hours, she clung to us, whining. She stopped eating and was too frightened to leave the house. Emergency doctors and specialists discussed possible causes—brain tumor, encephalitis, epilepsy, autism. My husband, Dave, and I were devastated. Over the next six months, these symptoms gradually subsided with no medical explanation or treatment. Although back to her "normal" cheery self, we started noticing subtle delays in her motor and communication skills as compared to her three-year-old playmates. Less than two years later, she was diagnosed with Asperger syndrome, a mild form of autism.

During Robyn's early years, I was a partner in a successful technical communication consulting firm. My hours were flexible and I worked from home. When Robyn's crisis hit, I'd already cut back on my workload, because her sister Karin was only six months old. Like Amy, I started reading autism books, joining listserves, trying alternative therapies, and hiring preschool workers. I soon stopped doing paid consulting altogether and started volunteering with a local autism advocacy group. There, and at a parent/child program that Amy taught, I met Amy.

Why We Wrote This Book

How did the idea for this book get started? While attending a disability conference, we browsed together at the book display tables. Although we saw plenty of "how-to-parent-your-disabled child" books, as well as collections of essays by parents, we couldn't find what we craved—a book answering questions about our own lives.

We wanted to know if we would ever get our lives back. Could we manage the intensity of raising our children with disabilities and still maintain our marriages, be good parents to our other kids, keep up our friendships, and have careers? How could we stay healthy—both physically and mentally? Would we always feel such grief, or would our lives move on?

We wrote this book to answer those questions. We've blended current research, our own experiences, and the wisdom of more than 500 mothers of children with special needs to offer advice, reassurance, and hope.

We are extremely grateful to the women who openly shared their successes, challenges, and emotions. We contacted disability organizations in the U.S. and Canada that kindly agreed to post our request for survey respondents in their newsletters and websites. We also connected with special needs parenting groups on the Web. Then, women completed online surveys about their home and work lives, their relationships, their ways of taking care of themselves, and their plans for the future.

To get a long-term perspective, we also contacted mothers of adults with disabilities. They described how they had changed over time and answered the question: "If you had to do it all over again—what would you do differently?" Soon, our request for respondents spread by word of mouth as far away as Israel and the Philippines. We are thrilled that the community of mothers of children with special needs have joined together to have a voice.

Initially, we feared that women wouldn't have the time or energy to complete our lengthy surveys. Fortunately, that wasn't the case. Their answers were rich, detailed, and honest. It seemed to be the first time someone had asked mothers how they, themselves, were doing. The quotes in our book are the words of these women—although their names have been changed to protect their privacy.

Reading about mothers' lives was the most rewarding part of our research. While some stories were inspiring and encouraging, others were heartbreaking. Some women described living with unsupportive relationships, poverty, exhaustion, and poor health.

In addition, some researchers who had studied mothers of children with special needs contacted *us*—excited about our project. As we dug deeper into published research, we found results that mirrored responses from our own surveys.

It has been deeply rewarding to research an issue we care so passionately about. Reading the advice of so many mothers, interviewing experts, and poring through studies have changed our own attitudes and behavior. Writing about future planning was particularly empowering. Peering into the lives of women and their adult sons and daughters encouraged us to start thinking about the future now. We've learned about small steps we can take now to plan for the years ahead.

In addition, we were struck by how mothers of children with such varying disabilities face such similar issues. When we set out to write the book, we wondered how we could make it equally relevant for mothers of children with physical, developmental, and mental health disabilities. We needn't have worried! All mothers of children with special needs shared similar joys, struggles, and transformed life perspectives. We are awed at the sense of community we share.

If you're the mother of a child with special needs, we hope you find your own experiences within these pages. You'll read about other mothers living challenging, sad, joyous, and fascinating lives. At the same time, you'll find practical strategies for adding balance, joy, health, and comfort to your own daily life, whether you're at home or in the workforce. And you'll learn that, over time, you'll grow stronger, richer (although maybe not financially), and more multifaceted because of the challenges you face.

A word about fathers: Of course, fathers' lives are also deeply affected by parenting a child with special needs. Many work extra hours to finance therapies, attend appointments, and do hands-on therapy and medical procedures. A few care for their children full-time at home. But, at present, it's usually mothers who bear the primary responsibility for managing home and family life (even when they are working full-time). So, in turn, it's the mothers who typically find their own lives most significantly altered. While both parents share common issues, there are also concerns unique to men and women. So we decided to tackle the issues singly—focusing, in this book, on mothers. We do think, though, that fathers, siblings, extended family members, and friends can all gain important insights from this book. In addition, this book can help service providers, professionals, and advocates better understand the families they work for.

Ultimately, we hope this book helps change our communities so that all mothers and their families can fully participate and thrive.

PART I

Welcome to our World

Parenting with a Difference

S everal times each weekday, Brenda receives a phone call from school. Her son has a connective tissue disorder that causes his joints to dislocate up to fifty times per day. He also has a life-threatening allergy to latex. Within minutes, Brenda arrives at school to perform a painful procedure on her son. Expertly, she "reduces" his dislocations by sliding his bones back together. Brenda's precision and confidence come from lots of experience—her other son has the same disabilities.

As the mom of two children with disabilities, Brenda says it's almost impossible to earn an income, or even search for a job. Finding time to be with her husband is also challenging. In their eight years of parenting, they have been away together only once—for an overnight at a bed and breakfast thirty minutes from their home.

Despite these difficulties, Brenda is proud of the strengths she's developed over the years. "I'm more confident," she says. Recently, she taught seminars about latex allergies to hospital department heads. As a Parent to Parent support volunteer for Easter Seals, Brenda also counsels parents of children with similar disabilities. "Life can feel overwhelming," she says. "But I've learned to treasure the good moments—even if it's just five minutes out of a really hard day."

Brenda's far from alone. The National Survey of Children with Special Health Care Needs (U.S. Department of Health and Human Services, 2001) found that one out of five families has at least one child with special needs.

Women like Brenda take on a parenting role beyond anything they'd anticipated. They become their child's case coordinator, nurse, therapist, and advocate. They learn psychological jargon, medical procedures, and teaching skills. While coping with exhaustion and frustration, they learn stamina. They care for their children with disabilities without formal training and with limited recognition and support from the community.

Only a few decades ago, many children with disabilities were in institutions. Today even the most fragile children are primarily cared for at home, usually by mothers. But sufficient community supports for families have not materialized. With medical advances, children whose conditions once meant early death now live well into adulthood. While parents cherish the extra time with their loved ones, they worry about how they will care for their adult child as they age themselves.

Parents face not only extraordinary caregiving realities, but also financial struggles. Even though dual income families are the norm in North America, there are few supports that enable mothers of special needs children to continue working. Quality child care is hard to find and often expensive.

Mothers at home face other challenges, such as isolation and lack of time to maintain their own health. Since respite funding and services are limited, it can be difficult for them to take a break. As a result, hobbies, fitness, friendships, and outside interests can diminish or even disappear.

Whether working outside the home or not, extraordinary parenting responsibilities can create extraordinary pressures. Mothers always feel they should be doing more—researching a new therapy or medication, making another phone call, advocating for an essential program. Even handling their child's paperwork takes endless amounts of time. Most also feel unable to balance out the time and attention they give to their other children. And for some, there is little time left to maintain a healthy marriage. The stress of juggling multiple roles eventually can take a toll on a mother's health and sense of well-being.

Yet despite the day-to-day challenges, women we surveyed stressed the positive ways parenting has transformed their lives. Mothers like Brenda learn to cherish the positive moments. Women who eventually re-enter the workforce benefit from the skills they've gained by special needs parenting. Some women explore new careers in areas related to their child's disability. Most find within themselves strengths they never realized existed. They describe themselves as stronger, more compassionate, and more knowledgeable about wide ranging issues.

If you're the mother of a child with special needs, the pressures faced by women in your position should come as no surprise. But often, when you're in the midst of a struggle, it's hard to appreciate the new strengths and wisdom you're gaining. It's even harder to pause in your battle for your child to take care of yourself. But you know you need to. Even if you won't do it for your own sake, it's essential to maintain your health and your sanity if you're going to successfully care for your child for years to come. This book was created to help you cope, adapt, and thrive while parenting a child with a disability.

"I often feel that my work takes a back seat to everything
else that happens in our family."

—Brenda, part-time early intervention worker
and mom to two medically fragile children

Chapter 1

Getting the Most
Out of Life

This book isn't just about "coping with" or "adapting to" the heavier parenting demands that have been placed on you as the mother of a child with special needs. This book is about helping you thrive, be happy, and carve out a fulfilling life for yourself.

Can you relate to Brenda's feelings (above)? If you're like most of us, when you became a mom you temporarily set aside some of your own plans for pursuing a career, hobbies, or other interests. There are, after all, only so many hours in a day. While fathers and other family members make sacrifices too, research shows that it's the moms who bear the brunt of caring for children with special needs. Your plans to climb the corporate ladder, finish your degree, learn photography, or make your first quilt can easily fall by the wayside, even as your children grow older.

In families with typically developing kids, this parenting intensity often diminishes over time. Children grow up and become more independent, allowing their mothers more freedom to pursue other activities. While this process may be delayed or stalled for years for mothers of children with special needs, eventually, each of us needs to reclaim lost dreams or embrace new ones. Whether it's work, hobbies, or community involvement, everyone needs an interest to call their own.

Your child may be the most important thing in your life—but you can't let her be the only important thing. When your child's needs are overwhelming, it's easy to let parenting become all-consuming. Kayla discovered that the year her adult daughter with Rett syndrome moved into a group home. "It hit me in the face when Lesley left—I had become an empty shell."

Maybe having your child leave home seems like a far-off dream. But every one of us needs a strong sense of self in order to feel competent and stave off depression. Otherwise, you wind up like Jane, the stay-at-home mother of a young child with a developmental disability and severe behavior problems, who's had little time to explore her own interests and strengths in recent years. She told us, "I feel like I've lost my confidence—I look back at the essays I wrote in University and wonder what happened to that person."

That doesn't have to happen. Even when parenting demands are intense, you can keep your own dreams alive. Or, if those old dreams have withered, you can revive them. But they may look different this time around.

If your child was recently diagnosed, you're probably feeling overwhelmed. If you've been dealing with special needs issues for a long time, you may feel you haven't had the luxury to consider your own hopes and ambitions. But sometimes, as your life changes to accommodate your child's needs, you'll find that your goals and dreams change as well. It's time to take a look at how your daily life fits with what's important to you now. This chapter will help you start to think about yourself—what you value, appreciate, or want to change—in order to live your life to the fullest.

How Life Plans Change

Twelve years after working her way up the ranks of her local police force, Louise got an exciting new job as the supervisor of the intelligence staff. Shortly after, she became pregnant with twins. At age two-and-a-half, her son was diagnosed with autism. To accommodate his many doctors' appointments and therapies, Louise took a voluntary $12,000 pay cut and demotion, so she could work shifts as a police dispatch supervisor.

Today, Louise says: "I no longer wish to aspire to a career—it is just a means for a short time." Now she is focused on helping her husband advance his career, so that she can achieve her new goal: "becoming a stay-at-home mom. Then I can help my son reach his full potential. Five years ago, I never would have thought I would feel this way."

For many moms, especially those of us whose children have special needs, our realities may not sync with what we were taught to believe when we were younger. If you grew up in the seventies or eighties, you were probably told you could have it all: You could work full-time, be promoted without limits, have an equal partnership with your spouse, enjoy quality time with your children, manage your household, and still have time to pursue your passions.

What no one mentioned was that, while you might be able to have all those things in your lifetime, you probably couldn't have them all at once.

Fortunately, people are starting to recognize that compromises have to be made. A recent study done by the Families and Work Institute found younger parents are far less willing to give work priority over family life.

How have your priorities changed? Think back to the days before you had children. What was most important to you then? In the first column of Table 1-1 on the next page, rank each of your pre-motherhood priorities 1, 2, or 3—with 1 being the most important, and 3 the least. Fast forward to today and do the same under the "This is Now" column.

Chances are, what you define as important has changed over time. And that's not only okay—it's natural. Like Louise, you may have once, but no longer, ranked a career at the top of your list. Or perhaps, after several years of being a stay-at-home mom, you're keen to return to school or try a new career. Tara, for example, never

TABLE 1-1

That was **THEN**	This is **NOW**
____ Family	____ Family
____ Friends	____ Friends
____ Career	____ Career
____ Social Life	____ Social Life
____ Schooling (yours)	____ Schooling (yours)
____ Volunteer Work	____ Volunteer Work
____ Health	____ Health
____ Religion	____ Religion
____ Hobbies	____ Hobbies
____ Housework/Yard work	____ Housework/Yard word
____ Other: _____	____ Other: _____

intended to work outside the home when her daughter was diagnosed with Rett syndrome. She says, "When my daughter was fourteen, I was offered the opportunity to work as a paraprofessional in a special education class. And I loved it. Through in-service training and night classes, I have learned about young people and computers. For this mom with only a high school diploma and no desire to attend college, I have accomplished more than I ever hoped or dreamed."

On the other hand, if you've been at home for many years, you may feel that maintaining your health or hobbies is now crucial. Our survey showed this to be particularly true for mothers of adult children with disabilities.

What effect has your child with special needs had on your priorities? Many women told us their values shifted after having children with disabilities. Some mothers said that their previous career choices and aspirations no longer fit with their life experiences, so they've started new careers or begun doing volunteer work in the disability field. Or they've gone back to school to study a related discipline. Many, like Tara, are thrilled that they can combine their life wisdom, professional skills, and passions.

Other moms told us they aren't concerned with careers right now, but value their religious faith more strongly than they had in the past.

Of course, some moms still value the same things they did before becoming a parent, but find it difficult to achieve their goals. It's hard to carry out your life plans when you face challenges such as financial constraints, insufficient services, and your child's medical crises.

DIFFICULT CHOICES

Many mothers said they have been forced to make difficult choices, often involving their careers. Louise stepped down from her intelligence supervisor position because her son required intensive early intervention—and there was no one else to provide it. Some moms feel they can't even consider paid or volunteer work because their children's needs are so overwhelming or because they can't find child care.

For others (especially single mothers), working full-time is essential, because of limited finances. Many remain in unsatisfying jobs—sometimes with inadequate child care—just so they can cover their child's expenses or keep their insurance.

Even those moms who were content at work found they had little time to exercise, enjoy hobbies, or nurture friendships.

Sometimes, when you're passing through life from crisis to crisis, there seems to be little time to consider our own goals. As a few mothers told us, they were just trying to get by day to day. If you've left your own goals behind, now might be the time to reclaim them. Or set some new ones. Each major section of this book will help you act on the present-day priorities you checked off.

The Keys to a Happy and Meaningful Life

You'd expect that mothers who had to put their own dreams on hold would be bitter and depressed. Actually, our surveys found that many had adjusted well to their unexpected life paths. While many mothers told us that having a child with special needs had derailed their professional lives, they also spoke positively about their situations. They were pleased that they could help their children progress and some had discovered new fields of work.

Despite the hard choices (or perhaps because of them), many mothers we talked with were amazingly upbeat.

To understand why, we turned to positive psychology, the science that examines what makes people feel happy and fulfilled. While most of us equate happiness with pleasure, e.g., relaxing on the beach or eating a chocolate sundae, researchers have found that happiness goes deeper than that. Surprisingly, having more money does not bring lasting happiness, nor does having more education, being younger, healthier, or better looking. "Relationships with other people are what make us happy," says positive psychology researcher Dr. Christopher Peterson, University of Michigan.

While relationships are the number one factor contributing to happiness, other factors identified by researchers include love, hope, and gratitude. Mothers we surveyed show immense love for their children and hope for their progress. No matter what their areas of achievement, most women said parenting their children gave them much gratification. Says one mom, "My strongest sense of accomplishment is seeing my daughter become an independent, competent, and well-rounded person."

When your child with special needs grows and accomplishes things in her own way—whether it's attending school, playing adapted sports, or learning to communicate with a picture board—you take great pride in her accomplishments. As one social worker says, "Moms start to see life in a different way. They never thought they'd be able to take joy in their children—but they do, over time."

According to research, the happiest moms are masters at accommodative coping—meaning they're able to set new goals if they find previous ones are unachievable. This flexibility is a key aspect of resilience—the ability to bounce back from setbacks. If you're resilient, you're able to face challenges and losses while understanding that the tough times will pass. You find ways to grow and develop from difficult experiences.

THE THREE LEVELS OF HAPPINESS

What about the mother who faces a devastating challenge such as watching her child endure constant pain or suffer through a degenerative and fatal disability? Can we realistically talk about her finding "happiness?" Actually, yes. Just because that mom's life may not be as pleasurable as others', doesn't mean it won't be as fulfilling—or more so.

Sometimes you must distinguish between a life that's pleasant and one that's meaningful, says positive psychology expert Peterson. "A life of meaning should revolve around rising to the occasion, meeting the challenge. These mothers love their children all the more and that's what meaning is all about. You can't undo what happened to you, but maybe you can help others. That's one way people rise above circumstance."

According to Dr. Martin Seligman, a pioneer of positive psychology and author of *Authentic Happiness: Using the New Positive Psychology to Realize Your Potential for Lasting Fulfillment*, there are three levels of happiness:

1. **The Pleasant Life:** This is what most people think of as "happiness"—having a life filled with positive emotion. These people know how to savor moments and be mindful of the present. Interestingly, though, people seem to have a genetically pre-programmed range for this type of happiness—you can't make yourself become a bubbly, always-smiling person if it doesn't come naturally (although that's not to say you can't learn to be a bit more upbeat than you currently are).

2. **The Engaged Life:** People who are "engaged" use their strengths and interests to the utmost. They become totally absorbed in the things that interest them—music, work, hobbies, friends, etc.—and pursue those interests with a passion. The most engaged life is one that exploits not just your talents and intellectual interests, but your character strengths (such as wisdom, curiosity, ingenuity, leadership, optimism, faith, or sense of humor) as well.

3. **The Meaningful Life:** At this highest level of happiness, people use those same interests and talents that engage them, but for the greater good—to help others and the community. They're pursuing what they love, while feeling a part of something larger than themselves.

The people most satisfied with their lives are those who pursue all three levels of happiness—pleasure, engagement, and meaning (with engagement and meaning being the most important).

According to this explanation of happiness, many moms of kids with special needs have rich opportunities for life satisfaction. You can experience intense joy while savoring your child's accomplishments, no matter how small they may seem to "typical" parents. You can use your personal strength—whether it's advocacy work, caregiving, researching, or sewing teddy bears—to make the world a little better for your own child and for others.

For some women we surveyed their sense of meaning and happiness stems from their religious faith or spirituality. Feeling that they and their family are part of something larger than themselves gives them hope and focus. In the words of one mother, "I am doing exactly what God intended for me to do."

Examining Your Life—How Fulfilled Do You Feel?

How many of us ever pause to consider how happy we actually feel in our lives? Is your life full with the three essential components of happiness? Do you feel you have enough opportunities to enjoy the moment, to use your talents, and to make your unique contribution to the world? Certainly these are overwhelming questions to ponder—especially if, realistically, a "balanced" day for you is one in which you have fifteen minutes to bathe! So, to get you started, we've developed a life contentment checklist, based on factors researchers have identified as correlated with people's sense of happiness and well-being. For each statement on the quiz on the next page, check whether you do the activity always, often, sometimes, or never.

If you checked off "always" or "often" to all of these, you likely feel a high level of life satisfaction. But if you mostly checked off "rarely" or "never," you're in a great position to make some positive changes in your own life.

Start to think about what "happiness building" strategies you can add into your life. For example, if you feel you seldom make use of your skills and interests, consider opportunities that might allow you to. It doesn't have to be a paid job (although it could be). You can also gain satisfaction from applying your strengths in a hobby, a volunteer position, or advocacy work. In the following chapters, you'll find more strategies to help you reach your goals to live a happy and fulfilling life.

LIFE FULFILLMENT AND CONTENTMENT QUIZ

1. I maintain strong relationships with family and friends (spend time with and support one another).

    O always   O often   O sometimes   O never

2. I take care of my body (get sufficient sleep, exercise, and nutrition, and schedule regular medical appointments).

    O always   O often   O sometimes   O never

3. I take care of my mental health (manage my stress, nurture family teamwork, call upon friends for support, find solace in my religious faith, enjoy solitary time to reflect, etc.).

    O always   O often   O sometimes   O never

4. I consciously count my blessings (in my head or jot them down in a book).

    O always   O often   O sometimes   O never

5. I perform acts of kindness and altruism (e.g., practicing random acts of kindness, doing favors for others, giving to charity, volunteering, etc.).

    O always   O often   O sometimes   O never

6. I savor sensory experiences (pay close attention to the vibrancy of the world—the beauty of sunsets, the smell of fresh bread, the feel of sand on the beach, etc.).

    O always   O often   O sometimes   O never

7. I know what my strengths are (what I'm good at and what I love doing) and use them regularly.

    O always   O often   O sometimes   O never

Experience Talks

"The happiest mothers are those who have made the journey through all kinds of emotions to a place where they accept the disability and embrace the life experiences it will bring them and their family. They are able to see the disability as a catalyst for immense personal and spiritual growth (including reassessing one's priorities and values in life)."

—Joyce, social worker at a children's treatment center

"Take care of your own health so you can be your best for your family. Keep active in activities you were interested in before, spend time with other women who support you but also who divert your attention away from your child for a while. If you had goals before your child came along, pursue them without feeling guilty. The better you are emotionally, physically, and spiritually, the better your family will be."

—Anne, mother of a daughter with physical disabilities

PART II

Taking Care of Yourself

"Don't feel guilty if you feel you have to get away from your child for a while. You are not a bad mother for feeling overwhelmed and frustrated. Remember that being energized and refreshed helps you be a better mother."

—Linda, mother of a teen with muscular dystrophy

If you're feeling exhausted and overloaded, you're in good company. Researchers have found stress to be more common in moms who have children with special needs than in those who do not.

For some mothers, stress is relentless; for others, it changes over time. So much depends on the type and severity of your child's special needs, your community and family supports, your temperament, and your coping strategies. Left unchecked, stress takes a toll on your physical and mental health. It can lead to symptoms such as headaches, sleeplessness, fatigue, stomachaches, chronic pain, anxiety, and depression. Fortunately, there *are* ways you can combat the impact of stress on your life.

In the following chapters, you'll read strategies for achieving a balance of healthy food, fitness, friends, work, and play in your life. You'll learn where to get support and where to turn if you're in crisis. And you'll read stories from women like yourself who try their best to look after themselves.

As so many mothers have reminded us, taking care of ourselves is a necessity, not a luxury. Today, commit to doing one new thing to improve your own physical, mental, social, or spiritual health. After all, we mothers are in this for the long run.

"I look at my energy and emotions like a big water pitcher. Every time I care for my family, I pour out of my pitcher. Unless I take time to put something back—by having my hair done, going window shopping, seeing a movie with friends, making Friday "date night" with my husband, or taking a community college class—my pitcher empties. You cannot give what you don't have in store. Exhaustion and frustration causes you to become irritable, edgy, and angry. Keep your pitcher filled!"

—Linda, mother of a teen with muscular dystrophy and developmental delays

Chapter 2

Put Yourself on the To-Do List

How do you keep your own pitcher filled? Especially when parenting your child is physically or emotionally exhausting, taking time for yourself is absolutely essential. In order to take care of your family, you need to continuously rejuvenate yourself.

For the sake of your health, you need to care for not just your body, but your emotional, social, spiritual, and intellectual sides too. As so many moms (like Linda, above) remind us, the better you feel, the better you can care for your family. Unless you take time to nurture your own needs, you can end up feeling resentful, burdened, and depressed.

If you're reading this book, odds are that you're struggling—maybe at home, maybe at work, maybe internally. The chapters to come will help you work through all these areas of possible conflict and stress. But let's start off by finding some relatively simple ways you can start improving your life *today*.

Keeping Your Pitcher Filled

Sometimes it's hard to know just what you need in order to refill your pitcher. Start by looking at how you typically spend your day, to see which activities you could add or subtract to help you feel more balanced.

Check off which situations best describe your daily life situation right now:

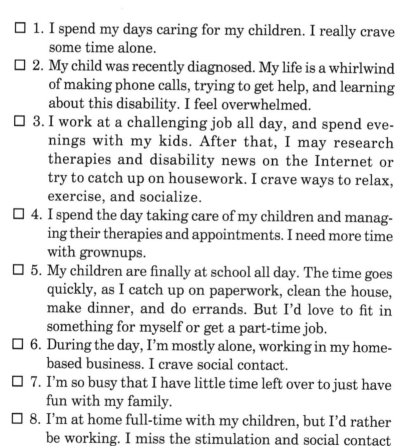

- ☐ 1. I spend my days caring for my children. I really crave some time alone.
- ☐ 2. My child was recently diagnosed. My life is a whirlwind of making phone calls, trying to get help, and learning about this disability. I feel overwhelmed.
- ☐ 3. I work at a challenging job all day, and spend evenings with my kids. After that, I may research therapies and disability news on the Internet or try to catch up on housework. I crave ways to relax, exercise, and socialize.
- ☐ 4. I spend the day taking care of my children and managing their therapies and appointments. I need more time with grownups.
- ☐ 5. My children are finally at school all day. The time goes quickly, as I catch up on paperwork, clean the house, make dinner, and do errands. But I'd love to fit in something for myself or get a part-time job.
- ☐ 6. During the day, I'm mostly alone, working in my home-based business. I crave social contact.
- ☐ 7. I'm so busy that I have little time left over to just have fun with my family.
- ☐ 8. I'm at home full-time with my children, but I'd rather be working. I miss the stimulation and social contact of the job I used to have.

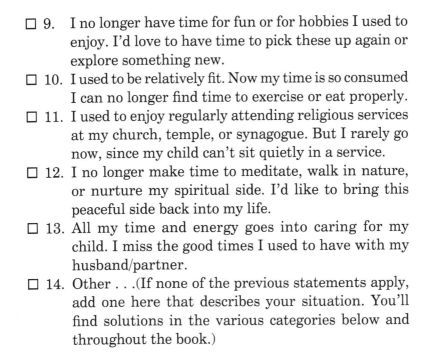

☐ 9. I no longer have time for fun or for hobbies I used to enjoy. I'd love to have time to pick these up again or explore something new.

☐ 10. I used to be relatively fit. Now my time is so consumed I can no longer find time to exercise or eat properly.

☐ 11. I used to enjoy regularly attending religious services at my church, temple, or synagogue. But I rarely go now, since my child can't sit quietly in a service.

☐ 12. I no longer make time to meditate, walk in nature, or nurture my spiritual side. I'd like to bring this peaceful side back into my life.

☐ 13. All my time and energy goes into caring for my child. I miss the good times I used to have with my husband/partner.

☐ 14. Other . . .(If none of the previous statements apply, add one here that describes your situation. You'll find solutions in the various categories below and throughout the book.)

Now that you've pinpointed what you're craving in your day, consider what you can add or change to meet your own needs. Take note of the number beside the box(es) you checked. Match the number beside the box to the numbers after each heading below, to read about possible solutions.

I Need a Break (1, 2, 3)

Getting a real break is essential, so that you can return feeling energized and capable. Try these ideas:

If you're going through an intense time with your child (such as a new diagnosis, or a medical or behavioral crisis), take short walks and stretch breaks for quick stress relief. Try deep breathing and meditation (see "I Need More Spirituality in My Life," later in this chapter.)

Get a mental health break by adding a little pleasure to everyday tasks. If you're driving your child to an appointment, for example, listen to music you both enjoy. When grocery shopping, buy yourself a magazine and a new kind of tea. Go for a brisk walk while your child is having a therapy or lesson.

When your kids are asleep, pamper yourself. Take a fragrant bubble bath, eat one fabulous chocolate, spend the evening in your softest sweater and favorite slippers, light a scented candle.

Take a weekly night off. When her children were young, Grace, a separated mom, took a dance class one evening each week after her daughter (with Asperger syndrome) was in bed. She asked her best friend to stay with her children. If you don't have friends or family who can pitch in and you have the funds, hire a regular caregiver instead. Some women prefer a night off at home. Fern has two young children with Joubert's syndrome. Her in-laws babysit while she scrapbooks, reads, or works in the garden. Tap into respite programs to give you a break, away or at home. For details on how to find respite, babysitters, and volunteers, be sure to see Chapters 9 and 18-20.

Swap child care with a friend so you can get out for exercise, errands, or fun activities. Bernie swaps an hour or two once a week. She says "it reduces feelings of guilt of doing something for myself, since it's free and I've 'earned' the time."

Write your own plans or time off on the family calendar. Sometimes, it's easiest to sign up for the same weekly night out or class. If your partner travels frequently, book weekly respite or child care. See Chapter 14 for ways to work as a team.

Get away by yourself. An overnight, weekend, or weeklong vacation without your kids can energize and renew you. Nel, who is a single mom, enjoys a few nights at a bed and breakfast twice a year, while family and friends cover the home front. She says these regular escapes help her to cope.

I'd Like More Family Time Doing Things We All Enjoy (7, 13)

While all of us benefit from time to ourselves, you also may crave enjoyable time with your family or partner. Women who work full time, in particular, told us they wanted to find family activities that would replenish them (not wear them out more).

Some women almost dread coming home—too many chores waiting to be done and demands waiting to be fulfilled. Others find coming home to their kids is the best part of their day. Ritva, mother of a child with a rare genetic skin disorder, has an unfulfilling job in sales. To make the job tolerable, she says "I focus on fun evening and weekend activities with my family."

Here are some ways to make your time with the family something to look forward to:

Once a week, unplug the phone, turn off the computer, and have a video or board game night with your partner and children. Schedule a regular family activity time and don't let other activities pre-empt it.

Increase the fun factor in errands. Play music or recorded books in the car, go out for ice cream after hitting the hardware store, or visit the pet store after grocery shopping.

Pick family activities YOU enjoy, too. Barbara, mother of a teen with Down syndrome, says, "I like to swim and so does my son. Going to the community pool allows him time for socialization and me a chance to relax."

Negotiate as much job flexibility as possible so you can coordinate work schedules to maximize family time. See Chapter 25 for more information.

Prioritize and share household duties among family members, so you'll have more time left over for fun activities. See Chapter 8 for advice.

For tips on making time for your partner, see Chapter 15.

I'd Like to Socialize More (3, 4, 6, 8)

If you're mostly home alone with your kids all day, or if you have a home-based business, you may feel lonely and isolated. You may not be able to attend typical parent and tot programs because of your child's needs or behaviors. If you work outside the home, it may be hard to find time to spend with friends in the evenings when you're busy with family and errands. Try these ideas to increase your daily social contact.

Try phoning a friend and making a date to walk or have lunch; email someone you haven't seen recently; attend church or synagogue and see your friends there. Sometimes even a quick "social fix" can make you feel more balanced. For example, when Amy works from home all day, she goes to a YMCA fitness class at lunch—not just for exercise, but to have a quick chat with regular class-goers as well.

Schedule a regular date to get together with friends; e.g., the first Saturday of every month you'll meet with your friend(s) for brunch or a movie. Arrange caregiving in advance and put it on your calendar, so everyone knows your plans.

Even though it can be a lot of effort to get out, do. Take your kids to the library or a park, even briefly. You'll likely see other parents there, and it will feel good to have a change of scenery.

Get away with friends. To renew her faith and self esteem, Sheila, mom of a child with Asperger syndrome, attends several church retreats each year. If you don't belong to a group, consider going with other moms of children with special needs. One weekend a year, Amy goes to a friend's cottage with three other moms. "Since we all have kids with autism, we vent, complain, and enjoy ourselves." Other low cost ideas include sharing a hotel room with several women, camping, or sleeping over at friends' houses. Request a getaway gift certificate (to a hotel, inn, or bed and breakfast) for your birthday, Christmas, Mother's Day, or wedding anniversary.

IF YOU'RE HOUSEBOUND AND FEELING ISOLATED:

Try a new craft, e.g., invite a friend over and get her to show you how to do a simple knitting project while your child naps, watches a video, or is being cared for in the house.

Invite another parent and child over for a play date or a sleepover.

Start an in-home mom-and-tot book club. Post a notice at your school or community center or gather some neighborhood mothers and host a story time.

See Chapter 3 for more ways to nurture new friendships.

I Miss the Stimulation of Work (5, 8)

Many mothers who quit fulfilling jobs to care for their children miss the stimulation and intellectual challenges of the professional world, as well as the breaks they got from constant parenting duties. Similarly, women who work at unfulfilling jobs—perhaps because they offer flexible schedules or necessary health benefits—crave opportunities to learn new things.

If that is your situation, volunteering, part-time work, or a challenging hobby may help you to exercise all of your strengths and talents—an essential part of feeling truly happy. Try these ideas:

Work part-time or volunteer in areas related to your profession. When Amy's daughter was diagnosed, she taught a college course one evening a week. Although it was hard to find time for planning lessons and marking assignments, she really enjoyed the break from parenting. By day, she was a desperate, exhausted mom, trying to "cure" her daughter. But one evening a week, she wore a skirt and jacket, and felt like the competent professional she used to be.

Find others who share your professional or intellectual interests and plan activities around them. For example, invite friends who share your love of books over for a book exchange. Each person brings two or three books that they've read and that they're willing to swap. Then, each person describes their books and why they enjoyed them. Eat something chocolate or fabulous while you're listening. Afterward, choose three books that sound the most appealing, and bring them home to read.

Try activities that develop professional and marketable skills. For example, if you'd like to improve your public speaking skills and confidence, sign up for a drama class. Or if you're interested in doing a book some day, try a writing or photography course. Look for hobbies that build upon your personal and professional goals. Sometimes, hobbies can open the door to new careers. Wendy, a musician in her community orchestra and mother of five (including one who has Angelman syndrome), says "Before, music was a hobby; now it's become a part-time career that I need as much as oxygen!"

Recognize the work you do with your child as both a labor of love, and *the skilled work of a professional.* When Heather's daughter Robyn was diagnosed with Asperger syndrome at age four, there were few relevant books, no proven therapies, and very few experts. With a toddler in tow, she spent hours researching interventions. After consulting with speech language pathologists and occupational therapists, she created a therapeutic program, hired and trained workers, and monitored her daughter's progress. Every year she re-applied for funding, re-hired and re-trained workers, and modified the program. Now that her daughter is fifteen, she can look back and appreciate what she accomplished. And today, as a support group coordinator, she advises others, using the knowledge and skills she gained helping her own child.

Consider whether you'd be less stressed returning to daytime work. Many moms welcome their work hours as a reprieve from parenting. Says Suki, mom of a child with Tourette syndrome, anxiety, and learning disabilities, "Going to work is my break. As much as I love my children, I am almost always relieved when Monday morning comes, and they go to school and I can go back to work." If the time is right to switch jobs, return to school or the workplace, or start your own business; see the chapters in Part VII: Redefining Your Work Life.

I'd Like to Reclaim Past Hobbies or Explore New Ones (5, 9)

Often we're so busy accomplishing things during our day that we don't take time to consider what brings us joy and pleasure. Instead, if we do have a spare moment, we fold another load of laundry instead of enjoying something that replenishes us.

But by enjoying leisure activities, you can reclaim a part of yourself, gain a new role, or enrich your sense of self. Maya, mother of three children with mental health disorders and ADHD, told us that "I truly feel centered when knitting. The world can be falling apart around me and I am able to stay calm and focused on my task. Reclaiming hobbies makes me feel like I'm still 'me.'"

A hobby can provide you with another way to be more than a mom—you become a reader, a dancer, a runner, a woodworker, etc. Your world can open up with more opportunities for learning, social contacts, and fun.

When you "indulge" a little in a hobby, you also act as a role model for your child. By following your own interests, you demonstrate to him the importance of life-long learning, and of caring for yourself. If your child seems to resent you taking a little time for yourself, this also offers an opportunity to teach him the importance of "giving"—in this case, the gift of time.

In our surveys, many women said they enjoyed crafts such as knitting, jewelry-making, painting, or sewing. So much of our work as moms is invisible and never finished. In contrast, crafts give you the chance to create a beautiful finished product—something substantial you can hold in your hand or hang on the wall.

Some women told us they explored their love of drama by volunteering to usher for community theatre (professional or amateur). They see plays for free and enjoy meeting people at the door. Others take the plunge and audition for community theatre.

Ready to try a new activity, just for the joy of it? Here are a few ideas to start you on your way:

> *Brainstorm activities you'd like to try.* In a blank book, jot down some activities you've always thought you might enjoy. Some possibilities include: photography, singing, playing an instrument, synchronized swimming, acting, baseball, painting, dance, basketball, tai chi, yoga, quilting, scrapbooking, rock climbing, hockey, skating, politics, gourmet cooking....

> *Make an action plan for enjoying your hobby.* (See our Sample Hobby Action Plan.) Often moms don't pursue hobbies because they face barriers such as lack of energy, time, money, equipment, or child care. In your plan, list ways you can enjoy your hobby that are low-cost and fast. (Be sure to include some ideas for things you can do when you're housebound.) Also, think about ways to schedule your new hobby so that child care is less likely to be a problem—maybe during the school day, or on Sunday evenings when your spouse is sure to be home. Or if your own schedule is truly unpredictable, find an activity that has flexibility built in. Carmelita, mother of a child with multiple needs, found a school that offers three-hour drop-in art classes for only ten dollars. "I can't afford to do it every week, maybe once a month," she says. But "just having the class to look forward to is helpful, because it is a long-term goal that distracts me from the daily struggles of mainstreaming, speech therapy, medication, ADHD, etc."

> *If you find yourself in a rut, ask a friend (or your partner) to try a new activity with you, just once.* Amy and her husband Jack, for example, went to a one-night sal-

sa dance class. Another time, they tried a one-evening cooking class.

Form a "Fun Night Out Club" with friends or couples. Once a month, each couple (or person) plans something fun, low-cost, and different for the group to try. Some ideas are indoor rock climbing, hiring a belly dance instructor to teach your group one class, having a wine or chocolate tasting, etc. If you meet at the same time each month, you'll have lots of notice to ask a friend, family member, or paid caregiver to watch your child.

Sample Hobby Action Plan: The Art Afficionado

Problem: I used to enjoy drawing and painting, but now lack time, space, and cash. I thought about taking a night class, but it's hard to find child care—and even if I could, I'm usually too tired at night!

Plan:

1. I'll make an "everyday" art kit: I'll visit the dollar store and art store to fill a box with supplies, including a sketch book, a pad of paper, watercolor paints, brushes, magic markers, pastels, and charcoal sketching pencils. Then I'll place the kit in an easily accessible place—like a kitchen drawer. When I have a snippet of time, I'll experiment with my art goodies at the kitchen table.
2. For inspiration, I'll take out books on drawing or painting from the library.
3. I'll check the local recreation department for any drop-in or one-time, weekend art classes, so I don't have to make long-term commitments.
4. I'll look into being a volunteer docent at the local art gallery. If I could volunteer, say, one afternoon a month, it'd give me the chance to catch up on the art world and meet other people with similar interests.

Note to self: I don't have to do all these things at once. Any one of them is a good start!

Sometimes I'd Like to Do Something Purely for Fun (9)

When's the last time you bought new clothes, had a facial, tried a new hairstyle? Amy recently got a gift certificate for a spa in town: "For the first time in my life, I enjoyed a facial, manicure, and pedicure. Decadent? Yes. Frivolous? No. I felt relaxed and rejuvenated." Feeling good about your appearance can be an energy and joy booster.

In addition to making time to reclaim old hobbies or to try new ones, you can consciously increase your moments of joy or pleasure. Social workers have told us that some of the most content moms they know find ways to increase their "pleasure points." Think of the countless things you do to make your family happy—cook their favorite meals, plan outings, read to them, etc. In the same way, plan ways to pamper yourself. Try these ideas:

> *Plan time for yourself each day where you don't need to "accomplish" anything (and when your children and other family are out of the picture).* Have a bubble bath, read, do needlework. Some moms wake up thirty minutes early to enjoy coffee and the newspaper by themselves. Others use early morning to walk, garden, or write in a journal.

> *Choose one activity that would help you feel more balanced in your day.* (See the box *"Thirty Cheap and Quick Ways to Have Fun,"* if you're short on ideas.) In your calendar, write down one thing you can do this week, to help you achieve your goal of increasing that activity in your life. Try an activity that combines several of your life cravings. For example, if you crave social contact, exercise, and time with nature, call a friend and make a date for a nature hike. Plan ahead, write it in the family calendar, and arrange child care (a spouse, friend, family member, or paid caregiver).

> *If time is tight, be creative in finding ways to fit in your "pleasure goal."* One mom who is home all day with young kids makes it a priority to read a few pages of an excellent book; instead of catching up on paperwork or cleaning up during nap time, that's her scheduled reading time.

30 Cheap & Quick Ways to Have Fun!

(Choose one and schedule it into your calendar this week!)

Great Escapes:

1. Spend an hour in your library reading current issues of the latest magazines.
2. Order a fancy coffee in a bookstore and browse while sipping.
3. Do a book swap with a friend for excellent low-cost reading materials. Meet for coffee and each of you bring a few favorite books to exchange for a few months.
4. At the grocery store, try a new exotic fruit, e.g., star fruit, guava, or papaya.
5. Get a nature fix to soothe the soul. Go for a walk in a wooded area and enjoy the trees.
6. Go to a pet store or shelter and admire the puppies and kittens.
7. Try something that you used to love but no longer make time for. When was the last time you ice skated, danced, skied, or rode your bike, for example? Do you still have a bike? Borrow from a friend, or buy one second hand.

Go Shopping:

8. Go ethnic—visit a grocery store that specializes in a culture you're interested in. Sample Indian pastries, Asian noodles, or Jewish latkes. Find an ethnic recipe online or from the library, and buy the ingredients in the store.
9. Hit a weekend garage sale and buy one inexpensive treat. A book? A vase? Used curtains?
10. Visit a secondhand women's clothing store and hunt for bargains.

Be a Tourist in Your Own Town:

11. Visit an art gallery, park, new tea shop, or walking trail.

(continued on next page)

(30 Cheap & Quick Ways to Have Fun continued)

12. Collect community flyers advertising art shows, community theatre, festivals—then write the events in your date book.

Join a Group:

13. Join a community theatre group, art gallery board, softball league, knitting club . . . .

Get Gorgeous:

14. Try a spa evening at home with drugstore goodies or free product samples.
15. Visit a department store makeup counter for a free makeover (but don't feel pressured to buy expensive cosmetics).

Housebound but Happy:

16. Offer to pet sit your friend's dog, cat, or bird. Enjoy having the furry company in your house.
17. Get out a book on massage from the library. With your partner or a friend, try out the techniques.
18. Put on a CD you haven't heard in a long time. Sing your heart out. Dance in front of the mirror.

Enjoy the Love of Learning:

19. Pick up a "learn a second language" video from your library. See what you can master in one night. Impress your kids and friends!
20. If you like to cook, try that new recipe for a chocolate dessert that you've been coveting. Share it if you like.

Make Your House a Haven:

21. De-clutter in order to de-stress and soothe. Start by cleaning out one drawer you use often. For example, throw out mismatched and holey socks in your sock drawer.

22. Buy fresh flowers or pick a few from your garden.
23. Plant a pot of fresh herbs for your windowsill (dill, tarragon, parsley) and snip off sprigs to add a gourmet touch to your meals.
24. Pick one wall of your house and fill it with photos of you, your friends, and family in happy times (or just plaster your fridge with photos attached by magnets).

The Pleasure of Giving:
25. Write a thank you note to someone who has given you a gift, invited you to dinner, helped your child, or just been a good friend—it will make you feel great.
26. Make a big pot of soup and wrap up one portion for a friend who is ill or who just had a new baby.

Be a Kid:
27. Next time you're with your child, forget the multi-tasking and take time to also enjoy the activity yourself. Squish your hands through playdough and make "hair" by pressing dough through a garlic press. Finger paint. Dance to goofy music together.

Savor Sensory Pleasures:
28. Create a nook for yourself with a comfy chair, a soft scatter rug at your feet, fresh flowers, fragrant candles, fuzzy slippers, and a cushy blanket.
29. Stroke your dog, cat, or child's soft hair.
30. Make a big bowl of popcorn topped with melted butter. Try seasoning it with dill or chili powder for a change. Munch it while watching your favorite show.

I Need to Get Fit (10)

Getting in shape—there's no overnight solution. (If we had one, we'd be writing a book on that!) Chapters 4-6 will help you get on the road to fitness by eating sensibly, exercising regularly, and getting enough sleep. Nevertheless, you may be surprised to find that a few quick little changes can give you a jumpstart to feeling healthier and more energetic. For example:

> *Packing portable snacks (like fruit, nuts, yogurt) for busy days*
>
> *Sneaking in quick walks during the day* (e.g., picking the farthest parking spot at work)
>
> *Walking your child to school or your dog to the park*

I Need More Spirituality in My Life (11, 12)

Another way we can help ourselves stay happy, balanced, and healthy is by nurturing our sense of spirituality. Religion brings meaning to some mothers' lives by making them feel part of something larger than themselves. Other mothers talk about the comfort and social support they receive at their place of worship.

Others no longer feel welcome at their place of worship because of their child's behaviors. Or, they are unable to find child care so they can attend on their own. If this is your situation, don't give up. Speak to your religious leader about your family's needs. Or form an informal prayer group with other moms. For more strategies on being included at your place of worship, see Chapter 10.

But you needn't attend services, nor be part of a specific faith group, to reap mental health benefits. Many women who answered our survey don't participate in organized religion. Some gave up after they failed to successfully include their child in services. Yet, most of these mothers still pray in a more personal way.

Recent studies link spirituality and prayer with increased mental health. In a study at Yale University of Medicine (2004), patients with high spirituality scores (e.g., those who believed in a higher power, the importance of prayer, and finding meaning in times of hardship) were less likely to suffer depression. Another study that year showed that, among patients awaiting cardiac surgery, those who prayed privately felt more optimistic than other patients.

Mothers we interviewed described numerous ways that they felt and expressed their sense of spirituality. The deep-felt love they developed through caring for their children was one aspect several mentioned. Says Roopa, mother of a fourteen-year-old with pervasive developmental disorder: "I really attribute my sense of spirituality to all the victories and challenges we have faced and realized with our son." Others described spirituality as the inner peace and calm they felt while meditating, experiencing nature, or enjoying family time.

Spirituality is really anything that makes you feel that there is a higher sense of purpose to your everyday life. For balance and health, explore spirituality in any way that is meaningful for you.

Try these activities to nurture your sense of spirituality:

Use meditation to help you relax, de-stress and to live in the moment. There are two basic components to meditation:

1. **Mind emptying**—ridding your mind of worries, fears. Examples are sitting quietly and paying attention to your breath, or counting to ten without thoughts interfering.

2. **Mindfulness**—a non-judgmental way of paying attention to what is happening in the moment. Recognizing that thoughts are not good or bad— they just are thoughts. You can refill your mind with what you choose to be there, such as positive affirmations (See the box "Quick Ways to Add Affirmations to Everyday Life.")

To help you meditate, get a meditation tape from the library, or tape your own voice doing a guided visualization of a favorite place. (See Chapter 6 for more information on meditation.)

Celebrate your blessings. Buy a blank book. At the end of each day, jot down experiences that you enjoyed during the day. Make separate lists of things you're grateful for.

For example, write one of these statements at the top of a page, and just come up with simple lists for each.

What I love about my children
Friends I appreciate
What I'm good at
The most beautiful places I've been
The most important things I've learned

You may even want to share your lists. Tina, mother of a child with fetal alcohol syndrome, says, "When the children rise in the morning, showing them my positive thoughts from the night before helps me to feel energized to start another day."

Be charitable. Pick a few items from your closet that you no longer wear, and give them to charity. Join your local

Quick Ways to Add Affirmations to Everyday Life

We spoke with Tzivia Gover, author of *Mindful Moments for Stressful Days*, who suggested these strategies:

Put affirmations or a phrase that comforts you on your computer screensaver (at home or at work).

When you're particularly worried, try repeating affirmations such as "We are whole," or "God is Good."

Choose a meaningful number or word for your computer password or bank pin number.

Try deep relaxing breathing, when stuck in traffic or waiting for an appointment. To get into the habit of slow and relaxed breathing, tie it to a common event in your day. For example, every time the phone rings take a deep breath or say an affirmation.

If you take comfort in religion and can't attend services, wear a symbol of your faith in a necklace. This is a tangible reminder of the bigger picture in life.

Add meaning to exercise: Think about a favorite prayer as you walk, run, or swim.

disability parents' group, and offer to be a "listening ear" to parents whose children are newly diagnosed.

If you didn't feel comfortable at your old place of worship, try attending services at a new one. Perhaps you might feel more welcome or connected with a different congregation.

Go on nature walks alone or with your family.

Read the Bible or books about spirituality.

Put on some music and dance with your kids. Moving and laughing together does much to reduce stress and increase your sense of wonder in your children.

Experience Talks

"Working lets me maintain some semblance of life outside of special needs. Having that time away allows me to build up strength to return to my parenting job."
—Regan, single mom of a child with multiple disabilities and a full-time social worker

"I go out with other 'autistic mothers' for a movie, dinner, drinks. I am satisfied because everyone who knows me understands I do much more than stay at home. I run my son's program."
—Charmaine, mother of a child with autism

"Take fifteen minutes a day to stretch or meditate or lock yourself in the bathroom and read words of wisdom from the Bible."
—Bella, mother of three children with multiple learning, mental health, and developmental disabilities

"Our family has no religious or spiritual practices, but we are very strong on 'doing as you would be done by.' Giving support to others in

need makes me feel better about myself. If you reach out to others with a helping hand, others reach out to you, too."

—Lise, mother of a child who is profoundly deaf and has fetal alcohol syndrome

"Exercise, socialize with friends, go to cultural activities, get outdoors, and do things outside your normal daily routine. For me, it's really important to not feel that I'm always chained to the house simply because that's where my special needs daughter is most comfortable. It can be challenging or stressful to take her out places with the rest of the family, but since I need to get out and see things and see people, I try to arrange ways to do that."

—Bernie, mother of a child with ADHD

"Get up early and make it a priority to do something for yourself a few times a week. There will always be laundry and cleaning available to be done. I tell myself that I can take better care of my family if I take good care of myself."

—Kuan, mother of a child who is blind and has cerebral palsy

*"I have established lifelong friendships that mean the world to me.
I feel I have a bond with a group of people who are special and
make me feel as though I'm part of something big."*

—Isabel, mom of a son with Down syndrome,
describing her friendship with other moms of kids with Down syndrome

Chapter 3

Ya Gotta Have
Friends

In your daily life, you may feel you have little time to enjoy and nurture friendships. But having close friendships is hardly a frill. Current research shows that close social relationships are absolutely crucial for happiness and health. Researchers have examined the characteristics of the happiest people and found, without exception, that the happiest people reported strong and positive social relationships.

Unfortunately, moms we surveyed told us that parents of children with special needs face some unique challenges when it comes to making and keeping friends. These can include:

Time and money constraints: Clara, whose child has spina bifida and epidermolysis bullosa (a rare skin disorder), says, "It's hard to maintain friendships when you don't have a babysitter or can't be spontaneous. We also have financial difficulties which make it hard to go out with friends or plan an evening out."

Friends who "just don't get it": Brenda, mom of two medically fragile boys, explains: "Sometimes friends will say, 'I wasn't sure if I should call you, because I didn't know if you could be bothered to call me back.' Meanwhile, they don't know I've just spent the last two weeks at home with my son on medication to keep him breathing, trying to keep him out of the hospital."

Not wanting to be pitied: We want our friends' understanding, but not their pity. Rose, who has a two-and-a-half-year-old child with muscular dystrophy, reports that "My husband and I have pulled away from many friends because they were always using 'that voice'—the one where they are constantly feeling sorry for you."

Dealing with our children's challenging behaviors: Says Paula (whose son has Asperger syndrome), "I have lost many friends—and opportunities for friendship—because of my son's behavior. People aren't much interested in being with my little family, and I have stopped reaching out, as the rejection is painful."

Living in different worlds: We want friends to appreciate our children's accomplishments. But as Moira, mother of a fourteen-year-old with autism, explains, "I started to feel like we were in a parallel universe . . . I can't expect them to understand how great it is when my child uses the past tense for the first time at the age of ten, when their kids perform in a band, are on the honor roll, and play soccer." Several moms told us that some friends stopped calling or inviting them over. Older moms sometimes find family friends back off as their children get older and move away. They no longer share the same interests. This was the experience of Myrna, sixty-four, who has a forty-two-year-old daughter with Down syndrome. "Friends and family have aged and have less time and energy for us," she says.

Living too much in the same world: Friendships with other moms of special needs children can be rich but, at the same time, limited. Friends may understand your issues, but you may share little else in common. Says Jeanne, mother of a twenty-two-year-old with Lennox Gastaut syndrome: "The friends I have now are those I have made through my daughter. My friends also have disabled children, so we are very limited in our interests."

Wondering what and when to disclose: Making new friends can be difficult as well. As one mom says, "If we let them in on the really challenging stuff, will they be scared away?" On the other hand, if you always put on the cheery, competent mother role, you can't really get close to people.

Nine Rules for Finding and Keeping Friends

It's true that rejection can be devastating. But it *is* possible to make and keep loving friends, despite the challenges you face. Many mothers we surveyed spoke of close, long-lasting friendships that have given them strength and comfort during difficult times. And even though some friendships inevitably dwindle, you'll find that new ones will be formed as well—especially with other mothers of children with special needs, and with people who are close to your child.

If you feel isolated, it's important to take action. These nine rules will help you develop and maintain the supportive friendships you need.

Rule 1. Give your friends time. Remember how long it took for *you* to adjust to your child's diagnosis? Your friends, who have less contact with your child, need time to appreciate your new reality. Giving your friends information about your child's disorder helps. Ritva, whose son has a rare genetic skin disorder, says, "Our friends were scared at first, but we spent a lot of time helping them become more comfortable. We trained them to do wound care and [now] they are the only ones we trust to babysit."

Rule 2. Recognize the different roles your friends play in your life. You might find your friend Anne is a lot of fun to go shopping with—her silly patter about office gossip and boyfriend problems takes your mind off things at home for a few hours. But if you start talking about your daughter's recent hospital stay, Anne starts fidgeting and quickly changes the subject. Julia, on the other hand, might be great for openly sharing concerns about your child—but she'd rather curl up with a book than blow an afternoon at the mall. There's no need to choose between the two friends— both Anne and Julia can play important roles in your life. And it's not fair to expect any one person to fulfill all your needs. Not all friends will be aware of the day-to-day challenges and successes you face. Try to find a mix of friendships. Special interests often bind people together. For example, Amy belongs to a reading club where members talk about books, not kids. For empathy, shared laughs, and acceptance, she also treasures her friends who have kids with special needs.

Rule 3. Cultivate friendships both inside and outside the special needs world. Other moms of kids with special needs "get it," and that's great. But friends outside the special needs community can offer support too, as well as diversion and new interests. In fact, researchers have found that mothers whose friends are primarily other caregivers report *increased* feelings of burden, in contrast to mothers with more diverse friendships. Many moms told us that their social networks expanded naturally when they returned to work or school, or when they took up a new hobby.

Rule 4. Combine friendship with exercise. Make a date to walk, attend a fitness class, or play a sport with a friend. As we'll discuss more in Chapter 5, exercise is a great form of stress relief. So while sharing a gripe session over lattés is fine on occasion, you'll get a bigger pick-me-up from a couple hours together on the bike trail.

Rule 5. Remember that everything is relative.
No matter what your family's reality is, there will always be others coping with more dire situations. And even "typical" families who seem to have it easy face challenges at times. Sure, it might be a little tough to sympathize when Judy's worried about paying for a brand new car for her sixteen-year-old (especially if you're struggling to pay for your child's medicine or therapies). But don't fall into one-upmanship. Roxana offers this advice: Just realize that the challenges and concerns of "typical" families are different from yours, and "just try to support your friends the best way you can." And sometimes, as Gloria suggests, the best strategy is to "put on a smile and pretend you live in their world too."

Rule 6. To combat envy, savor your child's successes.
Sometimes, it's hard not to envy friends with typically developing kids. Their lives (on the surface) look so easy. But while your days may be more complicated, you also can experience great joys. Amy remembers the first time Talia remained happy and calm through a whole meal in a restaurant: "For us, that evening was absolutely amazing. But for other families, it was just another dinner." Since our children's milestones are so hard-won, the elation we feel is intense, poignant, and life affirming. The next time you feel envious, hang onto the joys your child has brought you.

Rule 7. Actively seek supportive soul mates.
Start in places you're comfortable—your community center, place of worship, organized playgroups, or support groups. Meera became a stay-at-home mom (of a child with Down Syndrome), moved, and experienced her first "real" winter all at the same time. She felt isolated and down until she joined a community bible

group for mothers of preschoolers. "Over time I was able to form relationships with other mothers/women and begin to appreciate my role as a stay-at-home mother. In each situation, I felt that my son and I were always welcomed and accepted by the group." Others found friends at playgroups and support groups or through volunteer work.

Rule 8. Invite people in. When you feel over-whelmed, the last thing you feel like doing is having people over. But forget the dinner party—invite a few friends over for dessert instead. Don't wait until your house is tidy—just clean your kitchen, swish the toilet, and buy a cake. If friends want to bring kids, hire a worker or babysitter so adults can relax.

Rule 9. Communicate. A child with special needs can test a friendship. Sometimes, you may think your friend is rejecting you, while she may just think she's "giving you space." Maybe she thinks you're angry at her—when in fact you're just exhausted and may sound grouchy on the phone. Or perhaps she feels guilty, because she wants to help you and doesn't know how. You'll never find out unless you broach the subject. If, despite talking openly with your friend, your relationship is waning, perhaps it wasn't strong to begin with. It may be better to move on and actively develop other friendships.

Support Networks

"Support group members helped me see that I wasn't the only one going through these things—or having these feelings," says Tessa, whose toddler was born with a rare birth defect. "They helped me learn about my daughter's condition. With their support, I felt myself to be a much better parent and advocate for my child."

One of the most common ways for moms to meet new friends is through support groups related to their children's disorders. But the benefits of these groups go beyond making connections. One study by

McMaster University in Hamilton, Ontario found that belonging to a parent-run support group increased a parent's skills, feeling of power, and sense of belonging.

Support groups are sometimes most helpful for parents with younger or newly diagnosed children. In studies (and our own surveys), some parents of older children said they rely less on support groups now because they already have the information they need. Mothers of adult children were more likely to attend groups with an advocacy or action focus.

To find a local support group:

Contact local social service and disability agencies, your community hospital, library, volunteer center, or information center.

Look under "disability" in your phone book. Also check the section that includes government or social service agencies.

*Contact the **National Dissemination Center for Children with Disabilities** and ask for a State Resource Sheet that lists contact information for the agencies and organizations in your state relevant to disabilities.* In Canada, search the Canadian Abilities Foundation's website for links to disability organizations in Canada and around the world. (See Resources.)

Check national, state, and local websites for your child's disability. Often they include a list of local support groups on their sites.

Create your own network. If no appropriate group exists, ask your child's doctors, therapists, teachers, and community program leaders for names of other parents. If they can't give out names because of confidentiality, ask them to mail or email a flyer asking parents to contact you. If your child receives therapy at a center or attends a special needs class in a school, you may be able to contact other parents there. Many women have created successful support groups with the help of other parents.

FINDING SUPPORT ONLINE

Whether it's in place of or in addition to a "live" support group, the Internet can be a great place to turn for support from other parents. If your child has a rare disorder or you can't attend meetings because of scheduling and child care problems, email or Web-based support groups are ideal. You can log on at your convenience. It can also be less intimidating than airing your feelings in person.

Heather first "met" other parents of children with Asperger syndrome through an email listserv based thousands of miles away. "I learned more about the disorder during a few weeks of email than I had in the six months since the diagnosis. It comforted me knowing there were parents all over the world sharing my same concerns. Today I subscribe to a local autism group for information, not support. Like others, my needs have changed as my daughter has grown. I no longer need the emotional support, but I still rely on list members to point me in the direction of workshops, books, websites, etc., that might help me better understand my daughter."

If you don't own a computer, see if your public library offers Internet access. Some disability organizations such as the National Down Syndrome Society, The ARC of the United States, and United Cerebral Palsy have websites with online discussion forums. Yahoo, MSN, Google, and America Online have countless online support groups that you can join and post concerns, frustrations, and successes. Or you can "chat" in real time. If you don't find a suitable site, it's easy to create your own discussion group on one of the sites listed above. (See Resources.) Also check out websites and online discussion groups developed by parenting magazines, disability organizations, and families of special needs kids.

So, if you're feeling somewhat isolated, keep trying to connect with others—whether online, at a support group, at your church or synagogue, or out in the community.

Experience Talks

"Educate friends and families and take advantage of any offer of help. Give friends small tasks to do with your child. Remain present until they feel comfortable with your child. Be involved

with your child's life in your community and include them in every activity possible."
—Evelyn, mother of a twenty-five-year-old with Prader-Willi syndrome

"I have been involved with a Down syndrome group since it began fourteen years ago. We have a bond and friendship that goes beyond the norm. Our husbands have formed friendships, too."
—Dora, mother of a child with Down syndrome

"I have an informal network of moms in similar situations, and we gather occasionally to chat. I believe that not feeling alone, isolated, ostracized, and different is an important part of moving forward with our lives.
—Maya, mother of three children with learning and mental health disabilities

"My friends with 'typical' children will never understand my issues, but they are still friends. Sometimes it's nice to talk about normal kid issues, or not talk about the kids at all."
—Corrinne, mother of a child with bipolar disorder and OCD

"When I'm tired I often turn to coffee and chocolate. But then I end up with a sugar high, followed by more exhaustion. I want to eat well, but when I'm so stretched, who has the time or energy to eat properly?"

—Brianna, mother of a teen with autism

Chapter 4

Get Through the Day—
Fuel Up with Food

In times of stress, it's hard to resist cravings for unhealthy foods. In a 2001 study at the University of Alabama, 90 percent of the women participants identified themselves as "carbohydrate cravers," with chocolate being the food most craved. More than two-thirds reported feeling anxious, tired, or depressed before the cravings, but satisfied and relaxed immediately afterwards. That feeling of contentment may be due to the release of endorphins, the "feel good" hormones.

That contentment may be short-lived, though. Overindulging in sugary, fatty, or salty foods can lead to weight gain and associated diseases like diabetes and heart disease. And many mothers in our surveys said they struggled with weight control—an issue that seems to be tied with caregiving. Research suggests caregivers may be at particularly high risk for weight gain. A 1996 joint study by the University of Pittsburgh Medical School and the University of Washington found older caregivers of Alzheimer patients (especially *female* caregivers) gained considerably more weight over fifteen-to-eighteen months than non-caregivers.

But maybe stress affects you in a different way. Instead of over-eating, perhaps you lose your appetite and find it hard to eat enough. In a study at the University of Pittsburgh Cancer Institute and Brown Medical School, parents of children newly diagnosed with cancer reported consuming fewer calories over three months than parents of healthy children. As a cruel twist, they also gained significantly more weight—with those reporting the highest stress also gaining the most weight—probably because they spent more time in the hospital and less time exercising, according to the researchers.

Studies like these show how strongly stress and changes in eating are linked. Not surprisingly, the diagnostic criteria for clinical depression include changes in appetite and weight gain or loss. Researchers say that the primary stress hormone (cortisol) interacts with chemicals in the brain that affect appetite.

If you're worried about your own weight gain (or loss), you can improve your health with some easy and basic changes in exercise and diet. If you struggle with mood control, the next chapter will discuss how exercise can improve your mental health. But can diet also have such a positive impact? Some people think so. Compared to exercise, research in food and mental health is in its infancy. However, if you're feeling run down all the time, you should consider a dietary tune-up.

What Your Body May Be Telling You

Some researchers believe mood changes may be the first signs of subtle nutritional deficiencies. If you frequently feel irritable and depressed, try these few dietary changes that are based on preliminary research.

BOOST YOUR CONSUMPTION OF OMEGA-3S

Some studies suggest foods that contain Omega-3 Essential Fatty Acids, such as oily fish (e.g., salmon, albacore tuna, mackerel, lake trout, and sardines), may protect against depression. "Researchers refer to fish as the 'Prozac from the sea,'" says Liz Pearson, a registered dietician and author of *The Ultimate Healthy Eating Plan*. Pearson suggests eating fish at least once or twice per week. Other sources of Omega-3s include fortified eggs, walnuts, leafy vegetables, canola, soybean, and flaxseed oils. While the research on Omega-3s and depression is promising, the benefits for your heart are already proven. Omega-3s may also reduce inflammation for those with auto-immune disorders such as rheumatoid arthritis, Crohn's disease, and multiple sclerosis.

Concerned about mercury in fish? As of 2004, The American Heart Association (AHA) says that, for most people, the health benefits of eating at least two servings of fish outweighs any mercury risk. The AHA advises children or women who are pregnant, planning a pregnancy, or nursing, to avoid fish with higher levels of mercury such as shark, swordfish, King mackerel, and tilefish. You can also buy fish oil capsules containing Omega-3s such as DHA and EPA (look for labels that say "mercury free.") Before trying such capsules, or giving them to your children, ask your doctor, since large amounts of Omega-3s can cause stomach upset, and, in some people, excessive bleeding.

Some parents of children with ADHD, learning disabilities, or autism give fish oil capsules to their children. While research has reported lower levels of Omega-3 fatty acids in these groups, formal studies have not proven that supplementation reduces symptoms—although some parents report positive effects. Research in this area is still ongoing.

POP A VITAMIN DAILY

Take a good quality multivitamin every day. We know that most North Americans' diets don't provide the daily minimum requirements of many vitamins and minerals. To date, researchers have not spent a great deal of time looking at how vitamins affect mood and behavior. (There's not a lot of funding available for vitamin research, as opposed to pharmaceutical research.) But the limited information that's available suggests that vitamins are vital to more than just your physical well being:

> Deficiencies in folate, B6, B12, selenium, thiamine (B1) and Vitamin D have been linked to low mood and anxiety (the first three to dementia, as well).
> In a 1997 University of Wales, Swansea study of 150 women with "normal" thiamine levels, those who

took 50 mg of thiamine daily reported being more clear-headed, composed, and energetic than those taking a placebo.

In a 1998 Australian study on Vitamin D, participants taking at least 400 IU of Vitamin D3 over five days in the winter months reported a better mood than those taking a placebo. Vitamin D is produced in your body through exposure to sunlight and is essential for absorption of calcium. If you live in a northern climate, you'll need to get vitamin D from fortified foods (such as milk or margarine) or from a supplement, as there are few natural sources.

Finally, if you tend to get sick frequently, you may be deficient in one or more vitamins or minerals required for a healthy immune system.

Rather than trying to determine which vitamin or mineral you may be lacking, try taking a daily multivitamin. Taking a daily vitamin ensures that even on days when you don't eat properly, you're getting adequate nutrients. All multivitamins are not created equal—ask your doctor, pharmacist, nutritionist, or naturopath to recommend one.

PAY ATTENTION TO YOUR IRON LEVELS

Many women do not get enough iron. If you feel sluggish, have trouble concentrating, and feel down, your iron may be low. See your doctor, who can check your iron levels and recommend an iron supplement if needed. Foods high in iron include meats, eggs, dried beans or peas, green leafy vegetables (like spinach, kale, or broccoli), dried fruits, nuts and peanut butter, whole grains, and fortified whole grain breads and cereals. Eating foods containing Vitamin C at the same meal helps you better absorb iron from plant sources.

DUMP THE DIET!

Being "on a diet" may lead to actually eating *more* when times get tough. Research shows that dieters tend to overeat when they're under stress, while non-dieters eat their usual amount or less. Dieters are also more likely to eat for other emotional reasons.

Still, if you're gaining weight, it may be tempting to try the latest diet. Corrinne, whose son Zach has OCD and bipolar depression, describes her experience: "I decided that I wanted to lose about twenty pounds, so for four months I cut out almost all carbs and snacked on celery and cheese a lot. I lost the weight, have added carbs back in, and have gained back about five pounds." Now she wonders if she'll gain back the rest—a common problem, once dieters resume eating normally.

If you need to lose weight, forget about "going on a diet." Instead, think about eating healthy foods and increasing your exercise level. This is a plan you can stick with for life. Don't set your goal on becoming thin. Instead, focus on becoming fit, strong, and healthy. To help you make good food choices that will boost your energy level, consult with a nutritionist. Also see "Ten Ways to Lose Body Fat For Good."

DEAL WITH YOUR CRAVINGS

When you're stressed, that carton of double chocolate ice cream in the fridge can call your name. "Cravings are often hormonal," explains Pearson, a registered dietician and author of several books on nutrition. "You have to eliminate the competition," she says. "Whether your downfall is chocolate or chips, as long as it is in your cupboard, the apple doesn't stand a chance." Instead, Pearson suggests buying occasional treats in single-serving packages.

If your downfall is chocolate, take heart. Recent research shows that chocolate does more than make you temporarily feel good. It also contains disease-fighting compounds called flavonoids. Dark chocolate has about three times the amount of flavonoids as milk chocolate. Flavonoids are often lost in the processing of chocolate, so choose dark chocolate and check the label for high cocoa content or high flavonoids (easier to find in health food stores than in large groceries). Pearson recommends one daily serving only, which amounts to two to three squares of a bar.

When a craving strikes, walk around the block or up and down the stairs ten times. If the craving is for chocolate, reach for a treat (in individual portions) that is tasty, contains a bit of chocolate, and is nutritious. For example, try an individual cup of chocolate pudding made from skim milk. Or make up single size servings of trail mix that have nuts, raisins, seeds, and dark chocolate chips mixed in. When you have time, bake low fat muffins that contain fruit, fiber, and a few semi-sweet chocolate chips. Individually wrap them and freeze them. Reheat one in the microwave when you need a boost.

Ten Ways to Lose Body Fat for Good

1. **Exercise for thirty minutes, three times a week.** Walking counts.
2. **Eat small, well balanced meals (or snacks) every three hours.**
3. **Drink plenty of water.** Water takes the edge off your appetite and is necessary to metabolize fat.
4. **Never miss meals, especially breakfast.**
5. **Keep a food diary to keep track of what you're actually eating.** You may be surprised by some of your habits—such as frequent high fat, high sugar snacks. Then choose ways to modify your eating (such as increasing fruits and vegetables) and continue to write down what you eat each day. This will help you to see if you're eating foods from all the food groups and eating appropriate amounts.
6. **Keep to the calorie guidelines for your size.** For a rough estimate of how many calories you should consume each day, multiply your body weight in pounds by 15 (if you're active) or 12 (if you're not). If you're overweight or obese, multiply you ideal body weight by 15 (active) or 13 (non active) to find the number of calories you should eat to gradually achieve your ideal body weight.
7. **Don't lose weight too quickly; the slower the better.**
8. **Stick to the serving size on product labels.** (Note: That's not the same as restaurant portions, which can be equivalent to two or three servings or even more.)
9. **Reward yourself with a non-food treat whenever you reach one of your goals.**
10. **Be positive.** You can and you will.

Adapted from handout courtesy of Cheryl Guindon, personal trainer/manager, YMCA-YWCA, Guelph, ON.

If you crave salty foods, try popcorn, pretzels, lightly salted nuts, or healthier alternatives to regular chips such as baked potato or tortilla chips. Stick to the serving size on the bag.

If you're frequently fighting cravings, make yourself a Pamper Kit for stressful times. Fill a basket with flavorful herbal teas, a new magazine, a small bottle of rich hand cream, and a scented candle. Instead of caving in to stress-induced cravings, take a break for a few minutes to enjoy the goodies in your kit. As soon as you're able, pamper yourself with a bubble bath and an early bedtime with a good book.

Balance Your Intake of Fats, Carbohydrates, and Proteins

If you frequently feel drowsy after lunch, you may be overdoing it on carbohydrates or fats. A 1994 study from the Institute of Food Research in Reading, UK showed that participants who ate a carbohydrate- or fat-heavy lunch felt drowsier, more muddled and uncertain, and had longer reaction times than those who ate a more balanced meal (protein was the same in all groups). If pasta with cheese sauce puts you to sleep after lunch, try a whole wheat tuna salad sandwich instead.

Listen to Your Body

With our busy lifestyles, we may miss the signals our body is sending us about our eating or other habits. Heather, for example, used to feel hungry and irritable in the late afternoons, despite continually snacking on crackers, corn nuts, and other high-carbohydrate foods. Once she ate dinner, she felt fine again. Medical testing ruled out any blood sugar problems. Wondering if an unbalanced snack might be the problem, she started adding protein to her late afternoon snack (peanut butter with whole grain crackers, for instance). It worked. The protein rich snacks kept her hunger at bay until dinner and, more importantly, lifted her spirits so late afternoons became enjoyable again.

Getting Professional Advice

If you are frequently sick, moody, or exhausted, first talk to your doctor to rule out medical conditions. For personalized nutritional advice, visit a dietitian, nutritionist, or naturopath.

Dietitians (sometimes called nutritionists) study nutrition as it relates to health. A dietitian has, at minimum, a bachelor's degree specializing in food and nutrition as well as practical training in the hospital or community. If you have specific health problems such as diabetes, high blood pressure, or weight concerns, a dietitian can help you modify your diet. She can also answer your questions about nutrition and help you plan meals to keep you and your family healthy. (Be forewarned that in many states and provinces it is legal to call yourself a "nutritionist" or practice nutritional counseling without formal training.) To locate an accredited dietician, contact the American Dietetic Association or the Dietitians of Canada (see Resources).

Naturopaths are doctors trained in natural medicine. Their basic science education is similar to that of medical doctors', but the emphasis is on preventing disease and optimizing wellness (while the emphasis in traditional medical school is more on curing disease). Naturopaths use natural treatment methods such as diet and lifestyle changes, nutritional supplements, acupuncture, and homeopathy, rather than drugs or surgery, to stimulate the body's own healing powers. Naturopathic medicine has played an important role in maintaining Heather's health. She says, "I'd had frequent colds and bronchitis for most of my life. A few years after my second child was born, I developed migraines—despite following federal food guidelines, taking a multivitamin, and following an exercise routine. With the naturopath's guidance, I altered my diet and started taking natural supplements and vitamins. My migraines have lessened and I rarely get colds."

A word of caution. "Natural" does not necessarily mean "harmless." Talk to your doctor before trying any natural remedies, since they can interfere with any medications you may already be taking. Check out any health claims carefully. Don't rely on one source of information (the product manufacturer or the clerk in the health food store, for example). Look for information and studies on the Internet or in health journals. Ask your doctor or pharmacist about the product (many health food remedies now appear on drug store shelves). Better yet, take the product under the direction of a naturopath.

The practice of naturopathy is regulated in twelve states and four Canadian provinces. To be licensed, a naturopath must be a graduate of four years post-university training at an accredited school of naturopathic medicine. To locate a qualified naturopath, contact the American Association of Naturopath Physicians or the Canadian Association of Naturopathic Doctors (see Resources).

Fortunately, dietitian or naturopath services are typically covered under private health insurance plans. But many of the vitamins, supplements, herbal remedies, or homeopathies prescribed by a naturopath are not. Some special diets and supplements can be claimed as medical expenses on taxes or flexible spending accounts.

Seven High-Impact Ways to Improve Your Diet

Perhaps you're not ready to undergo a major dietary tune up. Even if you make no other changes, improve your health by trying these seven easy strategies:

1. **Eat more fruit and veggies** (aim for five to ten servings daily). Studies show a diet high in fruits and vegetables can reduce your chances of contracting cancer, heart disease, high blood pressure, diabetes and even the common cold. *If you can make only one change in your diet—this is the one to make!* Include dark green, orange, and yellow fruits and vegetables; these generally have the most disease-fighting potential. Keep frozen fruits and veggies in your freezer. Also include dried fruit. A recent (2005) study from the University of Scranton strongly recommended we eat more dried fruit (dried fruits currently make up less than 1 percent of our diet) as they are high in phenol antioxidants (believed to be important disease-fighting components) and other nutrients, especially fiber. Figs, prunes, and dates were among the best.

2. **Go for whole grain,** which helps protect against heart disease, diabetes, colon cancer, and even against long-term weight gain. A 2004 study from the Harvard School of Public Health found the more whole grains the participants ate, the less they weighed at the end of eight years. Buy whole grain breads, brown rice, and whole wheat pasta, bagels, hamburger/hotdog buns, pitas, tortillas, English muffins, and breadsticks. All of these can be found in the larger supermarket chains. Try barley, buckwheat, quinoa, millet, amaranth, and spelt (found in health food stores and large supermarkets). Read the ingredients label carefully. "Wheat flour" or "enriched wheat flour" usually means white flour. White flour is stripped of valuable minerals, vitamins, plant compounds, and fiber in processing. In "multigrain" products, white flour is

often the main ingredient—so that "whole wheat" bread would be the better choice.

3. **Choose your oils wisely.** Buy canola and olive oil, since both contain high amounts of disease-reducing Omega-3 fatty acids and monounsaturated fat. Limit your intake of tropical oils (coconut, palm, and palm kernel)—they're high in saturated fat, which increases your risk of heart disease. Choose non-hydrogenated margarine, salad dressing, and mayonnaise. The hydrogenation process results in trans fats, which increase total and LDL (bad) cholesterol levels. Eat out at restaurants that use non-hydrogenated oils.

4. **Steer clear of products containing trans fats.** That means packaged cookies, crackers, and other snack foods that list hydrogenated oils, partially hydrogenated oils, or vegetable oil shortening in the ingredients. Some large grocery manufacturers are starting to offer products with zero trans fats. The health food section of your supermarket or your local health food store is another good source of these products.

5. **Add beans!** Beans are loaded with nutrition and fiber. Soybeans are especially good. They're a great source of protein, they lower cholesterol, and they may help prevent some forms of cancer. Try soymilk (any flavor), tofu, textured vegetable protein (replaces ground beef in spaghetti or casseroles), or soy nuts. Look for a specialty soybean (edamame) in the frozen food section of your supermarket or health food store. Boil the pods lightly and eat the beans straight from the pod for a tasty snack or add the pod to salads, soups, or stir-fries. Add chickpeas to your salad or buy ready-made bean salads. Make or buy prepared bean soups such as pea, lentil, black bean, etc. Use hummus as dip. If you don't have time to cook with beans, heat up a can of brown beans once a week and enjoy them with whole grain toast.

6. **Cut down on meals of red meat.** (Pearson recommends no more than twice a week.) If you love beef, choose lean cuts such as loin or round. Cook meat dishes with extra lean ground beef and drain off the fat before adding to casseroles. Replace some red meat meals with poultry (skin removed), fish, or beans.

7. **Drink six-to-eight cups of fluid a day.** Most of that should be water. Teas (black or green) have disease-fighting properties. Start your day with a glass of orange juice (keep it to one glass, as juice is high in sugar content and has little to no fiber). And, don't give up on milk (low-fat or skim), which is necessary for strong bones and may prevent high blood pressure, gum disease, and colon cancer. If you can't drink milk for some reason, buy calcium-enriched orange juice or soy milk. Cut out (or at least cut back) on soda, which has no nutritional value, and may be linked to the rise in diabetes and obesity among children and adults. If you can't do without, treat yourself to the occasional diet soda or mix fruit juice with soda water.

Healthy Eating Tips for Time-Strapped Moms

When our lives are packed with appointments and our kids' needs, finding time and energy to cook is challenging. When stressed, we are even more likely to turn to easy-to-prepare, high-calorie snacks. As a result, heavily processed convenience foods and fast food restaurants become irresistible. Instead, try these easy ways to improve your diet:

Keep fruits and veggies visible. After grocery shopping, take a few minutes to wash or cut up fruits and vegetables. Keep vegetables like carrots, celery, green peppers, and cucumbers in a labeled container in the fridge. Put your washed fruit in a big bowl as a centerpiece on the kitchen table. To cut down on salad preparation time, buy pre-washed packaged salads. Fill your freezer with frozen broccoli, peas, corn, etc., so you'll be able to add instant veggies to meals. Frozen cranberries, blueberries, mango, strawberries, etc., can be tossed on your cereal, mixed in with yogurt or smoothies, added to a fruit salad, or eaten straight out of the bag.

Eyeball labels. If your kids are along at the grocery store, you likely need to speed shop. But, if you can shop alone (it can be a nice break!), slow down and read the nutrient labels (don't rely on words like "natural" or "light" on the product package). Generally, the longer the list of ingredients, the more processed and unhealthy the food is. Heavily processed foods contain additives and food dyes that children and adults may react to. Here are some general guidelines from the FDA, based on a 2,000 calorie diet:

Calories: a listing of 40 calories is deemed low, 100 is moderate, and 400 or more is high.

Saturated fat and cholesterol: a Daily Value (DV) percentage of 5 percent or less is considered low; 20 percent or more is high. When comparing two brands of products, add the saturated fat and trans fatty acid together and choose the product with the lesser amount.

Salt: the number should be as low as possible—especially if you use salt at the table. An upper limit is 2,400 mg (about 1¼ teaspoons) daily.

Sugar: make sure added sugars (which may be listed as corn syrup, high-fructose corn syrup, fruit juice concentrate, maltose, dextrose, sucrose, honey, or maple syrup) are not listed as one of the first ingredients.

Take time to eat. Many of our moms said maintaining a healthy weight was challenging. Remember to eat breakfast. One University of Massachusetts Medical School study found people who skipped breakfast were four–and-a-half times more likely to be obese than those who ate breakfast. Weight gain aside—we need breakfast for the stamina to get through our day!

Make yourself a daily snack kit at the same time you (or your kids) make their lunches. Buy an insulated lunch pack and a small freezer pack to keep food cool. In small baggies or plastic containers, package a few foods from each category to make a complete snack. So, when you're hungry, pick a snack from each bag (a fruit or veggie, protein or milk product, and a grain). This powerful snack combination will give you the most energy and prevent you from having cravings. Keep this kit in the car, at your desk, or at home on the kitchen counter.

Sup on snacks. The same study found that people who eat four or five times a day are leaner than those who eat fewer times throughout the day. Try eating four or more small *healthy* meals per day at home or at the office. Have ready-made food available (see "Your Snack Kit"). The rest of your family will benefit too—so enlist their help in preparing foods.

Shop smart. You'll make far fewer impulse purchases if you always use a grocery list and shop *after* a meal, when you aren't hungry.

Ask how a menu item is prepared in restaurants. Plan how much you are going to eat before you start eating. If the portion you are served is bigger than planned, take the rest home for the next meal. Refrain from sampling everything on the buffet table just because it's included in the price.

Start a cooking club. Here's a great way to save some time preparing meals—and you'll get in some socializing, too! Once a month, with five friends, choose three dinner dishes (casseroles, soups, lasagna, etc.) that you all enjoy. On an agreed-upon weekend, cook up a twelve-serving quantity of your assigned dish. That evening, gather at one of your houses (armed with your dish and containers) for a moms' night out. At the end of the evening, you trade dishes, each person taking home three four-serving dinners to store in your

Your Snack Kit

(Bring along a plastic spoon and some napkins or wet wipes.)

Fruits and Vegetables

Apple

Pear

Grapes

Banana

Mandarin oranges/clementines

Peach or nectarine

Fruit leathers (pure fruit, not "roll-ups")

Dates

Raisins

Dried fruits (figs, apricots, prunes, cranberries, apples, etc.)

Fruit cup (in juice)

Unsweetened applesauce

Fruit or vegetable juice

Baby carrots (pre-washed ones are easiest)

Grape or cherry tomatoes

Meat, Poultry, Fish, Dried Beans, and Nuts

Lean meat slices (turkey, chicken)

Imitation slices of baloney or turkey (made from tofu)

Boiled egg

Unsalted nuts (almonds, cashews, walnuts, peanuts, etc.)

Seeds (pumpkin, sunflower, etc.)

Trail mix (containing nuts, seeds, dried fruit)

Roasted soy nuts

Roasted chick peas (check the ethnic section of your supermarket)

Honey and sesame seed bars

Treats

Chocolate- or carob-covered raisins or nuts

Baked tortilla, pita, or potato chips

Fig Newtons

Ginger Snaps

Milk, Yogurt, and Cheese *(low fat)*

Yogurt cup, tube, or drink

Boxed milk, chocolate milk, or soymilk

Milk pudding cup

Individually wrapped cheese sticks (or slice beforehand)

Breads, Cereal, Rice, and Pasta *(choose whole grain varieties)*

Bread sticks

Crackers

Flatbreads

Bagel or bagel chips

Shreddies, Bran Flakes, Cheerios, etc., in a zip-lock bag

Granola bars (low fat)

Pretzels

Rice cakes or crackers

English muffin

Pita bread or pita chips

Tortillas

Whole grain muffins (low fat)

Popcorn (unsalted or reduced salt)

Corn nuts (unsalted or reduced salt)

freezer. If you have a large kitchen or access to a church or community center, you can do your cooking together and rotate the shopping among your members.

Plan your meals a week ahead. Write down each day of the week on a small piece of paper. (The back of the grocery list works well.) Check your calendar for evening activities and choose quick meals for nights when you need to be somewhere in a hurry. Write down each dish (include recipe book and page number if necessary). Add any necessary ingredients to your grocery list. The result is only one trip to the grocery store a week (only the occasional side trips to pick up items missed or amounts misjudged). You can reuse your meal plans if you like, saving even more time. And by planning ahead, you are less likely to give in to "impulse" buys or a fast food fix.

Double or even triple up your cooking when you have some extra time. Instead of making one casserole, make two and freeze the second. Keep a stockpile of dishes in the freezer so the next time a crisis hits feeding your family isn't an extra worry.

Investigate the new crock pots that enable you to cook side dishes of vegetables along with your main dish. If you don't have time in the mornings, prepare your ingredients the night before and refrigerate.

Rethink which foods are considered "dinner." Eat more "easy" meals that are just as nutritious (and delicious) as ones that take more time. By eating simply, you'll also avoid the excess sauces, condiments, and gravy that often add fat but few nutrients. Here are a few ideas to try. But you can probably come up with some more great ones on your own:

> Serve store bought or homemade bean dip with whole grain pitas, veggies, and fruit.
> Grill a cheese sandwich (soak it in egg and add a slice of ham or turkey for an added treat).

Serve peanut butter sandwiches (add sliced bananas and cinnamon to your filling or lightly spread
margarine on the outside and grill it up like a
grilled cheese sandwich).
For variety, try other nut butters from the health
food aisles (almond, cashew, soybean).
Mix cooked whole wheat noodles with sun-dried
tomatoes (oil-packed in a jar) and sprinkle with
Parmesan cheese.
Dress fish fillets with a bit of margarine, spices,
and lemon juice and cook in the microwave. Add
some fast-cooking couscous, a few carrot sticks,
and a glass of milk, and you have a complete meal.
Frozen meals (read labels to avoid excess sodium
and fat) can be fine, but round out the meal with
extra vegetables and whole-grain bread.

Get Help. Especially during tough times, make use of
your support systems to help with meals or food preparation. When Amy's daughter had back surgery, several
friends brought over soups and dinners. One friend
cooked an extra portion of her family's meals and
brought them over for the freezer. Don't be afraid to
ask for help—friends and family are usually pleased to
have a concrete way of supporting you.

Getting the Kids On Board with Healthy Eating

You may feel these ideas are not so "easy" if your child presents special meal-related challenges. If so, it's easy to get so focused on getting
your child to eat (or keeping harmful foods away from him) that you
forget about your own diet. First, focus on what you can do easily for
yourself—snacking on more fruits and vegetables or choosing whole
grain crackers, for instance.

If your child has dietary restrictions because of allergies, food intolerances, or other conditions, then obviously there's no wiggle room
on his meal plan. You'll have to decide whether it's easier to keep the
whole family on the same restricted diet, or to make separate meals for

the child with special needs. (And by "easy," we're referring not just to how many separate meals you have to prepare, but also to how many arguments and complaints you'll have to referee.) But keep in mind that no one "needs" junk food—so, for example, if one child can't eat dairy or food additives, you're not being "unfair" by keeping ice cream and candy out of the house entirely.

On the other hand, many children with special needs are just incredibly picky eaters. If so, you can take steps to subtly modify family meals to make them healthier. Amy, for example, threw in a handful of frozen vegetables and used whole wheat noodles in a cheese/tuna/noodle casserole. Her daughter, who is sensitive to textures and spices, ate it happily.

The average mother tries offering her child a new food three times or less before she gives up. But nutrition expert Pearson says you may have to offer that same food ten or even fifteen times before your child decides he likes it: "Accept that you will have to throw out uneaten food. But, don't give up. Introduce new foods again and again." Rather than trying to force your child to eat an entire serving of a new food, try having a "one bite rule"—if he doesn't like that first bite, he doesn't have to eat any more (until next time it's served). You'll have the best results if you give your child new or less-preferred foods when he's the most hungry. For example, try offering raw veggies and dip before dinner.

Remember, good nutrition is vital for everyone's health. If you and your family have gotten into bad eating habits, then it's reasonable to expect that you'll get some resistance on the home front when you start to implement changes. Take it slowly, and know that, over time, it'll get easier. Once you've gone a few weeks without donuts or cookies, you'll find that apples and oranges taste sweeter than you'd remembered.

Experience Talks

"What I find works for me is to prepare several meals/breads at one time and freeze things. I always have healthy snacks in the car with me: fruits, water, nuts.... This keeps my hunger at bay and limits the runs into the convenience store for that junk food."

—Maya, mother of three children with special needs (mental health, ADHD, and learning disorders)

"I keep the cookies in the freezer to make it more difficult to eat them. I try and buy healthy snacks and I always have fruit available. My best advice is to eat more fruit."

—Kuan, mother of a teen who is blind and has cerebral palsy

"Eat a salad every day—vegetable or fruit. If you miss it at lunch, have it for dinner or for a snack. Vary your vegetables: add mandarin orange slices (fresh or canned), walnuts, chick peas, or sun-dried tomatoes. Wash vegetables in advance, keeping them in a zip-lock bag, or buy ready-made. There are some great frozen fruit mixes. Thaw for a day and you have ready-made fruit salad. I've cut my colds down to one a year and I've never felt better."

—Debbie, mother of a child with Asperger syndrome

"Eat healthy for just one week. After that week, you will feel so much better and be so proud of yourself that you'll want to continue. Subscribe to magazines that emphasize fitness and healthy eating."

—Suki, mother of a child with Tourette syndrome, learning disabilities, and anxiety disorder

"I am having trouble balancing my life with all the demands of my work and my son's requirements. I have a weight control problem and I never find time to exercise anymore. Before children, I was physically active: cycled, downhill skied, and golfed. The special needs of my family now encompass so much time that I can't include these very important aspects of healthy living."

—Louise, whose son has autism

Chapter 5

Stay Strong and Healthy— Get Physical

If it seems like you get sick more than other moms—you're probably right. Only 12 percent of moms of children with special needs rated their health as "very good" in a Canadian study by the Roeher Institute (2000). This contrasts with the 40 percent of mothers nationwide who rated their health as "very good" in a 1996 National Population Health Survey.

Exercising is a great way to improve both your physical and mental health. But before you even start thinking about exercise, you need to take inventory. Sure, you've been busy taking care of your child. But have you used that as an excuse to postpone your own health needs? None of us enjoy getting in the stirrups or the dental chair, and it's easy to let these things slip when your child's special needs seem so much more pressing than your own. But think about it—do you really want to risk some minor problem becoming a major one? Who's going to care for your child if you wind up in the hospital because you were "just too busy" to spare an hour for a doctor's visit?

Today, schedule all the appointments FOR YOURSELF that you've been putting off—that might include a physical, pap test, dental checkup, eye exam/glasses update, or mammogram. Get that sore knee or annoying rash checked out by a specialist. If your hair's falling out, find out whether it's being caused by stress or by a hormone imbalance.

Plan ahead for your medical appointments, and book child care with respite workers, family, or friends. Take your daily planner with you to each appointment, so if you need a follow-up visit, you can make plans on the spot. (Waiting until you get home to check your calendar just creates one more opportunity for you get off track.) And once you're caught up on all your health care needs, put a reminder on the calendar for any long-term follow-up. Some women like to book their annual doctor's appointments around their birthdays, making it easier to remember each year.

If you won't do it for yourself, do it for your son or daughter. You don't want to someday have regrets like Lori, mother of an adult with developmental disabilities, who told us she now wishes she'd taken better care of her own physical and mental health: "Now that I am older, and my daughter's sole caretaker, it is beginning to take a toll on me."

Making the Case for Exercise

TO STAY HEALTHY

One of the best ways of taking care of yourself is by making time to work on your own fitness. It's now common knowledge that aerobic exercise (such as walking, jogging, swimming, or cardio fitness classes) plays an important part in preventing disease and maintaining overall health. Aerobic exercise trains your heart, lungs, and cardiovascular system to deliver oxygen more efficiently through your body. It also can reduce your cholesterol levels and aid in weight control.

Developing strength is another step towards wellness. Especially if your child needs extensive physical care or lifting, you need strong core and back muscles. Kuan, mother of a child with cerebral palsy, shares that "Yoga keeps me physically strong, which is very important as my son Jeremy weighs 70 pounds and I have to lift and transfer him in and out of his wheelchair."

Both authors take Pilates classes for strength and relaxation (and to recover from hours in front of the computer working on this book!). As we get older and start to lose muscle strength and bone density, activities like lifting weights, Pilates, and exercising on a fitness ball are essential. These activities also help to increase energy, control weight, and calm a racing mind.

Amy met with a trainer at the YMCA who developed a strength training program for her. "Over time, I was thrilled to see some muscle definition. But equally important, strength training was a confidence booster. When things were challenging with my daughter, the gym became my sanctuary. While I couldn't control my daughter's progress, I could improve my own fitness level and strength."

"Mindful" activities such as yoga and Tai Chi also help promote body confidence, relaxation, concentration, and flexibility.

For maximum health benefits, it's ideal if you can combine some form of aerobic exercise with strength training and stretching or relaxation. Fortunately, you needn't go to a gym to improve your health. By walking, lifting hand weights (or soup cans), and stretching, you can improve your cardiovascular fitness, strength, and flexibility at home.

Many mothers we spoke with say they just don't have time for a regular fitness program. The recommended bare minimum for maintaining heart health is thirty minutes of cardio exercise (such as brisk walking), three times a week. If you feel you can't schedule in this amount of exercise, could you manage several ten-minute workouts instead? Several university studies have shown that doing three ten-minute exercise sessions in a day provide similar cardiovascular benefits to doing one thirty-minute session.

TO IMPROVE YOUR MOOD AND MENTAL HEALTH

When you're feeling tired, stressed, or down, the last thing you may feel like doing is exercising. But exercise can also be the key to improving your mood and energy level. Current research shows that exercise lowers stress and has a protective effect against depression and anxiety. Especially during the tough times, exercise can be your lifeline.

Fortunately, exercise doesn't have to be an "all or nothing" activity. Even one session of exercise can improve your mood. In a study (1993) at the University of Athens, women who took a single aerobics class reported an improvement in their mood that lasted for at least twenty-four hours. But if you're not an aerobics fan, you still have countless exercise choices that will help you feel good. In studies, women have reported similar mood-improvements after walking, jogging, swimming, cycling, weight training, and even yoga. In a 2004 study at Pacific University in California, twelve women caring for relatives with dementia participated in a six-week yoga and meditation program designed to help them cope with stress. Most participants expressed reduced feelings of depression and anxiety and increased feelings of self-efficacy (capability).

And, you don't need thirty minutes of exertion to feel better. Some studies have shown that even short bouts of exercise can improve your mental and physical health. In a study at Northern Arizona University (2001), participants reported improvements in vigor, fatigue, and mood after a single ten-minute session on a stationary bike.

Even if you can't commit to regular fitness, it's important to allow yourself at least a ten-minute break each day to do something active. A quick walk around the block at the end of the day can do wonders to improve your mood and lessen feelings of stress.

Researchers have examined what kinds of exercises provide the biggest psychological boost. According to a recent (2004) Polish review of existing research, the biggest mood improvements have been shown by people who participate in rhythmic, aerobic exercises (such as walking, jogging, swimming, or cycling) for fifteen to thirty minutes, three times a week for at least ten weeks.

If you're feeling especially down, remember how powerful exercise can be. Those who start out feeling the lowest also have the most to gain. In a University of Wolverhampton study, participants who started an aerobics class feeling the most depressed went away with significantly less anger, confusion, fatigue, and tension, as well as more vigor, than those who started in a good mood. And women are shown in studies to make the biggest gains.

What's the bottom line? No matter what your fitness goal (mood improvement, strength, flexibility, or overall health), you'll look and feel better if you exercise. Start with whatever time you can spare.

Then, build up to doing thirty minutes of moderate exercise (in one session or in several short bouts), at least three times a week.

Getting Started

Fortunately, there are many easy ways to increase your fitness level. Your heart, lungs, and nervous system don't care whether you're jogging around a fancy track at the gym or through the parking lot by your toddler's school.

BE ACTIVE IN EVERYDAY TASKS

Before looking at more formal ways of exercising, look at simple ways of modifying your everyday routine to increase your level of activity. For example, Amy used to drive her daughter to and from school most days. Now, they walk instead. Even though the school is only a five-minute walk away, it adds up to twenty minutes a day. While your child has therapy or a lesson, can you go for a walk instead of sitting and waiting? If you are at home full time or work in an office, take a break to walk up and down the stairs a few times. While watching TV, can you march on the spot, or do stretch breaks during the commercials? At home, dance to your favorite CD.

Maya, mother of three children with special needs, including bipolar disorder, depression, ADHD, and learning disabilities, finds creative ways to sneak in exercise. She explains, "Exercise is often the hardest activity to find time for, but I always feel better afterwards. I take my dogs for walks at a brisk pace. I'll stretch/do sit-ups/push-ups/etc. while awaiting my kids in their karate class. The class is in one large open room with the kids on a mat and the parents sitting on chairs and watching. I just take a far corner of the mat or on the floor by the chairs and do my thing! I'll even jog in place while folding laundry!"

SET AN OVERALL GOAL

Once you've started to increase your everyday activity level, set some more formal goals for yourself. Start by looking at what motivates you. Write down your main reasons for wanting to exercise. Check off all of the boxes below that apply to you.

Through exercise I hope to:

☐ Reduce stress and improve my mood
☐ Increase my level of energy
☐ Lose or gain weight and tone body
☐ Increase muscle strength
☐ Decrease risk of heart disease and other illnesses
☐ Be able to carry out my daily activities with more ease
  (i.e., lifting my child, climbing stairs, carrying groceries)
☐ Socialize with others
☐ Spend more time outdoors or in nature
☐ Sleep better
☐ Increase my self-esteem and confidence
☐ Have fun
☐ Other _____

DETERMINE YOUR TARGET

Write down specifically where you hope to be at the end of the year. Sample goals could be to:

> Be able to play active soccer with my children for thirty minutes without feeling winded
> Lose twenty pounds
> Be able to lift and manage the care of my child without back and muscle strain

Then, work backwards. Where do you hope to be nine months, six months, and three months from now? What do you need to do *right now* in order to achieve your goal?

Next figure out exactly what activities you will do each week in order to achieve your goal. Schedule them into your calendar.

Sample exercise goals for a week could include:

> Add fifteen minutes of activity to my daily routine
> Choose one (one-hour) activity on the weekend that is active (e.g., walking, skating, swimming, attending a dance class)
> Walk for thirty minutes (accumulated in short bouts is fine) three times per week
> Walk with a friend for thirty minutes in the neighborhood one evening per week

In your datebook or family calendar, check off each day or week that you managed to meet your goal. If you weren't successful, look at the reasons why. Then you can look at ways of removing some of the barriers that prevent you from increasing your activity level. If you were successful, look at ways for increasing your goals. For example, if you're walking three times per week, increase the time or distance, or add hills to your route.

KEEP IT SIMPLE: FIVE IDEAS TO GET YOU STARTED

If your time, schedule, and money are tight, try these speedy exercise ideas:

1. **Get on the ball for ten minutes a day.** "The best all-around exercise for home is the stability ball," says Cheryl Guindon, personal trainer, and manager at the YMCA-YWCA in Guelph, Ontario. It's good for all ages, body types, and fitness levels. For ten minutes, do "ball squats" against a wall while lifting hand weights, soup cans, or empty containers filled with sand. For this exercise, place the ball on a wall and while standing, press your back against it. Then, slowly squat, so that the ball rolls down the wall. (Consult a book, trainer, or video for the proper technique.) If you do this exercise without resting between squats, you work 75 percent of the muscles in your body, says Guindon. Best of all, you're working on functional movements. You do the same moves when picking up your child or when hauling groceries. Plus, you're working on your cardiovascular system, as well as stress relief.

2. **Walk your way to wellness.** Buy a good quality pair of shoes and head outside. To maintain cardio health, you need at least thirty minutes of brisk walking three times per week. But if you're just starting out, it might be easier to try short bouts of walking (ten minutes). A University of Pittsburgh study of women who were overweight showed that participants who were advised to walk in short bouts were more likely to maintain their walking programs than ones who were instructed to walk thirty minutes per session. In fact, the short-

bout walkers actually spent more time walking overall and walked on more days than the others.

3. **Find a friend.** To increase your motivation, exercise with a partner or group. If you're active in a support group, suggest a walking club. For years, Heather walked with two other moms from a playgroup one or two evenings a week. "If one of us couldn't go, that still left two to walk. We always scheduled our next walk before returning home."

4. **Track your progress and stay motivated by using a pedometer.** Clip an inexpensive pedometer to a belt above your hip in order to count the number of steps you take per day. Health America recommends taking 10,000 steps per day for health benefits. To start, wear the pedometer for your daily activities and at the end of the day, write down the number of steps you took. Most people take 900 to 3,000 steps in a typical day of everyday activities. Then, find ways to increase the daily steps you take, eventually aiming for 10,000. Small changes will add up. Take an extra loop around the grocery store, walk to visit a friend, walk at lunch at your workplace.

5. **Go natural.** If you love the outdoors, find new, beautiful places to walk. Says Helena, mother of two teens—one with hearing loss, ADHD and depression, "I enjoy walking my dog in the woods with a group of other mothers early in the morning, just after my sons get on the bus for school. I really enjoy these early A.M. walks even in the cold and light rain. Afterwards, I feel pretty refreshed and it's very nice to talk to these other parents."

Add variety. Once you're walking regularly, consider adding different ways to exercise. For relaxation, flexibility, and strength, try a class (or home DVD) of yoga or Pilates. To build muscle, tone and speed weight loss, consider trying strength training with light hand weights.

Motivation 101

Even if you're initially enthusiastic about pursuing fitness, you may have a hard time sticking with your goals. To maintain your motivation, try these additional strategies:

Set specific goals and write them down. At the beginning of each week, write down in your calendar exactly what exercise you will do each day. Or at the end of each day, write down your activity for the next day.

Pay in advance. Says Bernie, mother of a child with multiple needs, "I've found that I'm more likely to get to class if I buy a class card and input the whole session of classes into my Palm Pilot—this makes it both a larger financial and personal commitment up front."

Commit to following your plan for three months. Once you've followed through this long, you're more likely to be hooked on exercise.

Write up an exercise contract with yourself. Have your partner or a friend sign and witness it.

Visualize what you will see and feel when your goal is accomplished.

Make visual reminders. Post encouraging slogans and exercise reminders at the door, on your fridge.

Tell friends about your goals so you'll be more likely to follow through.

Have a friend call (or email) you at the beginning of the day, to remind you to exercise, and at the end of the day to check back with you. Offer to do the same for your friend.

Take your own wellness and fitness seriously. Make an individual health plan for yourself (much like your child's IEP). For help, consult with a fitness trainer and nutritionist.

Keep adding fitness activities that are fun. Try skating, a dance class, water fitness, etc.

As reinforcement, every week jot down a list of "healthy pleasures" you're enjoying as a result of exercising. Examples include: better sleep, better fitting clothes, relaxation, and that "after glow" in your muscles after a strenuous workout.

But Who's Minding the Kids?

Many moms reported that fitness takes a back seat in their lives because they didn't have appropriate child care (or funds for child care). But if you're determined, there are ways around that.

When Heather's daughter was an infant, she made a deal with her husband that continues more than a decade later. "We trade off weekend mornings of child care. Originally, we used those mornings to catch up on sleep. Now we use the time to bicycle, cross-country ski, or walk. If children's activities crop up, the parent who's 'on' handles it."

If you work outside the home, try tying your workout to your work day. Take an extra thirty minutes to exercise before or after work, while your partner or daycare provider keeps an eye on the kids. Or try walking a few times a week during a break or lunch hour—preferably with a friend or co-worker. If your workplace has an exercise room, you (and other employees) can hire a fitness instructor to teach lunch time classes, or you can stick a workout video in the DVD player.

Many recreation centers, YMCAs, and fitness clubs have on-site child care. Meet with the staff and see if they can accommodate your child. Some also offer parent and tot classes, where you exercise *with* your child. Alternatively, request they run a class for children with disabilities concurrently with a class for adults.

Of course, you don't actually have to leave the house to exercise. If you have the time, space, and willpower to exercise independently, start a home routine. Hire a personal trainer, buy exercise videotapes, or borrow them from the library. If you'd prefer company, have a once-a-week "class" in your home and invite a friend. To keep your child occupied, set aside one favorite activity she may only do while you're exercising—whether it's time on the computer, that video that drives you up a wall, or the building blocks with 1,000 pieces. Strategize right, and she may start suggesting you need to exercise! But if that won't work, hire a babysitter to get your child out of the house while you sweat—maybe for a walk in the fresh air or milk and cookies at her house.

Consider buying new or used exercise equipment to use at home. Says Suki, mother of a child with Tourette's syndrome, ADHD, and learning disabilities, "After my kids go to bed each night, I use an exercise bike while reading or watching TV. My husband cleans up each evening, because he knows that exercise is important to me. On weekends, I sometimes exercise during the day when the kids are busy with something else, or I let them watch TV with me."

Make Fitness a Family Priority

GET THE EQUIPMENT

Can't leave your child alone so you can exercise? Instead, you can bring them along in an exercise stroller, wheelchair, or a bicycle cart while you walk, run or bike. Larger sport "joggers" are designed to hold older children with special needs.

Specialized bicycles, skis, and other equipment are available for older children. You may be surprised at how fast your child can meet your own fitness level. Gross motor delays kept Heather's daughter from riding a bike until almost nine but just three summers later she joined the family in a 60 km charity ride.

Check to see if your insurance will cover the cost of equipment that is used for mobility (such as a three-wheeled bike for a teen). If not, approach disability organizations, hospitals and rehabilitation centers, service clubs like Rotary or Easter Seals, foundations and trusts, or equipment manufacturers. For contact information, see the Resources section at the end of the book. Besides providing funding, some may rent or loan used or new equipment. See if a local bank has special financing plans for disability-related purchases. Some specialized equipment manufacturers may provide discounts, rent-to-own programs, or advice on getting the product paid for under insurance.

15 Easy Ways to Increase your Exercise

1. **Each night schedule a ten-minute or longer family walk.** Motivate your kids by increasing the fun factor. Play "I spy" or "spot the most dogs" type games as you walk. The winner gets to choose the bedtime story. Heather used to take her kids on a "book hike." She brought her kids' favorite books along. After every ten minutes of walking, they would stop for a reading break.

2. **Each weekend, schedule at least one family activity that involves fitness.** Take turns choosing the activity.

3. **Play with your kids.** Join in games of tag, hide-and-seek, Simon Says, etc. Play backyard croquet, horseshoes, or badminton. Buy or borrow a driveway basketball hoop, or shoot into plastic garbage bins.

4. **Park a ten-minute walk away from work.**

5. **Get off the bus to work a few stops early.**

6. **Do you have a favorite TV show you watch without fail? Take a twenty-minute walk before watching it.** Write both activities in your calendar.

7. **Park at the far end of the parking lot when doing errands alone.** Keep an umbrella in the car and dress for the weather. Whenever possible, walk rather than drive for nearby errands.

MAKE IT FUN

One way to increase friendships as well as fitness is joining a group. For instance, the American Volksport Association offers organized hikes and special family walking events in all states. In addition, they specify the level of difficulty of every trail, and whether it is wheelchair accessible. Or get motivated to meet your fitness and healthy eating goals by joining America on the Move, which is a national initiative helping people improve their health. You can register (for free) as a group or individually to receive tips and track your progress. (See the Resource Guide for more information.)

8. **Hit the outdoors.** To find recreational trails close to you, see Resources.
9. **Walk around your house and use the stairs while you talk with a friend on a portable phone.**
10. **Walk with friends instead of going for a coffee.**
11. **Avoid labor-saving devices at home.** Use a push mower instead of gas or electric, wash the car by hand, and use a snow shovel instead of a snow blower.
12. **If you're getting bored, try anything new** such as indoor cycling, yoga, belly dancing, kickball, etc.
13. **Instead of sitting while you watch your child's sports team practice, walk briskly around the field or arena.** Invite other parents along.
14. **Join a mall walking program**—especially when it's too cold to walk outside.
15. **Whenever possible, take the stairs instead of the elevator.** Amy recently spent a week on the fifth floor of a children's hospital after her daughter underwent surgery. Using the stairs instead of the elevator when she went to get meals helped Amy keep her stress level down and energy level up. If you work or live in a high rise building, walk up the first few flights and take the elevator the rest of the way. Gradually, increase the number of flights you climb.

Whatever activities you choose, it's a good idea to set goals. Create a family calendar with family exercise and activity written in. For each successful week, you can celebrate or offer awards such as certificates or special video nights.

Finally, if the thought of fitting any formal exercise into your life at this point stresses you out, don't give up. Life circumstances change. In the meantime, grab exercise at any opportunity. Walk your dog, garden, swim with your kids, run up and down stairs at home. Just keep moving.

Experience Talks

"Exercise helps me control my weight, feel more in control of my life, and bolsters my spirits. The most important thing is to find a way of exercising that fits into your schedule and lifestyle. Otherwise, you won't do it. Decide whether it is easier for you to leave the house to exercise (walk, run, hike, or join a health club), or to exercise at home (buy videos that motivate you and/or invest in the best equipment you can afford)."

—Suki, mother of a child with Tourette syndrome, ADHD, and learning disabilities

"My daughter is often up at odd hours of the night or extremely early in the morning, which interrupts my sleep. Sometimes my husband works late and inadvertently wakes me up when he comes to bed, so my sleep gets short-changed on both ends. Other times, I can't sleep because of worrying about my daughter or for other, unexplained reasons—perhaps depression-related."

—Bernie, mother of three, including a child with ADHD and a mood disorder

Chapter 6

Desperately Seeking Sleep

Are you getting enough? Sleep that is. Many of us are not. A 2005 survey from the National Sleep Foundation finds adults sleep, on average, seven hours per night. Some moms we surveyed coped with much less: only four hours for some shift-workers. You may feel that your sleep deprivation is simply a fact of life—an issue that can be solved by downing a few extra cups of coffee. But adequate sleep is just as important as good nutrition and exercise are for your physical and mental health.

Research shows that insufficient or interrupted sleep leads to concentration and memory problems, sleepiness, inability to work effectively (inside or outside the home), and to serious or fatal car accidents. In his position as medical director of the Texas Children's Sleep Center at the Texas Children's Hospital in Houston, Dr. Daniel G. Glaze sees many families of children who have special needs and sleep problems. "Frequently, the mom has quit her job because she no longer can function or is falling asleep while driving to her job. If you're not getting a good sleep at night, it impacts not only on you, but on the whole family."

If you struggle with maintaining a healthy weight, inadequate sleep could be a contributing factor. In a recent study at the University of Chicago, researchers found that partial sleep deprivation changes the level of hormones that regulate hunger. After participants (young men) slept only four hours each for two nights, they reported a 24 percent increase in appetite. And what they most craved: sweet, salty, and starchy foods. In another recent study, people who reported less than four hours of sleep a night were 73 percent more likely to be obese.

Several studies link insomnia with psychiatric and medical illnesses. For example, women with insomnia are at a greater risk of becoming depressed—and staying that way. Recent research at the University of Chicago suggests that sleep deprivation may be linked to a variety of physical problems, such as reduced ability to fight infections. Inadequate sleep can even foster insulin-resistance, which is a risk factor for developing type 2 diabetes.

Fortunately, there's much you can do to improve your sleep life. The first step is to determine if you're getting the amount of sleep that you need.

Are You Getting Enough Sleep?

While most people feel rested after eight hours of sleep, individual needs vary. Some people feel alert on as little as six hours of sleep, and others need as much as nine or ten hours.

To determine how much sleep you need in order to feel rested, keep a blank book beside your bed. For two weeks, jot down the hours you sleep each night and how alert you feel during the following day. If you're awake during the middle of the night, note that, too. If, for example, you only get seven hours of sleep per night, but you feel alert and rested, that amount might be right for you. But if you feel sleepy and rely on coffee or other sources of caffeine to keep you alert, you're getting insufficient sleep.

Speak to your doctor if:

You have a long history of being unable to fall or stay asleep.

You frequently feel you can't concentrate and maintain your alertness during the day, even though you got sufficient sleep.

Your fatigue and sleepiness are interfering with your ability to carry out and enjoy your daily life.

You have unexplained high blood pressure. Untreated sleep apnea (when you stop breathing repeatedly during sleep), for example, can lead to cardiovascular problems like hypertension, heart attacks, and strokes.

Sleep disturbances (e.g., insomnia, sleeping too much, or early-morning wakefulness) and problems with concentration can be signs of depression. But if your doctor rules out depression as the cause of your sleep difficulties, she may decide to refer you to a sleep specialist, who may order a sleep study at a clinic. This study will examine possible physical causes of your daytime sleepiness, such as breathing problems or nighttime leg movements. (See more about sleep studies towards the end of this chapter.)

Do You Have Insomnia?

Does it frequently take you more than thirty minutes to fall asleep? Do you often wake up in the middle of the night and have trouble falling back to sleep? If your sleep is disturbed by one of these problems three times or more per week, you share a common problem with many moms—insomnia. The good news is that you don't have to be doomed to toss and turn. Try these tips:

Only go to bed when you're really tired. Try going to bed an hour later.

If you're having trouble falling asleep (or getting back to sleep in the middle of the night), get out of bed and try a quiet activity, such as reading, in another room. Only return to bed when you're feeling sleepy.

Avoid taking a nap during the day. If you feel over-whelmingly sleepy, limit yourself to a short nap (twenty to thirty minutes) no later than 3:00 p.m. (Naps are okay if you want to catch up on sleep, and you don't suffer from insomnia at night.)

Try to go to bed and wake up at the same time each day, including weekends.

Avoid coffee, tea, caffeinated drinks, and chocolate after noon.

Take a warm (not steaming hot) bath before bed.

Make your bedroom a comfortable haven for sleep. Buy heavy curtains to block out sound and light. Keep the bedroom temperature comfortably cool. Is your mattress comfortable? If not, visit a mattress store for advice and to try out other mattresses. Try out various pillows, such as ones that are shaped to the curve of your neck. Treat yourself to soft sheets, a cozy blanket, or new duvet.

Reserve your bedroom only for sleep and for sex. Bill-paying, surfing the Internet, and reading heart-pounding thrillers should take place in other rooms. That way, you automatically associate your bedroom with sleep.

Avoid doing anything mentally stimulating (like working on the computer) or upsetting (like dealing with medical bills) before bed.

If you're kept awake thinking about what you need to do the next day, keep a blank book beside your bed. Before going to sleep, write down reminders to yourself, and then "close the book on them."

If worry about your child, family, work, health, etc., keeps you awake, choose from one of the meditation techniques in "Anti-Worry Meditation Exercises."

Exercise during the day (but not at night).

Try a progressive relaxation exercise before you go to sleep. Lie on your back in bed and start by tensing up your feet for a few seconds. Then, release the tension on your feet and let them relax. Repeat the tensing and relaxing sequence with your calves, thighs, etc., up through your body. Pay attention to which parts

Sleep Remedies—Naturally Speaking

If insomnia is a chronic problem for you, consider trying natural remedies (under the direction of a licensed naturopath). Teas made from mild natural sedatives such as chamomile, lavender hops, lemon balm, and passionflower are natural relaxants. The naturopath may also suggest homeopathic remedies.

Homeopathy is a system of medicine founded on the principle that a substance which produces symptoms in a person who's healthy can cure those symptoms in someone who's ill. Homeopathic medicines are diluted many times until the concentration can be so low that not even one molecule of the original exists.

Acupuncture as a treatment for insomnia also shows some promise, but more research is needed.

Never self-prescribe stronger sedatives like valerian and kava kava that have not been proven safe. Both the FDA and Health Canada advise consumers not to use kava kava due to concerns around liver toxicity. Also, don't self-prescribe melatonin, a hormone popular with travelers and shift-workers, which is thought to regulate sleep cycles. Be cautious if considering "natural remedies" such as melatonin, as there are few studies supporting their effectiveness. Since treatments like melatonin are not regulated by the FDA (Food and Drug Administration), there is no guarantee about the actual contents of the product you buy. (Never give alternative health supplements to your children or take them yourself without first checking with your doctor or naturopath, especially if you're pregnant or are taking any prescription or over-the-counter medications.)

of your body already feel tense. By the end of this exercise, you'll likely feel both physically and mentally more relaxed.

Skip the evening news, which is often filled with disturbing images and events. Instead, if possible, fill your head with images and thoughts that are happy and relaxing. Listen to relaxing music or read an inspiring book. Take a few minutes to jot down in a blank book five things from your day that you were grateful for and enjoyed. On a tough day, remember the small things—a great cup of coffee, an interesting conversation, a new flower blooming in your garden.

Try a glass of warm milk before bed. Milk contains tryptophan, an amino acid that converts to serotonin—a neurotransmitter that helps you feel sleepy.

Skip alcohol for four to six hours before bed. Although a glass of wine may help relax you initially, it can cause sleep disturbances in the middle of the night.

Avoid aerobic exercise before bed, as it raises your heart rate. You want to slow down your metabolism. Instead, try stretching, a relaxation exercise, Tai Chi, or a brief meditation (see next page).

Try herbal teas or other natural remedies (see box).

See your doctor. Occasional insomnia is normal. But if your insomnia carries on for weeks and affects how you feel during the day, speak to your doctor. She may prescribe short-term medication along with the behavioral strategies described above. Or the doctor may refer you to a sleep specialist. If anxiety or depression affects your sleep, she may recommend medication and/or counseling. (See Chapter 7 for more on dealing with anxiety and depression.)

Anti-Worry Meditation Techniques

Try these four meditation techniques to calm your worries:

Memorize a comforting poem or psalm that you can focus on in the middle of the night. Choose poems with meter, rhyme, and soothing images such as the water or the sea. If you can't sleep, silently go through the poem in your head. Every time, a worry "breaks through," simply start back at the beginning of the poem. Don't be frustrated if you aren't able to get through to the end of the poem. Completing the poem is not important. What matters is the process of focusing on the soothing words instead of your worries.

Slowly count to ten silently without any other thought interfering. Breathe in time to your counting—one breath for each number. If your mind strays from counting, start back at number one again.

If you're intensely worried, try this visualization. Picture the person you're worried about. Then, think back to a time when you were feeling joyful with them, or when they were feeling delighted. Now bring that image to mind and picture that person feeling happy, surrounded by a color that is comforting to you. Focus on that positive image and breathe slowly.

Escape. With your eyes closed, picture a beautiful place you've visited. Focus on all the sensory details around you. For example, if you're on a beach, smell the fragrance of coconut sunscreen, see the pelicans soaring above you, feel the sun warming your skin, and hear the waves crashing.

Source: Tzivia Gover, author of *Mindful Moments for Stressful Days.*

Sleep Deficit—Catching up on Lost Sleep

Even if you don't have insomnia, you may be suffering from insufficient sleep. Many moms *could* sleep more but don't—either because their children keep them up or because they're "too busy" to get sufficient time in the sack.

The result is sleep deficit—the total amount of sleep that you've lost over time. For example, if you need eight hours of sleep each night to feel rested, and you typically sleep only seven hours, you have a sleep deficit of seven hours by the end of the week. That means you've lost the equivalent of an entire night's sleep in just one week! If you're constantly living with such a sleep deficit, you'll feel the effects, which can include exhaustion, inability to concentrate, and physical/mental stress.

Are You Cheating Yourself Out of Sleep?

Many moms tell us they willingly let other activities stand between them and sweet slumber.

Do any of these statements apply to you?
- ☐ I frequently stay up late or get up early so that I can enjoy some time to myself. It's the only time I get to read, watch TV, cruise the web, return emails, or just relax.
- ☐ I have a home-based business, so often I work late at night when my kids are asleep.
- ☐ I can't stand it when my house is chaotic. So at night or early in the morning, I catch up on chores like doing laundry, paying bills, and completing paperwork for my child's needs.

If you're occasionally trading off sleep for personal time, it isn't a big issue. But if this is your daily habit, you could be accumulating a significant sleep deficit.

Instead, meet with your family to brainstorm ways to increase your daily time to unwind, to work on your business, or to tidy up. For example, can you designate an hour to yourself after dinner, while your partner or siblings watch your child with special needs? Can you hire a caregiver once or twice a week in the evening? Or schedule a weekend morning to yourself once or twice a month?

Is Your Child Robbing You of Sleep?

Many parents get up several times per night with a child who can't sleep, feels anxious, or requires turning, medication, or physical care. To cope when your sleep is frequently disrupted, try these strategies:

Nap when possible. Fara has four children, including a ten-year-old with special needs who is up most of the night. When her husband comes home from work, she naps. For many people, even a twenty-minute nap helps recharge batteries—early afternoon is ideal. But if your problem is insomnia, avoid napping or you won't be tired enough in the evening to go to sleep.

If you have a partner, share nighttime duty. Use your natural sleep rhythms to divide up responsibilities. Says one mom, "Since I'm a night owl, and my husband is an early riser, I'm in charge of any child fusses before 2:00 a.m., and he takes any between 2:00 and 6:00 a.m." Take turns wearing ear plugs so at least one of you gets a good night's sleep. Trade off weekend mornings to sleep.

If you're single, ask family and friends to take over for a night so you can sleep uninterrupted.

Hire help. Pay a qualified worker to look after your child or take them out while you sleep. Check out community options for occasional overnight respite.

Request gifts of sleep. Ask for "sleep vouchers" on your birthday or Mother's Day. One of the best gifts Heather ever received was a weekend off. Her husband took their two kids away to his mom's house. With the weekend to herself, she caught up on sleep and enjoyed "me" time as well.

Depending on your child's age and disability, can she be downstairs on her own (or with a sibling) for a couple hours on weekend mornings? As the mother of a child with Asperger syndrome explains, "My son is only allowed thirty minutes of video games on weekdays, but on weekend mornings, he is allowed unlimited play time, as long as he lets us sleep."

Tackling Your Child's Sleep Problems

"For the first four years that Jake lived with us, he slept in one-and-a-half-hour to two-hour bursts and then was awake and noisy for an hour or more each time before returning to sleep," recalls Cecile, whose son has fetal alcohol syndrome. "My husband and I were exhausted until we found a medication which helped with sleep. Looking back, I'm not entirely sure how any of us survived!"

Aside from the physical care duties that keep many moms awake (e.g., administrating medication or tending to equipment), many of us lose sleep (like Cecile) because our children have sleep problems. Although some kids may quickly bounce back from a night of bouncing off the walls, others become grouchy or listless. And, after countless sleepless nights, we moms often don't have the stamina to get through the day ourselves, much less deal with our exhausted children.

The most common sleep problems among children—especially those with special needs—are difficulty settling to sleep, frequent waking during the night, and rising too early in the morning.

The first step may be realizing that you have a problem. For over a year, Amy's daughter (who was six at the time) woke up every day between 4:00 and 4:30 a.m. Both Amy and her husband were perpetually exhausted, while Talia seemed energetic and unaffected. It never occurred to them to ask for professional help, for several reasons: They thought that sleep problems were typical and unavoidable for kids with autism. They didn't know where to go to for help. And they started to think that such bone-tiring exhaustion was normal. But none of that is true. If your child's sleep problems are affecting your quality of life it's time to get professional help.

Defining and Evaluating the Problem

If your child's sleep problems are disturbing your sleep, start by tracking how much time he actually sleeps. For a few weeks, keep a sleep diary:

Write down if and when your child naps during the day.
Describe his pre-bed routine each night and how long it takes.
Track how often and for how long your child is awake during the night and what time he gets up in the morning.

Does your child snore a great deal, even when he doesn't have a cold? Snoring isn't uncommon in children, but you'll want to discuss it with his pediatrician, so she can rule out allergies or sleep apnea.

If your child regularly takes medication or supplements, write down every one, including what time of day each is given. (Many medications, ranging from allergy remedies to even "non-stimulant" ADHD medications, can cause sleeplessness or early morning wakefulness.)

With these detailed records, you'll be able to see your child's sleep patterns and what changes might be needed. Also, you can bring this diary to a doctor or psychologist to show them how much of an impact your child's sleep is having on your lives. The sleep diary will prove, for example, that your child really is only sleeping for four hours a night—and you're not exaggerating!

Sleep Improvement Tips to Try with Your Child

Be a detective. Try and figure out the reason for your child's sleep difficulties. Perhaps your child is napping so long during the day that he isn't tired at night. Noise may keep other kids awake. (Amy's daughter, for example, woke up every time it rained or a heavy truck drove by.) Allergies or food intolerances may keep kids awake. Other children may be seeking attention, feeling anxious, or not understanding why and when they need to sleep. Sleep issues can also be a sign of depression. In many cases, though, a source may be hard to find; some conditions just seem linked to sleep disorders. Some children are kept awake because of physical challenges such as muscle spasms or breathing difficulties related to their disability (check with your doctor).

Cut out or cut back your young child's naps. If your child is in daycare, ask the staff how long your child is actually sleeping. One mom was puzzled when her three-year-old son was usually wide awake until midnight. She eventually found out that a preschool teacher was letting her son nap for three hours every afternoon!

Establish a predictable and soothing evening routine that enables your child to wind down. For example: snack (not a sugary one!), bath, tooth brushing, book, back rub, lights out. Try posting a bedtime schedule (in words or pictures, whichever is appropriate) to remind your child of the steps of the routine. Even teens and adults can benefit from a routine such as homework, reading or quiet activity, bath, and bed. For teens, try to make sure they don't sleep in too late on weekends, so they'll be tired at their regular bedtimes.

Teach your child relaxation or meditation exercises. Simple drawings or photos might help. An occupational therapist, for example, made Talia a simple picture book on the computer describing how to do progressive body relaxation.

Be selective about evening snacks. Avoid foods or drinks high in sugar (that includes fruit juices), chocolate, or caffeine, or other foods or food additives known to cause a problem in your child.

Increase your child's activity level during the day so that he is more tired. Exercise along with him and you'll both feel better. But no wrestling matches right before bed! (Make sure Dad knows that rule, too.) Running and bouncing is for daytime; stretching and slow breathing is for bedtime.

No scary books, cartoons, movies, or video games before bed, either. In fact, some children can't handle watching scary stuff at any time of day—although the fears may not surface until bedtime. (Hey, no one worries about the boogie man jumping out of the closet in broad daylight, right?)

If your child tends to wake very early, teach him strategies for keeping busy and quiet. Bernie, mother of a child with ADHD and a mood disorder, says that "in addition to the medication, I've worked with my special needs child to stay in her room and pursue quiet activities like reading, drawing, or puzzles, instead of coming into my room when she can't sleep. She understands concrete rules well—for example, 'Stay in your bedroom until 6:30 a.m.'"

Does your child have nighttime fears? Find out what they are and allay them if you can. If his toys look more like "monsters" in a darkened room, keep them in a closed cabinet or move them to the playroom. For those invisible monsters that live in closets and under beds, some parents find it effective to arm their children with cans of "monster repellant" (canned air, used for cleaning computer keyboards) or special "charms," or they perform "magic rituals" to keep the monsters away. Kids can have very active imaginations, and sometimes you need to find creative solutions.

Make sure you're not unconsciously rewarding your child for waking up in the middle of the night, say by letting him get in bed with you or telling him extra bedtime stories. Tabitha, mother of children with fetal alcohol syndrome, and mental health issues, says, "Don't talk to them if they get up, but swoop them up with a hug and take them immediately back to bed. You may have to stay by the bedroom door for a few nights until they realize they won't be getting up any more."

Look at what your child needs to feel safe and comfortable. For some children, a quiet dark room with just a mattress on the floor is best for sleeping. For others, sleeping under some sort of canopy feels more secure than looking up at a high ceiling. Some kids sleep better in a sleeping bag on top of the bed, rather than under sheets and blankets.

Childproof your child's room to ensure his safety. That way, even if he wakes up in the middle of the night, you'll be able to minimize the attention you give him. Kids who tend to wander at night might get into dangerous tools in the kitchen or even escape out the front door. To safely confine a child in his room, block off your child's room with a gate. If that doesn't work, use two gates stacked on top of each other. Some parents cut off the top half of the door and lock the bottom part. That way your child stays in his room, but you can easily check on him, and he can get your attention. For children who wander or sleepwalk, enclosed beds are available, and may be covered by some insurance providers. But you need to discuss this option carefully with your doctor to ensure your child's safety.

For some kids, it's ok to sleep with the lights on (certainly better than not sleeping at all!) If your child is afraid of the dark, a little night light may not be sufficient. Try instead leaving one light on at night, and lowering the wattage of the bulb in the bedroom lamp each time you replace it.

If your child is kept awake by noises in the house, soundproof his room with heavy drapes and carpeting. Also consider masking household sounds with white noise in the bedroom. Many drugstores and department stores carry white noise machines starting at around twenty dollars. One mother uses a cold water vaporizer to create soothing background noise. Air purifiers or window air conditioning units also fit the bill for some children.

Call in The Sleep Pros

If none of these strategies work and you're exhausted because of your child's sleep problems, get professional help.

First, talk to your child's doctor to rule out allergies and other physical causes, and to learn whether one or more of your child's medications might be causing the problem. Bring in the sleep diary that you have completed over the previous few weeks. The doctor also will need to rule out physical causes related to your child's disability and will screen him for depression or anxiety (especially if the sleep problems are accompanied by changes in appetite).

The next step is to ask for a referral to a pediatric sleep specialist. Often this specialist works together with a psychologist who has expertise in behavioral approaches to managing sleep problems. But if the child has symptoms such as snoring, leg movements during sleep, or excessive daytime sleepiness, the specialist may suggest a sleep study, which is typically covered by health insurance and Medicaid. If your son or daughter is an adult, consult a sleep specialist who has experience with adults with special needs.

Sleep Studies

Here's what typically goes on in a sleep lab. Families arrive two hours before the child's usual bed time. After explaining what will happen, a technologist uses paste to apply non-invasive sensors to the scalp, chest, and legs. Then, the child goes to bed at the usual time and is videotaped while he sleeps. Parents can sleep in the same room as their child. Outside the room, for eight to ten hours, the technologist records brain activity, heart rate, respiration, oxygen values, breathing, and leg movements. Afterwards, technicians and doctors review all the hours of sleep on a computer, prepare a report, and recommend a treatment plan.

You may feel that your child's behaviors or special needs will make it impossible for a successful sleep study. But a sleep clinic that specializes in children has many strategies for making kids feel comfortable. Experienced technicians distract children with videos and music. They ensure co-operation by making the procedure into a game, and by letting the kids help apply the sensors. Also, parents actively participate, so they can reassure their children. If necessary, technicians wait until the child is asleep before applying all of the sensors.

To find a sleep clinic near you that can accommodate your child, ask your physician, or see the Resources section.

OTHER PROFESSIONALS WITH SLEEP PROBLEM EXPERTISE

For more help in managing bedtime routines or nighttime wakefulness consult with a behavioral therapist. An occupational or physical therapist can provide relaxation exercises or other techniques or products that may help your child sleep better. For example, some children sleep better with heavy weighted blankets or quilts that are wrapped tightly around them—but consult an OT before trying one of these approaches. A naturopath may be able to suggest supplements or dietary changes that may help. (Heather's daughter Robyn started sleeping through the night after dairy products and food dyes were removed from her diet.) But be sure to have the ok of your child's doctors before making any dietary changes or, especially, before adding supplements (many herbal supplements interact with medications).

Also ask other parents, especially those whose kids have similar disabilities to your child's, about techniques that have worked for them. And remember that, over time, your child's sleep life, and your own can evolve and improve.

Experience Talks

"Lee did not sleep for the first three years of his life. I thought I would lose my mind. I had to hire night baby sitters because I thought I might hurt him. He is now almost thirteen and has been sleeping through the night for a while. I go to bed early, close my door, and have my other child or husband open the door before they go to bed."

—Kuan, mother of a child who has cerebral palsy, global developmental delays, and is legally blind

"I really think I am on the verge of getting lost. Well, I probably am lost.
Things that used to be important issues in my daily life—like my weight,
clothes, and all that material stuff—seem so senseless now."

—Courtney, mother of a preschooler with Down syndrome,
currently being treated for depression

Chapter 7

Fighting Your Inner Darkness—Anger, Anxiety, and Depression

Almost all the women we surveyed discussed positive ways that being a mother had transformed their lives. But some also described ongoing feelings of stress, resentment, blame, guilt, anger, sadness, bitterness, and rejection.

A few women, like Courtney (above), told us they feel hopeless. They can't even consider work, hobbies, or volunteering, because they are struggling just to meet their children's daily needs. For these women, even basic self-care, exercise, or breaks seem unattainable.

Most people manage stress by looking after themselves physically, saying "no" to extra commitments, and taking more time to relax. That's easier said than done if your child has extraordinary needs.

Of course it's "normal" to feel stress when you are going through difficult times. But "normal" doesn't necessarily mean it's "okay." If these feelings persist, you aren't managing your stress well. Do any of these statements describe you?

☐ I feel overwhelmed by emotions—sadness, anger, anxiety—and these problems have continued for several weeks.

☐ I find it difficult to concentrate and my family life, work, etc., is suffering.

☐ My thinking has slowed down; it takes longer or more energy to answer questions.

☐ I am irritable, edgy, restless, or angry a lot of the time.

☐ I worry excessively, can't get rid of persistent thoughts, and always expect the worst.

☐ I eat and sleep more or less than I usually do. I have gained or lost weight.

☐ I no longer have energy for or take an interest in daily activities, including those that used to give me pleasure (e.g., family activities, work, hobbies, sex).

☐ I'm frequently argumentative or aggressive to the point of physically harming or emotionally upsetting myself or others.

☐ I am abusing drugs or alcohol.

☐ I think about death or suicide.

Checking off even one of these boxes could mean you are suffering from anxiety, depression, or both. This chapter will explain more about these issues, but it's vital that you talk to your doctor.

Anxiety—A Primer

Most of us feel anxious some of the time, since anxiety is a normal response to stress. When Amy's daughter Talia was younger, for example, she had frequent screaming tantrums when out in public. Never knowing when Talia would erupt, Amy often felt stressed and anxious on everyday outings.

But immediate stressors—like trying to get through the mall without a meltdown—can be just the tip of the iceberg when your child has special needs. It's the longer term implications that keep a mom awake at night. (Will other children shun my child because of her behavior problems? Will she ever be able to live independently?) Worries about your child's future can cause enormous stress. Some of the most difficult times can be when your child's ill, when you're awaiting a diagnosis (or are in shock from just receiving it), or when your child's going to transition to a new school or life phase.

Physical signs of anxiety can include a racing heart, clammy palms, muscle stiffness, tiredness, stomach discomfort, and headaches. Emotionally, you may feel frustrated, edgy, fearful, worried, or sad. You may have a short fuse, use poor judgment, be overly active and impulsive, or slow down to a crawl.

Typically, anxious feelings like these come and go as difficult times pass. But for some mothers, the difficult times never seem to pass. At best, they have occasional lulls between crises.

It doesn't matter whether your child truly is in crisis or whether you think you tend to "blow things out of proportion." Your body doesn't know the difference—stress is stress, and it takes a toll. If a heightened state of anxiety has become the norm for you, or if your current state of anxiety is so high that it's making it difficult for you to function in your day-to-day life, you need to talk to your doctor (see the section "Getting Professional Help—You Deserve to Feel Better," later in this chapter). When you put off getting treatment, symptoms only tend to get worse and more difficult to treat.

When excessive anxiety lasts for at least six months, worries spread to many different issues (not just, for example, your child's health), and the anxiety is so intense that it interferes with day-to-day activities, it is considered a *generalized anxiety disorder*.

An extremely intense bout of anxiety or fear that hits suddenly (in the absence of any real danger) is called a *panic attack*.

Symptoms, which generally last only about ten minutes, can include shortness of breath, sweating, rapid heartbeat, dizziness, and more (see the box for additional symptoms). Panic attacks can be so severe that the person having them may think she's dying, having a heart attack, or losing her mind.

Fortunately, there are effective treatments available for anxiety difficulties and disorders. There's no reason to suffer—there's nothing noble about it. It just makes life more difficult for you, and for the people who love you, as well.

Panic Attacks

A *panic attack* is an abrupt bout of severe anxiety or fear that occurs in the absence of any real danger. During a panic attack, a person experiences four or more of the following symptoms:

- Rapid or pounding heartbeat
- Sweating
- Shaking or trembling
- Difficulty breathing
- Choking sensation
- Tingling sensations or numbness
- Hot flushes or chills
- Chest pain or discomfort
- Nausea or stomach ache
- Dizziness, lightheadedness, or feeling faint
- Feeling that what is happening isn't real, or that you're watching it from outside yourself
- Fear of losing control or going crazy
- Fear of dying

Although it can be extremely intense, a panic attack generally peaks in about ten minutes. Some people experience panic attacks in response to a specific trigger (e.g., the sight of blood), while others have "uncued" attacks that seem to occur spontaneously. A variety of conditions can be at the heart of a panic attack: anxiety, depression, medication side effects or substance abuse, or even some general medical conditions.

Depression

Clinical depression is more than just a case of the blues. Of course, if you feel sad or empty most of the time, that's a major sign. But sometimes the symptoms can be more subtle, such as no longer enjoying or taking interest in activities that used to bring you pleasure. Other signs can include:

Lack of energy
Restlessness
Insomnia
Excessive sleeping
Feelings of worthlessness or guilt
Difficulty concentrating or making decisions
Significant weight loss or gain (without dieting)
Thoughts of death (not just suicidal thoughts)

Do any of those symptoms sound familiar? If so, you're certainly not alone. Many studies have found that depression is far more common among parents of special needs children than parents of typical children. For example, in a 2001 Swedish study, 207 mothers filled out a multiple-choice questionnaire about any symptoms of depression they might be experiencing. Among mothers of typically developing children, only 4 percent scored in the depressed range, compared to 8 percent of mothers of children with intellectual disabilities and 16 percent of mothers of children with autism. Single mothers were the most vulnerable.

Other studies have shown higher rates of depression and anxiety among parents of children with brain injury, Duchenne's muscular dystrophy, schizophrenia, cerebral palsy, and other disorders.

You might assume that the parents of the most severely disabled children would be the ones who suffer from the most depression. But that's not necessarily true, says Dr. Peter Rosenbaum, Co-Director of the CanChild Centre for Childhood Disability Research at McMaster University in Hamilton, Ontario, "We traditionally think and assume if our kid's problems are more severe, we're under more stress. Not true. Much more important is children's behavior. Behavior can drive you crazy." ADHD, for example, isn't life threatening, but if your child has hyperactivity and little impulse control, every day can be a struggle (especially when an uneducated public tends to judge

Are you Depressed? Take This Test

Take the CES-D questionnaire (Radloff 1977) to determine how severe your feelings of sadness are. This scale cannot make a diagnosis of depression—only a trained professional can do that. A score of above fifteen may indicate significant levels of depression. However, if you score severe depression on this scale or have suicidal feelings (regardless of where you score), you need to seek help immediately. Skip to our "Getting Professional Help" section.

If you score above fifteen, consider re-taking the test in a week. If you're still scoring in the "moderate" depression range or above, it's time to look into getting help.

During the past week:

Rarely or none of the time (less than 1 day)	Some or a little of the time (1-2 days)	Occasionally or a moderate amount of time (3-4 days)	Most or all of the time (5-7 days)
1. I was bothered by things that usually don't bother me.			
O	O	O	O
2. I did not feel like eating; my appetite was poor.			
O	O	O	O
3. I felt that I could not shake off the blues even with help from my family or friends.			
O	O	O	O
4. I felt that I was just as good as other people.			
O	O	O	O
5. I had trouble keeping my mind on what I was doing.			
O	O	O	O
6. I felt depressed.			
O	O	O	O
7. I felt that everything I did was an effort.			
O	O	O	O
8. I felt hopeful about the future.			
O	O	O	O

	Rarely	Sometimes	Occasionally	Most of the Time
9. I thought my life had been a failure.				
	O	O	O	O
10. I felt fearful.				
	O	O	O	O
11. My sleep was restless.				
	O	O	O	O
12. I was happy.				
	O	O	O	O
13. I talked less than usual.				
	O	O	O	O
14. I felt lonely.				
	O	O	O	O
15. People were unfriendly.				
	O	O	O	O
16. I enjoyed life.				
	O	O	O	O
17. I had crying spells.				
	O	O	O	O
18. I felt sad.				
	O	O	O	O
19. I felt that people disliked me.				
	O	O	O	O
20. I could not get going.				
	O	O	O	O

Scoring:

Score each statement (EXCEPT for 4, 8, 12, and 16) as follows:

Rarely/none=0   Some/a little=1   Occasionally/Moderate=2   Most/all=3

Score statements 4, 8, 12, and 16 as follows:

Rarely/none=3   Some/a little=2   Occasionally/moderate=1   Most/all=0

Interpretation of total score:

0–9 Not depressed   10–15 Mildly depressed   16–24 Moderately depressed

24+ Severely depressed

Source: National Institutes of Research, Centre for Epidemiological Studies.

you for your child's unruly behavior). Not surprisingly, mothers of children with conditions such as autism or schizophrenia (which can cause severe or unpredictable behaviors) often have among the highest rates of depression.

CHRONIC DEPRESSION ("DYSTHYMIA")

Maybe you've felt "down" for a long time, but you figure "I'm functioning: I'm working, and taking care of my family. It's no big deal." But it *is* a big deal if it's preventing you from enjoying life. Long-term (two years or longer), milder depression is called *dysthymia*. Symptoms often include social withdrawal; lack of enjoyment or interest in activities; feelings of inadequacy; guilt or brooding over events that occurred long ago; irritability; low energy or productivity; and difficulty concentrating or making decisions.

Chronic depression doesn't tend to go away on its own. In fact, without treatment, it's more likely to decline into major depression. But the good news is that the same treatments that help with major depression—antidepressant medications and "talk" therapies—help with dysthymia as well. See the "Getting Professional Help" section later in this chapter.

Anger

Many women we surveyed described themselves as angry—angry at the disorders that affected their children, at uncaring health care and education systems, and at the people around them—even the well meaning ones. Antoinette, whose son has Down syndrome, told us, "If one more parent comes up to me and says 'Oh, you are SO blessed...' I swear I'll knock them over!"

Anger can play a role in both anxiety and depression. A 2004 Missouri State University study looked at how 514 women managed anger. The study found women who externalized their anger (directed it toward those around them) had higher rates of obsessive-compulsive behaviors and depression. These women, as well as those who internalized their anger (i.e., suppressed or denied it), also suffered from more frequent physical complaints and paranoid thoughts. On the other hand, women who used a more assertive approach—one that clearly acknowledged their anger but channeled it toward solving a problem—had the lowest rates of physical symptoms, anxiety, and depression.

Ultimately, it's not just the challenges you face in your life, but also *how you cope with them*, that can affect your state of mind. The good news is you can learn new ways of coping.

Coping Style–What's Yours?

How people respond to challenges can put them at risk for depression. For instance, how would you respond to the following situation?

A respite service in your community allows children with special needs to sleep over at a staffed group home for a weekend and enjoy recreational activities. During that time, parents enjoy some time to themselves or with their other children. Hoping to access this program, you've been on a waiting list for over a year. Now you're told that you must wait another six months. You're very disappointed, since you had planned to take your first weekend away with your husband while your child was at the respite program.

How would you react? Would you:

  a) vent to your husband and friends, then try to put it out of your mind for the next six months?

  or

  b) make a list of action steps to get the service sooner: e.g., call the respite agency and ask about an appeal process, phone other agencies that have caregiving expertise, and contact a local government official?

  or

  c) accept that the wait is inevitable and resolve to use the extra time to prepare yourself and your child for your first weekend apart?

If you chose option a) you have an *emotion-focused coping style*. That means you react to a difficult situation by wishing it away, venting about it, denying it, not acting upon it, or ignoring it (by distancing or distracting yourself from the problem).

If you chose b) you have a *problem-focused style*. You are more likely to devise and implement a plan of action, even if it means putting other activities aside so you can meet your goal.

If you chose c) you have an *accommodative coping style*. You can flexibly set new goals if your previous ones were unachievable.

If you used a problem-focused or accommodative copying style, you could probably find some upside to the situation, even if the outcome was not what you'd hoped for. For example, perhaps you meet other families and find other helpful services in town while advocating for respite.

Sometimes, especially in our children's early years, it's hard not to react out of fear and frustration. But as our children mature, so does our ability to take action. Carolyn, a mother of an adult with Rett syndrome, developed an accommodative coping style over time. She says, "Early on I wondered 'How would we manage and survive?' [But over time] I decided that I'd better not spend all my energy on things I had no control over. So, instead, I focus on making my daughter's life as full as I can."

Your style may not fall into any single category. You may vent first and then focus on the problem by attempting to solve it or revise your objectives. And that's okay—as long as you get past the venting. Studies have found that caregivers who use emotion-focused coping styles (venting, ignoring, etc.) have higher levels of distress and depression.

Interestingly, though, which style of coping—accommodative or problem-focused—is best for you may depend on your child's situation. Researchers at the University of Wisconsin-Madison and Brandeis University (1995) studied mothers of adults with either developmental delays or mental health problems. While problem-focused coping reduced the risk of depression in mothers of adults with developmental delays, it did not do the same for the mothers of adults with mental illness. A follow-up study by Seltzer et al. (2004) at the University of Wisconsin-Madison and Georgia State University found that parents of adults with mental health needs were less likely to be depressed if they used accommodative coping. For them, flexibility and the ability to set new goals in a difficult situation was key. The researchers hypothesize this may be because adults with mental illness have behaviors that are more severe, unpredictable, and cyclical—so parents would be less able to control difficult situations through problem solving.

Brenda, mother of a child who is medically fragile, learned to cope with major life changes in an accommodative fashion. Because her son had multiple health problems, she had to withdraw him from school for the year. To care for her son at home, she had to give up a job that she loved. But now, several months later, she realizes how much she enjoys home-schooling her bright son who explores concepts well-beyond his grade level. And Brenda knows she's developing teaching skills that she will use in future jobs.

Suzanne, whose child has a developmental disability and behavioral challenges, used to cry, get angry, or withdraw when things went wrong. But that approach accomplished little. Eventually, she learned to use a more problem-focused coping style. When her son was hit by another student in his classroom for children with high behavioral needs, Suzanne briefly vented her frustration to her husband and close friends, but then took action. She organized a meeting with the teacher, the principal, and the school board's special education consultant, at which she expressed her concern that the classroom was understaffed and therefore unsafe. Two weeks later, another assistant was hired for the class.

No matter what special need your child has, emotion-based coping puts you at risk of depression. Focus on action. Don't ignore the problem or try to wish it away. It's okay to vent to someone you trust, but then get on with what needs to be done. When a problem persists that is outside your control, adjust your goals and look for the positive. See the box "Taking Action" for steps to increase your self-confidence and your resilience.

Taking Action

1. **Realistically assess the problem.** How serious is it? (Often it makes sense to choose your battles.) How much control do you have over it? Accepting circumstances that you cannot change helps you focus on issues that you *can* influence.
2. **Draw up specific, achievable goals.**
3. **Create a realistic timetable.**
4. **Each day, try to move closer to your goal.** Ask yourself, "What's one thing I can accomplish today that moves me in the right direction?" Focus on what you're achieving, not on what remains to be done.
5. **Look ahead with optimism.** Take a moment each day to close your eyes and visualize a successful resolution. Or write down your goal in a blank book, and record the action steps you're taking.
6. **When the problem is resolved or abates, reappraise the situation positively.** Recognize that some good comes out of most challenging situations.

The Power of Optimism

Whether you see the glass as half-empty or half-full can also put you at risk for depression. University of Wisconsin-Madison researchers studied 520 mothers caring for adult children with autism, schizophrenia, and Down syndrome (2004). For all three sets of mothers, optimism was related to better mental and physical health.

A crucial factor in optimism is your "explanatory style"—the "self-talk" that goes through your head when something bad happens. A pessimist blames herself, generalizes the experience, and gives up trying. For example, if a pessimist's application for medical assistance was denied, she might tell herself:

"It's my own fault. I'm terrible at filling out forms."
"There's no help available for my family."
"We'll never get accepted, so I might as well stop applying."

An optimist, on the other hand, would attribute the same setback to circumstances outside her control. She'd tell herself the defeat was an isolated event, and worthy of another try:

"There must be high demand."
"We didn't get into this particular program, but that doesn't mean there's no help available to us."
"I can always appeal or try again next year."

Fortunately, even if you frequently use negative ways of thinking, you can train yourself to be more optimistic. But, you must do more than simply "think positive thoughts" about a difficult situation. Psychologist Christopher Peterson, a researcher in positive psychology at University of Michigan, says, "If (your positive thinking) doesn't lead you to do things, it's simply a mantra. Positive psychology is about doing, not so much about thinking."

So, how do you put positive psychology into action? Try using a cognitive behavioral technique to help you reduce negative thoughts. This technique, coined the ABC method, was pioneered in 1967 by clinical psychologist Albert Ellis. It's like detective work. When negative thoughts strike, examine the evidence for your beliefs and dispute them. (See the box "Using Positive Psychology to Combat Negative Thoughts.)

If you'd like help trying this technique as a form of cognitive therapy, consult a psychologist or psychiatrist. For help finding one, see the section "How to Find a Professional."

Using Positive Psychology to Combat Negative Thoughts—Situation: A Frustrating Meeting with Your Child's School

A	**Adversity** Describe your setback.	The principal criticizes your idea in a school meeting.
B	**Belief** What did you tell yourself?	He never supports me. Every time I ask him for an accommodation for my daughter, he makes excuses. He's not even trying to be helpful.
C	**Consequence** What was the result of your self-talk?	I was really upset. I sat in the meeting scowling, with my arms crossed—silently fuming. When the meeting ended I left without shaking his hand or even saying goodbye.
D	**Disputation** Is your belief really true?	Okay, it's true he didn't support me with this accommodation but he did work hard to get my daughter a Teaching Assistant last year. And he suggested alternative strategies at the meeting so it isn't like he isn't trying to be helpful.
E	**Energization** Take a positive step to set things right.	I'm going to call him and explain why I left the meeting so abruptly. I'll ask if we can arrange another meeting to brainstorm alternative ideas.

Adapted version of ABCDE model from *Learned Optimism*, Martin E.P. Seligman.

Preventive Maintenance for Mental Health

In addition to improving your coping style, it helps to have a tool-kit of ways to manage your stress. These strategies can help you manage your everyday lows so they don't turn into something more serious.

Take care of yourself. This advice is the most crucial. Eat well, exercise, rest, and most importantly, take time for yourself. Prayer and meditation help protect against anxiety and depression. To help calm angry thoughts, try deep breathing, visualization, yoga, vigorous exercise, or brisk walking. See Chapter 6 for some tips on relaxation, visualization, and meditation.

Foster family teamwork. Current research shows that family support and co-operation are the most important factors in the positive mental health of parents caring for a child with special needs. Your relationship with your son or daughter also affects your mental health. If behavioral problems are a source of distress, get professional help. See the chapters in Part IV: Family Ties for ways to strengthen family relationships.

Stay involved socially. Don't isolate yourself. Romantic and long-lasting friendships provide the best buffer against depression. Research shows that people who are married or in a close relationship are the happiest and have the lowest rate of depression compared to any other group. Don't let your child's needs overshadow your own need for companionship. Nurture individual friendships, but also involve yourself in community groups, faith-based organizations, or special needs groups that can provide social support and can make you feel more hopeful.

Write it down. Writing can be a therapeutic way of resolving sad or anxious thoughts. Just getting it down on paper can relieve tension or help you work out your feelings. Some mothers find keeping a diary or journal the best way to manage everyday stress. Time strapped? Try the quick, easy, but effective journal writing techniques in "Write It Out."

Distract yourself from negative or obsessive thoughts. Research shows that people who dwell upon negative feelings are more

WRITE IT OUT

"Freewriting" helps you to explore feelings and ideas that might not emerge with regular logical thinking or writing. Try writing quickly, non-stop, for five to ten minutes on whatever comes into your head. Or try free-writing based on a particular word or phrase such as Spring, Love, Hope, I Remember, Friendship. Keep your hand moving and don't pause to reread what you've written. Disregard proper punctuation and grammar. If you're stuck, repeat your last words or phrases. Afterwards, read your work and circle any ideas or words that interest or surprise you. Examine any ideas or questions you'd like to follow up.

Making Lists can help you explore feelings, intuitions, thoughts, and plans when you have little time. Lists help you examine problems and goals and to make them concrete, so they can be tackled. Try writing a variety of lists such as hopes, fears, successes, joys, frustrations, and plans. List "what went right" during the day. Trying to make a decision? Make a list of pros and cons.

Doodling can be therapeutic. Make a quick sketch of your day, some event, your loved ones, or yourself. Circle the aspects of the day that bring you the most joy. Can you add that joyful activity to the rest of your week?

likely to become depressed than those who distract themselves. If you tend to obsess or ruminate try these "thought-stopping" techniques used by therapists:

When stuck worrying or thinking negatively, snap a rubber band around your wrist or ring a loud bell to signal an end to your thoughts. Then find something else to do.

Say "Stop" to yourself. Or pull out a three-by-five card with a simple message such as "Stop," "Relax," or "Don't Panic." Then follow it up with a positive message, e.g., "I can do this."

Make a list of "distracting" activities to divert your attention when needed. Jackie, who has an adopted teen with fetal alcohol syndrome, told us "I have a list of "busy work" activities that send a message to my brain that 'Everything is okay,' when I'm feeling anxious or angry. I try crossword puzzles, sorting, pencil sharpening, talking on the phone, list making, word games, etc."

Mentally reschedule your thoughts to a specific time, e.g., "Stop! I will think about this at 8:30 p.m." Then, at that time, give yourself thirty minutes to focus on these thoughts or worries.

Pull out an important memento (e.g., a postcard, snapshot, or sentimental item) and focus on what it means to you.

Practice "mindfulness" by trying to stay in the present, instead of worrying about past or future events. When anxious, find time to yourself when you can focus on sensory experiences in the moment. For example, relax in a bath, drink soothing tea, listen to a relaxation tape of nature sounds, or wrap yourself in a soft blanket and read a book.

Increase activities that provide gratification. Pleasures such as watching TV, curling up beside the fireplace, or going out for a good meal are important. But, more important for protecting against depression are activities that bring meaning to our lives. These activities should be challenging and exercise your personal strengths and talents. Assess your priorities from Chapter 1. Are you working towards your life goals? Assisting others can also bring much meaning to one's life. The mothers who seemed the happiest in our survey were involved in activities such as advocacy work, volunteering, home schooling, therapy, and meaningful work or hobbies. But helping others needn't involve formal volunteer or paid work. Take small steps. For example, phone another mother who could use some support. Put some of the recommendations from Chapter 2 into action.

Increase the humor in your life. Many moms say that humor helps them cope with almost anything. To get through the tough stuff, consciously increase the humor in your life. Watch funny videos and read light-hearted books. Laugh at some of the outrageous stuff your child does. As Kristina, mother of an eleven-year-old with hydrocephalus and spina bifida says, "My son has a great sense of humor and has taught me how to laugh at things. He is learning how to misbehave. He can now reach his dresser drawers from his wheelchair, but he can't open them. So after I open them and leave the room, he pulls all his clothes out. Then he says, "Oh, Oh, Momma, I was bad. Come see!" Humor and laughter help us enjoy life and may also help us live healthier. Current studies associate a sense of humor or laughter with better immune function, increased pain tolerance, decreased feelings of stress, and even healthy blood vessels.

If you seldom enjoy a good laugh, consider trying "laughter yoga." Laughter clubs offered through The World Laughter organization were started in 1999 by psychologist Steve Wilson. Sessions offer structured laughing exercises developed by physician Madan Kataria of India. Each thirty-minute session includes breathing, stretching, and laughter exercises (some borrowed from yoga). See the Resources section for more info.

Confide in someone you trust when you're feeling down. If it feels risky to be open with friends or family, talk to your doctor, spiritual advisor (priest, minister, rabbi, etc.). Or, see a counselor. If money is tight, ask your doctor or social service agencies about free counseling services.

Mothers we surveyed offered their wisdom for coping during stressful times. They said: choose your battles (or worries), celebrate the "little" moments, and take one day at a time. Pay attention to the quality and enjoyment of each day. Many took pride in their children. Says one mom, "I try to celebrate my daughter's accomplishments as they come." Another mother tells us, "Every little victory for my child makes me feel useful."

Jill, mother of a nineteen-year-old with alcohol-related neurodevelopmental disorder offers this advice for days when you feel discouraged—"Think about your expectations for the day and try to simplify your plans so you can do less. Remember that this will be a temporary feeling and another day you'll feel better."

Getting Professional Help—You Deserve to Feel Better

So, you've tried the preventive measures we've suggested but you're still feeling overwhelmingly angry, anxious, or depressed. It may be time to seek professional help.

"I knew I was suffering from depression a few years back when I would find myself crying for no reason," recalls Maya, mother of three children with mental health issues, ADHD, and learning disorders. "The best thing I did, and advice I have for others, is to seek help for yourself. Exercise, eating right, and counseling are steps in working through your depression, and even medication might be needed. Drop the stigma of mental health as a weakness and seek help for yourself."

While most of us regularly visit the doctor with our physical ailments, we may hesitate to consult a mental health professional. A 2004 American Psychological Association (APA) survey found 20 percent of Americans feel there is a stigma associated with therapy and 21 percent cited fear of other people finding out as a reason they might avoid seeking it. Yet according to the same survey, nearly half of American households have sought out the help of a mental health professional at some time.

Mothering a child with special needs demands additional physical and emotional strength. Many mothers we surveyed have sought help from professionals. Several mothers of adults told us they regretted not getting help sooner, as they felt they'd be in better shape both physically and mentally if they'd done so. Research suggests they're probably right. A 2004 study from the University of California found that chronic stress can actually affect humans at the cellular level. Looking at parents of children with serious chronic illnesses, researchers found that those with the highest stress levels had cell characteristics the same as someone ten years older. Don't wait for stress to take years off your life.

If that isn't enough incentive to seek help, do it for your family. When you're under stress, so are your family members. Children are more likely to exhibit behavior problems when their parents are experiencing high stress. Children of depressed mothers are at a greater risk for social, psychological, and cognitive delays. These children are more likely to be depressed themselves or suffer from other mental health illnesses. While genetics is a factor, so is the role model that you provide for your children.

Fortunately, though, it's never too late to make positive changes with the help of a professional.

When you are depressed, your husband is also at an increased risk for depression. In a stressed household, there can be more marital conflict and tensions which can put your children at risk. In such situations, family counseling may be vital.

But most importantly, seek help for yourself if you need it. You and your family deserve to enjoy mental health and a sense of well-being.

WHERE TO GET HELP

Once you've decided to get help, it can be difficult to know who to contact. Start with your family doctor, who may diagnose and treat your problems or may refer you to a mental health professional for a more skilled assessment.

Psychiatrists are medical doctors with additional training in the diagnosis, treatment, and prevention of mental disorders and emotional problems. They are the only mental health professionals who can prescribe medication. For some illnesses (such as schizophrenia, severe depression, and bipolar disorder), medications are crucial. In addition, many psychiatrists do psychotherapy—therapies that help people change their behaviors or thoughts, explore past relationships, or improve relationships with families and friends. Some psychiatrists, on the other hand, prefer to concentrate on medication management, and refer patients to psychologists or other professionals for therapy.

Psychologists have doctorate degrees in psychology rather than medicine, and therefore can diagnose mental illness and provide psychotherapy, but can't prescribe medication. Other professionals such as social workers and counselors typically have master's degrees. They are licensed to provide psychotherapy, but not to diagnose mental illness.

Your family doctor can help you choose the right professional. If you decide on counseling, find a therapist or social worker who understands the special issues you're facing. Contact hospitals, children's treatment centers, family counseling agencies, and mental health agencies, and ask about their counseling services. Also, if you feel comfortable, ask friends you trust to recommend a therapist.

Treatments

MEDICATION

Psychiatrists may prescribe antidepressants for depression and anxiety. Drugs commonly prescribed due to fewer side effects are SSRIs (selective serotonin reuptake inhibitors) such as Prozac® (fluoxetine hydrochloride), Paxil® (paroxetine hydrochloride), and Zoloft® (sertraline) and newer antidepressants such as Wellbutrin® (bupropion) and Effexor® (venlafaxine), which have different chemical structures than other antidepressants. Two older classes of drugs used for depression, monoamine oxidase (MAO) inhibitors and tricyclics, have more side effects, but may be more effective for certain patients.

If your doctor prescribes antidepressant medication for you, it's important to realize that it's not going to work overnight. These drugs typically take a month or two before they reach their maximum effectiveness, and your doctor may need to alter your dosage, depending on how your body responds to the medication. Everyone responds differently to these various drugs, so if the first one doesn't work for you (or has unpleasant side effects), your doctor may try different ones until he finds the one that's the best fit for you.

Once you are taking an antidepressant, you shouldn't stop taking it without the consent and oversight of your doctor. Many patients cease taking antidepressants because they "feel better," when that's actually a sign that the medication is working. Moreover, some of these medications must be tapered off slowly, or they can have a "rebound effect" that could make you feel even worse than before you started them.

Many antidepressants are effective for the treatment of anxiety as well as depression, and, because they are non-habit-forming, are often prescribed first. But benzodiazepines, commonly known as tranquilizers, are faster acting, and may be prescribed instead of or in addition to antidepressants. Four commonly prescribed benzodiazepines for anxiety include Valium® (diazepam), Ativan® (lorazepam), Klonopin® (clonazepam), and Xanax® (alprazolam).

Medications can be extremely beneficial, but they can also have significant side effects and some like the benzodiazepines can cause dependency. If your doctor suggests a drug, ask about its success rate, side effects, and whether there are non-drug alternatives (such as therapy that can be tried instead or at the same time).

For adults with moderate or severe depression, medication is usually the first approach. Several mothers we surveyed who were suffering from depression said medication played a crucial role in helping them regain their sense of well-being. With the medication, they had more of an ability to exercise, see friends, eat healthily, and care for themselves.

PSYCHOTHERAPY

Generally, combining medication with psychotherapy is more effective than medication alone for anger, anxiety, and depression. And for some, psychotherapy alone may be preferable. You and your doctor should discuss what's right for you.

Before choosing a psychotherapist, you'll want to find out about the therapist's orientation. There are many different approaches to psychotherapy, including cognitive-behavioral, interpersonal, psycho-dynamic, and more. Many therapists today take an eclectic approach, drawing elements from several different schools of psychology.

Cognitive-behavioral therapy (CBT) helps you understand how your own negative thoughts and actions can contribute to your angry, depressed, or anxious state. The therapist teaches you to recognize when you're not thinking about problems clearly, or when you're sabotaging your own efforts. Then, through homework assignments and in-session work, you'll learn new, healthier ways to approach challenges. Treatment typically lasts three months or so, but varies with the individual.

A recent review (2002) of studies that compared medication and cognitive-behavioral psychotherapy (CBT) for individuals with major depression found an identical depression remission rate after treatment. Because CBT changes thought patterns that trigger depression, relapses may be less likely to occur. Cognitive-behavioral treatment can also help those dealing with anxiety disorders or anger control and in some cases eliminate the need for medication.

Interpersonal therapy looks at your relationships with those around you. If conflicts with family and friends trigger your depression, interpersonal therapy can help you improve your communication with others by teaching you assertiveness and other strategies that help raise your self-esteem. Besides relationship conflicts, it helps those dealing with role transitions (e.g., working mom to homemaker), social isolation, and loss or grief. Therapy is usually completed within three to four months.

Psychodynamic therapy, which has its origins in psychoanalysis, can also help people deal with role transitions, social isolation, and mourning but takes a different approach. It assumes mental illness stems from unresolved and unconscious childhood conflicts. This "talk" therapy can help some to understand and cope better with their feelings by talking about past and present experiences. Less intense than psychoanalysis, psychodynamic therapy usually involves less than a year of weekly visits (and some therapists use a short-term approach that can take only three to four months). It can, however, continue for much longer. Kuan, mother of a teen who has cerebral palsy and is legally blind, was in therapy for six years on a weekly basis. "The therapist got me to think of my other child who is well, myself, and my husband, and not totally focus on my son with special needs. She validated my feelings and was an impartial listener."

The general aims of psychotherapy are to help people regain a sense of control and pleasure in life. It's not a quick fix, but when successful, its effects can be long-lasting.

OTHER THERAPIES

Family or marital therapy may be useful to help a spouse or family learn ways to cope with depression of a family member. (See Resources for information on how to find a marriage or family therapist.)

Food supplements marketed for anxiety and depression such as kava kava or St. John's Wort should be taken only under the supervision of a licensed naturopath or medical doctor. Because of mixed results, most experts don't feel they have enough evidence on St. John's Wort to recommend it as an alternative to medication.

There is some preliminary evidence that acupuncture may bring some relief from major depression.

Take advantage of courses such as anger management, relaxation, yoga, meditation, etc., offered in hospitals and community health centers.

How to Find a Professional

Your family doctor should be able to refer you to a psychiatrist, psychologists or other therapist who will meet your needs (or see the

Resources section for other ways of locating mental health professionals). Your choice of clinicians may be limited by your HMO or insurance company—some may provide you with a list if you ask. If insurance coverage is an issue, see Chapter 11 for some advice on where to find free or low-cost counseling.

Before committing to a therapist, ask for an initial meeting to see whether you're comfortable with him or her. Find out what approach the therapist uses, and be sure it's what you want. If you don't like the first therapist you meet with, shop around! Psychotherapists are professionals, and you don't have to worry about "hurting their feelings" if you feel they're not right for you.

Beware of e-therapists (therapy offered via email); there is no way to check their credentials or ensure privacy. If you are unsure of the credentials of any professional, call the appropriate regulatory body and ask if the therapist is in good standing. Get the contact info from the national associations in the Resources section.

In Crisis? Act Immediately!

Some parents of special needs children face situations difficult for most of us to fathom. Some endure chronic sorrow as they watch their child deteriorate because of a degenerative condition. Marina, mother of a capable thirty-five-year-old with muscular dystrophy says, "I know that he will die before I do. The grieving is unbearable." Ongoing counseling is crucial for these parents. Other families experience ongoing, unpredictable, intermittent crises. Some parents suffer bites, bruises, and worse from children who may be strong, aggressive, and impulsive. If the situation escalates and gets out of control, both parents and children may be at risk of serious harm. Getting immediate help is essential.

CALLING FOR HELP

Here are some steps to take if you are in immediate crisis.

If your situation is life-threatening, call 911 or the emergency number in your phone book.

If you need time to regroup, call a neighbor, friend, relative, or trusted babysitter to come over. They can watch your child while you are planning what to do next.

Call the mental health crisis number(s) listed in the front of your phone book and tell them you or your family are "in crisis." Often services don't kick in unless families say the need is extremely urgent. Many social services have crisis response teams and funds for in-home or out-of-home respite if a family is in crisis. Do not "downplay" your needs. Commonly when parents make these calls, perhaps out of pride or guilt, they underrate their situation.

Once the immediate situation is under control, make an appointment with your family doctor. Your family doctor will be able to assess your situation objectively and decide whether medication or a referral to a specialist such as a psychiatrist, psychologist, or other professional is necessary.

Call your local support group or other families of special needs kids for advice. Do they have any contacts or know whom to call to get the kind of help you need?

As so many mothers have reminded us, taking care of ourselves is a necessity, not a luxury. Today, commit to doing one new thing to improve your own physical, mental, social, or spiritual health. After all, we mothers are in this for the long run.

Experience Talks

"I realize I'm not a victim and try to see the positive in whatever I do. If I am unhappy, I look at the situation and see what I can do to change it for the better."

—Ann Marie, mother of a twelve-year-old with Down syndrome
after getting help for depression.

"Previously, I relied on medication to help me through the stress, but now I stay in close touch with those entrusted with her care and remain involved in her life. When I feel overwhelmed, I just stop myself. I have better control of my thoughts now."

—Lorie, mother of a twenty-year-old who is non-verbal and lives in a group home

"I care about others and go out of my way to help people, animals, and nature. Doing so when things are rough personally/family-wise helps me feel good about myself. It allows me to have control over a situation, something not often felt at home. Therefore, volunteering in any way, even for short bouts of time, helps me feel happy and balanced."

—Maya, mother of three children with special needs, including bipolar disorder, depression, ADHD, and learning disability

"I have learned to breathe deeply when I am sad or angry. I tell myself everyday that the glass is half full. I also tell myself that I do not have control over what happens to me. I can only control my reactions to what happens to me."

—Kuan, mother of a thirteen-year-old who is blind with cerebral palsy

"I look at my life as a challenge to meet, not as a tragedy."

—Gail, mother of a child with multiple disorders

PART III

Daily Life

Reality Check

"I find that my house is not as clean as I'd like,

and we eat frozen pizza and hot dogs at times,

but the important thing is we spend time as a family."

—Corey, divorced mother of three,
including a teen with Duchenne's muscular dystrophy

Like Corey, we need to make daily choices about what is essential and what is "good enough" in our demanding days. For most parents of "typical" kids, daily meal preparation doesn't include inserting a gastric tube into their child's stomach or working around complicated food sensitivities. Most parents don't help their teen or young adult with toileting, feeding, and showering. And most don't spend hours arranging and attending medical or therapy appointments, managing insurance red tape, and advocating for their child in the school system. But many of us do—although our alternate reality may be invisible to the outside world.

Our lives can also be affected by extraordinary financial challenges. While other parents save for a special family trip, many of us must budget for car adaptations, wheelchairs, ventilators, braces, special diets, tutors, therapies, and our children's lifelong care. And while most parents look forward to their children growing up, moving out, and being independent, many of us have no such certainty about the future. Instead, we worry.

Despite this complicated and often rewarding alternate daily reality, we also manage "regular" family life—cooking, laundry, getting kids to activities, keeping a job. Sounds impossible doesn't it? It can be—especially if you're trying to accomplish everything by yourself. Even in families who share equally in household tasks, it's usually the mother who takes on the role of organizing and delegating all aspects of family life. But being a "good mother" doesn't mean you can or should do it *all*. Instead, you have to realistically evaluate the priorities for your family—what really matters, versus an unworkable ideal. And you need to put pride aside and ask for help from family, friends, community, and government.

Now, take a breath, make a pot of tea, and take some time out. In the following chapters, you'll learn practical ways to add ease to your busy days. You'll find real-world advice about finding help and funding, organizing your time and paperwork, advocating for your family, taking control of financial pressures, and planning for your child's future (instead of worrying about it!) Armed with this information, you'll have more time and energy in the day for yourself and for your family.

*"I spend approximately twenty hours a week completing
paperwork or making phone calls to insurance companies, doctors,
therapists, and nursing agencies. Because I work part-time and
I'm home more often, all these things fall to me."*
—Rose, mother of a child with muscular dystrophy

Chapter 8

The Time Crunch

L ike Rose, you may be working the equivalent of a second
shift, just to manage your child's special needs. A 2004 study
by the U.S. Department of Health and Human Services found that,
among children with disabilities or chronic illnesses, 13 percent of
their families spend eleven or more hours per week caring for their
special needs (administering medications and therapies, coordinating services, maintaining equipment, taking them to appointments,
etc.). Not surprisingly, HHS found that the more impact the child's
condition has on his functional ability, the more time the family
spends providing special care. The time burden tends to be greatest
in low-income families.

Some mothers we spoke to find it almost impossible to fit all the
special needs care into their day. Carmelita has a five-year-old with
ADHD, apraxia, and multiple motor and sensory issues, as well as a

three-year-old: "Troy is supposed to have six-to-eight twenty-minute "Floortime" (one-to-one therapeutic play) sessions with me per day. On days he goes to school, I only see him for three-and-a-half hours, including breakfast, snack, and dinner. It is crazy!"

To cope with such demands on their time, many women we spoke with use shortcuts and routines to simplify their days. Daphna, who has a ten-year-old with autism, says, "Every morning before I go to work, I do the dishes, make the beds, and sweep the kitchen floor. The rest of the work is done on the weekends, or I spend fifteen minutes in the evening cleaning. For the sake of sanity, my home is not a Martha Stewart model home. My slow cooker is my best friend, and I triple recipes and freeze lots of food. When I get home, I open the microwave. On Sundays, I put my children to work cutting vegetables for lunches and snacks, and putting cereal and snacks into baggies for school lunches."

Unlike Daphna, for many of us, sweeping floors and making beds may be occasional rather than daily events—especially if family members aren't actively involved. Your child may give you little time to even consider these household details.

Jane, mom of Mathew, who has developmental delays and ADHD, says, "Because I have three other kids (one of them a preschooler) I can't take care of all of them by myself. Mathew needs one-to-one shadowing in the house for safety reasons. I can't turn my back for a second. I can't make dinner unless my husband or a support worker is home."

Even if our children's needs aren't as extreme as Jane's, we all need strategies to help us get through our days with more ease. Read on for ideas.

Managing Your Time—Make a Plan

"I have finally reached a point in my life that I'm okay with everything not getting done," says Ilene, mother of a four-year-old with Fragile X syndrome. "I'd rather take the kids swimming or to the park than spend a beautiful day inside cleaning and doing chores."

The true key to managing your home life is realizing that *you can't possibly do it all.* Like Ilene, many moms we've talked to said they've learned to let go of the idea of having a perfectly clean house, for example. There are just too many things to do that are more important—or more fun—for your family.

By doing some planning, you can make more time for the things that count. As a planning tool, use our Household and Family Task Chart that shows typical household and family activities. Can you spot a few that you can skip, do less often, delegate, or hire out?

1. MAKE A COMMITMENT TO CHANGE

Use or adapt the sample chart on pages 132-33 to record the household tasks that you or another family member usually does. From your list, choose three tasks that you would like to change to make it quicker or easier to accomplish. What task causes you the most grief? Shoveling the driveway? Cooking?

2. DISCARD OR LESSEN ...

Can any of your most dreaded tasks be discarded or done less frequently. For example, must the kitchen floor be swept every day? If your child constantly mouths dirt from the floor, it may be a high priority—otherwise, perhaps it can wait. Could you ditch daily bed-making by buying your kids a duvet or comforter? Instead of tucking in sheets, they could simply pull the comforter up. Or you could decide to make beds only when company is coming!

Could you simplify your week by cutting out one of your child's extra-curricular activities? Sue and her husband, for example, decided to limit their soccer-loving daughter's games to once per week. They knew it would be impossible to manage their younger child's home therapies with "rep" level soccer that required four nights per week practice and weekend trips for tournaments. Instead, they promised more family "pick up" games at the park.

And what about volunteer commitments? Are you a person who seldom says no? To lessen your stress level and increase your time, look at each involvement critically. Aim to cut back commitments that don't rejuvenate you or help you grow as a person. Some ones to consider eliminating: school activities that don't include your child, social commitments that don't nurture supportive friendships, or inefficient committees that no longer match your passions. Once you've tamed your volunteer life, be cautious about filling up your calendar again. Before volunteering for anything, ask yourself: Will this help me reach my goals? Will this be fun? Will this obligation interfere with other important activities that are important to me (e.g., family, work, ex-

COMPLETED SAMPLE
Household and Family Task Chart

Household Task	Action Stop, Lessen, Delegate, or Hire Out	Plan
Tidying	D	Establish a ten-minute "tidy routine" for the kids in the evenings, starting tonight.
Sweeping	L	Instead of sweeping the kitchen nightly, sweep Mon. and Thurs.
Bathrooms		
Making Beds	D	This weekend, show John how to pull the duvet up over his bed.
Dusting		
Vacuuming	D	Next cleaning day, assign some rooms to family members.
Home Repair		
Lawn Mowing	H	Hire the neighbor's boy this summer.
Gardening		
Cooking	S	On Fridays, have kids make their own pita pizzas.

Loading/ Unloading Dishwasher	D	Loading: Have each family member clear and load his own dishes. Unloading: Show the youngest how to place clean cutlery in the drawer. (It's a great sorting task!)
Setting and Clearing Table	D	Have family members take turns, starting tonight.
Tending to Children	D	Swap child care with a girlfriend one evening per month.
Assisting Child with Special Needs Care	D	Teach Katie to help John brush his teeth.
Scheduling Appointments	D	Occasionally ask Frank or my mother to make the appointments.
Attending Meetings and Appointments for your Child		
Driving Children to Appointments and Activities	D	Have Frank drive for Tues. night soccer this season.
Helping Children with Homework		
Volunteer and Community Work	S	Give up helping with school pizza day next year.

Household and Family Task Chart
Complete YOUR chart.

Household Task		Action Stop, Lessen, Delegate, or Hire Out	Plan
Tidying			
Sweeping			
Bathrooms			
Making Beds			
Dusting			
Vacuuming			
Home Repair			
Lawn Mowing			
Gardening			
Cooking			

Loading/ Unloading Dishwasher			
Setting and Clearing Table			
Tending to Children			
Assisting Child with Special Needs Care			
Scheduling Appointments			
Attending Meetings and Appointments for your Child			
Driving Children to Appointments and Activities			
Helping Children with Homework			
Volunteer and Community Work			

ercise, seeing friends)? Or take Maya's advice: "Be willing to help at the last minute if you're available, but don't make advance commitments." Time freed from outside activities may enable you to designate one night per week for your own exercise or interest.

3. WHAT CAN YOU DELEGATE?

Delegate? Not so easy, especially since no one can do things as well as you do, right? Plus, there's the guilt factor. One mother told us, "I am horrible at delegating tasks to my family. I never want them to be burdened with mundane tasks." Remember that there is nothing mundane about learning how to live independently. Every child (to the best of his ability) needs to learn household and self-care skills. Mastering them will increase your child's independence, sense of competence, and self-esteem. Plus, keep in mind that a task that may seem boring to us can seem like fun for kids. Just ask a kid who is spritzing vinegar on a window to clean it, or one who is grating cheese for a favorite tuna casserole.

It may take some ingenuity and planning to teach your child a task, but it's worth the effort. Joanne taught her twelve-year-old Amanda (who has a developmental disability) to do her own laundry. In her room, Amanda has a three-bag laundry hamper (whites, darks, and reds). A few times per week, Amanda carries down a bag of clothes and does her laundry, guided by color coded instruction stickers her mom placed on the washer and dryer. Amanda is learning an essential skill and feels proud of her new abilities.

If you need help breaking tasks into steps that your child can master, ask your child's teacher, a life skills coach, or an occupational therapist. These professionals should have books that teach life skills (cooking, laundry, setting the table, etc.), in a visual, step-by-step way. Or check with your library, bookstore, or special needs organization.

What if your partner won't get onboard? Many moms we surveyed felt they were doing their share of housework and more. Refer to Chapter 14 for some ideas on how to better equalize the load.

Single moms tell us they lean heavily on their children, parents, and friends to help get things done. Divorced or separated moms like Jeanna take advantage of time when their children are away. "I try to do major home projects on Saturdays, when my kids are with their father. He also comes to visit them on Tuesdays and Thursdays, which gives me time to take care of bills, shopping, and laundry." Single parents should also make use of programs like Big Brothers or Big Sisters that both benefit their children and free up their own time. University or college students–especially those studying special needs-related subjects—can be ideal caregivers or volunteer companions. Besides having a special interest in your child, they often have flexible time available to care for him or help him practice new skills. Don't rule out mature high school students who may enjoy spending time with your child at home so you can complete chores or just relax.

Even if friends and extended family aren't heavily involved in your life, ask them to help with a specific task, like mowing your lawn, or driving your children somewhere. If it makes you feel better, offer a service in return. One mom cooks her friend a home-made meal in exchange for a few hours of child care. Two friends have a play date at one of their homes, and do some basic cleaning or cooking together. The next week, they meet at the other's home. Trading a service may not free up much time, but if you have more fun doing it, you'll be less stressed. See Chapter 17 for more ideas.

4. Could You Hire Out?

Brianne, mother of a child with autism, usually felt overwhelmed by her home's clutter, disorganization, and untidiness. Since the house looked so chaotic, the family avoided having friends over, which isolated them. After unsuccessfully trying everything—family meetings, children's chore charts, doing one chore per evening, Brianne and her husband decided to hire a cleaning company every two weeks at $80 per cleaning. To pay for this, they cut down on luxury daily expenses such as coffee and her husband's work lunches out. The impact on their family life was huge.

Drop other unappealing tasks that you could inexpensively hire out. For example, hire the preteen next door to shovel your driveway. You'll gain a free evening and a pain-free back. In the summer, many companies hire summer students to do tasks such as house painting. If you've put off painting a room for years because you don't have the time or energy, here's the chance to get the job done inexpensively.

Alternatively, hire someone to look after your children so you can do your household tasks more effectively, as Patti did. "Our oldest (with Down syndrome) was two when the twins were born. A caregiver comes in so I can have personal time to do the shopping, work out, go to volunteer meetings, etc. With her tending to the boys, I feel like I still have my adult life and don't feel overwhelmed with doing it all."

Not everyone has the resources to hire out. But friends, family and volunteers are often willing to help when they know you're feeling overwhelmed. Don't wait for the offer—ask.

5. Putting It All Together

Go back to the list of tasks you checked off. Brainstorm with your family ways that you can divide up the work, simplify the task, or hire out—considering the skills and priorities of each family member. Agree on the action that should be taken and the steps necessary to carry it out (fill in the Action and Plan columns on your chart). For example, if the task is bed-making and the action is to **D**elegate, the plan might be teaching your kids how to make their bed, this weekend. (See the Sample Completed Household and Family Task Chart for an example. We've intentionally filled out more tasks than it's really feasible to change, simply to give more examples.)

Now, tack up your plan on the fridge or bulletin board so that all family members can check it. Were you able to commit to making at least three time-saving changes during the week?

Your plan will likely need some tweaking. Reassess it with your family every few months as new tasks, commitments, or extra-curricular activities arise.

Everyone benefits when you work at your household tasks as a team. Your kids learn valuable life skills, your marriage is strengthened, and you all gain free time.

Dealing with the Drudgery—Cooking, Cleaning, and Laundry

Even if you simplify, delegate, or hire out, cooking, cleaning, and laundry are never-ending tasks. With your family, try these tips to minimize the time and effort required.

Cooking

1. **Once a week, make a basic menu plan for dinner.** One single mom, who works shifts, plans simple dinners with her two teens (one with Asperger

syndrome). Her kids help prepare easy meals such as scrambled eggs, grilled cheese sandwiches, spaghetti, etc. She rounds out each meal with a salad, fresh fruit, and cut up veggies. From your meal plan, make a grocery list and shop only once per week. You'll save time and money.

2. **Find healthy take-out food:** On a week when your time is tight, plan a take-out evening. But instead of pizza, find a place that makes home-cooked, healthy meals for take out or for home freezing. Ask at your local market or look for ads in your community paper. Typically, these meals cost the same or less than pizza. Or choose healthier take-out alternatives from your grocery store, such as cooked chicken and pre-made salad.

3. **Whenever you or a family member cooks a meal (spaghetti sauce, soups, casseroles, etc.), always make extra and freeze a portion or two.** That way, you'll save time cooking on busy nights, and still have home-made healthy frozen dinners.

4. **When you chop onions, grate cheese, cook dried beans, etc., always prepare more and refrigerate or freeze the remainder for another meal.** You can also brown extra ground meat, and store some in the freezer for future recipes.

5. **On grocery shopping day, let your kids individually wrap portions of crackers, cookies, carrot sticks, etc., for their lunches.** Then, in the morning, they can quickly grab a pre-made snack pack for their lunch bag.

6. **Make a huge salad:** Once a week, make a large salad filled with nutritious ingredients such as rice, beans, corn, celery, red pepper, etc. This will last for several days, and will ensure you have easy lunches for home or work. Only add the dressing right before serving.

7. **Make a crock pot meal once per week to free up your evening.**

8. **If you can afford it, get groceries delivered.** You can order groceries online and they will be delivered once per week. Typically, the groceries cost no more than they would from a store. You'll pay approximately 10 percent on top of your grocery costs for delivery. But, if this saves you an hour or two per week, it might be worth it for you.

LAUNDRY

9. **Buy some smaller bins or divided laundry baskets.** Have each family member sort their dirty laundry by color into bins kept in their own rooms. When a bin is full, a family member can collect the same-colored laundry from others and do a combined load of laundry. Then, the laundry person can sort clean laundry into each basket. Afterwards, everyone puts their own clothes away.

10. **To help young children put their own clothes away independently, label each dresser drawer** (use words, symbols, or photos of each type of clothing, as appropriate).

11. **If you'd like to do laundry less frequently, buy everyone extra pairs of underwear and socks** (the first things they always run out of).

12. **Stress to your kids that they needn't throw jeans or pajamas into the laundry if they've only been worn once.** Assign each family member a bath towel and wash them all once a week.

13. **Wash your sheets monthly unless your family has allergies, eats on the bed, etc.** Assign each child one day per month for his sheets and write it on his calendar. On that day, the child strips his own

bed and brings the sheets to the washing machine, along with a load of his own "whites" laundry.

CLEANING

14. **Get your family onboard by inviting guests over for a snack or for a play date.** Then, with a deadline, your family can rush through the house, do a quick pick up, toilet swish, and kitchen counter wipe.

15. **Put together a basic cleaning kit for each bathroom and kitchen.** Include paper towels or rags and a spray bottle with all purpose non-toxic cleaner. That way, it's easier for your child to be in charge of cleaning one room.

16. **Try using disposable wet sanitizing wipes and dusting cloths to make it easier for your children to help clean.** Also, consider disposable dusting cloths that your child can wear like a mitt on their hand.

17. **Make a list of basic chores that should be done daily** (such as setting the table, loading/unloading the dishwasher, feeding the pets, wiping kitchen counters and table). At the dinner table once weekly, have each person sign up for one chore for that week. Or let your kids keep the same chore they've mastered and don't mind doing.

18. **To avoid major clean-up hassles, clean as you go.** For example, after a meal, each family member rinses their own plate and loads it immediately into the dishwasher (if you have one). Enforce this rule until it is a habit.

19. **Cut down on the mess by making a "no eating" rule that applies to everywhere but the kitchen** (except for special occasions like movie watching or when guests come over).

20. **Break tasks into small blocks.** To tackle a big job, such as cleaning out a closet or child's room, try working at it for fifteen minutes at a time. Eventually, the job will get done.

21. **As often as you can, or even as little as once or twice a year, hire a professional cleaner to give your house a deep cleaning.** Or, ask for a cleaning gift certificate for the holidays.

Get Yourself Organized

"Simplify through organization," recommends Carmelita, mother of a child with ADHD, apraxia, and multiple motor and sensory issues. "Once things are organized and it becomes routine, you can concentrate on other important things."

To minimize stress and maximize time for what you want to do, organization is key. Even if you consider yourself to be a laid back, spontaneous kind of person, consider this: by adding better planning and more structure to your life, you can increase the time you have to relax! Try these ideas:

WEEKLY PLANNING

Each Sunday or Monday, sit down with your date book to plan the week ahead. Write down in your calendar what you'd like to get done that week. Highlight the tasks that are essential—such as medical appointments or school meetings, work commitments, etc. As you complete each task, cross it off. For your non-pressing tasks, delegate them, ditch them, or write them down in your calendar for the next week.

Each week, make sure you include activities that nurture your physical, social, spiritual, and intellectual needs. Make these activities a priority and write them down. They needn't be time consuming or complicated. For example, take a walk in the neighborhood, call a friend, and read a good book before bed.

Some moms say they color code their weekly activities, so they can see at a glance whether there is relative balance in their week.

For example, you could write work, appointments, social get-togethers, volunteer, church/synagogue, exercise, hobbies, family time, etc., in different colors.

USE CALENDARS AND DAY PLANNERS

If you're a high-tech kind of person, use technology to keep you organized. If you work at your computer most days, try using the calendar and task lists in Microsoft Outlook. It has pop-up reminders and alarms to remind you of appointments or commitments. Another option is using the calendar feature on your cell phone, if you have one. A pricier but effective alternative is a PDA (personal digital assistant).

If you're more of a visual person who prefers to see your day, week, or month all together, use a paper day planner instead. If you have only two or three appointments per day, you may prefer a book that has an entire month on one page. But to visually organize all work, home, and family commitments, a planner with a week spread across one or two pages, with spaces for each hour, will be more effective. Amy uses a calendar that has spaces for hourly appointments and a "reminder" section at the bottom of each day. She writes her daily "To Do" list and priorities in that section.

Professional organizers suggest using only one calendar and keeping it with you at all times, so that nothing gets forgotten. One mom, who has an hour subway commute to work each day, uses this time to review and plan her weekly schedule. Place a checkmark beside appointments and commitments once you have discussed them with your partner and/or family members. That way the checkmark tells you, for example, that your partner has agreed to drive your child to a medical appointment that week.

Involve your family in scheduling the week. Have a brief talk on a set day and time to discuss the week and who needs to be where. Some moms also use a family calendar by the kitchen phone that has each child and adult's activities written in. Try using a different color ink for each person in the family. If your kids are able to, have them write in their own activities on the calendar. If you use this system, don't forget to transfer activities into your own calendar. Get in the habit of checking the calendar each morning. Don't schedule appointments and commitments too tightly, as they usually take longer than you have anticipated.

Another way to clear your day and mind for things that matter is to get rid of paper clutter.

The Paper Chase—How to Conquer Endless Piles of Paper

"All the bills end up in the massive medical insurance folder and into the tax folder at tax time," says Maya, mother of a child with learning disorders and mental health issues. "I have started binders for each, but since I give up on filing when I run out of time and energy...the pile grows exponentially!"

The amount of paper we moms have to keep organized is staggering—our children's school, medical, and therapy records; insurance; household files; home business records; volunteer documents; etc. Inevitably, these papers land in endless piles that overtake our dining room table, or languish in an overflowing "To File" box. We asked Helen Montfort, a professional organizer, for advice. "Start by setting up a system for your current paper, rather than dealing with years of old paper," she says. "Otherwise it can be too overwhelming to begin." She recommends this system:

EVERYDAY SCHOOL PAPERS

For each child, get an inexpensive cardboard "banker's box" with a lid from an office supply store. Label the box with your child's name and school year. Toss all your child's papers, school flyers, PTA news, etc., into the box, without sorting or editing. Then, at the end of the school year, go through and throw out all unimportant paper. Some kids will be able to do the sorting and discarding independently.

IMPORTANT SCHOOL DOCUMENTS

Use a Binder. Place important information (your child's IEP and notes from IEP meetings, therapy reports, report cards, standardized tests results, educational/psychological assessments, important notes about your child from the teacher, documents related to discipline, etc.) chronologically in a three-ring binder that you label with the school year. So, the papers in the front start with September, and progress through June at the end. Just in case the papers get separated, pencil in the date on each sheet.

Or Use Hanging Files. Alternatively, put all important yearly school information chronologically in a hanging file labeled with the school year. Ideally, use hanging files that are housed in a filing box with a handle so that it is portable. Some moms just bring the whole box to school meetings. Alternatively, buy a "rolling" file system on wheels that is open on the top and waist high. This system is great for bringing to a table for you to organize papers. Of course, you can also use a traditional filing cabinet with hanging files and labeled folders.

MEDICAL INFORMATION

Your child's medical records can be filed using the same system you pick for important school documents (see above). Or try these suggestions offered by other mothers of children who are medically complex. Says Krista, "I keep a typed copy of all medical/social service/ school addresses and phone numbers in my purse. I have also developed a quick double-sided sheet listing all major hospitalizations, diagnoses, braces, etc., which I give to new medical providers and school personnel. That way I make sure that I don't forget to tell someone something I have come to consider normal."

If your child has multiple medical challenges, keep a current three-ring binder with your child's medical background and updates. At appointments or hospitalizations, you'll have all the information you need to complete the paperwork or answer doctors' questions. If you like, computerize this record and update it periodically. In your child's medical binder include: name, Social Security number, insurance identification numbers, dates and types of immunizations, drug allergies and reactions, medical problems, diagnoses, routine medications, medical treatments or equipment used, doctors' names and addresses, basic school info, agencies providing care, medical supply companies, surgeries (dates, procedures, and length of time in hospital), and past hospitalizations.

For a ready-made option, get copies of the *Care Notebook* and the *Care Organizer* developed by the Center for Children with Special Needs, a division of Children's Hospital and Regional Medical Center in Seattle (see Resources). The notebook is a three-ring binder with plastic pages for business cards, pocket dividers to store forms, and thirty-nine forms covering everything from your child's daily activities to medical bills. (All the forms can be downloaded for free.) The *Care Organizer* is a plastic expanding file folder with individual pockets labeled (in English, Spanish, Vietnamese, Russian, Chinese, and Somali) to help organize paperwork. Both the notebook and organizer are available for free to parents in Washington State. For everyone else, they are $20 each.

Other care notebooks are available from the American Academy of Pediatrics. Or, if you prefer to organize your paperwork online, check out the free Children's Medical Organizer developed by the Hospitals and Clinics of Minnesota. (See the Resources section for contact information on any of these products.)

Insurance Paperwork

Label a stack of file folders with the name of each health provider you deal with—doctors, hospital, lab, supplies, etc. Use the hanging file system or buy a large accordion folder. Keep bills, Explanation of Benefits (EOB) forms, statements, and any other correspondence in the corresponding folder. Sort by date with the most recent date at the front of the file. That will make it easier to match bills with EOB forms.

When an EOB comes in, paperclip it to the corresponding bill. That way, if you need to submit both to a supplementary insurance firm or a flexible spending account, they're together (don't forget to keep copies).

For each provider, make a tracking sheet by hand or on a spreadsheet that lists the date of service, account number, charge, amount paid by your insurance company, amount paid by supplementary insurance, and your out-of-pocket payment. If you pay a deductible or have an out-of-pocket limit, track this as well.

Information about Your Child's Preferences, Needs, and Abilities

Make an "All about Me" binder for your child. Include your child's diagnosis, likes, dislikes, strengths, favorite outings, etc., as well as general information about the disability, suggested ways to adapt activities, and relevant pamphlets. You can pass along this binder to any new respite worker, community program staff, or your child's new teacher at the beginning of the year.

Keeping on Top of Bills and Other Incoming Paper

Montfort offers this easy system for managing paper and the endless tasks they can generate:

Sort Your Mail

Don't leave your mail in one pile, in which important documents and bills can become lost. Instead, each day (or at least once per week), sort incoming mail into different baskets—one each for: magazines, catalogs, "odd" pieces of mail that don't fit another category, and bills.

Then, when you have to pay bills, you can easily find them in one basket.

Use a "Tickler" File to Remind You To Complete Tasks on Time

Professional organizers say this file "tickles" or reminds you to take action. Buy an accordion-type file that has numbered pockets and a stack of white 3 x 5 inch index cards. When you receive any piece of paper requiring action, pencil on it a number indicating its priority, and file it under that number. So, for example, write #1 on a top priority action, and file that paper in the #1 slot. Also, write the action (such as "Phone the dentist for an appointment") and the priority number on an index card. Keep the cards in your purse or a central place. Each day, choose two high priority cards, get out the corresponding paper from the file, and complete the action—such as making your child's dental appointment. Montfort prefers this system over lists, because it helps you to prioritize tasks. And cards are less likely to get lost than endless lists.

Alternatively, write a to-do list in your calendar, and asterisk the most important tasks. At the end of the week, write down any tasks you didn't complete to be carried over to the next week.

Routines Rule—Overcoming Daily Chaos

"We have a routine that minimizes morning chaos," says Brianne. "My husband programs the coffee maker the night before, and brings us coffee in bed before the kids wake up. My youngest (with autism) feeds the dog and fish and my eldest empties the dishwasher. My kids pour their own cereal and place their bowls in the dishwasher. I help my youngest get dressed and brush her teeth. I make lunches while she watches morning TV. Eventually, I'd like my kids to make their own lunches."

Like Brianne, you too can lessen stress and help your kids to be more independent by adding some routine to your family life. Try these ideas:

SCHEDULE IN ROUTINE TASKS

Ever wake up Monday morning, race out the front door, and discover your car's gas tank is empty? To avoid these kinds of unnecessary stresses, pick a specific time for mundane tasks and stick to it, as much as possible. Fill up your car with gas at the same time each week, preferably tied to a specific errand or outing. For example, always fill up your gas tank after your child's speech therapy appointment. By grocery shopping at the same time each week (and meal planning ahead of time,) you can avoid the expensive midnight dash to the convenience store for milk or diapers. Try assigning laundry, washing bedding, to specific days.

When you get a new calendar, pencil in weekly or monthly tasks like giving out allowance, changing your furnace filter, or replacing water filters.

To increase your kids' independence, help them establish routines too. For example, have each child (with help) lay out his own clothing. Says Carmelita, "My older child (with special needs) has a hanging cloth cubby in his closet that holds each day's clothing items (socks/underwear/shirt/shorts or pants). Then he can just grab them and get dressed by himself in the morning." Backpacks, diaper bags, and briefcases should be packed the night before and stored at the front door. Kids can also help to make their own lunches the night before.

Let your kids have a before-bed ritual of setting the breakfast table—including boxes of cereal. For younger kids, have a small easy-pour milk jug in the fridge at child level, so kids can help themselves to breakfast.

CONQUER THE CLUTTER

If you're not organized, you're not able to find what you want when you need it. It's hard to feel relaxed and productive if your home looks chaotic and you can't find your car keys. And there's nothing more stressful than rushing out to a school meeting or medical appointment when you've misplaced crucial documents or your child's shoes. Even if you're comfortable in a "relaxed" home, most kids function better when their environment is structured and orderly. Try these tips:

> De-clutter an area in very small chunks of time—such as fifteen minutes per day or week. Otherwise, it can feel too overwhelming to start.

Every item should have a designated home, so you're not searching for it. For example, your child's medications can be in a high-up locked box in the kitchen. Designate a shelf or basket for each child's toys, homework, therapy equipment, school permission forms, etc. In the front hallway or closet have a basket for each child that has hats, mitts, backpacks, sunscreen, etc. Label the basket with your child's name or a photo so that he can use the basket independently.

To eliminate last-minute searches for keys, keep a key hook or basket at the front door and always drop your keys there. In the same basket at the door, keep any outgoing letters that need to be mailed that day or library books or videos that need to be returned on the way to work.

Make a "Go Elsewhere" basket and keep it in a central place, such as the kitchen. Then, you can do a quick five-minute pick up of your house, and place items that need to be put away in the basket. Eventually, you or your family can put the basket items away. If you have a multi-level house, teach kids that if a basket is at the bottom of the stairs, they should take it up.

Try to deal with things immediately, so clutter doesn't build up. For example, when your child presents you with a permission form for a field trip, fill it out immediately, if possible. If that's not doable, file it in your in-basket and write the due date or reminder on your calendar.

Reclaim Your Weekends

"I spend all week looking forward to the weekend when I'll have more time," says Debbie, whose child has Asperger syndrome. But then, "the weekend hits and by the time I get through all the work that needs doing, there's no time left just to relax or spend time with my family."

Weekends should provide us with a chance to spend family time, rest, and have some fun. Too often, though, we're frantically catching up on errands, cleaning, and chores. Instead try these strategies:

Rather than grocery shopping on a weekend, when it's most crowded, shop on a weeknight. To avoid multiple trips, make a list based on your meal plan. If you like, take along a child for one-to-one time. If you have family members left at home, they are in charge of cleaning out the fridge and unpacking. Now you have a full fridge for you to enjoy family time on the weekend.

Don't leave all chores for the weekend. Schedule in basic chores and errands throughout the week for all family members, so that you don't lose a weekend day to housecleaning.

Schedule a block of time on the weekend for a fun family activity—even if you haven't yet planned the details. Don't let phone conversations, email, or errands eat into this family time.

Consider designating one day each month when everyone's home as a "do nothing" day. Be spontaneous that day or have everyone take turns choosing a family activity. Plan it well ahead of time so errands are done.

Plan something on the weekend and write it down, just for you. Lunch with a friend? An exercise class? A visit to an art gallery? Even an hour or two will give you something to look forward to.

Several moms said they had a regular weekend 'date night' with their partner, even if they lack the money or child care to leave the house. At the very least, take the time to enjoy a video or nice meal together at home.

We could spend every moment working with our child, researching therapies and attending disability meetings. There will always be another intervention, medication, or treatment we could try. Sometimes, walking the dog or heading to the park is the best use of your day. We moms have many aspects of life to balance: family, paid, or volunteer work, advocacy, and most importantly, our physical and mental health. See the chapters in Part IV: *Family Ties* and Part II: *Taking Care of Yourself* for ways to keep a healthy balance.

Experience Talks

"Make a priority list. Allow some time for yourself on the list, even if it's just fifteen minutes to go for a walk around the block or stop for a cup of your favorite coffee. I tell myself that what does not get done today will still be here tomorrow."

—Kuan, mother of a child who has cerebral palsy,
developmental delays, and is blind

"Asking for help was difficult at first, but as your child grows, you accept that you can't be "Super Mom." My husband and family are more than willing to pitch in when asked. Together, the work load is easy and we have enough time to get the work done, therapies accomplished, and still have fun."

—Denise, mother of a child with global developmental delay

"Consider giving up extra social and community commitments. Reduce the number of activities children are involved in, so you don't spend your entire life driving from event to event. Build margins into your life so that life becomes more simple, you are less stressed, and you can enjoy your family."

—Krista, mother of a child with hemiplegia and a hemispherectomy

*"We use respite several times a week. We would not have such a
positive outlook without respite. It saves our soul."*

—Julie, mother of a five-year-old with Angelman syndrome

Chapter 9

Find the Help
You Need

Programs that give you an occasional break from your special needs parenting duties can greatly improve your energy
level, optimism, and quality of life. Respite care was developed for just
that purpose. Other services such as early intervention, after-school
programs, or community recreation programs can give you some much
needed "down time" while your kids gain valuable skills.

Some moms told us they didn't know what help was available.
Says Juantia, mom of a four-year-old with Tourette syndrome, "I
know there is a lot more out there, but I don't know how to find it.
This is the toughest part for me." Other moms, if they did know, said
they were reluctant to ask for help because they didn't want to be seen

as accepting 'charity.' These days, the norm is that nuclear families function independently, so we feel we should "take care of our own."

Many moms told us they were frustrated by the "red tape" necessary to access programs. Julie says, "The hardest thing was filling out all the paperwork and all of the acronyms that were used. My husband and I are well educated and we still found the system confusing, frustrating, and depressing." In order to access services, we often must fill out forms describing our children by their diagnoses and difficulties, instead of by their personalities and strengths. That's pretty disheartening, especially when we're trying to teach ourselves and our families to focus on the positive.

If you're trying to hold down a job, or are a single mom, the search for support can be especially difficult. So you may wonder whether applying for services is even worth the trouble.

It is. Despite the hassles, you need to learn what's available in your community and take advantage of the programs offered. You and your family have much to gain.

To find out what supports are available locally, talk to other parents of children with special needs. Also ask teachers, doctors, therapists, and other social service providers. Look up "Disability" in your phone book blue pages and call organizations and agencies. Contact local, state, and federal government and request supports for families of children with disabilities. And as Filomena advises, "End EVERY call with 'Do you know anyone *else* that can help me in this matter?'"

In this chapter, you'll learn about some of the services that may help your child and family. If they're not available in your area, see Chapter 10.

Access Respite or Short-Term Care to Accomplish Tasks or to Take a Break

"We use respite every month to get away for dinner, for time to run errands or to spend with our older son," says Juliana, whose toddler Toby has Down syndrome. "This has been wonderful, because we can't use teenage babysitters—we need qualified adults and the cost is $10-plus per hour. We are reimbursed for about 60 percent."

Years ago, respite (a break from caregiving) was provided by extended family members who lived in the same house or close by. Grandmas, sisters, and cousins actively cared for the kids so parents could get a much-needed break. Now, family members often live far away or work full-time themselves, making it difficult for them to pitch in.

Formal respite services began to develop in the 1960s, when governments began closing institutions and moving individuals with special needs back to their communities, often back in with their families. The aim was to give families relief from constant caregiving, especially when informal supports weren't there. Today, the need is greater than ever.

Respite can be provided in many forms and funded in various ways. Respite can mean having someone come into your home to look after your child or having your child stay overnight at someone else's home. It can mean sending your child to enjoy activities in the community with a support worker, while you enjoy time to yourself. Respite can be provided during the day or overnight, short-term (a few hours) or a few weeks (while your family goes on a vacation, for example).

Monica sends her twenty-four-year-old daughter with Angelman syndrome to overnight respite camp for three weeks during the summer and seven weekends throughout the rest of the year. "Camps are wonderful respites! We go out to dinner with friends, go to the movies, and go on vacation ourselves for a week when she's at summer camp."

What often confuses parents is the fact that there's no one consistent approach to respite care. The services provided, the organizations that provide them, and the families that qualify can vary tremendously, depending on where you live. Respite may be funded totally or partially by the government or a community organization. You may pay part of the cost on a sliding scale according to income, or you may pay the full price of the service yourself. In some cases, private insurance may partially cover it.

As a parent of a child with special needs, you might be able to receive an annual respite stipend from your state or province, or receive a voucher allowing you to purchase respite services from a community provider. Or, in some states, you may receive respite in the form of a government-sponsored program such as a Medicaid waiver. Sometimes, respite is sponsored by a hospital, community agency, or service club (e.g., Rotary club, Easter Seals). In addition, respite programs may be offered by a church, school, or special needs association, or by a volunteer host family in their own home. A social service agency may even partner with a private business such as a hotel. While your child is cared for at home, you and the rest of your family enjoy a meal, swim, and overnight stay at the hotel.

If you receive funding to purchase your own respite services, you can usually choose and hire your own support worker (such as a university student, neighbor, or nurse). In most places, you are not allowed to hire siblings or other family members as respite workers. Some programs let you use the funds to access child care, after-school programs, adult day camps, recreational activities, or summer camps as respite. Or, when a local program isn't available, some families join together to pool their funds, hire a support worker, and start their own respite program.

Sounds great, right? There are some restrictions. Depending on where you live, respite may be limited to those with certain disabilities (e.g., physical and developmental disorders, but not mental health ones). The parent of a child with a "more severe" diagnosis such as autism might get respite, while the parent of a child with a "milder" diagnosis such as Asperger syndrome or ADHD might not. In addition, respite may be restricted to certain age groups, or to families with limited income

Even if you get some funding, there may be no qualified facilities or workers to provide the necessary care. Obviously, you're not going to leave your child with just anyone. Staci, like many moms we surveyed, says, "Sometimes you can't find a good, dependable person for that respite care." That's especially true for children who require intense nursing or behavioral support or for those who live in rural areas.

In many communities, there are long waiting lists for respite funding and programs. A 2003 Florida study of over 300 parents of children with special needs found less than half of families needing respite care actually received it.

RESPITE—GO FOR IT

Despite the challenges of finding and funding respite care, it's well worth pursuing. Respite time enables you to do errands, relax, or enjoy time with your partner or other family members. Building a relationship with a provider means you have a reliable caregiver for your child if there is a family emergency. Children enjoy trying new activities and making social contacts outside of family, especially as they get older. Amy's daughter, Talia, for example, goes out with respite workers in the community, and enjoys swimming, indoor rock climbing, library visits, hiking, skating, movies, and more with them. These outings expand her social world and give her a chance to gain independence from family members. Some day your child may live on her own, in a group home, or other supported care. Out-of-home respite care gives your child, teen, or adult a chance to test the experience of living outside the family home.

Ask other families of children with similar care needs to recommend respite staff or programs they have used. When meeting with respite agencies, ask about the qualifications of staff and whether you can choose the respite worker. For care outside of your home (such as respite spots in a group home), ask for details about the daily routine, meals, recreational activities, and emergency procedures. Also, ask about the other children who might be in respite care at the same time. Are their needs and diagnoses similar to your child's? What is the ratio of staff members to children? Does the program provide transportation? How far in advance can you book respite? And do they care for siblings? In addition, see the questions for child care providers in Chapter 20. If you are interviewing a provider to come into your home, use the sample child care interview in Appendix 5 as a starting point. Most respite programs have a detailed manual for parents and families that contains answers to many of your questions—so ask to see a copy.

We moms are often reluctant to ask for help, since we're so used to being independent. Yet, using services doesn't mean that you're not capable. By increasing your child's support system and people who know and care for her, you help her to be as independent as possible in the future. Plus, you help to ensure that the rest of your family stays healthy and happy.

WHERE TO FIND RESPITE CARE

Access respite services through a Medicaid waiver (see Chapter 11) or other government program, or through community agencies. Common sources of respite are listed in the box on the next page.

The nonprofit ARCH National Respite Network run by the Chapel Hill Training-Outreach Project has an online locator service that helps parents find respite agencies across North America (see Resources). The site lists for-profit home care providers, as well as nonprofit agencies, so be sure to get thorough information about the different options.

If respite is unavailable in your area, approach your community for help. One mother created a popular respite night through her church. Start your search by talking with your local contacts (other parents, your case manager, school teachers, doctors, therapists, and children's treatment centers). ARCH National Respite Network (above) also has information available from their website to help you start your own group.

Places to Contact for Information on Respite

State Departments of Mental Retardation

State Developmental Disabilities Councils

State Programs for Children with Special Health Care Needs (formerly Crippled Children's Services)

Departments of Health and Human Services, or Social Services

Departments of Mental Health

State and Local Departments of Education

State Protection and Advocacy Agencies

State and Local Disability or Support Groups

The Arc

United Cerebral Palsy Associations, Inc.

Autism Society of America

Brain Injury Association

Mental Health Association and Child and Adolescent Service System Program (CASSP)

Spina Bifida Association

National Easter Seal Society

Parent Training and Information Centers

Parent-to-Parent

University Affiliated Program(s)

Community Services Boards

YMCA/YWCA

Churches

Recreation Centers

Source: National Dissemination Center for Children with Disabilities (NICHCY).

Have a Small Child? Look into Preschool Special Education Plans

"We rely heavily on Tennessee's Early Intervention System (TEIS) because our insurance won't cover any of our daughter's therapy, since it is 'non-restorative,'" meaning it won't "cure" her speech deficit, says Christine, mom to a two-year-old with cerebral palsy. "They also have a program where they reimburse for mileage when you travel for therapy."

If you have a child with a disability or developmental delay who's not yet old enough to attend kindergarten, you may be able to get free or low-cost diagnostic testing, some therapies, and specialized instruction through your state's early intervention program or special education program for preschoolers with disabilities (see below).

Early intervention (or "Infant and Toddler") services are mandated under the federal Individuals with Disabilities Education Act (IDEA). In the past, infant and toddler programs only covered children from birth through two. However, when IDEA was reauthorized in 2004, states were granted the flexibility to allow children already receiving early intervention services to stay in these programs (with added educational components) until they're eligible to enter kindergarten.

Children are entitled to early intervention services if they have disabilities or developmental delays in cognitive, physical, speech/language, social/emotional, or self-help skills. Each state determines eligibility based on its own definition of "developmental delay," and may also extend services to children considered "at-risk" of a delay if intervention is not provided.

Early intervention services can include speech and language therapy, assistive technology devices and services, occupational therapy, physical therapy, psychological services, nursing, family counseling, transportation, and more.

If you are concerned that your child's development is not progressing as it should in one or more areas, your pediatrician or the pediatrics branch of your local hospital can put you in touch with your local early intervention office. You can also get contact information for your state's program from the National Dissemination Center for Children with Disabilities (see Resources), or look up your state's "Child Find" service (which provides free screening, referral, and initial service coordination) in the phone book or on the Internet.

If, on initial screening, it seems possible that your child may have a developmental disability, or be at risk of developing one, you will be assigned a case manager and your child will be given a free, multi-disciplinary assessment. Then, if your child is deemed eligible for services, an Individualized Family Service Plan (IFSP) will be drawn up by a multidisciplinary team (including you, the parents), specifying the kinds of services recommended for your child.

As part of the team, you have input into how services are carried out. Fortunately, services are mandated to take place in the most natural setting as possible. This minimizes the need for you to transport your child to various appointments. Instead, when possible, services are provided at home or in daycare.

Systems vary outside the U.S. In Canada, early intervention and preschool programs are primarily a provincial responsibility. The Ministry of Health or Children's Services usually determines what is available in each province (for example in Ontario, most larger communities have an "Early Years" Centre). Contact local agencies in your own community, so that you can access such crucial early help for your child.

Special Education Services Are Available for Preschoolers and Up

We usually think of "Special Education" as a service that's provided in elementary and secondary school. But special education services in the U.S. are actually available to children with certain disabilities or developmental delays starting at age three. In fact, some parents say their school systems are much more generous with services and therapies when children are still in preschool. (And if your child has been unable to attend preschool because of her disabilities, the school system may have a preschool program she can attend, or may provide services in your home.)

Special education today is very different from a generation ago. Not only does it include specialized instruction (often in a mainstream classroom) to address your child's unique learning needs, it may also include "related services," such as transportation, speech therapy and audiology, health services, psychological services, physical and occupational therapy, recreation, adapted physical education, assistive devices (ranging from low tech pencil grips to complex computers), or extended year schooling (summer programs). It may also include special adaptations or modifications that your child is entitled to, such as extended test-taking time, special technology, and more. (See info on Section 504, below.)

All special education assessments and services are free, regardless of the child's age, so you don't want to miss out on these valuable services. If you are concerned that your preschooler may need special help, and she was not enrolled in a state early intervention program (or if the program does not extend beyond age two in your state), contact your school district's special education office. Your local elementary school should be able to give you the phone number for a person who is knowledgeable about services for children ages three through five. If your child is already in kindergarten or above, request a special education evaluation by mailing a letter to the principal.

Of course, you can't just assume that your child will receive special education services, even if she had early intervention as an infant or toddler. Once more, IDEA establishes the guidelines for service. Special education services are only available to children with mental retardation, hearing impairments/deafness, speech or language impairments, visual impairments/blindness, serious emotional disturbances, orthopedic impairments, autism, traumatic brain injury, "other health impairments" that adversely affect a child's ability to learn (which covers a broad range of disabilities), or specific learning disabilities. Children aged three to nine without one of these labels but with a developmental delay (as defined by the state) may also receive services—but that varies by state.

Once you've requested an evaluation, your child's learning needs will be evaluated by various specialists (e.g., a speech pathologist, occupational therapist, and special educator). Then, a team that includes parents, the child (when appropriate), teachers, the specialists, a school administrator, and someone who can interpret and explain the evaluation results (e.g., the school psychologist) will meet and determine whether your child qualifies for special education. If she does, the team will develop an Individualized Education Program (IEP) that identifies learning goals and objectives for your child, as well as the services and accommodations that the school district must provide to meet your child's educational needs. The IEP specifies who will provide these services, their frequency, and duration.

If you don't agree with the IEP team's evaluations or recommendations, you can challenge them. Procedures vary by state, but the evaluation or IEP team should have given you a document that describes how to resolve problems; if they didn't, ask for a copy of the "procedural safeguards." An excellent resource for information on special education law and disputes is Wrightslaw, a website with legal and advocacy advice for parents of children with special needs (see Resources).

In Canada, provincial Ministries of Education determine what services students with special needs receive in school. If you have concerns about your child's progress, meet with your principal. If your child needs accommodations or modifications to the curriculum, an IEP similar to the American model will be drawn up. Procedural safeguards are also in place for appealing decisions. Contact your Ministry of Education or local school board for more information. If you still have concerns, contact your local disability association, which should be able to refer you to someone who can help you advocate for your child at school.

SECTION 504

Some children with disabilities who don't qualify for special education and related services under IDEA may still qualify for "accommodations" and "modifications" under Section 504 of the Rehabilitation Act of 1973. This civil rights law, very similar to the Americans with Disabilities Act, prohibits institutions that receive federal funding from discriminating against people with disabilities. (Section 504 defines a qualifying disability as a "physical or mental impairment which substantially limits one or more major life activities," including caring for one's self, performing manual tasks, walking, seeing, hearing, speaking, breathing, learning, reading, writing, performing math calculations, or working.) All children who receive special education under IDEA automatically qualify for Section 504 protections. In terms of a public school, Section 504 requires that the school make reasonable accommodations to allow a child with a qualifying disability the same "access" to a free appropriate public education (FAPE) that a child without disabilities has. It must also provide accommodations in any extra-curricular activities that the school sponsors.

Depending on your child's disability, "reasonable accommodations" might include:

    Administration of medications at school
    Extended time for taking tests or completing written assignments

Environmental modifications (e.g., wheelchair ramps, accessible bathroom stalls)

Allowing use of technology such as computers, tape recorders, or calculators

Reorganization of the classroom and students (e.g., seating child closer to the teacher or away from disruptive students or certain sensory stimuli)

Modification of the type and frequency of communication with parents (e.g., scheduled, periodic teacher meetings; daily or weekly behavioral reports; regular communication with teacher via email or telephone; providing parents with a set of text books to keep at home; etc.)

Appropriate behavioral management strategies

These are just a few examples of accommodations. But don't let the school system tell you that Section 504 "is just for giving medications at school."

Section 504 doesn't offer nearly as many protections as the IDEA does. But if your child has special needs and doesn't qualify for special education, ask your school district to evaluate her for a 504 Plan. If you disagree with the decision, you can request a hearing. As a last resort you can also file a complaint with your local Office of Civil Rights (OCR).

Before resorting to appeals, try to work out disagreements with your school district through negotiation and compromise. Many problems can be resolved through informal meetings that preserve your good working relationship with school staff. Taking legal action can be both expensive and emotionally draining. Appeal only after all other options have been exhausted.

Find Out about Your Community Resources

"I use the Boys and Girls Club three hours a week and use a Community Centre program on Saturdays for four hours," says Daphna, mother of a child with autism. "I have finally found a 1:1 worker who works five hours per week. I have also arranged with an agency for every-other-weekend of out-of-home respite."

Some moms like Daphna take full advantage of what their community offers. Your child may participate in a free, agency-sponsored program. Or you can use respite dollars to cover fees for community programs or to hire personal care attendants or one-on-one workers to enable your child to attend. Private insurance sometimes covers the cost of therapeutic community programs such as speech and language or physical therapy. As always, ask other parents, professionals, and agencies you deal with for their suggestions. Some examples of programs include:

> *Volunteer and friendship programs that provide social interaction for your child and free time for you.* Best Buddies, for example, pairs youth and adults with intellectual disabilities with secondary school, college/university, or work peers.

> *Specialized programs for people with disabilities provided by agencies or nonprofit-groups.* Examples include Special Olympics (sports and friendship), social skills groups, and specialized cooking classes. Often, volunteers pair up with professionals such as speech, occupational, or physical therapists, social workers, etc., to provide the service.

> *Day programs, after-school programs, or work programs.* Special job coaching agencies may help youth and adults find work or volunteer opportunities in the community.

> *Community recreation groups like those run by the local YMCA, recreation and parks department, or the Boys and Girls Clubs.* These may help with life skills and integration into regular programs. Often these groups provide volunteer one-to-one support for children with special needs.

> *Churches, synagogues, and other places of worship often provide support for children and adults with special needs who want to participate in regular groups.* Some offer specialized religious instruction or recreation for people with special needs.

Commercial recreational programs (such as dance, karate, basketball, music) sometimes offer specialized classes for children with special needs. Others help to include all children in their programs by providing volunteers for extra support.

Unearth Buried Treasure—Finding "Hidden" Grants and Loans

"The local Moose Club built a ramp on our house," Jalynn, mom of eleven-year-old twins, with cerebral palsy and cortical blindness, told us. "And our church diocese has a program that paid for our accessible bathroom."

In most communities, there are hard-to-find funding pots that can help pay for diapers, home and car adaptations, assistive devices, schooling, respite, one-on-one aides, summer camps, after-school programs, guide dogs, and more. Many community groups, religious organizations, service groups, individuals, schools, and newspapers offer funds or yearly grants. In Guelph, Ontario, for example, the local newspaper has a fund that pays summer camp fees for children.

Unfortunately, you must invest time and energy to discover the funds and to complete sometimes lengthy applications. And there are no guarantees that you'll get funding. But given the possible payoffs, it's worth trying.

ASSISTIVE DEVICES AND TECHNOLOGY

Wheelchairs, adapted homes or vehicles, specialized computers and toys, hearing aids, and other equipment all allow children and adults with disabilities to participate more fully in the community. If the equipment is medically necessary, such as a wheelchair, Medicaid or private health insurance is more likely to fund it. If it's needed for school or work (such as a computer), it may be funded under related services or vocational rehabilitation programs. For those who receive SSI benefits, the PASS (Plan to Achieve Self-Support) program allows you to save for expenses required to get a specific job or start a specific business—including housing modifications or equipment—without losing benefits.

Rarely is all equipment we need paid for. Often, you will need to borrow, lease, or purchase items yourself. Fortunately each state has a program that supports families needing assistive devices, thanks to the Assistive Technology Act of 1998. Services might include providing information on products, training, assessment, and funding.

Depending on the state, families can lease, purchase, or borrow equipment (sometimes you can even try a product at no cost for a short time). Or you may be able to take out low-interest loans with long repayment schedules. Some states also have Telework, a program that funds equipment such as specialized computers or accessible vans that enable employable adults to work from home or to visit customers. The Rehabilitation Engineering and Assistive Technology Society of North America (RESNA) provides contacts for Telework and other loan programs. (See Resources for more information.)

Canadian provinces have various assistive programs run under the Ministry of Health or Ministry of Social Services. For example Ontario's Assistive Devices Program (ADP) pays 75 percent of items like orthopedic braces, wheelchairs, and breathing aids. New Brunswick pays up to $8,000 for vehicle retro-fitting. You can find out more about different provincial programs through Service Canada (see Resources).

Housing

Housing modifications can also be expensive. Before modifying your home or apartment, explore all available sources of funding. For example, the Department of Housing and Urban Development (HUD) offers a couple of purchasing and rehabilitative loan programs that may help you finance the purchase of a new home or improve your existing one to be more accessible. The Federal National Mortgage Association (Fannie Mae) has loans geared to people with disabilities for accessibility modifications. Contact your local Independent Living Center for information about these and other lending sources (see Resources).

In Canada, the Residential Rehabilitation Assistance Program for Persons with Disabilities (RRAP—Disabilities) offers assistance to low income homeowners or tenants to modify their homes. Contact the Canadian Housing and Mortgage Corporation (see Resources).

Digging Deep—Have You Tried...?

If you've been unsuccessful at getting funding through public assistance or private insurance try these sources:

Ask other parents, local disability organizations, and social service agencies (and professionals) whether they know of any other funds earmarked for families of children with disabilities.

Your local Independent Living Center (ILC) may have funding for home modifications or other equipment.

Research large disability organizations such as United Cerebral Palsy, the Arc of the United States or Muscular Dystrophy Canada; besides information, groups sometimes provide services like respite care or fund disability scholarships or equipment loans.

Assistive technology manufacturers may offer guaranteed loans or "try before you buy" programs for equipment or technology. Also, they often have information on other funding sources.

Forty Alliance for Technology Access centers across the U.S. offer software lending libraries, toy libraries, product and vendor information, access to computer labs, training, free loan of refurbished computer equipment, and more. Some services may require fees (see Resources).

Service groups such as Easter Seals, Rotary Club, and March of Dimes sometimes have equipment loan, respite, vocational, camps, or other helpful programs. Other groups such as Kiwanis, Knights of Columbus, Masons, Optimist, Sertoma, and the Lions often raise money for individual needs in their community. Since many groups only focus on one type of disability, contact them individually by visiting their websites or finding their local contact in your community phone book.

*Children's foundations may help with specific cir-
cumstances,* e.g., the Make a Wish Foundation or the
Starlight Starbright Children's Foundation may help
a child with chronic, serious, or life-threatening disease fulfill a life dream (such as visiting Disneyworld).
Starlight may also fund a computer for a child who is
hospitalized for a long time. The Disabled Children's
Relief Fund helps children with inadequate insurance
pay for wheelchairs, orthopedic braces, walkers, lifts,
hearing aids, eyeglasses, medical equipment, physical
therapy, and surgery.

*Look for disability-related, charity, and foundation di-
rectories at your local library.* Most major libraries have
The Foundation Directory (Foundation Center, New
York) or, in Canada, the *Canadian Directory to Foundations & Grants* (Imagine Canada, Toronto). Each
provides eligibility criteria, the application process, and
deadlines for each foundation. Or for a fee, access them
online (The Foundation Center provides some basic information for free.)

*Universities, colleges, and other post-secondary institu-
tions often offer disability-related scholarships.* Check
with the Financial Aid office of the post-secondary institution. Federal and state/provincial governments may
provide aid under some circumstances. Consult your
Department or Ministry of Education.

*Check with religious charities, churches, synagogues,
schools, employers, chamber of commerce, hospitals, labor
unions, sororities and fraternities, or veteran groups, to
find out what type of funding they may have available.*

*For added clout, join with other families who have
similar funding needs.* It's easier to ask for money that
will benefit an entire group of children, rather than
just your family. For example, you can ask a company
to fund extra aides for kids with muscular dystrophy to
attend summer camp in your community.

With networking, research, and a good deal of persistence, you can find services, funding, and supports to enhance your child's day-to-day life, as well as your own and your family's. In a later chapter, we'll discuss how to sharpen advocacy skills, to ensure that your family actually receives the services you worked so hard to locate.

Experience Talks

"The only way to find out what is out there is to ask. If you do not get the answer you need, ask someone else. Your best resource is other parents."
—Roberta, mom of ten-year-old Jonathan with Down syndrome

"Funding might be scarce, but thanks to the Internet you can arm yourself with knowledge. Knowledge is power."
—Alana, mother of a five-year-old with craniosynostosis, CP, and Asperger syndrome

"Keep up to date on health and research issues. Get involved with other parents of special needs children, especially with those who have similar needs as yours does. Accept help. Don't think you have to do this all alone."
—Robin, mom of an adult with Prader-Willi syndrome

"Becoming a parent advocate is a full-time job."

—Marilyn, mother of a child who is blind and has cerebral palsy

Chapter 10

Advocacy 101— Speaking Up for Your Child

We usually think of "advocacy" as a letter writing campaign to Congress or a march on the capitol. But the fact is, the moment your child is born, you become an advocate—*your child's advocate*. If your child has special needs, you may spend more time on advocacy than a paid lobbyist does.

At the everyday level, we moms advocate when we speak up for our children in the school yard, in the grocery store, or on the street. We advocate in the doctor's office and the classroom, to make sure our children's needs are accommodated. When frustrated by a lack of services, we may band together with other families to create new programs. We become active in disability groups, PTAs, and daycare boards. Some of us eventually volunteer on the boards of the same agencies that we once struggled with.

And finally, we may join together to lobby the government to change laws affecting services for our child and thousands of others.

Our kids teach us that *we must constantly speak up*. If you don't advocate for your child, her quality of life will diminish, as will your own and your family's. It's impossible to be happy and productive at home or at work if your child's life at school or daycare is falling apart. Daily life is also unmanageable if community activities most people take for granted are impossible for your child to access.

It is empowering to advocate successfully for your child. When you succeed, you gain a much-needed service as well as confidence, control, and, in some cases, camaraderie with others in similar situations.

Advocacy 101

Wherever your advocacy takes place—in the state house or the daycare center—there are certain common tactics that will always serve you well. Mothers we surveyed who are seasoned advocates offer this advice:

Recognize your own expertise. Always remember that you know your child best, so you are the best expert to advocate on her behalf.

Be informed. Learn about your child's disorder so you can educate others. Read, talk to other parents, attend workshops, consult with professionals, and research on the Internet. Contact disability associations for information on trends, treatments, educational interventions, and legislation. Know your rights and your child's rights under legislation such as the Individuals with Disabilities Education Act (IDEA), the Americans with Disabilities Act (ADA), and Section 504 of the Rehabilitation Act. (Similarly, in Canada, be familiar with rights under the Canadian Charter of Rights and Freedoms, human rights legislation, provincial education acts, and, in Ontario, the Accessibility for Ontarians with Disabilities Act.)

Ask questions. Leave every meeting (and end every phone call) with the school, insurance company, or service provider with a clear understanding of what was said and what actions will be taken.

Be professional. Be courteous, respectful, and determined. Direct your indignation at the unjust situation, not at the person on the other side of the desk. Stay calm—don't rant or yell. Feel confident by looking professional—ditch the jeans for dress pants and carry a briefcase and notebook. Know the chain of command, should you need to escalate your concern or appeal the process.

Give praise when deserved. If you acknowledge people's efforts for your child, they are more likely to give you credit too.

Control tears and tantrums. Most of us have felt teary at meetings when disappointed, frustrated, or grateful. Most professionals recognize tears as a natural sign of dedicated parenting. But lose your temper and you may find yourself marked as "trouble." Ann Marie offers this advice: "If I find myself getting too emotional or defensive, I acknowledge this and tell them how I am feeling and why."

Network with other parents. Other parents can tell you whether others have encountered the same problem you're having, and how they've handled it. If you find others are currently dealing with the same issue, you can join together. A group of parents working towards a common cause effects change better than a single voice.

Know when to back down. Sometimes you have to give a little to get what you need. If your goal, for example, is to ensure your distractible child catches the school bus home, the method may be unimportant. Even though you may prefer that a teacher see her onto the bus, a responsible older student might also work well. Save your energy for the bigger battles.

Take your support team. Increase your power and control by bringing a family member, friend, professional, or professional advocate to important meetings. As Selena says, "An extra set of ears doesn't hurt. Not everyone hears the same thing." Ask your support person to take notes, so you can actively participate.

Document everything. Although time consuming, it pays off. Log all phone calls with professionals, maintain clear health records, keep copies of all forms and receipts, and record minutes of meetings. Keep everything in one place for quick access. Organize your paperwork before presenting your case. Says Daphna, who works for a disability agency and is also a parent of a child with autism, "The more documentation you can provide, the stronger your case and demonstrated need."

Be visible by volunteering. Don't only show your face when you're asking for something. Many mothers we surveyed volunteer or work part-time with schools, child care centers, hospitals, religious groups, community agencies, and disability organizations. Trish, a mother of four children with special needs, says, "When people see me in the class and on campus daily, they work harder for my children—they want to give more."

Seek out family-centered support. Philosophies such as wraparound or individualized funding encourage family, friends, and professionals to help advocate for your child.

Teach your child to self-advocate. As they get older, your children (if possible) need to speak up for themselves. Provide a good model and give them opportunities to practice. Nora's son with Asperger syndrome speaks to school board staff about how a teaching assistant helps him learn. These words carry far more clout coming from a child than a parent. If your child is unable to self-advocate, involve siblings, other relatives, or friends in your advocacy efforts—so they can continue when you're unable to.

The Real "Grassroots"—Advocating for Your Child in Public and Private

Children with "hidden" disorders—as well as their parents—are often harshly judged. Children with behavioral or mental health issues are sometimes avoided, yelled at, and even sworn at in public. Akemi's son is an adult now, but she vividly recalls outings with her son (who has autism). "A typical response to my son's behavior was 'Some mother you are! Can't you control this little *&#@!'"

If your child has ADHD, for example, well-meaning friends and relatives may deny that the disorder even exists. They may say, "All he needs is a little discipline!"

Because of the stress of feeling watched or judged, we may avoid family gatherings or social get-togethers with friends. We may hesitate to go out at all.

So what can you do?

EDUCATE THE COMMUNITY

Most people don't mean to be insensitive. Their attitudes are shaped by misinformation or generalizations (often based on books or TV shows). When talking about our own kids, the authors have been asked numerous times, "Autism—do you mean like Rainman?" Rather than get insulted or upset, we take that as an opportunity to teach someone new about the huge variations within the autism spectrum.

Some parents suggest carrying brochures or business-size cards that describe your child's disorder, relevant websites, etc., that you can hand out to people who are curious or critical. Or your child can deliver the card herself (there's nothing worse than being spoken about like you're not there). Ask your disability organization if it has cards available.

If your child has difficulties with teasing at school, consider giving a presentation to the children (and teachers) explaining her disability. (If you're uncomfortable doing this yourself, see if your local disability group has someone who gives such talks.) You might be surprised to see how understanding and supportive kids can be, once they understand why your child looks or behaves as she does.

It's important that you don't isolate yourself. Enjoy the community. The more you and your family are visible and involved, the more accepted you will feel. Carol says being involved in the community changes attitudes. "At the kids' school, I go on field trips and help monitor testing. It benefits me emotionally because people get to know who I am in relation to my children at the school. I am the 'mother with the little Down syndrome girl.' I get a chance to provide a good example. They see a happy, positive person. My life is not devastated. We are a normal family."

Join your local disability association to find like-minded parents. Most are involved in parent support, advocacy, and community education. Volunteer to support their events that increase community awareness about the disability. For example, offer to sit at an information booth, giving out info on your child's disability at community events.

PLAN AHEAD FOR THOSE AWKWARD MOMENTS

Still, we know, realistically, that no matter how hard you work to educate people, you may still run into uncomfortable situations from time-to-time. So plan ahead. Know what you will say to others if your child starts acting out during a community outing, such as: "I'm sorry if the noise is bothering you. My child has a neurological disorder, and sometimes it makes it hard for her to sit quietly." Or practice a response to an insensitive comment about your child. Keep in mind that you're not required to disclose information, just because someone else is nosy. For example, if a store clerk asks why your (non-verbal) child isn't talking, you can explain that she has autism, if you want to. But it's also OK to say "He's not allowed to talk to strangers."

You may find it helpful to commiserate with other moms of kids with special needs. Talking about upsetting incidents with moms who "get it" is great therapy. You could end up laughing together about the ridiculousness of the comments.

Feeling Heard in the Doctor's or Therapist's Office

"The medical doctors my son sees are fantastic," writes Donna, mom of a child with multiple disorders. Other women are less enthusiastic. Grace, mother of a teen with Asperger syndrome, says, "My son's pediatrician doesn't have a clue, and it's frustrating trying to talk to him and feel heard. I haven't figured out how to bring him around yet."

Many mothers complained that doctors pooh-poohed their concerns about their children's slow development—which meant their children were diagnosed much later than they could've been. That, in turn, meant they missed out on early intervention that could've made a significant difference.

It's also frustrating when your doctor understands the medical disorder, but can't point you towards the community resources you need. Says Alice, "My son's pediatrician, though knowledgeable in every other way, hasn't known much about appropriate respite for us." The medical journal *Pediatrics* published research in 2000 that compared the perceptions of doctors with the perceptions of parents whose children had chronic health conditions. Although doctors tended to rate the children's conditions as more severe than parents did, they also rated their unmet needs (for information, counseling, family support, household help, child care, etc.) as lower. Perhaps this explains why some parents like Grace feel their doctors just don't seem to "get it."

To maintain a healthy relationship with your child's doctor, try these tips:

Follow your instincts. Ilene, mother of a five-year-old recently diagnosed with Fragile X syndrome, says, "I went along with what my son's pediatrician told me for a long time, even though I knew in my heart that there was something amiss. Finally, to pacify us, he sent us to a specialist (all the while saying it was a behavioral issue)." As mothers like Ilene remind us—you are the expert on your child. If your doctor ignores your concerns, ask to see a specialist. If he/she refuses, consider getting another doctor, if possible.

Find a doctor who listens and respects your opinion. The best choice is not always the most experienced doctor, as Ilene found out. "It took me six months to find a doctor that clicked. While she may not be the most knowledgeable pediatrician on the subject of Fragile X...she is willing to listen and learn and respect what I have learned and what I know about my son." If you live in a small community or doctors are restricted by your health plan, your choices may be limited. Ellen must stick with her son's neurosurgeon, even though he's frequently negative. So, she sends her husband to the appointments. "I surround myself instead with people who think anything is possible."

Ask questions. Despite her PhD in Special Education, Tessa used to feel intimidated by medical professionals during her child's hospital stays. They'd use confusing jargon and made assumptions about what she already knew. Finally, she told them, "You deal with this all the time, but I don't. I need you to convince me that what you want to do is needed." Now she always asks as many questions as it takes for her to understand the situation.

Educate your doctor, if required. Not all doctors are experts in your child's conditions. Heather's daughter was diagnosed with Asperger syndrome the same year it was officially recognized as a disorder. "My knowledge far surpassed my doctor's, and I wanted his support in sending blood work to a University-backed research lab to investigate a dietary intervention that might help my daughter. After anticipating his questions, I gathered information, and I convinced him to requisition the blood work." Give your doctor time to read your materials or investigate your reasoning. Your doctor can help you determine what information is reliable.

Prepare for your appointment. If you think your appointment will take extra time or if you want to discuss an issue privately (without your child's presence) discuss this beforehand. Or give the nurse a note to stick on the chart, if you don't want to raise a topic in front of your child. If your child is likely to have a meltdown or be uncomfortable in the waiting room, tell office staff. They may schedule the appointment first in the day, call you at home closer to the appointment time, or find a private waiting room.

Take a notebook. Write down your questions and information such as instructions for medication or procedures for an upcoming surgery.

Be a liaison. If your child is going in for surgery, be the communication link between doctors, nurses, and specialists. Janessa has been by her twenty-month-old son's side for five surgeries, sleeping and eating at the hospital. "The only means of communication is this unbelievably thick chart. When your child is seeing many doctors with different specialties and his nurse is constantly changing (and overworked), you must be the one to ensure the continuity of care."

Track your child's health history meticulously, so if issues are raised about past history, you have accurate information at your fingertips. See Chapter 8 for some organizational tips.

Getting Bills Paid Through Insurance

"My biggest challenge is dealing with the crazy insurance system for Kenneth," says Neysa. "It's a constant battle." Neysa, whose five-year-old has Rett syndrome, is one of many parents who regularly battle insurance companies for coverage. Here are some tips for smoothing the way:

Know your health plan. Familiarize yourself with the services, equipment, medications, hospitals, and health professionals covered; rules about going outside the network; any deductibles; copayments (set fees, such as $10 per visit) or coinsurance (percentage of the charges you're responsible for, such as 25 percent of the doctor's charges); the limits of your plan (e.g., maximum number of visits, annual or lifetime dollar limits); and the procedures you must follow to get approval for services (including referrals or pre-approvals).

Record everything. Keep your policy number, individual number, and the name and phone number of your insurance agent somewhere handy, e.g., in an address book, a bulletin board by the phone, a file folder, etc. Know where your policy handbook is (the file cabinet is a good place, or, if your house is a disaster area, do as one mom does and keep it at work). If you're more organized on the computer, ask your insurance company if they can send you a copy of the handbook on CD-ROM; or check to see if it's available online.

Cover yourself. Call your health plan before you begin any therapy, see a specialist, get medical tests done, or undergo surgery to confirm the procedure and the provider are covered under your policy. Ask if you need a prescription, referral, or pre-approval.

Take Names. Note the full name of the person you talk to at your health plan. That information may come in handy should you run into problems later.

If you're having difficulties getting expenses covered on your own, contact your state Protection and Advocacy (P&A) system or SNAP, a Medical Insurance Empowerment Program for parents of children with special needs (see Resources).

Getting the Support You Need at Your Child's School and Programs

Whether it's getting a new therapy or service written into your child's IEP (Individualized Education Program), or just getting the teacher to be more understanding of her sensory defensiveness, you need cooperation at school. To really meet your child's needs, you need the buy-in of the therapists, the teachers, the aides, and even the playground assistants.

When we are surrounded by supportive, skilled people we feel happier, healthier, and more resilient. While some professionals are immediately supportive and empathetic, others need to be won over. As Brenda, mother of two sons with rare disorders, so aptly put it, "...with most professionals, the respect is there. I really felt like I had to earn it, though—I was not respected just for being a parent." But whatever their attitude is when you meet, your goal is to win them over to your side—or rather, your child's side.

Mothers who answered our survey offer this advice on maintaining your support team:

Be open. Openness builds trust and mutual respect. If you don't agree with a professional's advice, say so—respectfully. Monica, who has a twenty-four-year-old with Angelman syndrome, agrees. "I get it off my chest, out in the open. They know where I'm coming from and what I think." She managed to get her ideas incorporated into her daughter's day program, although professionals initially disagreed with the suggestions.

Be an equal partner. Acknowledge where their expertise ends and yours begins. You are the expert on your child's strengths, weaknesses, routines, motivation, history, and interests. Only you know how much time, money, and energy you and your family have to spare. Only together can you make an informed decision.

Show them you're a team player. Ask what you can do at home to reinforce what the staff does at school. But also be clear on how far you want to take that role. Some parents want to be consulted about everything; others prefer to let professionals make most of the decisions.

Involve them in your child's life. Keep your "team" informed of your child's victories and frustrations outside the classroom. "I try to get to know professionals personally and make sure to share all of my son's achievements with them—and give them credit for helping him get there," says Juliana, mother of a child with Down syndrome. Other parents share photos of their child to reinforce that he or she is not just the next "case" in a case conference. Show them your child has a life beyond the school.

Praise and acknowledge. Fanny, who has a sixteen-year-old with Asperger syndrome, says, "The professionals we deal with are amazing, and without their help, support, and caring my son might not even be in a 'regular' school." Make sure you share positive comments like this with the professionals helping your child (and with their bosses, as well!). Feedback gives professionals details on what works best for your child and also gives them incentive to go that extra mile.

Be patient. Sometimes we expect teachers, therapists, and other service providers to intuitively understand our children. Jasmine told us, "The assistant principal does not believe that a child with hydrocephalus has social skill problems and learning disabilities. She thinks he is just 'acting out' at school. I have provided information and set up meetings to explain what hydrocephaly is. I think she's starting to understand."

Accessing Community Programs

We heard from mothers who include their children in YMCA programs, swimming lessons, Girl Scouts, Boy Scouts, and other activities. Unfortunately, recreational programs are just starting to have supports (such as one-to-one assistants) that enable all children to participate. If your local ones don't, you may have to pioneer and help program leaders adapt the program. But the efforts are worthwhile—for both of you. While your child attends a program at the YMCA, for example, you may be able to exercise or swim at the same time. There are social benefits as well—you'll meet other families and increase your child's social contacts. As adults, these "typical peers" may become supportive friends, advocates, or business owners who may be able to offer your son or daughter employment. And by helping organizations be inclusive, you pave the way for other families to also participate.

Unfortunately, today, there are still far too few quality day programs and recreational opportunities for adults with disabilities. Lorie has a twenty-year-old with Rett syndrome. "I feel she needs more social gratification than just her immediate family. Aside from attending the Adult Center, there is nothing else available to special needs people." Recent studies also highlight these issues. A University of Wisconsin-Madison longitudinal study found that the biggest concern of parents of adult children with disabilities was filling the time outside of work or day program hours. As Lorie says, "When your child is young, everyone is enthusiastic about education, therapies, and activities, but as they grow older, the attitude seems to be 'What will be, will be.'"

Where programs don't exist, you may have to do some of the groundwork yourself. Start with your child's interests and see if an existing program could be adapted. Visit the program and list accommodations that will be needed. This may include room or equipment modifications; rule changes (such as requiring peanut-free snacks); use of visual instructions and schedules; additional personnel, such as a sign language interpreter or a one-on-one assistant; or education and training for the instructor. Anticipate objections such as cost, extra time, or inconvenience, and be ready to counter them. For example, if your child requires an assistant, see if local agencies can provide funding. Larger community recreation departments and YMCAs may already have inclusion coordinators to help modify programs and to support staff.

Once you know what you want, ask. Many community organizations are eager to accommodate. After meeting with Amy, the local YMCA staff agreed to provide a volunteer so Talia could participate in a children's fitness class. "Each week, the instructor emailed us the class activity schedule so we could prepare Talia ahead of time."

It's important to know your rights. Under the ADA, all public and private entities, whether the city, the YMCA, or a private club, must make programs accessible to those with disabilities unless the modifications would "fundamentally change the program" or result in "undue burden." They may not charge an extra fee for your child to participate, just because she has a disability, although they could require you to pay for a sign language interpreter or a one-to-one assistant—if doing so would cause an "undue burden" for the organization. Keeping that in mind, a large YMCA or city recreation program is more likely to provide paid help than a small private program.

If your child has a disability that affects her behavior, breaking program rules such as "no running on the deck" or "no swearing" cannot be used to exclude him or her. Only if a child is a direct threat to herself or others may she be excluded.

The Disability Rights Section of the Department of Justice offers free information on the ADA (see Resources). In Canada disability rights are not so clearly specified; however if you think your child has been discriminated against because of her disability, you can file a complaint with the Human Rights Commission.

Feeling Welcome in Your Religious Community

For many women, actively participating in church, synagogue, or another place of worship is a key part of their lives. Attending regular services can bring a sense of peace, spirituality, and comfort—that is, if you're not trying to supervise a bored, screaming, or wandering child at the same time.

Fortunately, many congregations open their arms to all children. Says Liz, "My church offered my son a one-on-one assistant for Sunday school without me even requesting one. His assistant has been an incredible blessing to my family." On the other extreme is Ilana's experience: "My son was not always quiet. The priest was understanding, but the other parishioners were not as tolerant. Hearing deep sighs and mutterings of, 'Why does she even bring him here?' were difficult to tolerate. We didn't go to church any more after that." Other families take turns attending services, leaving the child with special needs at home. Some families leave and search for a more inclusive spiritual community.

With advocacy, you can participate more actively in the religious community of your choice. Pamela, whose child has Angelman syndrome, says, "My son is included in a Sunday School program, and the volunteers that have come forward to help him are unbelievable. But it didn't just happen. I had to push for him, as the church could have just as easily left him behind."

Here are some ways to advocate within your religious community:

Be an active participant in your religious community. Amy volunteered to teach religious school—and even taught her daughter's class one year. "That way I could model what she needed. Now, temple members are familiar with my daughter and are understanding when she is chatty or flitting about during services."

Meet with your priest, rabbi, or religious leader, so they can get to know your family and your child's needs and strengths. Provide information about your child's disability, and how your child might act in services or in religious school programs.

Check into your church's or synagogue's resources for people with disabilities. Many religious groups have policies, resources, and, in come cases, complete ministries dedicated to those with disabilities. The Family Village website at University of Wisconsin (see Resources) lists worship resources to help parents and religious institutions integrate those with disabilities.

Educate congregants about your child and her special needs (depending on your comfort level and that of your child). Either speak to people individually, speak informally when you have a committee meeting, or include disability information in your church or synagogue monthly news bulletin. Also, invite congregants to participate with you in fundraising events, walkathons, etc., related to your child's disability. This involvement is a great way to build support and enjoy an inspiring day out together.

Be open and tell leaders in your community what you need. For example, perhaps a teen volunteer could supervise your child in the playroom while you attend services. Brainstorm ways to make religious services more accessible, such as providing a comfortable corner with pillows, children's books, or sensory toys.

Suggest new programs but be willing to do at least some of the groundwork yourself. When faced with an unsuitable Sunday school program, one mother started classes for kids with special needs.

Be prepared to modify ceremonies and rituals. For some families, religious ceremonies and life cycle events are a cherished part of life. Having your child experience First Communion, Sunday school or a Bar/Bat Mitzvah is possible with creative adaptation. Some children may not be ready to participate until they're a bit older than the norm. Others might require shortening or modifying prayers, changing the standard ritual, or changing the location and number of members present at the ceremony.

Advocacy on a Larger Scale

You can make many improvements by advocating on a local level at schools, organizations, and community programs. But sometimes, you're stonewalled by a law or precedent that is made by a higher level of government.

For example, in Ontario, after years of pressure and advocacy by parents and groups, the government agreed to provide one-to-one intensive behavioral therapy for children with autism under the age of six. But since the funding was inadequate, many eligible children never received treatment, because they turned six while still on the waiting list. Thirty-five families banded together to form a class action suit against the government, stating that denying their children the treatment on the basis of age violated their constitutional rights under the Canadian Charter of Rights and Freedoms. The Ontario Superior Court ruled in favor of the parents. The case has since been appealed by the Ontario government, but, if ultimately successful, it will mean millions of children with autism will get much-needed therapy.

Of course, class action suits are a last resort. They require a lot of energy and perseverance. In the end, you must be prepared to walk away with nothing—or worse, be on the hook for legal fees.

Letters and phone calls to government representatives, petitions, rallies, Capitol Hill visits, and media coverage are all effective ways of convincing the government to change policy. To advocate at this level try these strategies:

Work your way through the chain of command before speaking with someone higher up. For example, if an agency employee tells you there is a two-year waiting list for the service your child is entitled to, ask for the name and contact information of the employee's supervisor. Then, phone or write a letter to that person, and keep on going up the chain of command. If you aren't successful, *then* consider approaching your government official. Start with the service provider at the bottom, because they will know exactly what services are available locally. A politician will have many groups and issues to deal with and to understand. So your grievances will be competing with those of other constituents.

Learn who the players are. Know who your representatives are and what their responsibilities are, so you can direct your efforts to the right people. It may sound obvious, but with the complexities of government, it's easy to confuse federal, state/provincial, and municipal responsibilities.

Know how government works. How does legislation get passed? Who has control at each stage? What protocol must be followed? The more you understand, the better you can target and time your lobbying efforts.

"Face time" makes an impression. Meet with your local government representative to discuss the issue. Come prepared with arguments to support your case. Try to find out the representative's background or position on similar policies by searching their website or media reports. When possible, find a media angle that will make your issue attractive—for example, news that might be good publicity for the representative or an embarrassment to his opponent. Bring documents that will be easy for officials to understand, such as a short one-page handout that summarizes your main points. Follow up with a thank you, regardless of the outcome.

Quantity counts. Invite other parents to join you in a letter writing/email campaign for a common cause (such as inadequate school funding or lack of adult programs). Post a message on a local online group or advertise in a disability association newsletter. Provide a template letter and names and addresses of agency or government officials to make the job easier for parents. Send a copy of your letter to the media.

Join an established advocacy group. Your advocacy will have more success when you join with a recognized group. Often spokespeople from such groups are invited to give input to government reps when making policies. Many disability associations advocate at the government level or know associations that do.

Start your own. If there is no lobbying group for your cause, join with others with similar concerns. In Heather's community, an autism education lobby group started recently after one mother waited an entire school year for a suitable placement for her child. A group of twenty-five parents held an initial meeting and then engaged a lawyer to find out how they could improve educational services for all children with autism spectrum disorders in the community.

Go to the media. Newspapers, radio, and TV news are always looking for compelling human interest stories, especially ones that involve those with disabilities. Call radio or TV phone-in shows or email radio hosts. Write letters to the editor. If the issue gets enough attention, government is more likely to act.

Create a petition asking your representatives to take action on your issue. Circulate it at support group meetings, workshops, online groups, and make it available at a website. For a bigger impact, deliver the petition in person to the representative.

Hop online. If you'd rather contribute from your home computer, join an advocacy group that sends out information via the Internet. Groups often post information about their lobbying efforts on their websites or in electronic newsletters. Parents are increasingly invited to comment electronically on government policy. The best way to find out about these requests is to join online forums, which can be run as bulletin boards on organizations' websites or via free email discussion groups offered by Internet companies such as Yahoo, MSN, or America On Line. (See Resources.)

Join a research project. A less direct (and non-political) way to advocate for your child is to enroll in a research project. Research leads to treatments that improve the quality of our children's lives. Some large research projects allow you to participate from home. For example, the Autism Spectrum Disorders Consortium Canadian-American Research Consortium (ASD-CARC) posts questionnaires parents can fill out at their computer. If, though, you're considering enrolling your child in a clinical study for a medication, be sure to discuss it with her personal physician(s) first.

Need more information or training? Happily, you can find good information on advocating for your child online, in books, and at professional training session. For educational advocacy (to age twenty-two), contact your local Parent Training and Information Center or Wrightslaw Special Education Law and Advocacy. For Canadian advocacy groups, consult the Canadian Abilities Foundation's online Directory of Disability Organizations. (See the Resources section for contact information for these organizations.)

Hiring a Professional Advocate

Sometimes, it's difficult to advocate on any level (from personal to political) on your own, or even with the help of other parents.

If you're unclear on your rights (or your child's) or need assistance presenting your case, a disability advocate can help. Your local disability organization may have a list of school advocates, educational consultants, lawyers, or even trained volunteers, willing to assist (sometimes for free). Also ask parent support groups (online or those that meet in person) for recommendations. These local groups often can tell you which advocates have the most influence with the school board, the insurance companies, etc.

The Bazelon Center for Mental Health Law in Washington, DC publishes a state-by-state list of advocates on their website. Each state also a has federally-funded Protection and Advocacy (P&A) system designed to protect individuals with disabilities. Services vary by state, but might include referring you to an advocate, helping you access funding for assistive technology devices, or representing your case at a meeting. (See Resources.)

Occasionally, parents decide to tackle huge issues involving their child's rights. These fights can drag on for years and can consume hundreds of thousands of dollars in legal fees. Always start by seeing whether there are any advocacy groups already involved in similar fights and what they have (or have not) been able to accomplish. Rather than fighting alone, you may be able to work alongside others. Also, have a preliminary consultation with a lawyer who can advise you about the costs/benefits of a long, drawn out legal battle—and your likelihood of success. Then, you can make an informed decision about whether you want to fight the system. You may decide, for example, to send your child to private school rather than try to reform the school system.

Advocacy—The Double-Edged Sword

"I have helped other families advocate for their children and assisted them in getting services," recalls Ingrid, mother of a child with global delays. "I have used my personal contacts to raise awareness of autism through TV interviews and newspaper articles that I have done."

Mothers like Ingrid are proud of their efforts. But others find advocacy to be the most emotionally-draining and time-consuming aspect of their day. Heidi, mother of a twelve-year-old with Down syndrome, told us that "For eight years I fought the school system for every little thing; they wouldn't give up anything that they didn't have to. And I never felt like I won, which meant that my son lost. It was constant stress."

When services are scarce, advocacy that leads to services for some—but not others—can breed resentment. Penny watches younger children with autism get the intensive behavioral treatment for which she advocated for years, while her son does without. "I see families getting services I helped make possible—and still my own child cannot access this help . . . and we cannot afford it. I am happy about families getting the service—but have seen many of these people who are receiving it show little or no appreciation for what has been done for them. VERY few participate in and support the disability organization that was key in getting these services, and bristle at the mention of an invitation to come join—let alone support its efforts."

And, what about the time advocacy efforts drain from your work, your family, and your personal life? It's not uncommon for some mothers—even those who were once strong advocates—to pull back. When Amy tried to get help for Talia years ago, she realized there were huge gaps in services. "So I volunteered for several committees that connected parents and agencies—advocating for children's needs. I gave presentations at a rally and at meetings. It felt good to use my skills and to contribute. But, over the years, I grew frustrated that nothing changed. I realized I needed to back out and to focus on reclaiming my own career."

Studies confirm that advocacy *is* a double-edged sword. Researchers at Lakehead University in Thunder Bay, Ontario asked caregivers of twenty-six children with developmental disabilities whether their advocacy efforts increased or decreased their stress. Not a single person answered exclusively one way or the other. However, the researchers identified several factors that contribute to a positive advocacy experience. If you're optimistic about the outcome, and view advocacy as a tool (rather than a burden), you're less likely to feel stressed by your efforts. Other important factors include focusing on the future, being able to balance advocacy with your personal life, and having good relationships with professionals. Achieving success in advocacy also is exhilarating!

How do you know when to lighten your advocacy load? If you're unlikely to meet with success or if your personal, professional, or home life is suffering, consider backing off. Try and find at least one trusted professional (or parent) who can carry the torch for you.

The bottom line: focus on what's under your control. Find out what you are entitled to, seek out the help you're offered, and be persistent. If you have extra energy, advocate to make the system better.

Experience Talks

"Network with agencies—get involved with organizations that already advocate for resources. Working alone is not as effective."
—May, mother of a thirteen-year-old with autism

"I've tried to bring awareness whenever I can. For example, when an issue pertaining to home health care comes before a city committee, I will quickly email council members a message on how it affects our family."
—Bonnie, mom of a nine-year-old with severe physical and developmental disabilities

"Communicate your views very clearly when talking to doctors. Back up your ideas about care with logic and research."
—Giselle, mother of a nineteen-year-old with schizophrenia

"I have found that most educators and service providers who work with my daughter have really good intentions. Sometimes the bureaucracy puts us at odds. I try to distinguish between the individuals and the system that employs them. I try to remember to thank them often."
—Marilyn, mom of a daughter (age six) who is blind and has cerebral palsy

"My husband and I have tried to build a reputation as parents who try to work within the system and offer possible solutions/alternatives as opposed to just providing negative remarks.
—Bonnie, mom of a nine-year-old with severe physical and developmental disabilities

"We were in a two-story house with a second floor bathroom and with two growing kids. I couldn't keep carrying them up and down the stairs. The cost to do anything to the house to make it accessible was horrendous so we had to look at building from scratch. And in order for our kids to go anywhere we needed a $60,000 van that could fit two wheelchairs. In six months we bought two wheelchairs, a van, and a house. It was utterly overwhelming."

—Brenda, mom of two children who are medically fragile

Chapter 11

Taking Charge of Your Finances

Allegra has two adult children with myotonic dystrophy. Both need scooters at $2,200 each. She hasn't calculated the cost of the required ramp on her car.

A week at the local YMCA summer camp for Daryl's son with developmental delays will set her back $950 ($300 regular fees and $650 for the worker).

Louise pays $30,000 annually on intensive behavioral therapy for her preschooler with autism.

Raising a child with special needs is expensive. One out of five families experience financial hardship due to their child's special needs, according to the U.S. Department of Health and Human Services' *National Survey of Children with Special Health Care Needs*. One out of ten families pay more than $1,000 out of pocket annually for therapies, medications, equipment, hospital stays, etc.

Our children often require essential equipment, drugs, hands-on care, assessments, and/or therapies that are often covered—at least in part—by some form of insurance or government program. But then there are the hidden costs— things families with "typically developing" children take for granted. Most families have to pay for child care, summer camp, recreational programs, bicycles, toys, diapers, school supplies, etc. But when your child has special needs, you may need a practical nurse instead of teenage babysitter, a one-on-one attendant for community programs, adapted equipment or toys, specialized learning materials, or diapers into the teenage or adult years.

And of course, there's the cost of becoming a better advocate for your child. To learn the latest treatments, therapies, or medications, you may attend workshops and conferences, or purchase books and training videos.

When you want the best for your child, or feel you have the chance to "cure" your child, it's tempting to pay for any equipment or treatment that has promise. It might be a computer program for ADHD, hyperbaric chamber treatments for your child with CP, a weighted apron for your child's sensory issues, herbal or homeopathic supplements for your child with learning problems, or a gluten- and casein-free diet for your child with autism. Costs can easily run into the thousands annually. And those are the less expensive options. Others, like sophisticated assistive devices, adaptive equipment, experimental medication, intensive behavioral programs, or training conferences can cost tens or hundreds of thousands of dollars annually. Few if any of these costs are covered by government programs or insurance.

Where Do You Start?

Focus on getting your child the essentials first. Try to get all the financial help you're entitled to by researching what's available, filling out the necessary forms, and finding a financial advisor you can trust. If your family income is low, contact the Social Security Administration to see if your child might be eligible for SSI (Supplemental Security Income) and/or Medicaid. In Canada, contact the Canada Customs and Revenue Agency (see Resources) to see if your child is eligible for the federal Child Disability Benefit.

Is your child approaching age eighteen? If so, and his income is low, he may become eligible for SSI (and in most states Medicaid) on his birthday, because parental income will no longer be a factor. Similarly in Canada, your child may now qualify for government support. As Tara, mom of an adult with Rett syndrome, told us, "For our family, the financial pressures have decreased because she now has her own SSI income and that helps to pay for diapers, wipes, clothes, and some of the things she needs." See Chapter 13, "Legal and Financial Steps for Planning Ahead." Also check out Chapter 9 for ideas for other programs that may help you and your family.

Keeping Control of "Special Needs" Expenses

Don't shell out hundreds of dollars on treatments that aren't covered by insurance, a grant, or other outside monies, unless you've thoroughly checked them out. Check credentials of the seller, ask for references (and call them!), look up research studies, and speak with other parents, your child's doctor, and professionals you trust. Always seek financial advice before taking a large step such as moving, selling or mortgaging your house, or borrowing huge amounts of money to get your child a treatment. Of course you want the best for your child, but you don't want to put your family's future in jeopardy either.

Here are tips for controlling special needs expenses.

> *Buy in bulk to save money.* One mom on a listserv advises others when she's going to purchase an enzyme product and then places a combined order.

> *Shop around.* Special needs catalogues sometimes sell products that can be bought cheaper elsewhere. Amy paid $40 for a vibrating lady bug from a special needs catalogue. Just after, she found a similar product at the Dollar Store for $1. Similarly, you'll find inexpensive scooter boards, mini trampolines, hula hoops, balls,

etc., recommended for gross motor therapies at major discount chains. A speech and language pathologist Heather knows recommends board games that can be purchased through major discount chains to teach social and communication skills. Ask your child's doctors, special education teachers, and therapists if they can recommend low-cost alternatives to expensive "special needs" products.

Consider inexpensive home-made alternatives to factory-made products. For example, one mom saved $50 by making a foam wedge to prop her son up when he sleeps. A teaching assistant approached the local police department and asked for used bullet proof vests. She sewed bags of sands into the pouches to make a low cost weighted vest for children who are calmed by wearing them. Games to teach social skills or life skills can be drawn on poster board and laminated (but don't break copyright rules).

Save on conferences. Pay for workshops and conferences early to take advantage of "early-bird" prices. Ask if the presentations will be available on a CD or the Internet. Although nothing replaces networking with other parents in person, you may be able to get all the information and save costs by staying home. Special needs associations often provide discounts to members for workshops and conferences; it can sometimes be cheaper to join the association than to attend as a non-member (especially if you will be attending more than one event per year). Or band together with other parents to get group discounts. If you can't afford the registration fee, tell conference organizers; they may be able to offer a discount or scholarship. Or, offer to volunteer at the registration desk in exchange for admission to the conference.

Look into loaner programs. If your child needs specialized equipment, you may be able to borrow it from an equipment loan library offered by state Assisstive Technology Projects, or through service groups, disability associations, or other non-profit organizations. When your child is finished using the equipment, you return it so that another family can borrow it.

Don't buy retail. At least, not if you can trade, borrow, or buy previously owned equipment. Trade therapy supplies, medical equipment, etc., with families with similar needs. To contact families, post on special needs Internet groups, or advertise in association newsletters. On the listserv Heather belongs to, families post their requests for equipment and supplies. Then, often, families donate those they are no longer using.

Check out online auctions and sales. You can often find second-hand items, such as games and toys recommended by therapists, on Ebay.com, Craigslist.com, and other sites for a reasonable price.

Sniff out the discounts. Some museums, tourist attractions, and movie theatres provide a discounted admission fee for children with disabilities (or their attendant or support workers). Phone ahead to check. Sometimes you must apply for a special card first.

Research Rx assistance programs. If you don't have insurance or are struggling to pay for your child's medications, check out the Partnership for Prescription Assistance (see Resources). This service directs people to over 275 public and private patient assistance programs that may help.

Watch your prescription formulary. If you *do* have health coverage, ask your insurance company for their list of approved drugs—their "formulary." If the drug prescribed by your doctor isn't on the list—or is on the most expensive tier—you'll have to pay more for it. So keep the list with you when you visit your doctor, and ask if she can choose one of the less expensive drugs.

Seek out research programs. If you have the time and interest in medical or psychological research, evaluation and treatment costs are often included. Beverly, mom of nineteen-year-old Erin with Rett syndrome, had some medications and therapy covered this way in the past.

Don't assume care has to be costly. Look for free mental health clinics and other nonprofit clinics that offer free services or charge based on ability to pay. Many psychologists and psychiatrists offer sliding scales, where they charge lower income patients less money—ask.

Get necessary pre-approvals and referrals. Don't give your insurer an excuse to decline a claim. Call your carrier before you begin any therapy, see a specialist, take medical tests or undergo surgery to be sure it is covered under your policy. Ask if you need a prescription or referral.

Local service clubs can help. Approach local service clubs such as Lions, Rotary Club, etc., to help you fund equipment, programs, or modifications to your house (such as a ramp). See Chapter 9 for more sources of funding.

Use pre-tax dollars. Check whether your employer offers Flexible Spending Accounts for health care or dependent care. FSAs offer tax savings by allowing you to pay for out-of-pocket expenses with pre-tax money. You designate an amount to be set aside for the year, and it is then deducted from your paychecks in equal installments. The money you set aside in FSA accounts is tax-free. For example, if your salary is $45,000, but you put $4,000 into an FSA, your taxable income drops to $41,000. You then get reimbursed out of the FSAs for your out-of-pocket medical or dependent care expenses. The savings can be significant, and it can be useful to have costs spread equally across the year, but there are some catches (for example, if you don't use all the money you set aside in an FSA for the year, you lose it). The accounts affect what you can claim through your taxes, so check with your tax advisor.

No Health Insurance? Three Programs You Need to Know About

"We are caught in the 'Catch-22' of middle class," laments Maya, mother of a child with learning disabilities and mental health issues. "We have too much money to qualify for help, but too little money to afford the help we desperately need."

Medical expenses—either for chronic care or a sudden emergency—can wipe out a family's savings and run up unimaginable debt. It's hard enough to pay for some medical expenses when you do have health insurance. Without any insurance at all, the results could be devastating. While some low-income families get their health care paid for through Medicaid, most middle class families aren't eligible for the traditional Medicaid program. But don't immediately assume there's no help available.

STATE CHILDREN'S HEALTH INSURANCE PROGRAM

If you don't have health insurance through an employer, and your income/assets are too high to qualify for Medicaid, you may still be able to get free or reduced-rate health insurance for your child through your State Children's Health Insurance Program (CHIP). Some states use this federally funded program to expand Medicaid services to uninsured children from lower income families. A few states have plans for special needs—Connecticut, for instance, offers a plan called "Husky Plus" that provides extended services for physical and mental health for children under nineteen using the expertise of the Yale University School of Medicine. Connecticut also offers low-cost plans for children of higher income parents. Renee discovered her state plan met her family's needs: "Because my husband is self-employed, we searched for individual health insurance for our family. NO ONE would insure us because of my son's special needs. I struggled daily with worry over this. Finally, we found insurance through the state...Florida Healthy Kids...that helped us cover them."

"MEDICALLY NEEDY" PROGRAMS

Are your family's medical bills eating up most of your paycheck? Thirty-five states plus the District of Columbia offer "Medically Needy" Medicaid coverage, where eligibility is based on your income *minus medical expenses*. Children with large medical expenses (especially older children who wouldn't be covered under Early Intervention or other funding) may be eligible.

MEDICAID WAIVER PROGRAMS

Thanks to the parents of a toddler with multiple disabilities, many children who might have been institutionalized are cared for at home with the help of Medicaid. In 1981, parents wanted to bring their daughter Katie Beckett home from an institution permanently. While Katie was institutionalized, only her income and assets were counted for eligibility to Medicaid. But if Katie lived at home, her parents' income and assets would be too high to qualify for Medicaid, and too low to cover the cost of her care. To correct this inequity, in 1982 Congress enacted the Katie Beckett Waiver (Home and Community Service Waiver), which "waives" parental income for Medicaid eligibility for children who would normally be covered if institutionalized. So, only the child's income is considered (no more than $2,000 in assets).

These Home and Community Service waivers can cover services such as case management, homemaker/home health aides, adult daycare services, respite care, and even physical modifications to the child's home. They may focus on age groups, geographical regions, or specific disabilities. Some examples include Maryland's Autism Waiver, Pennsylvania's Attendant Care Waiver for those with physical disabilities, and Vermont's Mental Health Waiver.

For Jody, who has a twenty-one-year-old daughter with autism and a three-year-old son with Down syndrome, the DD (Developmental Disability) waiver in New Mexico is a godsend: "The DD Waiver pays my husband to stay home so that my daughter does not have to be in a residential facility. It covers the cost of us doing home instead of residential care, her therapies, medical costs, respite, and her personal monthly income."

Because the states are given a great deal of flexibility in how they design the above programs, you'll need to contact your state health or human services department for information on specifics (see the government pages of your phone book). For disability-related programs in Canada, contact Service Canada (see Resources).

How Low Can You Go?—Forty Cost-Saving Tips

As well as keeping your disability-related expenses under control, you can cut your everyday expenses in easy ways that add up over time. These savings can ease your financial pressures, or simply provide you with some cash for some family fun.

Try these ideas to cut costs and save money:

1. **For one month, keep a record of all of your expenses, including small daily items.** Then, look over your list, and place expenses into categories. Once you see where your money is going, you'll know where you can start to cut back.

2. **Identify key areas where you typically overspend,** e.g., clothing, household, gifts, dining out, etc. Define a monthly or annual budget for these items, and track receipts to stay on course. Use a ledger sheet from an accounts book, search out an inexpensive computer program, or use a spreadsheet like Excel.

3. **Eliminate items you have by habit, but no longer need or enjoy** such as magazine or newspaper subscriptions, cable television channels, or cell phones that you seldom use.

4. **To avoid high interest charges, never place more purchases on your credit card than you can pay off when you're billed.** Where possible, use cash so you only spend what you have. Or reserve your credit card for emergencies only.

5. **Clip coupons and follow through on rebate offers.** Many people choose a product based on a rebate

and never claim it. Even small savings add up over time. Also, save receipts in one file or envelope so you can return defective merchandise for a refund.

6. **Pay attention to your phone rates.** Limit calls during peak hours. Sign up for a phone package that best suits your calling pattern. Reserve cell phone use for emergencies.

7. **Combine your insurance.** Negotiate a discount by dealing with the same agent for your cars and house.

8. **Budget for holiday expenses at the beginning of the year.** Set aside money throughout the year, rather than paying off debt after Christmas. By setting a firm amount, you also are less likely to overspend on gifts.

9. **Take advantage of after-Christmas sales to stock up on birthday and holiday gifts for friends or family.**

10. **Involve your family, including children, in money decisions.** If your kids understand where your money goes, they'll be less likely to ask for expensive purchases. Telling them you're saving for a family vacation may take some of the sting out of not receiving a Nintendo.

11. **Start a clothing exchange.** Partner with several families who have children of different ages. Every season, exchange clothing or recreational equipment (such as skates) that are in good condition.

12. **Shop second-hand clothing stores and consignment shops for good-quality clothing at low prices.** You may be surprised to find your kids love this. Children who are sensitive to new "stiff feeling" clothing often find "broken in" clothes more comfortable.

13. **Sell your own clothes (and your children's) at consignment stores.** Or donate it to charity, but keep meticulous records—you'll be pleasantly surprised at how much you can deduct from your taxes.

14. **For your work wardrobe, avoid trendy styles that will need replacing in a year or two.** Stick to simple and basic colors in black, tan, blue, and gray that coordinate easily with blouses and shoes. You'll save money on simpler items and cut down on the amount of clothing you buy.

15. **Buy "wash and wear" clothes.** Dry cleaning costs add up.

16. **Buy a season ahead for huge savings.** For example, buy next winter's clothes at the end of the season. For kids, you can get excellent quality snowsuits at a bargain price.

17. **For family fun, buy second-hand equipment** such as skates and skis at sports stores or swap meets.

18. **For your own shoes, consider buying one high quality, pricier pair instead of several cheaper ones.** You'll save money in the long run with, say, an $80 pair of sandals that might last you for eight years. Also, with higher quality shoes, you'll be more comfortable and avoid foot problems.

19. **Instead of going shopping or out for dinner with friends, go for a walk, have a pot-luck dinner, or watch a video at home.**

20. **Limit your everyday luxuries.** If you buy a few coffees out each day, take home-brewed coffee in a thermos instead. You'll save $5 per day (lots more if you tend to splurge on fancy lattés or espressos).

Brown bag your lunch and you'll save even more (as much as $50 per week).

21. **Barter your services.** Maybe you're a whiz on the computer, but can't hang a picture to save your life. Some communities across North America have organizations that facilitate bartering. For example, The Time Dollar Institute helps communities set up a system where you provide an hour of service for another person, which earns you one "time dollar." Then, you can spend your "time dollar" and receive a service (such as child care, computer help, household repairs) from another member (see Resources).

22. **Scrimp on entertainment costs.** See movies at the inexpensive repertory cinema, if you have one in town. Or catch a flick at matinee prices (which often extend up to 6:00 p.m.). Skip the pricey in-theater snacks. Buy an entertainment coupon book (often sold by charities as a fundraiser) with two-for-one coupons for restaurants and entertainment. Also, they have discount coupons for services such as car and home repair.

23. **Always carry an insulated lunch pack in the car with bottles of water, fresh or dried fruit, nuts, crackers, etc., so you'll be less tempted to stop for snacks for hungry kids.** Where allowed, bring in a small pack to movies, sporting events, etc., to avoid buying expensive refreshments.

24. **Simplify your children's birthday parties.** Instead of a pricey outing, try an old-fashioned home-birthday with simple games, a craft, make-your-own pizza, and ice cream sundaes.

25. **If you'd like to treat yourself to a restaurant meal, go out for breakfast or lunch instead of dinner.** Or eat dinner at home, and go out for dessert and coffee.

26. **Buy household staples such as toilet paper, detergent, and diapers in bulk at big box stores.**

27. **Plan what you're going to buy (make a list) and how much you'll spend before going shopping (grocery, department store, hardware store, etc.).** Buy only those items. If one spouse tends to buy more "discretionary" items during shopping trips, send the thriftier one.

28. **Buy generic brands.** You'll save approximately 25 percent compared to brands with flashy packaging.

29. **Buy meat and poultry in large family packs.** Freeze portions you don't use for later.

30. **For high quality, less expensive fruit and vegetables, shop at farmer's markets during the summer months.**

31. **When considering rental or lease-to-own products, such as furniture or appliances, do your homework.** Calculate the total cost of payments, and ask about extra insurance costs and penalties for missed payments. What happens if the product breaks down? Do you get a replacement? Are your payments stopped? Know when you can buy the product outright and at what cost. Compare costs of renting, buying on credit, borrowing, or buying before making any major decisions.

32. **Once a week, make a big batch of simple muffins with whole grains and freeze them.** This eliminates the needs to buy costly (and less nutritious) granola bars, fruit rollups, etc.

33. **Instead of buying expensive commercial greeting cards (around $3 to $4 each) buy a package of blank notecards and write personal notes.**

Make homemade cards out of your children's art-work. Or send personalized e-cards.

34. **Take time to repair.** Instead of hiring someone, see if any family members can paint, sew, or fix something, to avoid having to buy something new. If no one's handy with a needle and thread, your local dry cleaning store probably offers inexpensive cloth-ing repairs or alterations.

35. **For friends and family, make a homemade batch of cookies and a card instead of a pricey gift.**

36. **Don't feel obligated to support fundraisers** (e.g., school chocolate bars or charity drives) pitched by relatives, friends, and neighbors.

37. **Borrow videos and DVDs from your public li-brary instead of renting them.**

38. **Check out Ebay (www.ebay.com) to buy second hand toys and games.**

39. **Try before you buy.** If you're considering buying expensive equipment, rent or borrow it before decid-ing to buy it. Also, consider splitting the cost with a neighbor for equipment that you can both use, such as a lawn mower or snow blower.

40. **Resist the temptation to shrug off small sav-ings by assuming they won't add up to much.** If you work at it, those small savings could easily add up to $100 or more a month. Over a year, this results in significant savings.

Share Your Financial Struggles

Despite cutting back on expenses, you may face times when you're unable to make payments. In those situations, request help or modifications when you need to. Many individuals and organizations will allow you to delay or consolidate payments or even waive them. Banks and utility companies may agree to defer payments or renegotiate lower monthly amounts. Most are willing to help if they know you intend to pay. Don't simply stop making payments or you risk facing a collection agency at your door.

Organizations that run recreational and therapeutic programs usually make allowances for families with financial difficulties. Angie, mother of an eight-year-old with autism, says recreational programs allow her to delay payments. She also volunteers her time in exchange for partial payment. Some community recreational programs offer free or discounted membership for families with low income. School principals typically have discretionary funds used to assist families in paying for school supplies or field trips. Some child care centers have similar emergency funds for parents. These safeguards are rarely advertised, so you need to ask.

Seek Advice from the Pro Team— Financial Advisors, Accountants, Tax Advisors

Whether finances are tight or not, you must meet with trusted professionals for financial advice. They will save you money in the long run and will also give you peace of mind about the future.

MINIMIZING TAXES

Your tax advisor can make sure you take advantage of all possible tax relief. There are credits and deductions geared specifically to disability. Tap into these in the early years—if your child progresses, they may no longer qualify. Medical expenses that exceed a certain amount, such as home modifications, health insurance, hospital and doctor's fees, adaptive equipment, guide dogs, special diets, special schools, conferences, and tutoring, may be able to be written off. For children with special needs, child care credits and deductions may continue past the age of twelve.

Financial Planning

A financial advisor can help you manage expenses, set aside emergency funds, establish savings, and maintain adequate life insurance. Most offer an initial consultation for free. To find financial advisors with disability expertise, ask other families or local organizations. Or contact the National Association of Personal Financial Advisors in the U.S. or the Canadian Association of Professional Financial Advisors (Advocis). The Arc can also recommend financial planners. See Resources.

Experience Talks

"One of the hardest things is to ask for help. It feels like you're admitting to a sense of failure—that 'I can't do this.' But it's really a sign of strength to say 'We're doing all we can, but we can't afford all of it and we need more help.'"

—Brenda, mom of two children who are medically fragile

"We don't have a lot of money. We don't keep up with the Joneses, but the bills are paid and we have food on the table every day. The kids are spoiled with love and attention rather than money."

—Carmen, mother of a child with Down syndrome

"I am very worried about her future. We have joined the local ARC trust, but otherwise haven't made many plans for the future with her. I am hopeful that she will be able to live in a supported setting as an adult, and that we might regain a little freedom, although that might be overly optimistic!"
—Judith, mom of a thirteen-year-old with multiple disabilities

Chapter 12

Create a Positive Future

Many of us worry about what will happen when our children grow up. How will they cope when we're gone? Will they live with brothers or sisters? And what if there are no siblings? Who will love, care, and fight for them as intensely as we do?

Those of us with more able children also worry. Even if we expect them to live independently, we wonder how they'll manage their finances, hold a job, and take care of their health. Will they be isolated, or enjoy friendships or marriage? And if they have their own children, how will they navigate the complicated world of parenting?

In our surveys, we asked parents if they had planned for the future. This question was particularly disturbing for moms of young children. "Frankly, it scares me to death," says one mom. "The thought of my two children not having me around to take care of them sends shivers up my spine!" says another.

Other mothers said they have no way to foresee yet what their children will be like as adults—making planning for their future even more baffling. Says Toni, mom of a child with a pervasive developmental disorder, "At six, I don't know that we can visualize where he will be in a few years as he continues to progress."

Future planning may seem scary, but it doesn't have to be. Nor does it have to cost a lot of money. Planning ahead is more than having a will or setting up a trust fund. It's developing a network of supports for your child, so others can assist her if you're unable to. Planning means developing your child's independence to the best of her capabilities. If your child is a teen or adult, it may mean investigating new living arrangements, college, day programs, volunteer opportunities, or employment. It also means encouraging your child to be independent as much as possible.

The best way to battle fears of the future is to take action—no matter how small. You can work on these strategies over the long term. Here's how to get started.

Practical Everyday Steps for Preparing for the Future

"My daughter is included in everything, everywhere," says Roxana, mother of a nine-year-old daughter with Down syndrome. "She is learning how to have a relationship, to be a friend. I hope some friendships will be lifelong. This will help her in the future."

As Roxana realizes, community involvement and learning how to socialize are key skills for the future. Another mom, Carmel, doesn't have enough cash to set up a trust fund for her twelve-year-old son with spina bifida. For now, she has a "care plan" that involves teaching him life skills such as laundry, housecleaning, and cooking. Josie believes her daughter with ADHD and a non-verbal learning disorder will go to college, get a job, and live independently some day. To prepare, she teaches her teen organizational strategies such as using a day planner to pencil in appointments and deadlines and establishing effective routines to minimize stress during the day. In addition, all three moms teach their children to self-advocate by involving them in school meetings.

No matter what our child's level of ability, she will do best in the future if we help her develop practical skills now.

TEACH YOUR CHILD IMPORTANT LIFE SKILLS

When your child is struggling, it's natural to want to jump in and help. But often, the best way to help your child isn't by taking over the activity she's wrestling with. After all, you won't always be there with her. Instead, you want to teach your child to be as independent as possible. As the Chinese proverb says: "Give a man a fish, and you feed him for a day. Teach a man to fish and you feed him for a lifetime."

But we moms also know that "teaching" can be easier said than done. Maybe you're rushed. Maybe you're tired. Maybe your child is going to fight you every step of the way (especially if she's used to you "doing" for her). But that's OK. Take it one step at a time. You don't have to tackle everything at once, or you'll both be overwhelmed.

Start by listing the activities your child is involved in or needs help with in a typical day. Then, you'll know which areas to focus on. If you begin with something your child is interested in, she'll be more enthusiastic about learning. In other words, if you want your child to learn to cook, it might be more motivating to start with brownies than with broccoli. If you want her to learn to go places independently, the movie theater or the donut shop is a better place to start than the dentist's office.

If your teen or adult is headed for college, make sure she has her own bank account, can manage her own money, and knows how to live within a budget. Encourage her to sign up for practical courses such as accounting, home economics, or shop in high school. Starting in childhood, have her help with cooking at home so, by the time she graduates high school, she'll have a repertoire of nutritious, easy meals she can prepare herself.

If your child has trouble with "executive functions," i.e., attention and organization, encourage her to consistently use a day planner or electronic organizer. If she has difficulties adapting to new situations, give her "scripts" to use. (Presented as a series of pictures or words, a script can explain an unfamiliar situation and how to appropriately deal with it.) If your child is blind or has physical challenges, teach her how to navigate the community independently. These are just a few ideas—you know your child best.

Be sure to access school and community supports to help you teach essential skills to your child. For example, an occupational therapist can help teach your child self-care skills by breaking down the steps for showering, tooth brushing, etc. Consult a speech therapist who specializes in pragmatics for ideas on how to increase your child's social skills, teach her to express her feelings, etc. A physical therapist can help increase mobility to further your child's independence. And a teacher may mentor your child on how to self-advocate.

Sample Life Skills Plan

Having a written plan that details your child's present skills will help you know what areas to work on. Tailor yours to your own child's interests, abilities, challenges, and age. And talk with your child to make sure the plan helps her meet her own goals. For example, a teen with a physical disability may want to learn how to use special transit so she can get to a summer job or to a friend's house without Mom's help.

Here's a sample life skills plan for twelve-year-old Chris, who has a developmental disability.

1. **Determine the child's special interests.** For Chris, these include cooking, pets, and computers.

2. **Check off how independently the child can do each activity**. (Sample on next page.)
   I (Independently) or **H** (with **Help**)

3. **Set some goals.** Chris has some good life skills and strong areas of interest. While he is independent in some areas of self-care and dressing, he needs to learn how to brush his teeth and take a shower independently. Also, since he's interested in cooking, preparing simple meals would be a good goal to start with. Most libraries have excellent cookbooks for children with photographs of step-by-step instructions.

To tackle the goal of helping Chris increase friendships, his parents could build on his fascination with cooking and animals. For example, there may be cooking classes for children offered in the community. Perhaps he could volunteer at the local SPCA, Humane Society, or pet store. Or he could offer to walk the neighbor's dog after school, which not only would be fun for him, but also give him exercise, a sense of responsibility, and experience that might help him get a paid job working with animals some day.

Sample Life Skills Plan for Chris

I	Toileting, washing hands and face
H	Brushing teeth
I	Choosing appropriate clothing for the weather
I	Dressing—including doing up buttons, zippers
I	Preparing breakfast—getting bowl and spoon; pouring cereal and milk
H	Preparing lunch—making sandwich, packing fruit, juice, etc.
H	Walking or taking bus to school
H	Preparing after-school snack
I	Choosing and enjoying leisure activities at home (music, TV, computer, reading)
H	Exercising at home or in the community (walking, biking, playing basketball, visiting YMCA, etc.)
H	Interacting with a friend (visit, phone, email)
H	Asking for help
I	Setting the table for dinner
H	Preparing simple dinners for the family (pasta and sauce, salads, sandwiches, eggs)
H	Carrying on a conversation at the dinner table
I	Clearing plates and loading the dishwasher
H	Doing a chore (laundry, sweeping floor, dusting, taking out garbage, watering plants, etc.)
H	Doing homework
H	Showering or bathing
I	Putting on pajamas
I	Relaxing and winding down before bed (music, reading, etc.)
I	Falling asleep easily

Since carrying on back-and-forth conversations is difficult for Chris, his parents could contact a speech therapist for resources and ideas on how to increase conversational and social skills.

To help Chris learn a task or self-help skill, he needs written or pictorial step-by-step instructions, so he's not dependent on an adult for reminders. An occupational therapist can provide more ideas on learning skills to help in his daily life.

TEACH SELF-ADVOCACY

Self-advocacy is not so much taught, as modeled. In order to effectively advocate for herself, your child must be confident and have self-respect. Be a good role model by acknowledging your own accomplishments and pursuing your own interests.

Encourage your kids to follow their own interests and talents (no matter how quirky they may seem to you!) Heather's daughter is passionate about world history and comic strips. To support this interest, her parents point out new history books in the library and schedule historical TV documentaries on the calendar. They encourage her to tell comic strip jokes at the dinner table. But to help her learn conversational skills, they set the rule that the joke must be relevant to the dinner conversation. Eventually, these kinds of passionate interests could lead to friendships or enjoyable employment. Even if they don't, they are interests that bring pleasure and meaning to her life.

Teaching our kids to take care of themselves is also important. Model and encourage healthy ways of managing stress by exercising, seeing friends, and eating healthily.

Bottom line, our kids need to be able to ask for help when they need it. Whether it is through sign, picture board, or verbal communication, a child must be able to access help when a parent is not there to intervene. This objective appears on many children's IEP (Individualized Education Program) plan. In middle school and beyond, more capable students are expected to seek assistance from resource teachers to help develop their IEP and to meet with teachers to discuss teaching modifications they need. To increase your child's confidence, have her role play with you the discussions she wants to have with teachers. This practice is essential, especially if she will continue to college, where parents are often discouraged from advocating for their children (due to "privacy" concerns).

As children become teens and adults, sometimes we have to hold ourselves back from trying to solve every problem. And, like all kids, they need the chance to experience "acceptable risks" in life and try things out independently.

Fashioning a Future That Fits for Your Child:

Include your child in planning for her future. As children grow into adulthood, most can help make life decisions based on their own hopes, dreams, and abilities. Including them in decisions all along helps them learn to advocate for themselves.

Think ahead to housing, transportation, education, and employment supports that she may require.

RESEARCH FUTURE LIVING ACCOMMODATIONS

"I plan on getting my child into a group home or supportive living environment before the age of twenty-one, so he can access programs as soon as he finishes school," says Daphna, whose ten-year-old son has autism. In her agency job, Daphna sees adults regress while on waiting lists and she's determined the same won't happen for her son.

While some mothers like Daphna anticipate their son or daughter moving out, others expect their children to live at home as long as possible. This is an individual decision that depends on available housing and community programs, finances, family support, and, of course, your child's preferences and abilities.

If you expect your child to someday move into a group home, residential facility, or a supported independent living situation, research what's available. Contact your special needs agencies and put your child on a waiting list for services as soon as possible. If you are able to volunteer in the nonprofit disability sector, as Daphna does, you may get more of an inside look at what is available for adults.

More able adult children may require limited support (other than you or a friend checking in with them occasionally). If your child's finances will be limited, look into public housing (where rent is based on income) and co-operative housing through your local housing agencies. Since subsidized housing depends heavily on government funding, expect limited availability and long waiting lists (often ten years or more). Contact your local public housing agency (under "Housing" in the phone book government pages).

A housing co-op is a nonprofit organization whose members collectively own or manage a multi-family development. Members purchase shares and then lease their units from the co-op (some units are subsidized). Look up "Co-operative Housing" in the Yellow Pages.

Through the co-operative structure, individuals share the responsibility of maintenance and repairs. Those with disabilities both have a voice and benefit from the close-knit community of a cooperative.

Sometimes, two individuals with disabilities can rent an apartment together (or live in a house purchased by the parents) and pool their staffing hours so they have adequate support. For example, if the government funds ten hours per person, two roommates will have twenty hours of combined support. If this option appeals to you and your child, try to find other interested parents through your own networks or local disability association.

Other individuals with special needs live in their own apartment or house with a roommate who has their own full-time job, but who provides live-in night time support. The roommate lives rent-free in exchange for helping in the evening. Ask respite, support workers, or personal attendants you've used in the past. Or, try advertising through your disability organization's newsletter.

Home Ownership Programs

If you have the resources, you can purchase a home for your adult child without jeopardizing her government payments. You can buy a house or condominium in your name and have your son or daughter pay rent to you. Or you can buy it through a special needs trust (or leave it as an inheritance to your son or daughter in trust). If set up properly (your child might need to pay rent to the trust), the home shouldn't jeopardize future Social Security or Medicaid benefits (or, in Canada, provincial disability benefits). Because trust laws are complex and changing, ask a lawyer who specializes in special needs trusts about the best ways to designate ownership before you buy or bequeath a home for your child. (We'll get into more issues on trusts in Chapter 13.)

Some parents purchase a duplex or multiplex (two or more apartments) and use the rent from the other unit(s) to fund their child's home.

Another option is to check out home ownership programs geared toward low-to-moderate income first-time buyers. Programs might include subsidized interest, help with down payments or closing costs, mortgage insurance, and more flexible lending criteria. One to look into is The Federal National Mortgage Association (Fannie Mae) HomeChoice mortgage loan program, which helps people with disabilities finance their own homes by partnering lenders with public housing agencies and community groups (see Resources). One mother told us she obtained a subsidized loan that enabled her son to purchase a town home. She moved in too and provides him with some assistance.

Contact your local housing agency (see "Housing" in your government and yellow pages) and special needs agencies for housing possibilities. The section "Consider Creative Options for the Future," later in this chapter, offers more ideas on creating a home for your son or daughter.

Post-Secondary Schooling Options

"I get extremely stressed out when I think about my daughter going to college next fall," confesses Alison, mother of a seventeen-year-old with hydrocephalus. Her daughter won't be living far away, "but not really close enough to help her remember the things she forgets."

Parents of typical teens are often anxious when their young adults go off to college. That anxiety is multiplied for parents whose children face extra challenges. Some young adults choose to stay close to family for support. Ginger's twenty-one-year-old son with sensory integration dysfunction is living at home while he attends college. "He feels he needs all the support he can get," she explains.

Other students are ready for the independence. Thankfully, there are programs that can ease the transition away from home. Some colleges and universities offer summer transition programs for students with disabilities. Students stay on campus for several weeks and undergo an orientation program that introduces them to campus life and to study skills. Ask a guidance counselor about this possibility.

Transition from high school must be addressed in your child's IEP starting by age sixteen in the U.S. (required age varies in Canada; consult your province's education act.) Don't let the school system dictate the transition plan. Be involved in this process, making sure you and your child agree with the end goal (e.g., more schooling, career, sheltered work, etc.), and the courses and services offered along the way (such as vocational classes, life skills, job training, etc.).

In most jurisdictions, children with qualifying disabilities can stay in high school until they are at least twenty-one. Some communities even offer continuing education programs that continue past twenty-one for students with special needs.

A growing number of colleges offer specialized courses designed for adults with disabilities who would have difficulty meeting the academic, social/emotional, or cognitive demands of standard college course work. The Life Skills Transitional Program at the Houston Community College, for example, offers a transition life skills course geared to students primarily with developmental delays, autism, speech and language difficulties, and orthopedic impairments. Selkirk College (British Columbia) offers varying courses across campuses, one with a work placement component.

Don't leave your search to your child's final year of high school. In the first year or two of high school, ask (or have your child ask) the school guidance counselor about colleges that have such programs. If there aren't any appropriate programs in your area, that will give you time to join together with other parents to lobby for them.

For students who are academically able, but need extra support to successfully access a post-secondary curriculum, there are more options available—but these can vary widely from school to school. Most colleges and universities have an office of disability support services. But it's important to understand that, once your child reaches college, the IDEA no longer applies. A student with a disability is only entitled to appropriate accommodations and modifications under Section 504 of the Rehabilitation Act and the Americans with Disabilities Act (ADA). (See Chapter 9.) Even having an IEP or 504 plan in high school is not a guarantee of receiving accommodations in college. Documentation of the disability and its functional impact (including an up-to-date evaluation), as well as documentation of the accommodations provided in high school, is typically required.

Of course, some colleges go above and beyond federal regulatory requirements when it comes to accommodating a disability. Some (more often, publicly-funded universities) offer many free services, while others offer extensive services, but with a high price tag. Sadly, still others balk at providing accommodations, and tend to offer only the minimal amount they can get away with. You and your child need to research different colleges' reputations long before its time to start filling out applications.

In order to receive services, your child must self-disclose her disability (although not necessarily on her college application) to the university and to individual professors. The more a student understands her strengths and needs, the more she can access useful accommodations. For example, if she has fine motor difficulties, she can request a note taker or copies of the professor's notes. If she needs academic support, there may be essay writing labs or tutoring available. To navigate the complicated social world of college, she may need courses in social skills, stress management, or time management. In addition, she might benefit from technological support such as tape recording lectures, and computer programs such as voice recognition software.

There are several sources available with information about special college programs for young adults with disabilities, as well as information on the different accommodations and services available at different universities. See the Recommended Reading and Resources sections for books and websites that will get you started.

Is There a Job Out There?

Employment rates are significantly lower for adults with disabilities. The 2000 U.S Census showed 80 percent of all males aged sixteen to sixty-four were employed, while only 60 percent of those with a disability were. For females, these figures dropped to 67 percent and 51 percent. It's encouraging to know that these numbers are actually improving—in the 1994-95 National Health Interview Survey only 36 percent of those with disabilities were employed.

While employment can be challenging for many with disabilities, it's not impossible. Along with tales of employment struggles, we hear inspiring stories. Recently a young man with Asperger syndrome graduated with top honors from a journalism program and received an internship with a major national newspaper—quite a "coup" for an individual who used to struggle with the most basic social skills. Fortunately, the ADA limits discrimination in hiring, legislates supports such as physical access to buildings or equipment, and encourages attitudinal changes towards all those with disabilities. There's no single legislation that does the same in Canada; however, disability protections are found in the Charter, human rights acts, employment acts and the Accessibility for Ontarians with Disabilities Act.

Depending on the person, full-time, long-term employment is not always the goal to strive for. Retaining the same job for years is no longer the norm for many people. Instead, home businesses, part-time jobs, and career changes are much more common, as people pay greater attention to work/life balance. In the same way, your child can fashion a rewarding life that mixes employment, volunteer work, leisure, fitness, and involvement in the community.

Mark, a thirty-five-year old with moderately severe autism, has a very rich and balanced life. He lives independently, with his parents' personal and financial support. His mother Christine relates that "in nearly seven years of living in his own home, Mark has developed more initiative and independence." His hours are divided among caring for himself, his home, his garden, and his service dog; going to the gym and pool, riding his bike, and hiking; using a computer-assisted learning program; participating in a spirituality group with friends and by email; earning cash by delivering the newspaper and working for a family friend who owns a business; and volunteering with his dog at a senior living facility.

While sheltered workshops still exist for those with developmental disabilities or mental health issues, more communities are closing them down because of their "segregated" nature. But finding other jobs in the community can take much advocacy. Depending on her disability, your adult child may need a job coach to support her in learning and completing her work responsibilities. In most communities, agencies offer a job transition or job search and support program.

Transportation to work (and elsewhere) can also be a problem if your adult child doesn't drive (something to keep in mind when she's choosing where to live). Parents and siblings can't always juggle their own jobs and lives around their children's various commitments. Larger communities often have para-transit systems or wheelchair accessible buses, while more rural communities may not have any public transportation. If your child will need transportation assistance, contact your nearest Independent Living Center. (ILCs are local non-profit community centers run by and for people with disabilities.) Centers sometimes offer vouchers for transportation through arrangements with local transit authorities, cab companies, volunteer drivers, etc.

Employment services offered through Social Security and other government programs can help your teen or adult with resume writing, interviewing, and job coaching. For those able to start their own business, grants may also be available through programs such as Canada's Opportunities Fund for Persons with Disabilities.

Ask high school guidance counselors, special needs agencies, and disability organizations about local hiring programs. Also look under "Disability" in the government section of your phone book. Many communities have volunteer centers that help people find volunteer opportunities at non-profit organizations. Look in your phone book under Volunteer Services.

Sometimes moms don't just plan for their children's future careers—they create them. A few mothers we surveyed say they will start or buy businesses that will employ their children. One plans to purchase and operate a hotel her children can work at; another is registering her chocolate-making business as a charitable organization that will train and hire adults with disabilities.

Keep in mind that paid employment can affect SSI and Medicaid benefits (or, in Canada, provincial disability benefits). Medicaid and other benefits can sometimes be continued under special work incentive programs through Social Security and each state or province. For example, PASS (Plan to Achieve Self-Support), offered by the Social Security Administration, allows you to save for expenses required to achieve pre-approved work goals such as retraining or starting a business (see Resources).

Consider Creative Options for the Future

Historically, adults with special needs were expected to fit into programs and supports that existed in the community—usually sheltered workshops and day programs. With government cutbacks, these programs became insufficient in quantity and quality to meet the needs of families today. Plus, families and individuals wanted more choices in how they lived, worked, and enjoyed their leisure time.

What's evolved in recent years is more "person-centered" planning (known as "wraparound" in mental health circles). In this approach, the individual with special needs—along with family, friends, and community members—designs a future that fits her interests, strengths, and desires, rather than getting plugged into whatever existing program has openings. With this model, there is less reliance on government programs and more on family initiative.

PERSON-CENTERED PLANNING MODELS

Two person-centered models that give individuals and their families more control over their futures are personal networks and microboards.

Personal Network (sometimes called a circle of friends or a circle of supports). A personal network is a group of people (friends, neighbors, church/synagogue members, co-workers, etc.) who have a personal relationship with the individual with a disability and are committed to improving her quality of life. They support the individual with employment, housing, education, friendships, and community activities. Even when parents have passed away, the network continues to support the person with a disability. This solution is a comfort for parents who fear for their children's future—especially if there are no siblings. For assistance developing a personal network, ask special needs agencies or your local disability organization. They can also tell you about local non-profit organizations that assist with creating personal networks and other life planning (for a fee). Often, you can hire a facilitator who will help initiate and maintain the circle of support.

Microboard. The microboard is an innovation started in Manitoba, Canada. A group of five to seven people (including the person with a disability, if she so chooses) joins together to form a non-profit organization. Family and non-family board members volunteer to work with the individual with special needs to address her planning and support needs. The microboard makes decisions about care and pays for that care. Government funding (Home and Community Waiver, Medicaid, etc.) is administered through the microboard instead of a government agency. This arrangement allows individuals and families more control over care.

While creating personal networks and other supports, be aware that it takes a fair bit of family time and initiative for these to succeed. But most communities have families who are already designing such supports. Connect with these families and organizations to access information and make your efforts easier to accomplish. See Resources for more information on organizations that can help with person centered planning.

INNOVATIVE COMMUNITY SUPPORTS

While initiatives like microboards and personal support networks are promising, you need supports to make it work. In most communities, there are long waiting lists for supported housing and employment. But families are pooling ideas, funds, and resources to come up with innovative living and employment arrangements. To find out about innovative community projects in your community, contact special needs agencies, disability organizations, housing agencies, and Independent Living Centers. Here are a few examples of innovative ideas put into action (see Resources for contact information):

The Rent-to-Own Network is a loose-knit group of agencies and individuals across Ontario who developed a plan for private investors to help people with disabilities become homeowners. An investor purchases a home and is responsible for utilities and household maintenance costs. The purchaser (individual with special needs) pays a small down payment, legal fees, and land transfer tax in order to start the Rent-To-Own Agreement. Then, the individual pays monthly rent to the investor, part of which goes toward equity in the home. Typically, the agreement can be finished within five years, when the purchaser has enough equity in the house to qualify for a mortgage. For more information contact the Ontario Association for Community Living (see Resources).

The Share Equity Housing Project in Ottawa, Ontario is a partnership between a developmental disabilities association and a Canadian federal housing agency. Families invest money towards the purchase of an apartment building, which is then rented out to individuals with disabilities for the rate each receives for housing from the government. Part of the rent goes toward a support worker to help with meal planning, cooking, and other activities of daily living.

Community Bus is a unique collaboration among school districts, local transit companies, and disability and other social service organizations (sixty-four partners in total) in Mason County, Washington, that makes use of school buses after hours. The buses transport people with disabilities, as well as teens going to and from after-school activities, and commuters coming home from work.

As these programs show, new ideas are developing all the time—but they take the involvement and energy of committed families. To help shape your child's future, stay involved with parent and local disability groups. While you may not be able to envision your child as an adult, you still can take action now.

If your son or daughter is already an adult, continue to advocate for services and access agency supports. And most importantly, network with other families to create innovative ideas for quality adult living. It's not too late to create a future with promise.

Experience Talks

"I am trying to treat my son more like an adult roommate, and less like a child. His dad and I give him more choices in all areas of his life, consult with him more, and talk often about when he will leave home. It is now our job to help establish supports for his independence in the community, to involve our extended family more, and to help our son achieve what he wants from his life."

—Laura, mother of a twenty-year-old with Down Syndrome

"Develop your child's powers of communication (by whatever modes), 'listen' to them, and develop their abilities and interests. Find and cherish friends for your child and yourself. These things are the best preparation for adulthood."

—Christina, mother of Mark, an adult with autism

"I am very nervous about my son's long-term plan of care. I try not to think about it, even though I know that is the wrong attitude to take."

—Rose, mother of a preschooler with muscular dystrophy

Chapter 13

Legal and Financial Steps to Planning Ahead

Rose is not alone. A 2005 MetLife survey of 1,718 parents of children with special needs found that nearly a third had done no legal or financial planning at all, despite the fact that over half (60 percent) believed their children would never be financially independent. The survey found:

> 68 percent of surveyed parents had not written a will.
> 53 percent had not agreed upon a guardian for their child, should they die.
> 72 percent had not named a trustee to manage the child's finances.

84 percent had not written a letter of intent outlining how they would like their child with special needs to be cared for in the future.

88 percent had not set up a special needs trust to ensure entitlement to government benefits, such as Medicaid and Supplemental Social Security.

Women we surveyed said planning for the future was not only overwhelming, but also confusing. "I really don't know how to start," Valerie, mom of an eight-year-old told us. Especially when we're already overloaded with things to do every day, it can be hard to make that first step.

Even though you may not have the time, money, or willpower to think about the future, taking action will help you feel more in control.

Start by gathering information about future planning. Ask other families what they have done, surf the Internet, and call your disability organization for advice. Watch your local paper for free or low-cost workshops on special needs planning.

The Basics—A Will and Guardianship

"My husband and I have been going back and forth on making out our wills because we have NO idea who would be willing to take in our son," laments Betsy, whose child has muscular dystrophy. It can certainly be difficult to think of someone who would have the ability, personality, and commitment to act as guardian for your child. You can reassure close friends or family by telling them you have planned ahead with a will, letter of intent (instructions for the care of your child), life insurance, and/or money in trust. Of course, few could care for your child as well as you can. But you're better off choosing a capable loving guardian than leaving it to the courts to appoint someone.

At the minimum, you must set up a will, assisted by a lawyer. Preparing a will yourself or from a home kit is risky if your child may require assistance in the future. Without a legal will, your child's inheritance may jeopardize any government assistance in the future. As little as $2,000 in assets can disqualify your child from SSI and Medicaid. An inheritance, personal injury settlement, or monetary gifts from family could make your child ineligible for government assistance when he turns eighteen.

Some parents think they've solved this problem by leaving everything to siblings instead, with the understanding that they'll look after their brother or sister with special needs. But not all siblings are capable of (or want) this responsibility. Worse, if no special provisions are made, should the sibling divorce, remarry, or die, the money you earmarked for your child with special needs could be distributed legally to others. Protect your child's future assets. (See "Creating a Trust Fund for Your Child," later in this chapter.) Find a lawyer who specializes in estate planning for special needs. Ask other parents and your local disability organization for names.

If money for lawyer fees is scarce, put a little aside each month. Even if you have to wait several years, at least you're taking a step. Or consider asking your extended family for a contribution (in lieu of holiday gifts) for lawyer fees to secure your child's future. If family support is unlikely, ask your special needs agency or parent group if they know a lawyer who does pro bono work.

It's hard to make a will, as it forces us to think about our own mortality and about our children living without us. But procrastinating on such an urgent need causes more anxiety than taking positive action. Book a caregiver, meet with a lawyer, and go out and celebrate afterwards. By taking that first step to guard your child's future, you'll feel a real sense of relief.

Writing a Letter of Intent

If you were to suddenly die or become incapacitated, that alone would be traumatic for your child. The last thing he would need would be for his own medical needs, routines, and daily life to be thrown into upheaval as well. You can guard against that by writing a Letter of Intent, providing your child's guardians with practical information to guide them in making decisions and interacting with your child (see Sample Letter on pages 225-226).

Your letter should include your child's likes, dislikes, daily schedule, and medical treatment. Include future plans for your child such as education, employment, and living situations. Talk with your child about his preferences and plans to make sure the letter accurately reflects his needs. Share copies with those who might be involved in future care, e.g., older siblings, appointed trustees, guardians, etc. Update it once yearly (perhaps on your child's birthday). Put the original letter in an accessible place in your home and tell key people (such as your child's identified guardian, siblings, a case manager, a friend or neighbor) where the letter is located.

Writing a Letter of Intent requires no lawyer, costs nothing, and could save your child much distress during a difficult time.

Creating a Trust Fund for Your Child

"My parents have set up a special needs trust, instead of a college fund," Shareem, mother of a fourteen-year-old with spina bifida, told us. "It will help with whatever my son needs as an adult."

If you have the resources and you think your child will be unable to fully support himself in the future, consider establishing a trust fund for him. A trust fund is an arrangement where your assets are transferred to another person (the Trustee) who manages them on behalf of your child. Remember, if you leave money directly to your child in your will, that money could prevent him from receiving supports from the government. Government funding for those with disabilities covers only living and medical expenses. Money in a trust could be used to increase your child's quality of life—to pay for vacations, entertainment, hobbies, vocational training, a car, furniture, etc. Or, it could be used for household expenses such as hair cuts, home repairs, lawyers, a housekeeper, etc.

But you must be sure to set up the right kind of trust. If you have a traditional support trust, the government may bill the trust for government benefits. To avoid this, see an attorney who specializes in special needs estate planning, who can set up a special needs or supplementary trust that allows you to leave money for "supplementary" needs, not covered by the government. Tell grandparents and other relatives considering leaving money or gifts to your child to bequeath them to the trust, as well.

In Canada, these disability-related trusts (called discretionary or Henson trusts) have rules that vary among provinces. Provinces also may have their own trusts, such as Ontario's Disabilities Expense Trust with their own set of restrictions.

To follow through with the instructions in your letter of intent, you need to name a "trustee," who is trustworthy, comfortable with financial affairs, and lives close by. Often a family member or close

Sample Letter of Intent

This sample gives you an idea of what should be covered in a letter of intent. Your actual letter would contain far more details than are indicated here.

To Whom it May Concern:
Re: Our daughter, Lori X

1. **Contact the following people if anything should happen to us:** *Names, addresses, mail and e-mail addresses of other children, extended family, case manager, and a close family friend.*

2. **Current situation and family life**: Lori is a thirteen-year-old with autism who lives with her brother and parents. At home, she enjoys reading, playing computer games, cooking, and helping with chores. She enjoys family outings such as hiking, swimming, visiting friends, and going to restaurants and movies. At least once a week, she goes out with her support worker *(name and contact info)* to outings in the community such as swimming and basketball at the YMCA. She is a happy, engaging, and highly verbal child who enjoys the chance to socialize. In addition, she loves animals and spending time with her family cat.

3. **Education**: Lori is included in a regular class at James Madison Middle School with one-to-one support. Her strengths are reading, memory, and music. Since she is unable to print by hand, she uses a laptop computer. When class lessons are too complicated, her assistant allows her to access related computer games and programs instead. In the future, she could attend (with support) a high school that offers vocational opportunities such as cooking or animal care. Alternatively, she could attend a self-contained class at the high school level with students who have high functioning autism or a mild intellectual disability.

4. **Future Residence**: Lori would like to someday share an apartment with a roommate. She will likely need a support worker to check in with her daily (or less frequently) to help with activities of daily living, banking, or general support. Lori's name is already on a waiting list for the Supported Independent Living Apartment Program offered

through *Name of Agency*. Contact our case manager (*name and contact*) for details. Alternatively, she could move in with her brother, who plans on having a basement apartment for Lori in his home.

5. **Employment**: Lori has a keen interest in animals and cooking, and is skilled with computers. She would probably enjoy working or volunteering at an animal shelter, a pet store, or in the food service industry. Perhaps she could also find work requiring some computer expertise.

6. **Medical Care**: Lori has no medical challenges. She is seen for a yearly check up by Dr. Smith *(contact information)*, who is familiar with Lori's strengths and challenges. In addition, she sees an eye doctor (*name and contact information*) and dentist (*name and contact information*) with special needs expertise.

   Lori is not allergic to any medications. However, in the past, she has experienced adverse side effects from the following medications, which should be avoided in the future: *(list drugs and adverse reactions)*.

7. **Behavior Management**: Lori occasionally pinches and gets teary when she is anxious. The best strategy is to provide her with a written schedule or calendar of what will be happening in the day. Also, she has been seen by a behavior therapist at the *Name of Clinic* (*contact info*). They have agreed to consult on any future behavioral issues that may arise.

8. **Social**: Lori participates in several community programs, including YMCA sports for kids *(day, time, location),* a community cooking class *(day, time, location)*, and therapeutic horse back riding (day, time location). She also greatly enjoys visiting our close family friends (*name and contact info*) at least once per week.

9. **Religious/Spiritual Life**: Most Sundays, Lori attends services with us at the (*Name*) Church. In addition, she occasionally attends youth group social programs for pre-teens.

10. **Guardian and Trustee**: Guardians and trustees have been assigned in our wills, which were last updated on *(insert date)* and are on file with (*attorney name, contact info)*.

Both parents' signatures.
Date

friends takes on this role. If family and friends aren't comfortable with the financial aspects (such as investing or accounting), you can hire a corporate trustee from a bank or financial institution to serve as a co-trustee or to manage the trust on your child's behalf.

Funding a special needs/supplementary trust can be done in several ways. Set up a regular savings program or make small monthly payments to a life insurance plan (ask grandparents and other family members to contribute in lieu of gifts). Don't name your child as a direct beneficiary of any life insurance, retirement or savings investments, bank accounts, property, etc. Most people name their spouses as their primary beneficiaries and their children's trust funds as their secondary beneficiaries. That way, the trust fund only receives the property and benefits if both parents die.

A less expensive option is to join a pooled trust, where several families combine their money to decrease administrative costs and increase their principal (the amount invested). A higher principal allows access to better quality investment funds that may pay a higher rate of return. Beneficiaries of the trust usually earn proceeds based on their share of the principal. Pooled trusts are only available in some states. Some disability organizations such as the Arc operate pooled trusts. (See Related Reading for the Arc's handbook on pooled trusts.)

You and others can fund a trust while still alive or through a will. A "living" trust takes effect now. Typically, a parent is the trustee. With this type of trust, parents, grandparents, and others can make regular gifts. Grandparents or other family can also leave inheritances to the trust. A testamentary trust, which protects your inheritance for your child, takes affect upon your death. Each has different tax implications; your lawyer can help you make the right choice.

Rules for trusts differ by state or province. Setting up a special needs trust requires an attorney with expertise in this area, knowledge of government programs, and sensitivity to disability issues. Ask your local disability organization to recommend a lawyer or estate planning professional.

Power of Attorney and Guardianship after Age of Majority

Under age eighteen (nineteen or twenty-one in some states), your child is considered a minor and you are allowed to make legal decisions for him. (If you should die, the guardian named in your will assumes this responsibility.)

Once your child is of age, however, it is assumed that he is competent enough to make his own decisions. You may assist with decisions informally. However, you have no legal right to sign documents like leases, etc. unless the court gives you that power. You may not be allowed to receive school or medical reports or participate in planning meetings without his permission. You cannot force him to attend school if he decides to drop out. Nor can you prevent him from giving his money to or moving in with people you think may exploit him.

A "competent" individual with a disability may grant a family member or friend power of attorney to make medical or legal and financial decisions for him. This may take effect immediately or when the individual becomes incapacitated. Each state and province has its own laws for power of attorney—consult an attorney for more information.

Guardianship is usually considered a last resort (i.e., after other less restrictive options, such as power of attorney, have been considered or proven inadequate). If your child is severely disabled, the decision may be clear cut. However, the majority of individuals with disabilities, including those with developmental disabilities, are capable of judgment on many issues. With the help of family, friends, a case worker, and perhaps a restricted bank account, they can often manage their own finances. Writing and depositing checks can be simplified by having direct deposit and automatic bill payment. For government checks, your child can designate you or someone else as a representative payee (talk to your Social Security office). If you have set up a trust, the trustee takes care of decisions on how to invest and spend money in the trust fund.

If, despite these modifications, your adult child is unable to make sound decisions related to his own safety, shelter, finances, or health care (or some subset of these), you can apply to the court to formally be made his guardian or conservator. With a "general guardianship," you would have the right to make all your adult child's decisions; a "limited guardianship" would be limited to certain decisions (such as medical ones). In contrast, with a conservatorship, you would usually have control only over your child's money or property.

Because you go before a court, you need to hire a lawyer and prove you are asking for the least restrictive measure required. Each state and province has its own specific laws on guardianship.

If you are named as your adult child's guardian, specify someone in your will to take over if you die or can't fulfill the role.

Other Things to Keep In Mind

Besides the important topics already discussed, here are some additional issues to be aware of:

If divorced, ensure your custody agreement doesn't affect government assistance in adulthood. If your child will continue to receive support payments after eighteen, consult your lawyer to ensure the wording of your custody agreement doesn't jeopardize future government support. Otherwise, support amounts could be considered income for your child and result in lost or reduced assistance.

Don't neglect disability insurance for yourself. (Purchase it through your employer or through an organization.) You are much more likely to become disabled than to die while your child is young.

If you have a health plan through your employer, check out when your dependent coverage ends. Many health plans end dependent coverage when a young adult turns nineteen. However, some extend dependent coverage to age twenty-two or twenty-five. And some cover to different ages, depending on whether or not your child is attending school full-time. Often, plans will continue to cover totally disabled dependents as "adult disabled children" beyond the usual end date for dependent coverage. Check your benefits handbook, so you have time to seek continued insurance for your adult child, if necessary.

A child with special needs destined for college is more likely to need financial support. Investigate education savings plans (Section 529 plans in the U.S.; Registered Education Savings Plans in Canada). Most plans allow you to transfer funds to a family member if your child doesn't go on to post-secondary education. A financial advisor or life insurance agent can help you set up a plan.

Finally, make sure you and your partner have adequate health insurance and life insurance. Take care of your-self—someone's depending on it.

Plan for Changing Needs

Planning for the future is a process that evolves as your child ages. Your will may require occasional updating—your carefully selected trustee or guardian may no longer be appropriate. New issues may arise in adulthood, such as finding a health insurance plan for your child after they no longer qualify for yours. Changes such as your adult child marrying or moving out of your state or province could also necessitate revising your plan.

Staying on top of things takes time, energy, and often money, but the relief in knowing your child will be well cared for makes it a worthwhile investment.

Experience Talks

"At a minimum, make sure your child is taken care of in your will, in the event you die suddenly. And, get to know what the options are for the future when your child turns eighteen."
—Ann Marie, mom to Heather, twelve, with Down syndrome

"Long-term planning is very important to us and we do have a plan in place for Tracey. We have burial plots, plenty of life insurance for the three of us; we are setting up a trust, and we maintain the friends we've had since Tracey was ten months old and we discovered she was disabled. We also maintain long-term friendships with the parents of her day program."
—Monica, mom of a twenty-four-year-old with Angelman Syndrome

PART IV

Family
Ties

*"When we decided to have another child, we
pictured Leah playing happily with her new brother or sister.
But by age two, Leah's sister was far from a playmate. Talia was a
screaming, unhappy, and remote child. Instead of enjoying family picnics
and outings, we were desperately searching for answers and help. Nobody
plans to have a daughter with autism. Now, Talia is thirteen, and our
life is a different kind of normal. Recently we dropped off both
girls at the movies—for the first time alone together—
while we browsed at the mall. It felt like a miracle."*

—Amy (co-author)

While our children may be different than we envisioned, we each manage to find a rhythm to family life that works for us. A study at the University of North Carolina, Chapel Hill, involving 165 families of children with mental retardation demonstrated what we've known all along: We are resilient and adaptable. While study participants all reported additional stresses, most families successfully coped with the challenges in a variety of ways.

According to this and other research, the following strategies help families remain healthy and cohesive:

Communicate openly, problem solve together, and negotiate.

Maintain a strong marriage (or support system, if you're single).

Take care of yourselves as parents. Seek counseling and help if you're suffering from depression.

These goals aren't always easy to accomplish. Especially when you're coping with your child's latest crisis or setback, your family life can fall apart. But even during tough times, the key to strong families is open communication. Keep talking about what works in your family and what needs changing. Make sure that family members feel safe to express all feelings—including negative ones.

To encourage open communication, you need time to connect with all family members. In the following chapters, you'll learn ways to nurture your relationship with your spouse, children, and extended family.

"Having a special needs child either makes or breaks your relationship. It caused us much stress and many arguments at first, but we've been able to build a better relationship through our mutual love of our child."

—Liza, mother of a seven-year-old with a rare chromosomal disorder

Chapter 14

Who's Minding the Marriage?

According to the U.S. Census Bureau (1997), if the past trend continues, 50 percent of today's first marriages will likely end in divorce. If you have a child with special needs, you may wonder if your marriage is even more at risk.

It's true that your marriage probably will be stressed by additional financial, emotional, and physical challenges. Some parents take on additional or unappealing jobs to pay for expensive therapies, equipment, or medications. A child's behaviors or declining health can leave little room for romance in a relationship. And if your child is awake and disruptive most nights, you may be constantly exhausted. Even your hours in bed with your partner are disrupted.

These challenges can stress some marriages to the breaking point. The divorced women we interviewed told us their marriages broke down for these reasons:

One parent was left doing most of the child care/parenting. As one mother phrased it: "One person parents and the other does their own thing."

Parents couldn't agree on parenting strategies, a child's needs, and/or diagnosis.

The marriage was already weak. Especially with additional family difficulties such as unemployment, alcoholism, or infidelity, the demands of special needs parenting were the "last straw." Several women said "The marriage wouldn't have survived anyhow."

So is your marriage doomed? Absolutely not. There is no evidence that special needs in the family increase risk of divorce, according to Dr. Peter Rosenbaum, co-director of the CanChild Centre for Childhood Disability Research at McMaster University in Hamilton, Ontario, who co-authored a study of almost 500 parents of children with cerebral palsy. The Wisconsin Longitudinal Study (2001) included surveys of more than 10,000 men and women at ages eighteen, thirty-six, and fifty-three or fifty-four. It found no difference in marital status between parents of children with disabilities (developmental or serious mental health problems) and parents of typical children.

Other researchers have shown that your marriage can actually be enriched by your special needs parenting experience.

When Kate Scorgie and Dick Sobsey of Azuza Pacific University surveyed eighty parents of children with disabilities (2000), 52 percent said the experience made their marriage stronger, 26 percent disagreed, and 22 percent were uncertain.

Many women we surveyed described their marriages as strengthened. In order to work together as a team, couples learn to communicate openly, to problem solve together, and to comfort each other. As Jenna, mother of a child with a rare disorder, explains, "It has made us stronger as a couple. We've had to face many problems and uncertainties, but we have always held on to each other and leaned on each other for strength."

Of course, even in strong marriages, women reported conflicts that frequently arose. Many mothers of adults told us they wish they had given more time and energy to their marriages all along. Fortunately, there are many strategies for dealing with the common stress points that occur in a marriage.

Different Reactions to Grief

Grieving for your child is cumulative over time. At each age and stage of development, parents mourn what "should" be going on in their children's lives. This sadness can be particularly intense, since we tend to anticipate future losses as well. Some conflicts arise because husbands and wives may grieve in different ways or at different times. Often women have been brought up to talk openly about their feelings, but men believe they should keep their feelings inside, or try to "do something more concrete" than talking. It's helpful to remember that your partner probably feels the same grief and anxiety that you do—but expresses them differently. Your spouse may feel that he must be stoic in order to support you.

Of course, each couple and family is unique. So, sometimes it's the husband who wants to talk about his feelings, while the wife may be ready to take action.

To manage your different reactions to grief, try these strategies:

Keep the lines of communication open. Check in frequently to ask how your partner is feeling and coping.

Rely on each other for support. Trade off times for being with your children, so you balance the extra work of parenting.

Seek help. At some point, you may need to go outside the couple relationship for support. Individually, or as a couple, consider counseling or attending a parent's group. (See "Help from the Pros," later in this chapter.)

Make time for each other. Going out for a movie "date" or even just a walk together helps nurture your relationship.

Attend some of your child's appointments together. If your partner tends to distance himself from the situation, going together allows him to get direct answers to his questions. As a social worker at Bloorview MacMillan Children's Treatment Centre in Toronto stressed "Every clinic appointment could bring on a new reaction of grief. If the father is not privy to the appointment information first-hand, he could distance himself even further, and that may make him feel disempowered to do anything about it."

Give each other time. Realize that each of you will grieve in your own time and way. Have patience and don't try to force your partner to change. Find emotional support elsewhere if your partner isn't yet ready.

Try hands-on tasks instead of talk. Your partner may find it more therapeutic to do something concrete. For example, building a ramp to your house or an accessible swing set in the yard together could be positive. Also brainstorm activities that you both can enjoy with your child.

Different Understanding of Your Child's Challenges and Strengths

Have you heard these words from your partner?
"You baby him."
"There's nothing wrong with her—she's just lazy."
"She'll outgrow it."
"You're too soft on him. He just needs to be disciplined."

When your partner denies or diminishes your child's problem, you can feel like a single parent. When Grace's daughter was diagnosed with Asperger syndrome, her husband said the child just needed stricter rules and a firmer hand. "We could not reconcile the differences," she says. "Hence the term 'ex.' We love each other desperately, but we can't tolerate each other's parenting views. It became unworkable, as I wasn't prepared to sacrifice my daughter's mental/emotional health to pacify him."

While not all situations are as extreme as Grace's, disagreements about your child's condition can seriously stress a marriage. If your partner believes there is nothing "wrong" with your child, you're left as the sole person trying to get help for her. Some women in this situation must manage all therapies, appointments, school meetings, etc., by themselves. Connie has twin preschoolers with hearing impairments. "When our second daughter became hearing impaired, he said that she just had 'selective hearing.' We still go weekly for auditory verbal therapy and he doesn't get involved at all. He is not dealing with the reality of how much work goes into caring, teaching, and working with them."

In our survey, women were most often the ones taking on the role of actively seeking help. As one social worker explains, "There are exceptions, but in my experience the mother throws herself into action: seeking answers and therapies, thinking about the disability and its impact, providing the special care required, and expressing many emotions. But the dad often retreats to the safety and consistency of his work."

Some can't even discuss the "special needs side" of their lives with their husbands, who deny that their children even have disabilities. As a result, these moms feel alone, resentful and exhausted.

If you're dealing with this conflict, talk openly with your partner. Then, work through the steps below to develop a common understanding of your child. These steps also are helpful to follow, even if you and your partner already work well as a team.

Learn about your child's disability together. As much as possible, both of you should meet with doctors or professionals together. To accommodate your schedules, request school meetings or appointments in the early morning or evening. If only you can attend an appointment, schedule a quiet time later in the day when you can provide updates to your partner. Sometimes, have your partner take your child to appointments, instead of you.

Ask for information sheets or books to share. Read the same book or watch a video together about your child's disability. (Many social service agencies and support groups have lending libraries with books and videos/tapes/DVDs).

Increase your partner's involvement one step at a time. For example, ask your partner to telephone a therapist requesting information about your child. Attend parent training, a disability organization meeting, or a conference together. As Mikaela writes, "My husband used to think that, if I was harder on my son, he would behave differently. The turning point for us was attending a national Fragile X conference together. This opened my husband's eyes to see that you can't 'time out' or 'yell' your son into normalcy."

Connect with other special needs families. Perhaps the most powerful key to understanding is to meet other parents who have a child with similar special needs. To find these parents, attend a support group, disability association meeting, or fundraising dance together. If those situations are too intimidating, arrange a dinner out with another couple who has a similar child. If you're used to "going it alone," it can be a revelation and comfort to find other parents dealing with challenges and thriving.

Get outside help. If you can't agree about your child, meet with a marriage therapist or counselor to talk through these issues. (See "Help from the Pros," later in this chapter.)

Accept what you cannot change. Some moms we surveyed say they can't change their partner's denial of their child's disability. Instead, they accept that they are the sole parent managing the disability issues in their child's life. If that is your reality, take excellent care of yourself to avoid burn-out and exhaustion. Exercise, enjoy hobbies, and connect with other moms of kids with disabilities to share ideas and support. And seek counseling if you need it. In time, your partner's understanding of your child may change.

Different Approaches to Parenting

Even when you agree about your child's abilities and challenges, you may have different parenting approaches. Women described these disagreements:

> "He takes the professionals' opinions as gospel, while I question everything."
> "I deal with things and he avoids things."
> "I expect more 'typical' behaviors and insist that we work towards that. My husband is more likely to do everything for our son."
> "My husband is less protective of our daughter. He pushes her harder to do things."

First, remember that it's normal to have different parenting approaches. As Wendy, mom of a child with Angelman syndrome, recalls, "We used to argue over medical decisions, but I finally realized that we are two individuals, one with the job of 'Daddy' and one with 'Mommy.' Though we may come to the same conclusions eventually, our feelings may be very different and we each have to be allowed to feel them." In order to ensure that your different approaches are positive for your family, take these steps:

Strengthen your identity as a parenting team. There are few role models for parents of kids with special needs. You seldom read about our concerns in typical parenting magazines or books. So how do you learn to parent as a team? In Amy's case, "We try and attend some of our daughter's appointments together. We occasionally book a sitter so we can attend an autism parenting workshop together. And sometimes going out with another couple who has a special needs child helps to 'normalize' our parenting experience. We enjoy a night out and swap stories of the bizarre situations our kids get into. All of these strengthen our feeling as a team and a couple. When we don't manage to do this regularly, we feel it. There's more tension between us."

Celebrate your differences. Compromise and try each other's ways of handling things. As Jenna says, "I tend to be overprotective, while my husband is more relaxed with her—this allows her to try new things. We reconcile this by me backing off sometimes and allowing my daughter to expand her experiences. Other times, my husband trusts my intuition and let's me handle certain situations with her."

Remember the big picture. Even though you may differ in your everyday approach, always discuss long-term dreams for your child and for yourselves. Rochelle emphasizes that you must "have a common vision for your child. We have a separate 'partnership' that is above and beyond our marriage. We realize that we are responsible for ensuring our son has a stable and happy life, and that the best way to do that is together."

Uneven Parenting Responsibilities

"The important thing is working together. Don't try and take everything on yourself."
—Toni, mom of a son with a pervasive developmental disorder

Without teamwork and planning, we can get stuck in roles that no longer work. For example, perhaps you decide to stay home with your infant for the first year. So you take on the primary parenting role. Over time, you may also take on most of the parenting, advocacy, and household tasks. This unbalanced situation can continue for years unless you frequently re-evaluate what works for all of you. Some mothers we surveyed are resentful. They say:

> "I seem to be the one who has done all the classes, read the books, and done the home parent training—he hasn't."
>
> "He does not understand why I'm depressed. I'm drowning in a sea of special needs."
>
> "Resentment comes when one person makes all the sacrifices and the other doesn't."

If you are handling the home front while your partner works full-time, you may be managing most of your child's care, paperwork, and appointments. While it's rewarding to be your child's primary parent and advocate, it can also be exhausting and stressful.

Of the women we surveyed, this uneven parenting was a relatively common complaint. Let's look at some reasons why this pattern may develop, and what you can do about it:

IS HE WORKING LONGER HOURS TO BRING HOME MORE MONEY?

Sometimes men feel extraordinary pressure to be the family breadwinner, especially if their wives are no longer employed. They may take on unappealing work, second jobs, or work longer hours to generate income for support workers, medical supplies, and therapies, or to maintain medical insurance. That means they work longer hours away from home, and when they return they're exhausted. Even fathers who are active parents at home start to burn out. Some dads feel they never get a break—they go from work to home, where there's child care and chores awaiting them. Some eventually retreat to work even longer hours at their jobs.

Suggestion: Trade off parenting responsibilities. To even the load, swap times when one of you is "on" for parenting. Take turns with tasks such as getting up with your child in the middle of the night or taking her to appointments. While co-author Amy manages most of the paperwork and meetings with therapists and teachers, she has always disliked taking her daughter to the dentist, hairdresser, and doctor because of her behavior. So, Amy's husband Jack takes Talia to these appointments. With his calmness and sense of humor, he distracts her and gets her through it (and Amy gets a break).

DOES HE CONSIDER TAKING CARE OF THE KIDS "WOMEN'S WORK"?

In some families, men aren't very involved because they never expected to be hands-on dads. Some hold traditional views of parenting, where the wife is primarily in charge of the home and children. If that's the case, he may see the extra disability tasks as just part of good mothering. Sometimes, spouses just aren't aware of how much behind-the-scenes work is going on—especially if they have a partner efficiently maintaining a smooth home life. They may be unaware that their wives are resentful about the uneven responsibilities.

Rochelle was exhausted when her preschooler (who has autism) insisted that she do everything for him (instead of his dad). But Rochelle was able to change this pattern and also her partner's attitude. "I finally insisted my husband start doing more with him," she recounts. "The first time he took my son to buy shoes without me, our son screamed the whole twelve miles to the store because I wasn't with him. After that, my husband began to realize how dependent our son was on ONLY me and began to make more of an effort, which gave me a much needed break. It also gave him a new perspective on how frustrating my day could be and why at the end of it I just wanted to 'veg out' or sleep."

Like Rochelle, you can take action. Try these strategies:

Suggestion #1: Take a good look at your own attitude and expectations about shared parenting. For example, when your husband is caring for the kids, do you say he's "babysitting"? That implies that he's doing a special favor or job that's not part of his parenting responsibilities.

Suggestion #2: Make a list of all of the tasks you do in order to support your child. Include areas such as personal care (feeding, toileting, dressing, bathing, etc), making special food, operating and maintaining your child's equipment, arranging and attending appointments, calling agencies and service providers, arranging child care, meeting with school staff, managing paper work and bills for funding and insurance, tutoring your child, going on community outings, etc. Ask your partner to choose at least one of these tasks for a week, and then sit down and talk again. What additional tasks can he take on?

DOES HE SEE HIMSELF IN A SEPARATE-BUT-EQUAL ROLE?

Some dads, although frequently absent from home, may be active in the world of disability advocacy. While you're home, preparing dinner and parenting your kids, is your spouse out attending board meetings or weekend disability conferences? If so, it's great that he's involved in disability issues, but he may not realize that he's enjoying the high-profile, social meetings while you're holding down the fort at home.

Suggestion: You've got to talk this issue through with your spouse. Tell your spouse what frustrates you. If it's the fact that you get all the "grunge" work, make a list and divide up some of the household tasks. If you both hate certain jobs, take turns on them, involve your kids, or hire someone to do them.

If you need to get out of the house and have some "grownup time," trade off the advocacy or educational meetings between you, or hire a babysitter so you can attend some together.

DOES HE ACTUALLY KNOW WHAT NEEDS TO BE DONE?

Some fathers aren't as involved with their kids because they honestly don't know how to help. If you've been the primary contact for medical appointments and professionals, he may not know how to handle a meeting or who to phone. If you're constantly in charge of bath time, your child's medical routines, or therapies, he may not know the drill.

Suggestion: Be specific about what you need. Some partners aren't involved because they don't know what's needed—either they're oblivious, or they assume that you've got things under control. Even if you're home full-time, it doesn't mean you're solely responsible for your child. With both your schedules in mind, talk about specific ways your partner can help. This strategy worked for Rhiannon, who is at home full-time and co-ordinates activities, therapies, etc., for four children. She had to decide on an appropriate school for her son. Since her husband works full-time, she visited several schools herself, but she didn't want to make the decision alone. Finally, she spoke with her husband, who took time off work to visit various classrooms. After that, they made the decision together. Sometimes you must ask for what you need.

DO YOU CRITICIZE HIS EFFORTS WHEN HE TRIES TO HELP?

Some women admit they are uncomfortable sharing household or family care responsibilities because their partners "don't do the job right." They may be reluctant to relinquish some parenting duties, especially if they see being mothers as their full-time jobs. If a husband feels you're nitpicking, he may completely back off. And, if he's looking for an easy way out of helping, you're giving him one. (There are even rumors of the occasional foul husband who will deliberately screw up jobs, so his wife will never ask for his help again!)

Suggestion: Is it really important that he do the job "just right"? If he's inserting a feeding tube, of course care is essential. But does it matter if he loads the dishwasher differently, or picks out rather creative clothing options for your child?

No matter what the reason, if you and your partner are deep in a rut of uneven parenting, you need to address the problem to avoid drifting further apart. Set time aside to talk about it. If possible, have someone watch your child so the two of you can go out and talk without interruption. Without accusing, tell him how you're feeling. And listen openly to his concerns and feelings. Chances are he could be feeling overwhelmed and exhausted as well. Often what comes out in these discussions is a sense of loss and sadness about your child. Once you've both expressed your feelings, you can brainstorm solutions. Then, choose one action to try to change the situation.

And don't forget to thank each other for the considerate things you each do. Too often, we save our thanks for the "paid people" in our children's lives.

Help from the Pros

"My husband and I have been to counseling together and separately," recalls Monisha, mom of a teenager with ARND (Alcohol-Related Neurodevelopmental Disorder). "It has helped us stop blaming each other for problems, helped us communicate better with each other, and helped us put our marriage first more often."

To make sure that communication stays strong and open with your partner, consider having a yearly "well-spouse" counseling session with a marriage and family therapist that you trust. A counselor can help you look at your typical patterns of communication, what is working well in your relationship, and what you'd like to work on. Then if, at some point, your marriage becomes stressed, you'll already have a counselor on board who has worked with you.

If tensions and differences in your parenting approaches are damaging your family life, don't hesitate to seek counseling as a couple or family. If your spouse refuses to go, seek counseling yourself. As Rhiannon says, "I now see a therapist for myself—mostly to keep my marriage healthy. I can't dump all of my frustrations on my husband—that's where the therapist helps."

See the Resources section for information on how to find a marriage or family therapist, or other mental health professional.

Experience Talks

"When my daughter moved into a group home, my husband and I were shocked at how we had become strangers consumed by 'survival techniques.' But going to a marriage counselor helped us to relearn how to be a couple."

—Kayla, mother of an adult with Rett syndrome

"Every time we have to work something out, we get better at communicating. To maintain a strong marriage, spend time together away from the kids. Also, make sure that both partners (especially Mom) spend time by themselves, away from other family members."

—Beatrice, mother of a child with hydrocephalus and seizure disorder

"Don't blame one another. Your strong, happy marriage will do wonders for a stable secure life for your child."

—June, mother of a child with autism

"Communication is the key. The moments we spend together when the kids are sleeping or when we have a sitter are the glue of our relationship. Go out on dates, talk, have sex. Be open with each other about everything. Love each other and your children unconditionally."

—Riva, mother of nine-year-old child with epilepsy and developmental delays

Chapter 15

Just the Two of Us— Finding Time and Energy to Nurture Romance

While many of the conflicts described in the previous chapter are common, they all seem to worsen when you and your partner haven't had time together. Without time to have fun together, you can feel like the romance in your relationship is fading. In fact, marriage can start to feel more like a "partnership" as you efficiently divide up the tasks of daily life.

When writing this chapter, Amy realized how frequently she and Jack trade off time. For example, she goes to her book club and fitness classes while Jack stays home. And Jack goes to piano lessons and fitness while Amy is home. While this arrangement enables them to be home with their kids, they slip into a pattern of enjoying most of their leisure/social time separately.

What's wrong with this situation? If you spend your most enjoyable time separately... what kind of romance is that? The danger of mostly separate recreation is that you look forward to being apart from each other, because that's when you have the most fun. But by doing enjoyable activities together, you increase your feelings of pleasure and intimacy—important aspects of a strong marriage. Of course, one way you support each other is by trading off parenting responsibilities, so the other can enjoy personal time. But, it is also important to enjoy time together.

But many moms we surveyed said couple time was rare. Comments like the following were typical:

"We're lucky to get dinner out for two hours every other month without kids. That's it for time alone."

"Our family is too far away on both sides to be supportive or helpful with regard to child care."

"We haven't had an overnight vacation in six years, unless it included bringing the three kids with us."

Others describe the difficulty of enjoying a sex life when their child's support worker is outside the bedroom door.

A particularly trying situation is when parents work opposite shifts, so one of them is always available to cover the home front. While shift work can be a more economical solution than trying to pay for special-needs child care, there are definite drawbacks. It can be practically impossible to enjoy a marriage with someone you hardly see. Several women said working opposite shifts was a significant stressor in their marriage. And a few said it was a factor in the breakdown.

For all couples, and especially those working opposite shifts, you need to strategize how to spend time together. You may have to re-arrange your work life, re-prioritize your activities, and cut costs somewhere else—but the results are worth it. As one friend quips, "When people ask how I can afford dates and holidays with my husband, I tell them 'It's cheaper than divorce.'"

Keeping the Connection

John and Stacy are the parents of a child with multiple disabilities who requires total care. Each season they sign up for a fun night class together to try something new, such as ballroom dancing. They remind us that to be good parents, we need to enjoy and cherish each other first. Children benefit when their parents' marriage is strong and loving.

Mothers who know what it's like to try to juggle a marriage along with your special needs parenting duties shared the following tips for nurturing your relationship.

Make time to connect. Moms in strong marriages advised making daily time to talk with each other when the kids are asleep. Don't let this time slip away, as May tended to. She says, "My kids usually get to bed around nine or ten. After we return phone calls, check email, and tidy the kitchen, my husband often watches the news, while I retreat to bed with a book." Eventually, she and her husband realized that several days could slip by with them barely having a real discussion. They nipped that in the bud, and "now some nights, when the kids are asleep, we sit down together with a glass of wine." If your children are teens or adults, set the alarm to enjoy some early morning weekend time together while they sleep in.

Talk about what's important to you—besides **the kids.** Of course it's important to talk about our children. But to stay close, we also have to share other aspects of ourselves. There are more things to discuss with your spouse besides therapies and school problems. Instead, try asking open-ended, personal questions, such as:

> What was the best/most frustrating part of your week?
> What's been most on your mind recently?
> If you could travel anywhere, where could you go? (Can we make that trip happen?!)
> What's one change we could try to make life easier/ more fun?

Eventually, these kinds of questions can get you thinking about your hopes, dreams, and plans for the future—as a couple.

Add some playfulness to your relationship. It *is* possible to "keep the fire lit" when the demands of parenting are relentless. Some low cost, in-house, romantic ideas include:

Enjoy a candlelit breakfast.

Have a comedy night by reading joke books and watching funny movies.

Savor your favorite flavor of ice cream—with one spoon.

Celebrate your own private anniversaries (first date, etc.) with a glass of champagne.

Write each other loving post-it notes and place them strategically around the house.

Borrow a how-to-ballroom-dance video from the library and try it out.

If you're the more adventurous type, try decorating each other with chocolate body paint or try some vanilla scented massage oil.

Try mini-dates. Schedule a regular "date night" with your husband—weekly, monthly, or whatever you can manage. Find it hard to get away for a whole evening? Even an hour or two out together can be a welcome relief. Besides the regular babysitting sources, check out places with short-term (one or two hour) child care and see if they can accommodate your child. For example, many fitness facilities offer babysitting while you (and your partner) work out together and go for a quick coffee at the snack bar afterwards. Also check shopping malls that have supervised playrooms so you can stroll the mall together. Most provide a pager, so that staff can contact you if needed. After Amy met with the local shopping mall playroom staff, she decided to try it out with Talia. "After five minutes, we were paged and had to retrieve her. But one year later, she happily stayed in the playroom for an hour." So revisit places to see if they might work as your child's needs change. For teens and adults, tap into programs that pair volunteers with individuals with disabilities. While your son and daughter is out doing activities he or she enjoys, you and your partner can plan your own fun.

Schedule regular "in-home dates" if you can't leave the house. Schedule the time in your calendar. Deanna has a hard time finding child care for her three children with special needs, so after they're in bed, "we get a video from the library and just cuddle on the couch. Not the best date ever, but it'll do in a pinch," she says. Other couples enjoy cooking a special dinner together, playing cards or musical instruments, or sipping wine and listening to music by candlelight.

Arrange your work schedules to be together when your children are in school or at their day program. For example, we heard from one mom who has every Friday off, while her husband works every other Friday. Every two weeks, they enjoy a "date day" while their kids are in school. Or both schedule a vacation day for the same time. Several mothers suggested going out for breakfast or lunch on school days as well.

Plan an overnight, weekend, and/or week-long getaway. Getting away can be challenging to arrange, especially if you don't have extended family available to care for your children. But it's worth the effort. If you're eligible for respite funding (see Chapter 9), use it to hire a caregiver to come to your house for the weekend. Also, some community children's group homes have overnight and weekend respite spots. You enjoy a break and your child enjoys a "sleepover party." As Mikaela writes, "Initially it was very stressful to leave our children overnight. However, it has helped us to remember why we are married—we actually like each other on dates!"

Swap child care with another family. Depending on your child's needs, a child care swap with another family who knows your child well may work beautifully. Invite their children to a "sleepover" one weekend at your home. Next month, your children spend the weekend at your friends' house. This way you can enjoy time alone together at your own home, without having to pay for a hotel. Alternatively, if your child is more comfortable at home, the other parents could care for him there instead.

Encourage your older child to attend social events. For your teen or adult child, take advantage of inclusive weekend retreats offered through Church and synagogue youth groups, agencies, and community organizations. Typically low-cost, these outings foster independence in your son and daughter and give you and your partner time to reconnect.

Escape with your family. Modify your family getaway so you have some "alone" time. Some hotels and most family resorts offer full-day programming for children. Others provide babysitting services. If you speak to the establishment in advance, they may be able to accommodate your child's special needs.

MORE LOW-COST IDEAS

High child care or respite costs can leave you little cash to enjoy a date. Try low-cost fun instead. As one couple tells us, "Never underestimate the healing properties of book browsing for a few hours" without children interrupting. Other low cost ideas include hiking, biking, picnicking, antiquing, window shopping, skating, going out for dessert, seeing a movie at a repertory theater, attending community theater, etc. Or walk in your neighborhood together. Just go.

If finding someone to watch your children is a problem, see Chapters 18-20 for more solutions.

The Single File

If you're a busy single mom, you may feel you lack the time or energy to pursue a romantic relationship. As Allegra, mother of two adults with myotonic dystrophy, says, "I have no time for dating. I only have Saturday night from eight to midnight free and I want it to myself. I couldn't imagine having to juggle a guy too!" It's fine to be single, and you may feel you have no time for a relationship, but you still need/deserve a social life.

In fact, your child will also benefit if you put some energy into expanding your own social contacts. Single mothers who don't have life partners or supportive best friends are in danger of becoming enmeshed in their relationships with their children, say several social workers we've spoken with. An adolescent, for example, may not explore his own needs for peer friendships because he fears leaving his mom alone and isolated.

Since single mothers often also have financial difficulties, they often have fewer resources. Without a car, for example, getting out in the community can be difficult.

To avoid isolation and an overly intense relationship with your child, investigate ways to bring more people into your child's life. Start with organizations that support single parents such as Big Brothers/ Big Sisters, which can provide a volunteer adult to spend time with your child. Also contact senior centers and request names of people interested in acting as surrogate grandparents to local children. Ask your local disability agency if it provides a matching service that pairs a volunteer (or volunteer family) with an individual with disabilities. Special Olympics is also an organization where children and parents make life-long connections.

To meet other moms and dads tackling child rearing alone, contact Parents Without Partners. This international organization offers education, family activities, and adult social and recreational activities.

Ironically, some moms say their free time and time to "date" increases once they separate. Women sharing custody with their ex-husbands often have weekends or evenings to themselves. If that's your situation, look carefully at how you're using your alone time. It's a great chance to explore activities that bring you pleasure and balance. And you can use that time to get connected with others.

If you're interested in dating, meeting someone suitable can be a bit of a challenge. Pia, a divorced mother, says, "I have no partner—they aren't exactly lining up either!" To increase your odds of meeting someone compatible, keep active in the community. Get child care/respite and take a night class or attend meetings for a committee that interests you. Join a single parent organization and bring your kids to one of their family activities. Stay involved in special needs parent support and advocacy groups. Also, get the word out to your friends that you are interested in dating. But be sure to specify what qualities you're looking for in a partner.

Even if you do meet someone, how will they react to your child(ren) with special needs? Mothers we surveyed advise being open from the start. Being upfront about your child also helps to "weed out" someone who wouldn't fit well with your family. Sue, divorced and remarried, says, "I married a man who is very supportive of my activities and who my disabled son thinks is wonderful. It was a major criterion for me that any "new" husband would be understanding of what families with a disabled youth endure."

If you are not interested in becoming involved romantically with someone, or the time is not right for you, a good friendship can provide the social support you need. For tips on finding or strengthening relationships with friends, see Chapter 3.

Experience Talks

"Always talk things out and tell each other 'I love you.' Try and do things just for each other—maybe a special meal or ten minutes alone."
—Chan, mother of a child with severe cerebral palsy and a seizure disorder

"My son is part of the package. I placed it up front from the start. We go together—no discussion. My partner, when we met, didn't race away. He stayed, learned about my son, and won my heart."
—Riva, a divorced mom, now in a serious relationship

"My sister gives me unconditional love all the time.
She cheers me up when I'm sad. I love teaching her new things.
She helps me see the world in different ways."

—Samantha, teenage sibling of a child with a pervasive developmental disorder

Chapter 16

The Joy of Siblings

Even if your marriage is strong, you probably still worry about making time for your children. Of course we love our kids— all of them. But just as our relationships with our kids with special needs can bring special joys, so can our relationships with our typically developing children. When one child struggles with communication, you appreciate being able to converse with your other children. And if one child struggles with physical challenges, it can be a relief and pleasure to enjoy a bike ride with your other kids.

While all of our kids have abilities and talents, some will never be able to enjoy certain experiences that other children take for granted. If you have a child without a disability, she can be your ticket into the "regular" parenting world—the one where moms discuss movies and carpools, instead of therapies and medications. There's a special joy that comes from watching your child perform in a school play, or score a goal for the hockey team. When we have parenting experiences in common with other typical families, we can increase our friendships and social supports. Our family life feels a little more normal.

And the Guilt—

Women we interviewed also described many worries about their other children. They wonder how such a different family life affects their kids. Penny, whose son, Jeffrey, has severe autism and extreme behaviors says, "A valuable card collection of one of my young teenage boys was damaged—because he ran out to his room to answer the telephone and in his eagerness didn't take the time to lock his door. In the time it took him to have a chat with a friend, Jeffrey ruined it. He was heartbroken and sobbing because one small act of forgetfulness can result in so much."

Coping with behaviors of brothers and sisters can be difficult. A 2000 study from the Children's Hospital of Western Ontario compared siblings of children with autism spectrum disorders, Down syndrome, and typical children over three years. Researchers found that siblings of children with autism showed more adjustment problems, and their parents were more distressed and depressed.

Mothers also feel guilty when they can't provide equal time for each child. Serena says her typical three-year-old is acting out. "I know a lot of his behaviors are a spin off of not getting more one-to-one attention." Her other son has muscular dystrophy and developmental delays.

In families with several children with disabilities, time is even more limited. Norma has two teens with mental health issues and says whichever one is in crisis at the time gets more attention than the other. "It goes back and forth, but it's always a struggle to be balanced," with the healthier child resenting the extra time she must spend on the sick one.

Moms also feel guilty when they ask siblings to help more—both with daily chores and babysitting. They worry that siblings will become resentful.

If your child with special needs has behavioral challenges, it can make commonplace family outings impossible. Then you feel guilty that your children are missing out on the normal childhood they deserve. Deanna, a mother of three, says, "Our most involved child definitely makes doing things as a family more difficult. We don't go out to dinner; we don't go on trips together; and we really can't even go to parks together."

For children with physical challenges, it can be exhausting just to get out the door. When children have complex medical needs and/or use a wheelchair, some activities are severely restricted. Not only are family outings curtailed, but siblings' activities may be as well. When one child can't be left alone, it's hard for a mom to play chauffeur.

The cost of therapies, equipment, and medication can also cut deeply into family funds. So, you may need to say "no" to your other children's requests for hockey equipment, piano lessons, or the expensive basketball shoes that "everyone else at school" has.

And moms' worries extend to the future. You may wonder if you can count on a sibling to care for your child with special needs after you're gone. And is that an unfair expectation?

The following sections provide insights into siblings and how you can best support them.

The Sibling Experience—What Do Siblings Worry About?

To counteract worries about your other kids, it's helpful to understand their perspectives and feelings. Or as one mother describes, "Be aware that 'normal' siblings, by virtue of the fact that they have special needs siblings, have special needs themselves."

Siblings may love their brother or sister with disabilities, but also resent the extra attention they receive from parents—and feel guilty about that resentment. Young children may be afraid of "catching" their sibling's disability. Some blame themselves for their sibling's condition. They may become angry or act out. And as they grow older, they wonder if they will be totally responsible for their brother or sister's care.

Fortunately, you can do much to support your children and to maintain a strong family life.

Provide information. Give your children accurate information about their sibling's disability. Check the library, bookstore, or online to find children's books. As your child grows older, update them with more detailed information.

Model open communication. Assure your children that it's okay to express all their feelings to you. Your kids may try to censor their resentment or worry because they don't want to alarm you. Gently ask questions and check in with them informally and regularly. If sitting down for a talk doesn't work, make other time that you can be alone together. Some kids open up most when they're helping you with chores or riding in the car.

Children can feel less resentful when they understand why their sibling consumes so much of your time. Lee has two children with different disabilities. She says, "They both understand that I have to do things differently with the other sibling. I am completely open and honest with my children. It helps if they know what to expect, when and why to expect it."

Have realistic expectations of your typical children. Some siblings feel they must behave perfectly and excel at school, sports, and extracurricular activities in order to "make up for" their brother or sister with special needs. Again, keep talking, listening, and be wary of pressuring your kids to excel.

Celebrate the accomplishments and achievements of all your children. Did you break out the champagne when your ten-year-old child with special needs used a spoon for the first time? Great—celebration is in order. But make sure that her sibling doesn't feel that her own accomplishments are ignored or taken for granted.

Encourage siblings to have interests outside of the family. Your typically developing child doesn't need to be enrolled in endless lessons, as many kids are today. But an outside activity or two can help build friendships, skills, and self-esteem. Plus, it can give you a chance to expand your own friendships with parents involved in the recreational organizations. One mom signs each of her kids up for a different activity—e.g., one in choir, one in dance, and one in flute lessons—so they all develop their own strengths. Some moms find it easier to schedule all their kids' activities at the same time/location, so they're not constantly on the road. If the school offers extracurricular activities, that's a great opportunity—you don't have to drive your child to it, and the friends she'll make will be ones she'll see in the hallway each day.

Strengthen your child's support system. Find an adult outside of the family (e.g., a guidance counselor or social worker at school) for siblings to confide in. Contact the school or social service agency and let them know about your family.

Help your child establish a peer group. Introduce your child to others who also have a brother or sister with a similar disability. It's important that siblings have peers to talk with who understand their experiences. Contact your case manager, social service agency, or local disability group to see if there are local peer-support groups for siblings of kids with special needs. These groups also have a positive effect on the child with special needs. Siblings who feel supported and well informed are more likely to want to remain involved in their brother or sister's life for the long run. If no sibling group exists locally, lobby agencies to get one started.

You could also create your own sibling support group. One mother created "The Downstairs Gang," a group of eleven families that get together several times a year. Each family has a child with Down syndrome. After seven years of meeting, parents and kids share both friendships and practical tips. Don't know similar families? Contact your local disability association and ask if you can mail a flyer to families to invite them to get together. Serve pizza, let siblings talk informally, and exchange phone numbers or emails. If you'd like more structure and guidance in forming a sibling support group, check out the Arc's Sibling Support Project (see Resources). It provides information and training to start your own group, and is adaptable for any disability.

If your child is often angry or acting out, seek counseling for her. Contact your local social service and mental health agencies for referrals.

Pay attention to any gut feeling you may have about your "typical" child—especially if her teacher approaches you with concerns. Sometimes a sibling may have a milder or related "shadow" version of their brother or sister's disability, which may have been overlooked.

Spending Time with Siblings— Finding Family Balance

Why do we, as mothers, always feel pressure to put the needs of our children with disabilities ahead of everyone else's? Two reasons, says Barbara Gill in *Changed by a Child: Companion Notes for Parents of a Child with a Disability*: "One is the anxiety and guilt that push us to do everything possible for this kid. The other is that the things we do for our child are prescribed and often monitored by professionals. Each time the physical therapist comes, she asks whether we've been doing the range of motion exercises, but no one comes by to check whether Mom and Dad have been out to dinner lately, or whether our three-year-old is getting her bedtime story every night."

As Gill says, it's difficult not to put your child with disabilities first. But when parents get burned out, kids can start to show emotional and behavioral problems. If you feel that your family life is mostly centered around your child with special needs, all of you may feel resentful. Don't sacrifice your family's needs for the sake of your child with a disability.

Be a role model for your children by taking care of yourself through exercising, maintaining friendships, and having interests outside of your child (see the chapters in Part II: Taking Care of Yourself for ideas). Try these strategies for regaining family balance and increasing "quality time" for everyone:

Divide and conquer. If you have a partner, one of you can care for your child with disabilities, while the other takes a child to lessons, on outings, or does a special activity together at home.

Mix errands with quality time. One-on-one time doesn't have to be a spectacular outing or activity. Take advantage of everyday errands by including one child while your partner or caregiver is home with the others. Chat, listen, and catch up on their news as you drive, shop, etc. At the grocery store, let her pick out some of her favorite foods. Errands can work well if your older child doesn't want to do "an activity" with you. As Teresa says, "I used to try too hard to do things with my 'typical' teen, but it just backfired and made things worse."

Make your children's schedule work for you. When your child with special needs is busy with a therapist or attending a program, use that time to interact with your other kids. Choose activities that you all enjoy. You don't need to be the perfect mom. Maybe you don't have the energy to play endless rounds of "Candyland" with your other child. It might be best to curl up on the couch together and watch a movie. Or find an activity that pampers you both. One mom takes her six-year-old daughter out for a "girl's afternoon" of lunch and manicures! Or exercise together. Grab your kids and walk the dog, bike, garden, or shoot baskets. (Or skate, toboggan, or shoot pucks in winter!)

Choose your time wisely. You don't always need a lot of time to show your child that they're special. Find out what's most important to your children, and be there for them. Rhiannon hired a support worker so she could watch her "typical" son play on his baseball team. Rochelle left work early to watch her daughter's ten-minute audition for the school orchestra.

Arrange dates with each child alone. Planning and enjoying a special activity with your child can strengthen your relationship, and do wonders for your own morale. Elisabeth plans a "date night" once a month with her teenage son. He chooses the food, the activity, and whether or not he wants a friend to join them. One mom occasionally takes her daughter out of the school for a "hooky day" of shopping, lunch, and movie going, while her child with special needs is at school.

Plan overnight or longer adventures. One parent can take a child away for an overnight adventure. But arranging a vacation for your typical children and both parents can be very special. Amy and Jack took Leah (then age twelve) on a trip to Eastern Canada for a week one summer, while Talia attended day camp and was watched overnight by a trusted respite worker. "For the first time on a family trip, we were relaxed and spontaneous. We were able to try activities based on Leah's interests—such as challenging hiking and caving." Other families send one child to a week of summer camp while they vacation with the other kids. Or see if grandma and grandpa could take your child for a few days.

Bring a support worker along on your vacation. Sometimes it feels bittersweet enjoying a vacation and missing your other child. Instead, try bringing your child's respite worker or personal care attendant along. That way, you can also enjoy activities with siblings that may not work for your child with special needs. The disadvantage can be cost and loss of privacy as the respite worker stays with you.

Siblings as Caregivers

Even though you're sensitive to your children's needs, you may also rely on them for caregiving help. It's hard to know what to reasonably expect of siblings. What if your teen wants to join the after-school drama club, but you need him to "babysit" his older brother while you work? How can we get the help we need from our other children, without overburdening them? How can we involve them with plans for the future, without overwhelming them? Experienced moms recommended several suggestions:

Keep your perspective. Are you worried that your older child assumes too many caregiving responsibilities? Remember, in most "typical" families, older siblings frequently babysit younger brothers and sisters.

Pay them for caregiving. Sometimes it's appropriate to pay your teen. If you've booked your teen for an evening babysitting, and she's later offered a paying job the same night, try to pay her the wage she would have received. If finances are tight, show your appreciation in other ways—make her favorite dessert or let her pick a video that you'll watch together.

Give them a say. Siblings may feel they have no control over the amount of family responsibility they have to accept. Each week, have a family meeting and discuss each person's plans, needs, and responsibilities.

Limit their caregiving. Don't overload children with caregiving responsibilities. Arrange child care or respite care so that siblings can take part in after-school clubs, homework, friendships. With younger siblings, be careful about how much responsibility you give them for caring for an older brother or sister with special needs. Make sure the tasks are age appropriate. For example, a young sibling could help by playing with a brother or sister for a few minutes (with a parent nearby). But a small child shouldn't feel she's been made responsible for her older sibling's safety—that's too much.

Show your appreciation. Show that you're not taking your children's assistance and support for granted. Regularly thank your children and tell them how their efforts are helping their brother or sister.

Involve them in planning for the future. Continually provide your children with up-to-date information. Even if you avoid discussing the future with them, teens will still wonder what their responsibilities will be. So it's important to openly talk about plans. Siblings who are lovingly included in their brother or sister's life are more likely to be involved when they are adults. (See Chapters 12 and 13 for more information on planning for the future.)

The Positive Aspects of Having a Brother or Sister with Special Needs

Still worried about your kids? While research is mixed, most studies show siblings of children with disabilities are indistinguishable from their peers. They report few differences in behavior, self-esteem, or competence. Researchers note positive effects too—such as maturity, responsibility, and cooperation. Other studies find siblings of children with disabilities and chronic illness show more warmth, tolerance of the differences of others, empathy, affection, and helpfulness as compared to siblings of non-disabled children.

Mothers we interviewed pointed out additional benefits. Some children are enriched by being exposed to their sibling's therapies. Says Randi, "I spend time with my four-year-old (with a pervasive developmental disorder) teaching him to count, the alphabet, sign language, etc., and my one-year-old daughter sits with us. I believe she will be advanced for her age, as she learns when I teach my son." Other siblings enjoy being the "expert" and educating other people about their brother or sister's disability. Many siblings continue their commitment by working in the disability field.

As adults, Seltzer and colleagues from Wisconsin-Madison University found siblings of individuals with developmental disabilities tend to maintain strong ties with their brothers or sisters. Forty-one percent of siblings reported at least weekly in-person visits. This did not hold true for siblings of individuals with serious mental illnesses—they tended to keep more distance—so your child's disability may influence whether her brother or sister stays close. Generally, your children will mirror you. If you model life balance, coping, and communication, your kids will likely follow your example.

Experience Talks

"My youngest son does not have the same close bond with me, but I just try to be there for him. I learned to sit back and wait until he comes when he needs something and then we have an enjoyable moment."
—Aileen, mom to a ten-year-old with autism and a nine-year-old with ADHD and speech and learning disabilities

"To make time for the other children, I either take them out for something fun one at a time, or get my husband to take our child with special needs out, so we can have fun at home.... I also try to make sure that I compliment the other children as they try to help with our special needs child or help me."
—Jenna, mother of four children, one a six-year-old with hydrocephalus and a seizure disorder

"My daughter is older than her brother and it was really hard at times to make special time with her. Now that she is older, she understands it better. I feel it has helped her to be a better person. She has always given a hand to someone that needs it."
—Nadine, mother of a teenager with fragile X and a twenty-year-old

"People told us to have another child to take care of our daughter when we are gone. I try to make people understand that my son is separate from his sister. He is her baby brother—not her personal aide or caretaker."
—Maxine, who has a five-year-old daughter with cerebral palsy and an infant son

"My family lives close by and attends sessions with my son's therapists for early intervention—this includes grandparents, aunts, cousins—just about the entire family."

—Sara, mother of a toddler who is developmentally delayed

Chapter 17

Grandparents and Extended Family— Getting Them on Board

Some mothers receive tremendous hands-on support from their parents, in-laws, and other relatives. Many women we surveyed said their mothers were their most vital support. Victoria, a single mother, says, "My mother has stepped in as a babysitter when nobody else would help. She has insisted that I join her on vacation. She helped me to buy a house. I owe my sanity to my mother."

But perhaps this kind of family involvement is not your reality. Your parents and extended family may be too elderly, too sick, too needy themselves, or too far away to offer practical or emotional support. Such is the case with Fiona. She says, "My father has cancer right now and mom is taking care of him. Two of my brother's kids have special needs as well. I wouldn't even ask them for help—I'd feel guilty!" Or perhaps your family is too busy to offer support as Judith describes: "My mother is so involved in her own life that I might talk to her once a month at best."

If your children are adults, your parents may be deceased or lacking the strength or energy to help you. Some extended family may feel you no longer need support. Says Kayla, mom to an adult with Rett disorder, "to family and others, we seem okay, because we have done it for so long."

Although family may seem indifferent to your child, they really may be overwhelmed by grief and confusion—especially if your child has just been diagnosed. Some, even over time, simply don't know how to help. In order to maintain those relationships, it helps to understand what grandparents and relatives may be feeling.

Why Grandparents and Others React the Way They Do

Marion was distraught when her newborn granddaughter was diagnosed with severe cerebral palsy—her grandchild would never speak and would need total care. She was heartbroken watching her daughter suffering with the news. "She'll always be my child and I feel guilty that I can't protect her," she says. Like Marion, grandparents of children with special needs can experience a kind of "triple grief." Grandparents grieve not only for their child and grandchild, but also for themselves. They have lost the grandchild they expected. They may have envisioned playing baseball and baking cookies. But how will they interact with a child who may have limited abilities to move, speak, or understand?

Many grandparents and other close family members have no idea where to turn with their feelings and concerns. While you may be joining parent groups, reading disability books, and attending appointments, grandparents may have no access to support and information. Without this support, they have no way of working through their own grief or fully understanding your child's special needs.

Without proper support and information, family members may react in ways that seem hurtful to us. To avoid facing sorrow, they may deny that there's anything wrong with your child—especially if the disability is invisible. Hope, mother of a child with autism, says, "In our family, grandparents believe our son is a perfect child with no disability. It's a very hard situation to deal with." In the case of "invisible" disabilities, such as autism, ADHD, mental health disorders, or learning disabilities, some family members may deny that your child even has special needs, blaming you, instead, for not disciplining the child sufficiently. They may insist that if you simply set limits with your child, their behaviors would magically disappear. Or that your child would catch up with their peers if you weren't so "overprotective."

Family members may trivialize the disability or avoid the pain by saying your child will "grow out of it." If your own parents or siblings react this way, you may be enduring constant advice or criticism about your mothering skills. Gina has a son with muscular dystrophy. She says, "Because our son did not develop symptoms until the age of seven, I think it has been harder for my parents to accept it. I don't think that they 'get' the everyday challenges, and they think I should have more time on my hands."

In addition, the information they have about disabilities may be years out of date. Martha has a grandson with Down syndrome. In her generation, she says, there were no children with disabilities in the schools. Your parents may have low expectations for your child—or recommend institutionalization—especially if that was the norm in their day.

Some grandparents and extended family react to their grief and bewilderment by backing off and remaining aloof from your children. Meg, who has a child with muscular dystrophy, says: "My husband's family is not involved. They never call or write."

Keep in mind that, often, family members want to help, but have no idea what to even offer (see "Ask For What You Need," later in this chapter). If you're disappointed with your family's level of involvement, try the ideas in the following sections.

Communicate and Share Your Feelings

To increase family members' support and understanding, share accurate information and your feelings. Be ready to ask for specific things that you need.

Grandparents and extended family may feel they need to offer strength by hiding their emotions. Although they may appear removed or cold, they may be trying to protect you. Keep the door to genuine communication open by sharing your own sadness, fears, and joys. Quiet and secrecy can only intensify the grief families may be feeling.

Amy learned how important it is to be honest with her own parents. She says, "I didn't tell my parents we were testing Talia for disabilities because I didn't want to worry them. So I felt stressed and tense when they visited. When I finally broke the news of the test results my mother said, 'I knew all along that something was wrong with her. But I didn't tell you because I didn't want to worry you.'" Your family might also benefit from talking to a social worker, counselor, or clergy member.

Be upfront with your family if they are behaving in ways that are hurtful. Especially if they don't understand your child's disability, they may offer unhelpful advice. One grandmother, for example, criticized her granddaughter with autism for flapping her arms. She also criticized her daughter, Deb, for being too lenient with this behavior. After months of resentment, Deb explained that her daughter needed to flap as a harmless outlet for her stress and provided some reading materials about "stimming." The grandmother stopped commenting and visits became more relaxed.

If, despite your explanations, your family is critical to the point where you feel attacked, you may have to think about protecting yourself and your own nuclear family. See the section "When Things Don't Work Out" for strategies.

Increase Their Comfort Level—Involve and Educate

Especially when you're just starting to learn about your child's disability, you may have little time to also educate your family. But sharing information is crucial. One mother says that education helped her parents be more involved and less judgmental of her son's "nontypical behaviors." If your child has complex medical issues, family members may be genuinely frightened. One woman whose daughter has severe cerebral palsy showed her mother what to do if the child should choke or have a seizure. Now that the grandmother knows how to handle an emergency, she's comfortable spending time alone with her. We've also heard about grandparents who invite their grandchild with special needs for sleepovers every few weeks.

Sounds wonderful—but what if your family situation isn't as rosy? Perhaps your parents or siblings don't have the interest, skills, or ability to take your child for an overnight. With information, and with contact, your parents and family may feel more connected to your child, and more willing to be involved. Try these ideas:

Call or email family members frequently to update them about your child. A group email is helpful if you have a large extended family.

Recommend disability websites. This is especially useful for out-of-town family members.

Pass along useful books or articles, which can open the door to discussions about your child.

Provide disability association contact information. Family members can then contact the agency or association in their area. Some associations have family or grandparent support groups. Most have lending libraries with disability related books.

Invite them to disability seminars, conferences, and fundraisers. By attending these events together, you'll learn about your child's disability, meet other families, and possibly even have fun. One mother said she felt supported and accepted when her whole family walked together in a Down syndrome walkathon.

Invite them to your child's therapy sessions or doctor's appointments. Joseph, whose grandson has Down syndrome, carefully observed early intervention therapy sessions. Eventually he felt comfortable doing therapies on his own and enjoyed helping his infant grandson learn to sit and to crawl.

Demonstrate how to connect with your child. For example, show how to successfully communicate with your child who may use an eye-gaze communication system or symbol board. Suggest activities that your child enjoys and doesn't get frustrated with.

Bring a support worker to family gatherings. That way, if the visit gets overwhelming, the worker can take your child for a break or attend to his physical needs. When they visit Grandma's house, Jemma brings a support worker for her child (who needs total care). In this way, Jemma enjoys chatting and gardening with her mom, while her daughter is assisted.

Arrange adults-only outings. Try a dinner out with your parents/family members without your kids in tow. This way you can nurture your relationship without having to focus on your children. You can also update your family members about your child, without having to talk in front of him or her.

Ask for What You Need

Once you've established frequent communication and ways to enjoy time together, ask for what you need. When we're used to being independent and strong, it can be hard to ask for help. Sally, after trying to do everything herself, finally asked her parents to babysit her "typical" child, when she had to take her child with special needs to a long-awaited appointment with a specialist.

Sometimes family members may not know what kind of help they should offer. If that's the case, give them specific tasks. Try these suggestions:

Caregiving. Ask grandparents or family members if they can watch your son or daughter for a few hours, an overnight, or longer, so that you can have a break by yourself or with your partner. If your parents are elderly or uncomfortable with your child, start with a short (hour or two) visit. Bring along your child's favorite movie, music CDs, or games. If your child is staying with grandparents more than a few hours and you have the funds, hire a respite worker or personal care attendant to give your parents a break. Or ask a friend who also has a child with special needs to drop by to assist with your child.

Cash. If your parents are far away or are uncomfortable watching your child, they may be eager to help in other ways. If they ask what gift you'd like, ask for babysitting/respite money. Let them know that you enjoyed their cash gift, and make sure to tell them how you spent it—for a dinner out, perhaps, and a favorite caregiver for your child. Some grandparents might want to pay for their children's sleepover or day camp with a one-to-one assistant. In addition, they could help out by setting up or contributing funds to a special needs trust. If your child is an adult, parents can still contribute by helping finance your child's education, housing, or recreational activities.

Other kinds of help—the gift of time. If you're short on time, ask your parents or family members to make phone calls for you to inquire about services. If they live far away, ask them to do research on the Internet or at the library for a new therapy that may help your child. Armed with this knowledge, your family and parents may feel more a part of your child's team. Amy's dad and relatives show support by acting as a "clipping service." They regularly pass along articles about autism they've found in magazines and newspapers.

When Things Just Don't Work Out

Sometimes, despite all of your efforts to educate your family, to communicate openly, and to establish closeness, you still don't get the support you need.

If you feel that you and your child are being harshly criticized, you should frankly discuss your concerns with your family. But if it gets to the point that extended family contact feels especially distressing, you need to take control of the situation. Deal with family on your terms by specifying how and when you will make contact. For example, you may decide to skip stressful holiday visits and instead plan a brief family outing at another time. Serena, who has a child with Duchenne's muscular dystrophy and a developmental delay, says, "We choose not to visit some family members because of issues related to my son. But they are welcome to our house anytime."

Or you may decide to temporarily limit or cease contact with those family members causing emotional harm. If that is the case, keep the door to communication open, so that you can re-establish regular contact if and when you choose. Instead of visits, try brief emails, cards, or phone conversations.

Perhaps, over time, as they get to know your child as an individual, they may become more actively involved in your life. In the meantime, actively seek support from friends, other families, and from professionals who are in your life. See the chapters in Part II: Taking Care of Yourself for more ideas.

Experience Talks

"I cannot control my family's acceptance. I can only control my own."
—April, single mom of three children with Duchenne's
muscular dystrophy and ADHD

"I keep a chart up on my parents' refrigerator of all of the things that my son is working on in each area. This helps his aunts and cousins know what kinds of games to play with him."
—Trudy, mother of a child with Down syndrome

PART V

Overcoming Barriers to Quality Care

Childhood through Adulthood

*"I took my son with me to a daycare center that he would
have attended before and after school. I could see the looks on their
faces. I received a phone call a couple of days later stating they didn't
think they could accommodate him—although he has no
limitations or specific requirements."*

—Whitney, mom of a son (age eleven) with Down syndrome

Most mothers say finding appropriate child care is difficult. But if your child has special needs, the search for child care can be especially frustrating. Caregivers sometimes resist including children who require specialized medical equipment or procedures, behavior programs, building modifications, or adapted teaching strategies. And unlike most parents, many of us need to find care or meaningful activities for our sons and daughters even when they're adults.

When children have more severe challenges, parents face additional barriers. Julie Rosenzwieg and colleagues from Portland State University studied the caregiving arrangements of forty-one families of children with serious emotional and behavioral disorders. None of the children were being cared for in a daycare or after-school center—although a number of them had been expelled from one. Parents shared care with each other, relied on siblings (with parental support in emergencies), or hired in-home caregivers, resulting in increased care and training costs.

Even when you're lucky enough to secure a spot, it often comes with strings attached. Mothers we surveyed describe unreasonable expectations, such as paying extra for aides, training, or transportation. Often parents must miss work or school hours as they train caregivers and help their children adjust.

The fact is, many of these problems shouldn't occur—they're illegal. The Americans with Disabilities Act (ADA) prohibits child care centers (including family daycare) from turning away a child with disabilities unless the child poses "a direct threat to the health and safety of others" or requires a "fundamental alteration" in the center's programs. Child care centers are required to make "reasonable" modifications to integrate all kids. While a private program is not required to pay for one-to-one support for a child, it must accept an aide that the parent, government, or another organization provides. And, since each child must be assessed on an individual basis, a child may not be refused admission just because caregivers assume her needs will be too great.

Despite this progress, families still have difficulties finding care. What's "reasonable" is open to interpretation. When they are told a program is full, or their children are placed on waiting lists, parents sometimes suspect they are being excluded. Many parents are unaware of their rights. Others may not have the skills or stamina to fight back. As no comparable legislation exists in Canada, parents there are left with even less recourse.

Of course, it's not just parents who are stressed by child care hassles. Since child care providers aren't given money for training or to hire specialized professionals, they often aren't equipped to provide individualized attention to children with special needs. At the same time, many child care providers lack training on the ADA.

With such obstacles, it's not surprising that despite the ADA, the majority of mothers we surveyed rely primarily on family members for child care. A 2003 survey by the Minnesota Department of Children Families and Learning found that 34 percent of parents of kids with special needs said they had to "take whatever child care arrangement they could get," as compared to 20 percent of other parents.

As children grow, your need for care changes. Many parents struggle to find appropriate activities and care for after school and summer. Summer camps, respite programs, and leisure activities are important, but not always accessible.

Parents of adults worry about finding fulfilling work, volunteer opportunities, or day programs for their sons and daughters. When their children no longer attend school, many say they spend so many hours each week seeing to their adult children's needs that they're left with little time to work, pursue their own interests, or even maintain their own health.

But it doesn't have to be that way. By investigating all available options and networking, you can often secure an arrangement that works. In the following chapters, you'll learn how to determine your needs for care, where to find it, and how to pay for it. You'll also read about care options for older children and adults that offer enrichment and support for your whole family.

"The year my son started school I had five caregivers—two that I removed him from and two that expelled him. The fifth caregiver is an intelligent, experienced, educated caregiver and my son has remained with her for two years. However, it was the first time I explained clearly to an agency how difficult my child was, rather than gloss over it and hope for the best. I think I would have been more successful had I taken more time in finding care—I tended to take the first person I met who would accept him. Eventually I decided to state all the issues, and take my chances on it taking longer to find the appropriate person."

—Monique, who has a son with oppositional defiant disorder

Chapter 18

Figure Out What Type of Care You Need

Whether you need child care in order to work, volunteer, or take some well-deserved time off, finding someone to look after a child with special needs is not always an easy task. It may be tempting, as Monique (above) did initially, to hire the first caregiver who says yes, especially when your child has difficult behaviors. But, you'll have more success and stability if you plan your approach.

The first step is assessing your child care needs. Consider the following:

Your child's needs. List your child's needs and strengths. What enables her to thrive? Does she need structure? Are noisy environments a problem? Does she need specialized equipment, therapy, or a prescribed environment? Are there situations that upset her? Does she require special transportation?

Your family's needs. List your family's needs related to your child's care. Too often, parents choose a placement based solely on their child's disability. But for a situation to work for the long term, it needs to suit the whole family. While you might be thrilled to land a spot in a therapeutic nursery school, if it's located too far, the extra commute could increase everyone's stress. If you are employed, what hours do you and your partner need covered? What flexibility do you require for holidays and summer? If you are at home with your child all day, you also need caregiving relief. How much time do you need to re-energize? Does the rest of the family need time away? How will child care arrangements affect sibling activities?

Your supports. Can you rely on family and friends to help with child care? Are they available for backup or emergency care? Large daycare centers may only close for holidays. But nannies and in-home daycare providers can get sick, leaving you scrambling.

Finances. How much can you afford for child care? Factor in costs such as transportation, field trips, craft supplies, specialized equipment, extra personnel (e.g., special needs workers or personal care attendants), etc. With a child care center, you may also have to pay for holidays, or for days your child is sick and can't attend. With a nanny or other private caregiver, you'll probably have to pay for vacation and sick leave, holidays, plus Social Security taxes, and, possibly, health insurance. If you have a child who requires one-on-one care, will you need a second caregiver for your other children? What will it cost to train caregivers? As you work out your budget, keep in mind whether you can a) utilize a flexible spending account, or b) get some costs covered by government programs (see Chapters 9 and 22).

Your child care preferences and philosophy. Once you've considered the factors above, think about the care that appeals most to your own values. For example, you may want a home-like environment, a program offering religious education, a specialized therapeutic program, an inclusive setting, or individualized care in your home. Also decide what compromises you're willing to make. By keeping your goals in mind, you're less likely to make an unsuitable choice.

Sometimes, you may need to cobble together several different options to create a program that meets your needs. Amy had a lot to balance when looking for child care. "My daughter needed a structured program, contact with typical peers, and time at home with therapists. I needed child care so I could teach part-time. While I liked the program and structure of a daycare center, most wouldn't take my daughter part-time. (Full-time was impossible, since our disability agency would only fund a few hours a week for Talia's support worker at daycare.) A home caregiver would offer more flexibility, but wouldn't provide the structure and therapies my daughter required. I realized that I had to combine several part-time solutions. Through word-of-mouth, I found a daycare center with special needs experience that would take Talia part-time. I also arranged a part-time nursery school spot, and hired home workers to take my daughter out in the community. And I arranged my own schedule so I could drive Talia to the various programs as well as be home part-time for her therapy appointments. The drawbacks were that it took extensive research, planning, and interviewing to find these solutions and communicate with staff. And juggling it all required lots of time and energy."

Segregation vs. Inclusion

In your hunt for care, you may have to choose between a segregated setting (i.e., one that includes children with disabilities only) versus an inclusive one (one that has children with and without disabilities). In recent years, the trend has been towards including children with disabilities wherever possible. Legislation sometimes mandates it. For example, the Individuals with Disabilities Education Act (IDEA) dictates that all early intervention services for children with special needs (birth to three) must be delivered in the most natural setting possible; i.e., places where normally-developing children are found. Similarly, children eligible for special education at three years old must be served in the "least restrictive environment" appropriate for the child. This has resulted in more child care options for parents and more opportunities for children to be with their normally-developing peers.

There may be times, though, when a segregated program is the best or the only way to access specialized services, quality programming, or adequate supervision. Quality of the care should always be the most important factor, regardless of the setting. Choose your care based on what's right for your child and family. And frequently re-evaluate your choice to make sure it continues to offer the most advantages. Over time, your child may benefit from both segregated and inclusive child care and recreational programs.

The Pros and Cons of Your Various Care Options

Even if you don't have an outside job, you probably still need some kind of child care so that you can run errands, attend your own appointments, accomplish tasks, exercise, and enjoy some time to yourself. There are a variety of options for young children such as daycare centers, preschools, nannies, and respite care. In addition to making your time more manageable, these options also provide an opportunity for your child to learn and develop. If your child is older, she also needs opportunities to socialize, learn new skills, and work or volunteer. Recreational activities, volunteer placements, and work programs may meet this need. Each of these options has it own set of strengths and drawbacks.

Relatives As Caregivers

You may be fortunate enough to have parents, siblings, or other family members who will care for your child for a reduced rate, or even for free. Among the mothers we surveyed, grandparents were the most popular choice.

Over a quarter of all children under the age of thirteen are regularly cared for by relatives, according to the 2002 National Survey of American Families. Other studies suggest that parents of special needs parents may use family and relative care more than parents of typical children. The Minnesota Child Care Survey (2002) found 41 percent of parents with special needs children say it is "very important" to have a caregiver who is a relative or family member, as compared to 32 percent of parents with typical children. Many mothers told us they trusted *only* their families to provide quality care.

Availability: Full-time; part-time; occasional; overnight

Pros:
> Your child is cared for in a familiar setting by those who love and are intimately familiar with her (making it an easy adjustment for the child).
> Knowing your child is in loving care provides peace of mind for you.
> The caregivers are often available outside standard working hours (especially important if you travel for business; or work shifts, irregular hours, or long hours).
> Relatives are more accepting of spontaneous requests and shorter notice to run errands, or drop your child off unexpectedly.
> They are often willing to look after sick children (which means you miss less work).
> Generally, relatives provide care at a much lower cost than other options.
> Relatives are willing to look after older children after they "age-out" of child care centers.

Cons:
> Not all families have relatives close by.
> Relatives may not have the strength, stamina, confidence, or skills needed for special needs care.
> If the relative gets sick or goes on vacation, you require backup care.
> Relatives, especially grandparents, may not provide your child contact with other children.
> Older relatives may not be up-to-date on child development.
> If relatives undermine your authority, it may be difficult to deal with (you can't just fire them and be done with it).

What Moms Say: "When I leave them, I know that they are in an extremely loving and supportive environment."

CHILD CARE CENTERS

A child care center is designed to provide care to groups of children while parents are at work. Daycare centers are nearly as popular as relatives for the care of preschoolers and are the primary care arrangement for five-year-olds (1999 National Survey of America's Families). Some centers provide before- or after-school care; a few provide around-the-clock care for those who work shifts, or offer backup or sick-child care (for children who are mildly ill). A growing number are located in employee workplaces.

Availability: Usually full-time; sometimes part-time or occasional (rarely overnight)

Pros:
Centers offer the reliability of confirmed days and hours of operation.
They offer children consistency in routine.
As licensed programs, centers abide by minimum health, safety, and training standards set by the state or province.
Programming is geared to the development of the child.
Children have the chance to socialize with others.
Children can often access needed therapy or early intervention services.
Some centers cater specifically to special needs children (offering expertise and specialized services in a segregated setting).
Caregivers are likely to have formal training on special needs and child development.
Centers are more likely to make physical and structural accommodations for your child.

Cons:
Costs are prohibitive for some (especially for infant and toddler care).
Centers may be unsuitable for children who get sick often, especially ones with compromised immune systems.
Parents must keep children home when they're ill.

They are sometimes resistant to children with behavior or medical issues.

Quality centers often have long waiting lists.

Payment is required even when the child is absent due to appointments or illness.

Centers rarely include children over age twelve, and spots for infants are limited.

What Moms Say: "They were 100 percent reliable, always there, always on time, the financial portion was clearly spelled out, and my child was given the opportunity to model typical children's behavior. It helped give me an accurate point of reference also."

Family (or "Home") Child Care Providers

Family daycare providers look after your child in their own homes. While some offer enrichment and structured learning comparable to daycare centers, others offer little beyond basic adult supervision.

Availability: Full-time; part-time; occasional

Pros:
Home child care is usually more affordable than a center.

A familiar home-like setting suits some kids best.

Caregivers typically care for fewer children and a wider range of ages (meaning they might be able to accommodate siblings and older children).

When numbers are low, the caregiver can provide lots of one-on-one attention.

The child (and parent) can develop a stable relationship with a caregiver (as opposed to a daycare center, where your child may move to a different teacher every year or two).

Cons:
Caregivers often lack training on special needs.

Home child care is often unlicensed (meaning there's less enforcement of health and safety issues).

Experience, enthusiasm, and qualifications vary considerably.

Caregivers are less likely to have resources to make physical or structural accommodations for special needs.

Home child care is less likely to have a lot of playground equipment, computers, etc.

With mixed age groups, caregivers are less likely to be able to provide developmentally appropriate activities for all children at all times—they might plop kids in front of the TV/video a lot.

If the one and only caregiver is ill or has a sudden emergency, you may suddenly have to scramble to make other arrangements. You'll also need to make alternative arrangements when she goes on vacation.

There may be pets and other family members in the house while your children are cared for. If the caregiver's children are home sick from school, your children may be exposed.

What Moms Say: "I really like this option because I am able to develop a relationship with this person who is so very important in my son's development."

PROFESSIONAL HIRED CAREGIVERS IN YOUR HOME (NANNIES, AU PAIRS, ETC.)

Dual income parents with excellent wages may be able to afford a live-in or live-out nanny. It's expensive, but if you have two or more children under age three, it may actually be cheaper to hire a nanny than to use a child care center. If you can find and afford the right person, this may be a good fit for your child. In-home care may be the only option for working parents of children with complex medical needs or emotional and behavioral challenges.

For full-time care, nannies are a popular choice. In addition to child care, some nannies do housekeeping as well, which can take a load off a mom's shoulders. A *certified* nanny is trained in child development from a nanny school and views her job as a profession. The vast majority of nannies, however, are not certified, and may have no specialized training. To work legally in the U.S. or Canada, nannies from abroad must obtain the appropriate work permits.

Au pairs are young people (eighteen to twenty-six years old) from abroad who want to learn about a different culture. During their year-long program, au pairs live with a host family and provide up to forty-five hours per week of child care and light housekeeping. They also take part-time college courses. Only a few agencies are authorized (by the Dept. of State) to bring au pairs to the U.S. Some students may call themselves au pairs but are not part of this program. If you want an "approved" au pair, go through an agency on the Dept. of State's list (see Resources).

In Canada, there is no official au pair program. Caregivers from abroad may work under the Live-in Caregiver Program run jointly by Citizenship and Immigration Canada and Human Resources and Skills Development Canada. They may renew their position for a second year with the option of applying for permanent residence in the third year if certain conditions are met.

Availability: Full-time; part-time; occasional; sometimes overnight

Pros:

Convenience—Care in your home eliminates the hassles of the morning drop-off and evening pick-up.

Your home is already set up for your child, so adaptations and modifications to the physical environment aren't necessary.

Parents often feel more at ease about the health and safety of their children when they're cared for at home.

You have more control over the structure and routine of the day, providing consistency to a child who doesn't cope well with change. If your child receives medical or other specialized care, you have more control over its delivery.

Your child receives one-on-one attention.

An in-home provider can look after sick children.

Providers are more likely to be available for occasional overnight care. In-home nannies may provide child care support on family vacations.

The caregiver may be able to oversee therapies at home and/or drive your child to appointments.

An au pair or nanny from another country can help your family learn about another culture, and may be able to teach your child a second language.

Cons:

This is the most expensive option. In 2005, the average cost of an au pair was $13,000, plus room and board. A nanny can easily cost double that—and up. A certified nanny, or one trained in special needs, can be especially pricey.

Most nannies will require training for special needs. Au pairs aren't allowed to work with children with special needs unless they've had prior experience, nor can they provide care that would normally be done by a practical or registered nurse.

Qualifications vary tremendously.

Most in-home caregivers aren't regulated, although some states regulate nanny-placement agencies.

Special visas are required for overseas nannies or au pairs (may take months to complete the paperwork).

Tax obligations can be extensive; e.g., as an employer you are required to calculate and withhold tax, prepare returns quarterly and remit employer and employee taxes.

Expenses besides salary and taxes may include worker's compensation, car insurance, health insurance, vacation, overtime, paid sick days and agency fees.

Some parents feel a lack of privacy having a non-family member in the house.

You will need backup care should your caregiver become ill or go on vacation.

Your child may have less contact with other children.

You will need an extra bedroom for live-in help.

Less expensive nannies may demand to be paid cash "under the table," opening you to various legal risks.

Nannies may have language barriers (although regulations specify au pairs must be fluent in English (or one of English or French in Canada).

Many nanny and au pair applicants are young, and possibly immature.

Care may be temporary; e.g., au pairs are only available for a year, nannies on work visas may return home, etc.

What Moms Say: "An in-home caregiver has worked the best for me because my daughter is in her own surroundings.

Things are different enough for her with her disability. She feels more in control."

"An au pair was the most reliable and steady [option], and very needed before my son entered five-day-a-week preschool at age three. The au pair attended all therapy sessions in our Birth-to-Three program with me, and we took a child CPR class together."

"We have used professional (college educated) nannies from day one. We have had great results as we have found that young/fresh out of college and energetic young ladies are very interested and invested in our children."

PARENTAL CARE USING SHIFT WORK

In 2004, 8.2 percent of employees worked shifts for family and child care reasons, according to the U.S. Department of Labor. When you have children with special needs, it can be hard to trust your child's care to another. Working different shifts allows parents to provide the bulk of the caregiving themselves and also save on child care costs. Shift work is most manageable when employees are given flexibility and choice in their work hours (e.g., shifts can be changed or shortened). Weekend jobs work well for many mothers, especially when fathers work regular hours during the week.

Availability: Depends on both parents' work situation

Pros:
> It's inexpensive; in some cases, parents manage without any child care costs; others supplement with child care for a few hours per day or week.
> A parent is always with the child.
> Both parents can have more equal involvement with their child's care, appointments, and therapies.

Cons:
> Parents often experience little or no time together as a family.
> Working shifts can affect your sleeping patterns, which can be exhausting for parents already carrying a heavy

load. Said one mother, "I would be in a fog, putting my kids on the school bus, with only three hours sleep." There may be fewer opportunities for the child to interact with other children.

What Moms Say: "My son and my husband are incredibly close, which is wonderful to see, but we don't have much family time."

Preschools/Nursery Schools/Kindergartens

Preschools, nursery schools, and kindergartens provide school readiness programs for young children (typically three- to five-year-olds). Preschools and nursery schools may or may not be licensed. Sometimes they are run cooperatively (organized and run in full or part by parents). They run in settings such as schools, community centers, churches, YMCAs, etc. Some follow philosophies such as Waldorf and Montessori. Almost all school districts offer kindergarten programs within the elementary schools (as do some private schools). Some states and provinces offer government-funded pre-kindergarten programs for three- and/or four-year-olds through public schools or private programs. Most programs are geared to low income or at-risk students but some are open to all children.

Availability: Usually part-time, mornings or afternoons during the school year. (Some are full-day programs, daily or every other day.)

Pros:
Schools offer academic programs taught by early childhood educators or teachers.
Children get the chance to socialize with others.
Schools provide a part-time arrangement suited to parents who go to school, work part-time, or need a break.
Some may be specialized to provide care to children with disabilities, and related services may be covered by school districts under the child's Individualized Education Program (IEP).
Parents are typically encouraged to be involved (in co-ops participation is mandatory).

Government-funded kindergartens (and pre-kindergarten programs offered in some states and provinces)
are free.

Cons:
Preschools and nursery schools may not be licensed (kindergartens are regulated by school boards or districts).
These programs generally follow the school year, so
they're unavailable in summer (although many preschools offer affiliated day camp programs).
Young children who get sick frequently may not be
suited to attending schools.
Preschools and nursery schools may be resistant to children with behavior or medical issues.
Quality programs often have long waiting lists.
Parents must pay for absences due to appointments,
sickness.

What Moms Say: "When my daughter goes to a private
nursery school, the school district will pay for a one-on–one
[aide] if she needs it—or a SEIT (Special Education Itinerant
Teacher) to be with her part of the day."

After-School Programs

Some schools, YMCAs, Boys and Girls Clubs, child care centers,
etc., offer before- and/or after-school programs. Activities such as
sports, crafts, games, and homework tutoring are often provided. After-school programs held at other locations typically provide busing
to and from the school.

Availability: Before/after school; sometimes during
school breaks.

Pros:
Usually programs are in the school or transportation is
provided.
May be open full days when school's closed.
School-based centers are more likely to carry over
IEP goals.

Programs allow socialization opportunities in a non-academic setting.

Cons:

Programs rarely accept anyone over age twelve.

The staff may lack disability-related training.

If the program is relatively unstructured, it may not suit your child's needs.

School-based programs are often held in the cafeteria or gym, which results in too much sensory stimulation for some children.

For some kids with special needs, school is exhausting—so group care at the end of the day can be overwhelming.

What Moms Say: "My daughter attended after-school day-care for a couple of years through the school district. There was a lot of resistance on their part in the beginning... [but] in time, it worked out wonderfully! She attended the program during the summers also. It was to give me a break and for her to socialize with other children."

SPECIAL NEEDS/DISABILITY WORKERS

Special needs workers such as personal care attendants/aides, home care workers, and support or respite workers fill in child care gaps and help children with special needs gain independence. They might provide medical, therapeutic, life skills, recreational, or routine care. Some may provide light housekeeping duties. Those whose costs are covered by Medicaid must pass a competency test. Some workers may be certified through organizations such as the National Association for Home Care (NAHC) or, in Canada, the National Association of Certified Caregiver/Personal Support Workers (NACPSW). Some workers may have taken related college courses or degrees in early childhood education or social work.

Support workers can be hired privately, through community agencies, or through a home health agency or registry. While it's less expensive to hire someone on your own, an agency is better equipped to run background checks and screen applicants.

Availability: Usually part-time; occasional, sometimes overnight

Pros:

Very experienced aides may have a high level of expertise, since they see their jobs as "careers" as opposed to temporary "babysitting."

Workers often have access to additional training offered by a community agency.

They come to your home.

They enable your son or daughter to participate in community activities without having to be accompanied by a parent.

Some may be able to work with your child for several years. Often university students work with a child or adult part-time while they complete their education over a period of several years.

Some workers establish a friendship with your child and provide informal support to your family even when they no longer work for you.

You can often find excellent workers by word-of-mouth if you have a strong network of other families who have children with special needs.

Cons:

It's expensive, although fees are often subsidized through government programs.

Qualifications vary. Anyone can call themselves a special needs worker or aide.

You're letting a stranger care for your child, unsupervised. Background screening can be difficult, even for agencies, as criminal records are not centralized in the U.S.

If you use an agency, you may not get the same worker every time.

Turnover can be high. The best workers often are en route to higher level social service jobs. And because pay is low, aides will often switch agencies to get a small wage increase.

If your (privately employed) worker is sick or away, you're left with no child care.

What Moms Say: "I was able to find a developmental service worker at my daughter's school for respite at home. While she is not medically trained, she is very comfortable with my daughter and will play with her and take care of other needs. This allows us to be outside or in another room so she can call us if Darlene needs a suction, etc."

"A nurse comes at 8:00 a.m. and takes Clara to school on the bus. [She then] returns at 3:30 p.m. and stays until 5:00 p.m. We also have a nurse at night from 11:00 p.m. to 7:00 a.m., which allows us to sleep. We really have no choice, as Clara requires RN care. It can be hard dealing with different personalities that don't always mesh with your family's. Other cons are the costs, and the frustration of having to deal with agencies."

CASUAL BABYSITTERS, MOTHER'S HELPERS

High school and college students, neighbors, retirees, and others who may be between jobs or looking for a little extra income may provide care or companionship. "Mother's helpers" care for your child or help you around the house while you're at home.

Availability: Usually part-time; occasional

Pros:
Babysitters, especially high school students, are typically easy to find (unless you live in a rural or isolated area).
They come to your home.
Babysitters may help your child build long-term supportive relationships with neighbors and other community members.
Seniors who take a special interest in your child could become "surrogate grandparents."
University or college students working in related fields often view their work with your child enthusiastically.

Cons:
Applicants may be young and immature.

Casual babysitters are unlikely to have any special needs experience and may not be an option for parents of children who need specialized care or have behavior problems.

Turnover is high as students and others move on in their lives.

What Moms Say: "I once had a group of female babysitters who were roommates and studying child development/psychology/education/etc. at the local university. They were great because they really paid attention to Megan. When they all graduated, I lost a valuable resource that I could never replace."

EARLY INTERVENTION PROGRAMS

Early intervention programs are federally mandated programs for infants and toddlers who are developmentally delayed or at risk of delay. If your child qualifies, these programs provide services such as speech and language therapy, assistive technology, occupational therapy, physical therapy, psychological services, nursing, etc., inside or outside the home (in a child care center, nursery school, playgroup, specialized center, etc.). For more information on early intervention programs, see Chapter 9.

Availability: Usually part-time

Pros:
Personnel have specialized training.

Therapies are delivered where most appropriate (e.g., at home or a daycare center).

Transportation to a center may be provided or reimbursed.

Fees are based on family size and income (typically free for low-income families and priced on a sliding-scale basis for others).

The setting and programming is geared to the needs of the family and child (including one-to-one workers, if required).

Parents have access to specialized support and referrals. Says one mom "our Early Intervention Coordinator recommended the 'Mother's Morning Out' program, as well as our physical therapist."

Cons:
>   Availability may be restricted to certain locations, days,
>   or hours during the day.
>   Not all children qualify.
>   Some programs (especially in-home ones) require par-
>   ents to be in attendance.

What Moms Say: "Currently my daughter attends a center-based program for children with Down syndrome and all
services are covered by Early Intervention."

HEAD START PROGRAMS

Head Start and Early Head Start are federally funded programs
that provide education, health, nutrition, and social services to low
income families. The goal is to increase the school readiness of children (birth to age five) in low-income families. Some jurisdictions have
policies of accepting children with special needs from higher income
families if spots are not filled. In Canada, the Public Agency of Health
runs a similar Head Start program just for aboriginal children. See
Resources for contact information.

>   **Availability:** Part-time during the school year (at least
>   three-and-a-half hours, four to five days a week).

Pros:
>   The program is free.
>   Head Start has many of the same advantages as child
>   care centers (e.g., reliability, training, etc.).
>   Ten percent of program spots are set aside for children
>   with special needs from low income families.
>   Head Start provides parents access to specialized ser-
>   vices and referrals.
>   Parental involvement in the program is highly encour-
>   aged.

Cons:
>   Head Start is usually available only to lower income
>   parents.

If you work full-time, you may need to arrange transportation or find other child care arrangements (although some offer transportation or full-day programs).

What Moms Say: "The Head Start teachers didn't have any preconceived notions about Down syndrome—they worked with him as they did with any other child. They listened to what I had to say."

Recreational Programs, Clubs, etc.

Recreational programs (through local parks & recreation departments, YMCAs, Boys and Girls Clubs, sports groups, Special Olympics, after-school clubs, etc.) often offer activities that kids, teens, and adults can participate in without parents. Programs can range from one-hour weekly art classes to all-day workshops or teen nights out. While participants learn new skills (or improve on old ones) and make new friends, at-home moms get a little down time and working moms get a secondary source of child care.

Availability: Part-time; occasional

Pros:
Facilities often hire paid assistants or volunteers to support those with special needs.
Organizations may have specialized programs for children and adults with disabilities.
Recreational facilities are more likely to have programs for youth and adults.
Sports or exercise programs, with appropriate adaptations, can improve participant's health—both physical and emotional.
Participants get to interact with others in the community.
Participants learn new skills, meet others with mutual interests, and gain some independence from parents.

Cons:
Programs are often of short duration, requiring the child or adult to meet and get used to new people.

An individual's experience is highly dependent on the personnel running the program, who may have little or no training in special needs.

It can take a lot of work to advocate for your son or daughter to attend the program, to train the staff, and to adapt the activities.

Your son or daughter may not have the abilities, attention span, or interest to attend a particular program.

What Moms Say: "The YMCA is the best thing that has happened in our life. They are willing to provide a one-on-one without charging any more than for other children. My child is with his peers and experiences many new things. They take him swimming, bowling, and on many other life enriching outings."

DAY AND OVERNIGHT CAMPS

When school's out during the summer and school vacations, many parents rely heavily on camps. Some offer a variety of outdoor, sports, and arts activities. Others specialize in offering expert instruction in computer instruction, wilderness camping, religious instruction, etc. Some camps make a point of including children of all abilities. Some even employ inclusion coordinators to help children with special needs attend successfully. Other camps are designed especially for children with physical, developmental, or medical special needs. There are even camps that offer vacation programs designed for adults with special needs.

Availability: Full-time (during the summer or during school breaks); part-time; overnight

Pros:
Day camps have similar advantages to recreational programs.

Overnight camps foster independence.

There is increasingly more choice in overnight camps that cater to special needs or integrate children with special needs into their programs.

Many special needs camps offer scholarships.

Camp programs for children with specific disabilities often hire college or graduate students (or even teachers on summer break) to provide specialized care.

Cons:

Counselors may be young and relatively inexperienced in special needs.

The success of a camp program may be highly dependent on individual counselors (who often turn over from one summer to the next).

Costs may be higher if your child requires one-on-one support at a privately run camp. Parents may have to pay support worker costs in addition to camp fees.

What Moms Say: "The day camp has an inclusion program for children with special needs. Hooray! Our son participates in all of the camp activities with the other children in his group, but he has a counselor assigned to keep an eye on him and to send home a report every day. Cons: It is expensive (but worth it)."

"Ten days of sleepover camp was a huge confidence builder for my twelve-year-old (with autism). She tried activities for the first time such as water-skiing, kayaking, and climbing a high ropes course."

EXTENDED SCHOOL YEAR (ESY) PROGRAMS

Children with special needs who would significantly regress without year-round schooling are entitled to attend special summer school programs under the IDEA. There is no extended school year requirement in Canada, although some larger districts provide programs.

Your child's IEP team (including you, as the parent) determines whether your child qualifies for ESY. Be an active member of the team. See Chapter 9 for more information on IEPs.

Availability: Part-time

Pros:

ESY is mandated in the U.S., so it should be available to any child who meets the criteria.

It can provide the stimulation and structure that your child needs to learn.

Cons:
Programs vary greatly, and can be as short as one hour per day.
Children with a variety of disabilities may be grouped together, so that it can be difficult to meet individual needs.

What Moms Say: "During this summer my daughter was in the extended school year summer program four days/week. It has allowed me to dedicate all of my time to my business and give me a little downtime in between."

RESPITE FACILITIES AND PROGRAMS

Mothers may use formal respite programs to get a break, run errands, spend time with other family members, or do paid work. See Chapter 9 for more information on respite care.

Availability: Part-time; occasional; overnight; weekend; sometimes one or more weeks

Pros:
Programs are geared to disabilities, so they're more likely to have needed medical equipment and expertise.
The program hours are likely geared to the family's needs.
Overnight care gives your teen or adult a chance to test the experience of living outside the family home.
Extended care allows parents to go on a vacation with other family members or attend to a family emergency.
Some programs provide a fun, safe, and positive "sleepover party" experience for children to enjoy.
Respite may be low cost if the program is government sponsored.
Care may be free if your child participates in an "Extend a Family" type program (where the child spends time or an overnight with a volunteer family).

Cons:

>   Some options are expensive—though costs may be covered through government vouchers, paid on a sliding scale, or covered at least partially by insurance.
>   There may be a shortage of highly trained workers or facilities for those with severe needs.
>   Programs in your area may be limited to a few disabilities or there may be long waiting lists.
>   Turnover may be high, meaning you must frequently train new staff and your child must adjust to new people.

What Moms Say: "We used respite care in a hospital setting. It allowed us to 'get a breather.' They also took care of my daughter while I attended a funeral out of state."

ADULT DAYTIME PROGRAMS

Programs geared to adults with disabilities may include recreation, work, volunteer experiences, and therapies. Some work programs may include training or job coaching in an agency office, along with practical work experience. Others may offer work in sheltered workshops geared to those with specific disabilities. In "person-centered" programs, adults (with the support of families or paid staff) create schedules that fit their own interests and strengths. During the week, they enjoy a variety of paid work, exercise, community outings, etc. (See Chapter 12 for details.)

Availability: Full-time; part-time

Pros:

>   Community programs offer individuals the opportunity to meet and socialize with others in the community.
>   Programs offer participants consistency in routine.
>   Most offer the reliability of confirmed days and hours of operation.
>   Work programs offer some adults financial independence and skills that may lead to regular employment.
>   Counselors typically have experience in special needs.

Cons:

>   Programs may have limited hours.

Supported employment is often temporary.
Transportation is often the responsibility of the adult
with the disability and may fall to the parent.
Some programs may offer little more than basic skills,
instead of opportunities to grow and develop.
Sheltered workplaces may limit your child's involve-
ment in the non-disabled community.
Programs for adults may be limited to one or two options.

What Moms Say: "Because my daughter is in a group
home, she has a work placement to keep her busy during the
day. There is not enough paid work for her at her work place,
but she is happy there. "

By now you'll likely have several options to investigate. The next
step is to find out what's available in your community. With the strategies in the following chapter, you'll be well equipped to find quality
care for your child.

Experience Talks

*"We had a nanny until [our twins] turned four years old. She was
warm and loving, and the kids adored her. Once the children turned
three and went to preschool for a half day, it was difficult to pay for
both the nanny and the school. In addition, our nanny needed a full-
time income, but did not want to do housework or run errands when
the children were in school. Therefore, when they turned four, we
found our nanny a new family and expanded to a full day at their
preschool. We were worried that the children would not like it, but it
was an excellent preschool, so they loved it.*

*"Once they started elementary school, we enrolled them in
a reputable after-school program. Their policy was to provide a
quiet place for homework, but they did not help the children with
homework. My son needed help with homework, so I changed my
work schedule so that I could be there after school."*

—Suki, responding to changing needs of eight-year-old twins,
one with Tourette syndrome, ADHD, and learning disabilities.

"Right now, some of the moms and local therapists are trying
to organize a group/organization that would help provide incentives,
training, and additional funding for daycare providers to
service children with special needs."

—Betty, who has a preschooler with Down syndrome

Chapter 19

When Regular Care
Options Don't Work—
Custom Care Ideas

If child care options in your community don't work for you, you
can advocate for needed changes as Betty is doing (above). But
sometimes, even with modifications, existing programs don't fit for
your family. Perhaps your child requires nursing attention that can't
be provided in the local child care. Maybe your work schedule is erratic and you can't find anyone who can cover your hours. Or, there
may be no suitable teen or young adult programs in your area.

If that's your situation, join with other parents to pursue some unconventional solutions. To find like-minded families, use your contacts, approach schools and agencies, advertise in community papers, etc.

Here are some examples:

Shared Care. When two to four families share, a nanny or live-in caregiver may be affordable. There are other advantages. Your homes will be physically adapted for your children, and you can pool skills and training materials. Since the caregiver remains constant, children may adjust successfully to a rotation schedule—if not, you can use one home as the center. The challenge is finding interested parents that live nearby. Ask families with and without special needs children to join your group. For more information, ask your child care resource center. Or order the booklet *Parent-Created Child Care—Shares* from BANANAS, Inc., the resource and referral center for California's Northern Alameda County (see Resources).

Co-op Care. If you have a flexible schedule, contact other parents who work at home, or have part-time jobs or flex hours. Together, take turns providing child care yourselves. This trading off might work well for before- or after-school care, for emergency situations, or for planned nights out for parents.

Custom-Tailored Programs. A group can hire and train students from a local college or university to coordinate an after-school or summer program for children or teens with special needs. For additional staffing, hire high school students or siblings to assist. Depending on the ages and needs, activities could take place at several sites or be concentrated in one location. Because there are several families involved, there is more expertise to draw from. Also, contact senior and volunteer centers for instructors who might offer their time. They could enrich the program by teaching skills such as music, crafts, or cooking. Contact your disability association to see if they can help with marketing, accessing grants, providing space, or administering and eventually taking over the program. Parks and recreation departments, YMCAs, and Boys and Girls Clubs are often willing partners in these ventures. They may also provide information about licensing requirements and activity/lesson plans that you can adapt for your children.

The Teenage Dilemma

"Now that my daughter is older, she's too old to be allowed to attend any of the child care programs," says Bridget, whose twelve-year-old has cerebral palsy. But her daughter "still needs child care support, as she is not mentally able to stay alone."

Unfortunately, after-school and summer programs for teens with disabilities are rare. Even where programs do exist, adults must drive them there—making them unsuitable for working parents. Teens with milder disabilities may be reluctant to participate in "special needs" programs, yet be unable to participate in age appropriate after-school activities.

But before giving up on organized care, check with the local child care resource center, local special needs agencies, your disability association, and your school district. If such care exists, it is likely run by a special needs agency, a service group such as Easter Seals or the Rotary Club, a disability organization, or by the local parks and recreation department.

After-School Care

Here are a few ideas you might consider for teens needing after-school care or activities to keep them busy:

Local High School Students. If your teen has relatively low needs, you could look into hiring peer "buddies" for after-school or summer activities. Some moms contact teens through their school principal or directly. (Some teens may already have friendships with mature peers that can extend into after-school or summer hours.) In some cases, students who work with your child may apply their hours to extra credit or volunteer requirements at their school. Several moms told us that students who have siblings with disabilities make particularly good sitters.

Formal Match-Up Programs. Ask your school if they know of any formal programs such as "Best Buddies" which match up high school/college students with youth and adults with developmental disabilities.

Model Programs

Still haven't found the right match? You may need to advocate for services in your community—or build them yourself. To get you started, here are a few model programs you may want to check out (see Resources for contact information).

The Arc of Montgomery County's "After All" program for pre-teens and teens provides after-school care in an integrated setting at a Boys and Girls Club in Silver Spring, Maryland.

Easter Seals runs recreational after-school programs for children with disabilities throughout Orange County, California.

A partnership between the Pangea Foundation (a not-for-profit technology organization) and the community agency Kids Include Together provides after-school computer classes for teens with disabilities in San Diego, California.

SUMMER PROGRAMS

Like after-school programs, summer programs for teens can also be difficult to find. While most summer programs end at age twelve, more camps are extending their camper age to fourteen, especially specialty camps that focus on golf, art, computer science, math, etc. Search online, and check out programs run by local museums and colleges.

If these types of camps don't work for your teen, try the following ideas that other moms have used successfully.

Have your child attend summer day/overnight camp as an older camper. If your child's favorite summer camp is only for children up to age twelve, it may still be developmentally appropriate for him. We know of several young teens (ages thirteen to fifteen) who continue to attend summer camps and are grouped with the oldest campers (usually twelve-year-olds).

Enroll your teen as a Counselor In Training (C.I.T.). Many camps have programs that train younger teens to be future counselors. Supported by a counselor, volunteer, or peer buddy, your teen may be successfully included in the leadership program. Some cities have C.I.T. programs specifically for teens with special needs.

Enroll your teen in a summer program for youths with special needs. If your teen is not interested in working or volunteering with younger children, he may enjoy an activity program instead. Many agencies, or parks and recreation departments have summer youth programs with age appropriate activities such as hiking, music, crafts, and community outings. Often volunteers provide additional one-to-one support.

Post a job ad for a high school or college student with an interest in working with a teen with special needs. Try your local youth employment center, college, high school, community bulletin board, or Church/synagogue/temple. This hired buddy can keep your teen busy by taking him to the pool, movies, lunch, etc.

Parents and agencies can work together to create some innovative options. Approach an organization such as the Boys and Girls club, Parks and Recreation, or Easter Seals who may be willing to design or adapt a program with your help. Or band together with other families and create a custom-tailored program.

. . . And Into Adulthood

"I have less time now, because finding someone to watch my older daughter is very difficult," Beverley, mother of a nineteen-year-old with Rett syndrome, told us. "When she was young we could still get a babysitter. I rarely have time to go out with friends, since it also involves working out a way for someone to be with my daughter."

When sons or daughters still require constant care or supervision, the years following high school can be taxing. The shortage of suit-able housing and day programs leaves some mothers housebound. Working moms who used to rely on school as child care may find it especially difficult.

While some day and recreational programs for adults exist, be prepared to advocate for care beyond the school years. Parents of adults may rely much more on special needs workers (personal care attendants, aides, etc.) to fill in caregiving gaps, as well as provide life skills training, recreation, and routine care.

For summer activities and vacations for your son or daughter, contact your Independent Living Center and other agencies for disabilities. Often there are summer camp, lodge, or cottage programs geared towards adults. Ask local agencies about community programs that pair volunteers and individuals with special needs.

See Chapter 12 for tips on preparing for and managing adulthood.

Experience Talks

"Check out summer youth centers often run through Parks and Rec. My daughter went for the last two summers. The program ran late afternoons and evenings. She liked the fact she didn't have to get out of bed early and that she could control if or when she wanted to attend. I liked the fact that she was with other kids. The counselors were great—usually it was a small group of kids, so they got to know her really well."

—Gertie, mother of a teen with social anxiety disorder

"I have had a hard time finding a place for my daughter. It's not easy finding child care for a child with special needs. We are still looking."

—Juanita, mom of a six-year-old with Down syndrome

Chapter 20

The Hunt for Care

If you have other older children, you may have plenty of experience in searching for child care. In fact, you may already know caregivers who might be perfect for your child. Emily, for example, started her search at the center where her older child had attended. She says, "We were afraid the center might not accept our daughter, but they said 'of course' they would take care of her. They have always been supportive of our needs and we have been able to work out compromises."

If you have willing and reliable relatives, neighbors, or close friends available, your search is simplified. The first caregiver for Heather's daughter was her next door neighbor, who she already knew and trusted. Arranging care was as easy as calling over the fence. Unfortunately, it's usually not that simple—especially when children require more specialized care. But it is doable.

Get the Word Out

In our own experience, the most effective method of finding child care is networking. Ask relatives, friends, neighbors, and especially other parents to recommend child care centers or caregivers.

Other parents are your best referral source, especially those who have kids with special needs. When Amy needed child care for her pre-schooler, she asked two friends who have children with autism. Both used part-time care at the same daycare center—so clearly that center welcomed children with special needs. When Talia started the program part-time, the child care staff already had special training in autism. They were used to implementing programs suggested by visiting therapists.

If you don't know other parents of children with special needs, join a support group in your area. Most disability and social service agencies can tell you about local groups and who to contact. Also, for quick help, post your request for advice on online support groups. For more information on support groups and how to find them, see Chapter 3.

The professionals you deal with such as your child's physician, therapists, and teachers may be especially good sources, since they know your child well. Early intervention staff and support workers are well aware of local resources.

If you have a college or university nearby, contact the professors who teach related subjects. For example, Amy often phones a professor who teaches a course in autism, who informs her class of an opportunity to work with a child who has autism. This announcement often results in a few excellent child care candidates. One student (now a social worker) provided part-time child care for Amy's daughter for more than six years.

Consider placing an ad in your local community paper or advertising bulletin. That way, you can describe exactly the help you're searching for. Always mention that your child has special needs—and if space allows it, the severity or type. Most papers provide you with a post box number so you can maintain your confidentiality. Moms who have tried this method say they are deluged with applicants (many unqualified). They warn it can be time consuming and frustrating. To save time, request a resume to be mailed or emailed to you so you can screen people to be interviewed.

Other referral sources include:

Local schools or school districts. Some provide a list of caregivers available for students with disabilities.

Local churches, synagogues, or temples. Many operate daycare centers, nursery schools, or parents' "morning out" programs. Ask if you can post an ad on the bulletin board.

Community newspapers and bulletin boards in community centers and local stores. Also try bulletin boards at nearby colleges or universities—especially in relevant departments such as psychology, social work, education, etc. Post your ad for a caregiver, and also check for ads posted by centers or caregivers.

Online groups. University students, recent graduates, and established special needs workers often post that they are looking for work.

The telephone book. Most daycare centers and nanny placement agencies are listed in the yellow pages of your phone book under "Child Care" or "Nannies."

The Internet. Search for your community name, "special needs" and "child care" to uncover further options. Many nanny agencies and some child care centers also have websites.

Employer child care referral services. Some larger companies provide information about child care options, cost, availability, and qualifications of local care providers. While some companies offer this service internally, others contract it out.

Nanny or child care referral services. These businesses match your requirements to a caregiver for a fee. Before paying, ask for references, and try to speak to a family who has a child with disabilities and has used their services. Find out what their policy is if a referral doesn't work out. (Do you get your money back? Or a replacement nanny for no additional fee?) Check the company out with the Better Business Bureau (or equivalent) before parting with any money.

Help from the Not-For-Profits

In addition to mining community connections, contact local child care resource centers for advice. Often referred to as Child Care Resource & Referral (CCR&R) centers, these organizations can refer you to local child care providers and integration support services and provide information on state licensing requirements and subsidies. They also help build quality child care by helping caregivers to meet licensing requirements, and by providing low cost or free training on child development, safety, etc. To find the nearest center, contact Child Care Aware (see Resources).

Child care in Canada is handled provincially. Provincially-funded programs include British Columbia's child care resource and referral program and Ontario's Early Years Centres (up to age six).

Services are free or low cost. Since a referral is no guarantee of quality, it's up to you to check out each program carefully. (See the section "Making Sure It's Quality Care," later in this chapter.)

In some child care resource and referral agencies, there are perks for parents with children with disabilities. In Maryland, for example, parents can use a free service called "LOCATE: Child Care Special Needs Enhanced Counseling Service." Counselors trained in the special needs field help you explore child care options. They explain how the Americans with Disabilities Act (ADA) affects your choices, and inform you about tax credits, subsidies, and agencies to contact for respite and parent support. They even call child care sites for you. Even if your local resource center lacks these specialized services, all will have counselors to point you in the right direction.

Your local public health unit may also be helpful. Many offer parenting programs that focus on child health issues. They may be able to refer you to appropriate child care facilities.

Through networking, advertising, and researching, you'll likely find some excellent options. Give yourself plenty of lead time, as the search also requires visiting and interviewing. Also, many centers have waiting lists or may take a long time to assess your child's application. In the case of au pairs, it may take three months or more to process the paperwork.

Making Sure It's Quality Care

Once you've located some possible providers, how do you decide what constitutes quality care for *your* child? Some parents look for caregivers with specific skills. Susan, who works part-time, says "I won't leave my daughter with people who can't use sign language with her. She should be able to express herself, be understood, and understand what others are communicating."

Others describe quality care in a more general way. Says one mom, "My first concern was that the person caring for my son would treat him well and give him the extra time and attention he needs."

Quality, in general, means a trained caregiver providing care that is appropriate to a child's physical, developmental, and emotional state in a safe and healthy environment. It's not about where the care is given, but about how it is carried out. What we all hope to find, ideally, is someone who will love our kids and want the best for them. When our children require specialized therapies, medical procedures, or teaching, we want child care to accommodate those services.

There are many resources to guide you in your decision. Take advantage of free publications from the organization Child Care Aware to help you find, evaluate, and pay for child care. Their publication, "Choosing Quality Child Care for a Child with Special Needs," includes information on where to look, what questions to ask caregivers, and a checklist for determining quality care. They also have general pamphlets on infant and toddler care, after-school, summer camps, and safety and health guidelines. (See Resources.)

Contact your local child care resource center for more advice and information.

IS THE CHILD CARE CENTER REGULATED, LICENSED, OR ACCREDITED?

Don't assume that regulated or licensed care automatically is high quality. While, it's true that regulated care is more likely to result in quality care—it is no guarantee. Most regulations ensure only basic health and safety standards, and enforcement of these standards may be almost non-existent.

Some states and provinces have specific licensing provisions for care of children with special needs. For example, in Arizona, licensed family care providers must write a service plan for each child, provide diapering in privacy for children older than three, attempt to integrate children into activities, and have the physical ability and training to care for a child with special needs. In Ontario, licensed family care providers can care for up to five children ages twelve and under—but no more than two can have special needs (fewer, if toddlers are also in their care).

Check state/provincial and local regulations for the type of care you are considering by asking at your local child care resource and referral center (for adult care, contact local departments of health or social services). It varies in each state whether various care programs are licensed or not. Most states don't license in-home caregivers, and not all license adult day programs. Some states license nanny placement agencies. And part-day programs like nursery schools and after-school programs may not be licensed at all.

The regulations governing family daycare are the least stringent. Some states provide "registration" or "certification" which does not require any outside inspections. Instead, the caregiver reads the provisions and signs off on them. Most family daycare centers are unlicensed. Those that are licensed may only be inspected every year or two. For these reasons, use checklists to thoroughly evaluate a family daycare.

If caregivers are licensed, you can contact your county licensing office to see if any complaints have been lodged against them.

Ask whether your potential caregiver is accredited by national child care organizations such as The National Association for Family Child Care (NAFCC) or the National Association for the Education of Young Children (NAEYC). Accreditation by one of these groups requires that the provider meet standards well beyond licensing requirements. Canadian caregivers are unlikely to be accredited—there is no national accreditation program in Canada. (Only Alberta has an accreditation program for centers and family care providers—Alberta Child Care Accreditation Program (ACCAP.)

If you are hiring a nanny, ask if she (or her agency) is a member of a professional association such as The International Nanny Association (INA). Some organizations, such as the INA, offer certification after a required number of hours of self-study and a written exam.

Although none of these accreditation organizations have standards specific to special needs care, their underlying principles include accommodating every child's unique needs. You can also use the online search tools provided by these organizations to see whether there are members in your area.

Of course, lack of accreditation or an association membership need not rule out a candidate, but it could be the deciding factor in the choice among several candidates. At the minimum, professional affiliation shows a caregiver is willing to learn and to conduct herself professionally. You might ask a candidate whether she'd consider joining an association or, if you can afford to, offer to pay a share of her membership fees.

Checking licensing and accreditation is important, but the most useful information comes from an interview and site visit.

CHECK OUT EACH PROGRAM OR CAREGIVER

After your networking and research, you'll likely have several options to pursue. Call each program or caregiver and set up an appointment to visit for at least one hour—preferably during activities (as opposed to nap time).

What to Look for at the Site

Whether you're considering a daycare center, nursery school, family daycare, recreational program, after-school program, adult day program, or a neighbor's house, note the following during your visit:

Is the setting clean and bright?

Are there separate areas for active play, quiet play, meals, and naptime?

Do they have books, posters, toys, games, activities, etc., that reflect diversity in religion, culture, families, and abilities?

Do the children or adults in care seem happy and involved?

Does the caregiver(s) look calm and appear to have everything under control?

Does the caregiver(s) have a rapport with the children? Does she get down to their eye level and seem fully engaged and happy to be with them? If caring for adults, does she speak respectfully to ones in her care?

Is the space open and free of hazards? Those using wheelchairs or walkers or who have coordination difficulties should be able to move comfortably and safely.

Is the center or home secure? Does it have a fenced in yard? Durable outdoor equipment?

For a more detailed checklist, see Appendix 4. Adapt the checklist to your needs or combine it with one from Child Care Aware. Be sure to fill it in soon after each visit, while your memory of the program is still fresh.

Some programs, such as summer camps or day programs that aren't currently in session, may be impossible to visit. Try to at least have a telephone discussion and a meeting with the director (with your child present) before the program starts. Visit their website and get references from other parents.

After your visit, you should have a gut feeling for the suitability of the center or program. Most importantly, you need to feel comfortable with the staff or individual caregiver.

What to Look for in the Caregiver(s)

During your initial phone call, visit, or follow-up interview with the caregiver, you will get clues about the suitability of the match. Make sure you take all the time you need. For instance, after your visit with a home-based program, set up an interview time in the evening (without children) if all your questions haven't been answered.

To judge their experience with children with special needs, ask these questions of the center director or caregiver:

> What training does the caregiver or staff have in child development? In special needs? Ask about specifics such as early childhood education, nanny certification, special needs certificates or courses, CPR, and first aid (for teenagers, insist on a babysitting program). Do they have practical experience; i.e., have they cared for children or adults with similar needs now or in the past?
> If a center, does it provide ongoing training in child development and special needs? If a family or in-home caregiver, will he take a course or do further reading if required? For example, many nannies have extensive on the job experience, but little formal training. In that case, ask if she'd agree to enroll in child care, development, or safety-related courses or workshops. Inquire about courses at your local child care and referral center or community college.

To learn about a candidate's knowledge and attitudes, present some scenarios that could occur with your child, and ask how the caregiver would deal with them. (You can adapt questions from the Sample Caregiver Interview Questionnaire in Appendix 5.)

During the interview, ask yourself:

> Do the personnel seem interested in your child's strengths, abilities, and interests—not just her disability?
> Do they seem enthusiastic about caring for your child? Or do they speak negatively of other children or families who have been in their care? Are they receptive to requested changes, such as providing space for specialists, changing the room layout, or installing safety catches?

At some point, introduce the child care staff or the caregiver to your child. Watch how they interact. Is the potential nanny warm and engaging? Does the daycare teacher pick up on your child's temperament, for example, speaking softly and reassuringly to a shy child? How does your child react? If they hit it off, that's reassuring. But if there's not an immediate bond, that doesn't necessarily spell disaster, if your child is tired or slow to warm up with strangers. If you are unsure of "fit," you might want to schedule a second visit. But if your gut says "no way," it's probably best to drop that candidate.

Making the Final Decision

Check at least three references—even if you love the person immediately. Some caregivers present well in the interview, but are less successful on the job. On the other hand, some more introverted candidates don't interview well, but do excellent work with children. So, calling references is essential. Ask questions such as: How does she react in a stressful or emergency situation? Can you give an example of a situation he handled well (and not so well?) How reliable is she? Some previous employers are hesitant to say anything negative about a person. So, if they've only said positives, say something like: "She sounds wonderful, but of course no one is perfect—if there is one area in which she could improve a little, what would it be?"

Even if you've given a caregiver or center a high score on your checklist, you still may feel hesitant. Feeling apprehensive is normal—

especially if this will be the first time you've left your child in someone else's care. Our kids are especially vulnerable.

Thankfully, there are strategies to monitor your kids in care. Many mothers and fathers drop by unannounced to see how their child's day is going. Alternatively, ask a trusted support worker or family member to drop by to check on your child. (Warn your caregiver that you may do this at some time, or the caregiver may not allow the person access to your child—as she shouldn't.) If therapists or early intervention specialists visit your child during the day, ask them for feedback on what they observe with the caregiver, as well.

Finding Backup Care

Even with reliable care, you'll need an alternative when your child or caregiver is sick. Parents of children with disabilities often require more backup care. Some children are medically fragile and prone to illness. Children with Down syndrome, spina bifida, muscular dystrophy, and other conditions may undergo surgeries and medical procedures with lengthy recovery times. Some parents require emergency care for when their children with behavioral challenges act out at child care or school.

To cover these situations, many parents stay home, using sick time or vacation days, or making up the time later. Research shows that mothers usually cover emergency backup care. According to a 2001 survey by the Kaiser Family Foundation, 50 percent of mothers say they don't work when their child is ill, versus 30 percent of fathers.

To lessen work disruptions, investigate all options before you need them. Some employers make arrangements for backup care with in-home caregivers or daycare centers—and share a portion of the cost. If you live in a larger city, you're more likely to have access to short-term care facilities. You'll be required to pre-register before using an employer's program, so take that opportunity to interview staff and visit the center just as you would for your regular care provider.

Additionally, there are more than 300 "sick care" facilities in the U.S. that care for children who are mildly or chronically ill or recuperating from illnesses or surgeries. Highly contagious children aren't permitted. Most of these facilities are in hospitals; some are in centers or homes that set aside space for mildly ill children. Usually a nurse is on staff or on call. Some home care agencies offer caregivers or visiting nurses who will care for your child in your home.

For more information, call your local child care resource center or contact the National Association of Sick Child Daycare (see Resources).

Dealing with Rejection

When Jordana decided to go back to school, she needed after-school care for her preschooler with autism. "I literally called every daycare center in the yellow pages. Some of them had spaces available until I told them about Lisa's needs. Then it was all 'I'm sorry, there really is no room for her right now. Call back in a few weeks' or 'I don't think we can accommodate a child with your daughter's special needs.'"

If a caregiver or child care center should reject your child without doing an assessment, you should (politely) inform them of their obligations under the ADA. If they still refuse to comply, or if you feel the findings of their assessment were inappropriate, consider filing a complaint with the Department of Justice. The process doesn't have to be difficult, since the majority of complaints never go to court. In many cases, the Justice Department resolves the issue with just a phone call to the child care center or provider. (See Related Reading and Resources.)

In Canada, your provincial Human Rights Commission can advise whether your child's rights have been violated.

Use every strategy to check out your caregiver, and as all mothers we surveyed advised, trust your gut instincts. If you're uncomfortable, go elsewhere. Worrying about your child will affect your work and health.

Experience Talks

"I have found care by asking, asking, asking. The answer may often be no, but it can also be yes. My son's school aide was very pleased that I asked her to look after him for summer mornings."
—Paula, mom of a preteen with non-verbal learning disabilities

"Get bold! When you see a child with a competent-looking support worker, introduce yourself, ask if they have any more time available, and give him/her your number."

—Nidia, mom of a preschooler with global developmental delays

"Realize you won't find the perfect situation. Figure out what is most important to you and find those things. Drop in unannounced if possible to get a different view of the situation. Never settle for a situation that doesn't seem/feel right. Trust your instincts."

—Marnie, mom of a five-year-old with Down syndrome

"I looked at maybe twelve daycare centers when I knew my son would have to go to daycare. I spoke with the providers. I looked at the facility. I looked at the children, the food prep area, and diaper changing area. I asked for a schedule of the day, and how they communicate with parents about daily activities (our son wasn't talking, so he couldn't tell us). I relied on gut instinct as well. I visited the ones I liked best several times, sometimes with my mom, mother-in-law, husband, and, finally, our son.

—Carmelita, mother of a child with ADHD, apraxia, and multiple motor and sensory issues

"Be realistic but open and honest about the special needs your child has. No point in disregarding some significant concern or need, only to have it pointed out to you a week into the program."

—Rosalinde, mom of a child with Down syndrome

Chapter 21

After the Hunt— Keeping the Care, Once You've Found It

Time to switch roles. Put yourself in the caregiver's shoes on the first day of your child's arrival. You're all prepared and are ready to care for a new child who has special needs. You've consulted with the child's parents and with professionals involved in his care. The child has visited, so he's familiar with you, the environment, and the routine. With all necessary equipment, adaptive devices strategies, accommodations, and emergency contacts on hand, you're all set!

Or are you? Perhaps, for example, the parent didn't mention that her tot regularly flushes toys down the toilet. Or that he bites other children. Or that he's not really completely potty trained. Suddenly you realize that this child's going to entail far more work than you anticipated, and you don't know how you're going to handle all his needs without neglecting the four other children in your care. By the end of the first day, you're frazzled, exhausted, and more than a little resentful.

When parents aren't completely honest with caregivers, everyone suffers. But sometimes, because we fear our child will be rejected, we tend to leave some details out. We hope that, by the time our kids' challenges are discovered, the staff will already love them and appreciate their uniqueness. Unfortunately, that's not how it usually plays out. A caregiver is more likely to be "up to the challenge" if she knows what she's getting into when she agrees to care for your child. Moreover, if you're not upfront about your child's difficulties, you immediately lose credibility. What else aren't you telling her, the nanny or teacher may wonder.

Several moms told us they regretted underplaying their kids' behavior difficulties when looking for care. And we heard from some summer camp directors that parents are notorious for omitting crucial information about special needs on the application form.

Provide accurate information on applications and in interviews, so that your child can succeed, rather than being "expelled" from child care or summer camp, or going through a series of nannies who won't stay.

Take Care of Training, Equipment, and Modifications Beforehand

Just as you need to prepare the caregiver for your child, you need to prepare the environment. Make sure all equipment and accommodations are in place before your child starts in a new program, even though you may have to pay for them. Although caregivers are expected under the Americans with Disabilities Act (ADA) to provide "reasonable" accommodation, this varies among situations. What is a reasonable expense for a large, financially secure daycare center that serves many children with special needs may be unreasonable for a small in-home daycare. If your child needs additional security in a home daycare, offering to pay for extra locks would be reasonable. Your caregivers may see this as added value and may (or may not) choose to contribute. But, if your child needs a ramp, for example, it would be unreasonable to expect a homeowner to build one.

Training is crucial for all staff who will be dealing with your child. If your child's disability is fairly minor, it may be sufficient to provide the caregiver with an article, book, video, or fact sheet about your child's disorder. Offer a list of relevant websites, if she'd like to do more research on the Internet. Also remind your caregiver of available supports. One mom told us, "I had my daughter's therapists introduce themselves to the staff and make it known that they were open and available to answer questions."

You can also ask your caregiver (whether a nanny, a home day-care operator, or a teacher at a large center) to attend training to accommodate your child's needs. You may need to pay some or all of the costs. While a child care center will likely pay for staff training on disability issues, this expense is unreasonable for a family daycare provider. Alternatively, offer to pay your caregiver a higher fee if she gets additional training. Training any in-home workers is your responsibility, as they are not covered by the ADA.

If your child needs routine medical intervention, such as injections, bandaging, or tube feeding, provide plenty of time for training before you leave your child alone with staff. Demonstrate the procedures and use instructional videos to increase your caregiver's confidence.

Once you've provided training opportunities, don't just assume it's a "done deal." While you won't want to quiz your caregiver (who would probably resent it,) you will want to discuss what she's learned from the materials/videos/workshops. Ask if she has any questions, and bring up topics that you think are particularly relevant to your child. If you gave the caregiver a pamphlet about sensory processing difficulties, but she looks at you blankly when you talk about your child's sensitivity to bright light and certain textures, you'll know she either didn't read what you gave her—or didn't understand it.

Nurturing a Relationship with Your Caregiver

Even if you arrange wonderful care, you may wonder how long you have until the arrangement falls apart. In one study, more than half of parents of kids with special needs cited this as an ongoing worry. Nurturing a good relationship with your caregiver is key. Offer to carry a cell phone so she can call you in an emergency or if she has questions. Supporting your caregiver professionally is also important.

Be sensitive to the amount of reading or training you are expecting. Some caregivers may feel overwhelmed or feel that you don't trust their abilities.

Ask if they will use a daily communication book. Caregivers (including relatives who provide care) jot down brief highlights during the day—such as your child's new skill, a troubling behavior, or a request for something from home. You return the book each day with your own comments describing your child's time at home. This book also provides a useful record of your child's progress.

Again, be aware of your caregiver's time constraints. If she has little time for written communication, chat briefly at the end of the day or talk occasionally by phone in the evening. If problems arise, talk openly with your caregiver and brainstorm solutions together.

Take time to nurture your relationship with your caregiver. Ask about her day or weekend and always thank her for her efforts. Help her celebrate her birthday with a card (and perhaps a small gift or bonus). If you have a live-in nanny or au pair, make her feel welcome in your home. Respect her off-duty hours and make sure your children do, too.

If you're dealing with a school or center, respond to their requests for parental involvement, read their newsletters, and be as active as possible. Realistically, you may not have time to join the board, edit their newsletter, or supervise field trips. But simply showing interest in their activities and respecting their policies (e.g., picking up your child on time) can better your relationship. Occasionally volunteering on a project unrelated to your child's special needs—say "School Clean-up Day" or the annual book sale—not only makes points with the administration, but gives you a chance to meet other parents and get your mind off disability issues for a few hours.

If family and friends provide child care for you, take special care to nurture those relationships, as it's easy to take them for granted. Acknowledge a special person's efforts with a gift certificate to a restaurant, movie, or store, and a card of thanks. Even if they refuse any kind of financial reimbursement, they'll appreciate your thoughtfulness.

Dealing with a Bad Situation

Sometimes, despite diligent searching, planning, and training, your plans go awry. Here are situations you might encounter in your child care setting.

> *The caregiver doesn't understand your child's needs.* For example, they see your child's lack of toilet training as willfulness, as opposed to developmental delay.

> *The caregiver is overwhelmed.* This happened to Filomena, who has two children with EMT, a disorder that causes severe skin breakdown. Her caregiver (experienced in emergency care) quit after only one day—saying she couldn't provide that level of medical attention.

> *Your child is not placed with similarly aged peers.* Brooke was told moving her daughter (with Down syndrome) out of the toddler room would result in "too much work" for the teachers. Says Brooke, "My daughter was only two at the time and didn't require any extra work." Many mothers said their children were held back in rooms for babies/toddlers because they weren't toilet trained, or were delayed in other ways.

> *Essential accommodations are not implemented.* Some children, for example, don't receive the one-to-one support or the therapies they need. Lenore's son, who is non-verbal, developed behavior problems when he attended a special needs preschool. "They left him to sit at the window all day, flapping vertical blinds in front of his face," she says. Or perhaps caregivers refuse to deliver your child's therapies, as Francine describes, "The head teacher said it would be too much work—as a result, my son was largely ignored and left to his own devices."

> *You face unreasonable demands.* Caregiver insists on extra fees or excessive amounts of your time (to attend every field trip for example).

BEFORE YOU BAIL OUT...

Before removing your child from the program or home, ask yourself if the situation is solvable. Here are some solutions to these challenges:

Offer more training and assistance. Start with an open discussion about the challenges the caregiver is facing. If she seems overwhelmed, would bringing in equipment, activities, or other materials from home help? What about sending the caregiver to a specialized workshop—or even attending it together? Nadia brought in experts. She called various agencies until she found someone to "go in and assist the teachers and make recommendations as to how to care for my son effectively. The daycare appreciates my efforts and my son is now thriving there."

Provide one-on-one support. If additional training, consultation, or equipment don't help, your child may need more individualized attention. Several parents contacted a volunteer resource center to get volunteer support in daycare. Some mothers, instead, paid privately for a worker to accompany their child. A lucky few had it paid for through an early intervention or Medicaid Waiver program. See Chapter 9.

Wait it out. Sometimes it takes time for caregivers to adjust—even after special training. Yvonne's daughter requires continuous oxygen. Staff at her daycare center "were convinced that she would stop breathing completely if she pulled her nasal cannula off of her face," but after they took care of her a few times, "they realized she wasn't that much different than any other baby."

Exercise your child's rights. Using your child's disability as an excuse to exclude him from activities or to charge extra fees is prohibited under the ADA. Schools and daycare providers must (with some exceptions) graduate your child along with his peers to age appropriate programs, provide simple medical treatment, and make reasonable accommodations. Contact the ADA Information Line (see Resources) for more info.

When It's Time to Move On

Sometimes, the problem just isn't fixable—or isn't worth the time and effort it would take to fix it. Ambereen made that decision: "When it came time to transition Keely to the "walker room" (for toddlers), I met much resistance, although it was subtle. I was told that she would be moved and then she never was. I had many meetings with the director and staff. I made numerous phone calls, always assured that she would be moved up soon. I decided I did not want my daughter somewhere she was not wanted, so I began to look for another center."

Even when a child care situation works well, eventually it may be time for you to move on. For example, your infant, thriving with a nanny at home, may need more opportunities to socialize with peers when he reaches preschool age. Then it may be time to investigate center-based care instead. When that time comes, give your caregiver or center reasonable notice. (If you signed a contract with a daycare center or school, make sure you give the required notice, or you could owe a fine.) If you've had a particularly helpful nanny or other in-home helper, consider offering to help her find a new position. (Which shouldn't be hard, as an experienced special needs nanny is a hot commodity!)

But as long as your situation still works well for your child, keep doing everything you can to communicate, advocate, and work as a team with caregivers. In that way, you can hold on to the excellent child care that you worked so hard to find.

Experience Talks

"I try to always be on time. If I'm running late, I call. Most important, I always thank the babysitter at the end of the day. In any kind of relationship, it's often the little things that count."
—Michelle, mother of a child with obsessive compulsive tendencies

"The complex medical needs of our children and their life-threatening allergies mean that we must rely on someone to come to our home. Financial assistance for such care is very limited and does not meet our needs adequately."

—Brenda, mom of two children who are medically fragile

Chapter 22

Paying the Price for Quality Care

Even if you manage to arrange quality care, you must pay the price. According to the Children's Defense Fund 2000 survey, the cost for a four-year-old in a child care center averaged $4,000 to $6,000 annually (with some centers charging more than $10,000). In all but Vermont, average tuition for a four-year-old attending an urban daycare center was actually higher than tuition for an in-state public college. In a quarter of the states, the cost was twice as high.

If, like Brenda, your child requires an in-home provider, you can expect to pay much more. Nannies' salaries vary depending on where you live, their responsibilities, and whether they "live-in" or "live-out." Caregivers that live out generally make a higher salary, but you must provide live-ins with free room and board. In a 2003-2004 nationwide study of over 600 nannies, The International Nanny Association found that live-in nannies earned on average $532 per week; live-out $590 per week or about $30,000 annually.

When children require specialized support, child care costs are even higher. Marjorie, a banker and mother of a child with physical and developmental disabilities, shells out hundreds of dollars per week to cover extra staffing costs on top of regular child care fees.

Of course, parents of children with special needs rarely can afford these extra expenditures. Research shows they typically have lower incomes and extra child-related expenses. To cut child care costs, many mothers turn to relatives and friends, work opposite shifts to their partner, or rearrange their schedules.

Sussing Out the Subsidies

Whatever your income, it is possible to obtain quality child care—but only if you're willing to advocate, innovate, and research programs and funding sources. With a low-to-moderate income, you may qualify for scholarships, child care vouchers, sliding scale fees, or specialized programs like Head Start. Since you may face a lengthy waiting list, though, apply immediately. Call your child care resource center for details and advice.

If you live near a college or university, that's a great place to start your search. Many operate quality child care programs and day camps at reasonable or subsidized rates. Some also operate innovative preschool programs at "lab schools," where their child studies students get practicum experience. Employees and students of the institutions may have first dibs on the programs (perhaps with special scholarships or discounts offered), but any spaces left are often open to the community.

Some daycare centers partner with school districts or educational cooperatives, reserving spaces for children with disabilities in exchange for training, equipment, or supplies. Ask your local Infants and Toddlers or preschool special education teams if they're aware of such a program. (See Chapter 9.)

Local government, service clubs, disability organizations, churches, and private donors may also provide subsidies or scholarships. The child care resource center can inform you of local government subsidies. For the lesser known sources, try your case manager or local disability organization. Also, look online or phone local service clubs, religious organizations, etc., to ask about scholarships.

Whatever option you pursue, always ask if there are subsidies for children with disabilities.

Funding Additional Supports for Your Child in Care

When children have high needs, the cost of care prevents many moms from re-entering the work force. Justine, whose teen has cerebral palsy, epilepsy, and asthma, told us she'd love to go back to work, "if I could get a [Medicaid] waiver, so my whole paycheck wasn't going to pay for a Registered Nurse."

While private schools and child care centers are required to make "reasonable accommodations" under the Americans with Disabilities Act, they're not required to provide a child with one-on-one care. That usually comes out of the parents' pockets.

Fortunately, this cost may be covered if your child (under age three) is enrolled in an Early Intervention program. Once your child is age three or over, some school districts will pay for a one-to-one paraprofessional within a preschool or school setting. These programs may also pay for assistive technology, therapy, nursing, and transportation. If your child needs these supports, make sure they are documented in the Individual Education Program (IEP) or Individualized Family Service Plan (IFSP). Of course, problems often arise when the parents and the school district disagree on whether a child needs one-to-one care.

For an individual who might otherwise need to be in an institution, Medicaid or a Medicaid waiver may pay for nursing support, a personal attendant, assistive technology, training, or specialized therapy that would enable him to participate in community programs such as child care or adult day programs. Private insurance may also pick up some costs. (See Chapter 9 for more information on accessing supports.)

But not all supports require funding. Betty found a volunteer support worker to help her son at daycare by calling a local nonprofit agency. Child care or adult care centers may be open to recruiting and training volunteer assistants. If a volunteer—or a group of volunteers—could be trained to provide the degree of care your child needs, offer to help your center place an ad or call volunteer agencies, schools, and community groups.

Some states and provinces provide financial support for child care or recreational programs to children and adults with complex needs through "wraparound" grants as part of a wraparound plan (also called person-centered planning). Contact your state agency or ministry responsible for children's services. Ask your case worker or try looking up "Child Care," "Child and Family Benefits," "Disability," etc., in the government pages.

Many child care centers are eligible for extra government subsidies when they care for a child (at least to age eighteen) with special needs. These funds may pay for extra staffing, special training, supplies, equipment, environmental modifications, or transportation. In some areas (Ontario, for instance) certain recreational programs are also eligible for subsidies. To qualify for subsidies, your child's needs must be well documented (by physicians or other specialists). While most subsidies are based on income, some states and provinces have child care assistance for families with special needs, regardless of income. To investigate special needs subsidies, ask your child care resource center.

Programs geared to disabilities rarely cover the full cost of child care, but by covering extra supports, they can make child care affordable for those who work and provide much-needed respite to others. Apply early—most programs have lengthy waiting lists.

Take Advantage of Any and All Tax Relief

Some U.S. employers offer Flexible Spending Accounts (FSAs) or Dependent Care Assistance Plans (DCAPs), which allow you to set aside up to $5,000 (as of 2005) for child care in pre-tax dollars. Your taxable income is reduced by the amount you set aside, and the federal government estimates these plans can save most families between 20 percent and 40 percent of the cost of covered expenses (meaning $1,000 to $2,000, if you use the maximum $5,000 allotment). Estimate your needs conservatively, though, because if you don't use the entire amount you set aside within the year, you forfeit the balance (some employers offer a two-and-a-half month grace period).

Most child care options you choose for your child (under age thirteen) or for older dependents unable to care for themselves will be eligible for the program, including care by relatives (except your own child under nineteen, or someone you claim as a dependent), daycare centers, family daycares, after-school care programs, in-home caregivers, au pairs (including agency placement fees) nursery schools/preschools, adult day services, etc. The services of a house-keeper, maid, etc., who cares for your child while you're working (or attending college full time) can also be included. As long as services are considered at least partly for the protection or well-being of your child, you can claim the full amount. You cannot claim for an over-night camp, lessons, private school tuition (not even summer school), or recreational programs (though, if therapeutic, you may be able to claim these as medical expenses).

It's important to keep in mind that you can only set aside money in a FSA/DCAP for child care expenses that allow you and your spouse (or just you, if you're single) to work, look for work, or attend school full-time. You will need to pay for all care up front and submit receipts to be reimbursed out of the plan.

A small number of family-friendly employers provide non-taxable matching funds directly to employees to help with child care expenses. Matching is based on a sliding scale, depending on income. For example, at Northwestern University, a family earning $50,000 or less annually who sets aside $5,000 in the dependent care FSA can receive up to $3,000 from the University.

Both employee and employer save money on FSAs; if your employer doesn't offer flexible spending accounts, you may want to suggest it.

Ask your human resources department whether they provide any other forms of financial assistance, such as reimbursements for child care during business travel or overtime, or vouchers for child care providers.

For those without employer plans, the federal child and dependent care tax credit allows you to reduce your federal taxes by up to 35 percent of the first $3,000 you pay for child care (the first $6,000 for two children or more). The size of your tax credit depends on your income. The tax credit normally applies for children under age thirteen. But, if your dependent is physically or mentally unable to care for herself, the age rule doesn't apply. Eligible expenses are the same as for the FSA (see IRS Publication 503 for a complete list).

Whether the tax credit or the FSA is more advantageous depends on each person's tax situation. Generally, middle to higher income families benefit more from the Flexible Spending Account, while lower income families benefit more from the tax credit. For more information, consult the Internal Revenue Service or your tax advisor. Many states also offer a child and dependent care tax credit and/or accept FSAs. Contact your state's Department of Revenue or Taxation.

Child Care Tax Assistance for Canadians

Canadian parents who work or go to school full- or part-time are eligible to claim a federal child care deduction. Parents can claim deductions for children up to age sixteen or dependents of any age who have mental or physical infirmities. Eligible expenses include both day and overnight care (to a maximum amount) and include personal attendant care. You may also be able to deduct advertising expenses and placement agency fees. Parents who are eligible for the disability amount (a non-refundable tax credit) because their children have severe or prolonged disabilities qualify for larger child care deductions. Caregivers of children over age eighteen who have disabilities can also claim a tax credit. For more information, contact the Canada Customs and Revenue Agency (see Resources).

Emergency Situations

If you think you'll be unable to pay next month's fees because of unforeseen expenses, tell your child care provider as soon as possible. A center or your local child care resource agency may have funds set aside for emergencies. For example, if your child has to undergo surgery or is hospitalized for an extended period, these funds may enable you to hold her spot in her daycare center.

If you're facing tough times financially, it can be embarrassing to be open about your family's situation. Remember that your family is dealing with extraordinary costs—far beyond what most families must deal with. On top of that, you may bring in less money because you need to dedicate more time to your child's care. It's nothing to be ashamed of. By continually seeking out services and financial assistance, you're helping your child to thrive. And realistically, your child may need both practical and financial help throughout her life—so get over any self-consciousness, and get to working finding the help you need.

Experience Talks

"My family has received funding from a parent disability association that pays the salary of a support worker so my son can attend camp. We always try and give back by participating in the association's fundraising events (such as Walkathons, community barbeques)."

—Sonya, mom of a child with autism

Career and Home

The Ultimate Juggling Act

"My work used to be my career—now it's just a job
in order to bring in money."

—Joanne, part-time worker with developmentally disabled adults
and mother to a child with a communication disorder

For a career-oriented woman, the birth of a child with special needs can force an upheaval in her work life that she'd never anticipated. Shelley, for example, never planned on giving up her career. For eleven years, she studied at night school to increase her skills and marketability. As a result, she received steady promotions in her company's accounting department. "My job was interesting," she recalls. "I enjoyed the people interaction and also flex hours." But after her daughter was diagnosed with autism and neurofibromyalgia, Shelley had little time or energy to focus on her job. "I stopped working so that I could get therapy programs up and running for my daughter. Since I couldn't go back to the type of job I was doing, I began a new career working with other special needs children. This was at a greatly reduced rate of pay. Unfortunately, I have had to stop this position also, due to time restrictions with my daughter's therapy."

Shelley's story is hardly unusual. Many highly qualified professionals are forced to take lower paying, part-time jobs that provide no benefits. Some find their new positions boring or unchallenging. Their opportunities for advancement are few. Others like Shelley give their jobs up entirely.

Mothers often see their work lives derailed by their children's disabilities—at significant financial and personal cost. Researchers at the University of Wisconsin-Madison found parents—particularly mothers—decreased their work hours shortly after their children were diagnosed with disabilities and continued to work fewer hours for at least the next fifteen years. While the Bureau of Labor Statistics says that 70 percent of U.S. mothers are employed, a 2000 survey by Family Voices and the Heller School at Brandeis University found that only 52 percent of mothers of children with special needs were employed—and half of those were working part-time. In the general population, 75 percent of working women have full-time jobs.

Of course, ironically, the family of a child with disabilities may need the second income more than ever. And the benefits to working outside the home can be more than financial. Dr. Alice Home of the University of Ottawa in Ontario interviewed forty mothers of children with ADHD, each of whom works at least ten hours a week, and found these moms frequently cited the emotional and "sanity saving" benefits they get from their paid jobs. The mothers we interviewed concur. "Working lets me maintain some semblance of life outside of special needs," say Regan, a social worker and single mom of a child with multiple disabilities. "Having that time away allows me to build up strength to return to my parenting job." Kuan, who sells insurance, agrees: "I find work relaxing, compared to the stress in my daily life of parenting a severely disabled child."

So, how do you maintain a professional life when the needs of your child are so pervasive? The barriers to employment can be significant—finding appropriate child care, making time for your kids' therapies and appointments, and keeping job skills current. How can you work in an employment culture that is only beginning to recognize family challenges?

Mothers we surveyed show it can be done. Many continue to work full-time by negotiating flexibility within their workplace and/or relying heavily on family and friends. Others opt to better balance their lives with part-time work or self-employment.

The key, say moms, is *flexibility*—both the mother's and the employer's. Overwhelmingly, women told us that flexibility, confidence, and willingness to compromise were key in negotiating accommodations. Most importantly, successfully employed moms said they had to prove they were excellent, dedicated, and reliable workers who were committed to their jobs. One mom told us "I work with my employer as well. I try to schedule [my child's] appointments in the evening or around the daily work." Another mom said "I have been known to go in over the weekend if I have unfinished work, especially if I know that in a certain week I may need to be gone a few times for different reasons."

But before you even start thinking about negotiating changes in your work situation, you first need to understand your rights as the parent of child with a disability or chronic illness.

"I tell every supervisor who I am assigned to that I may need to take as much as one day a month off to attend to my son's needs. I make it clear that I will finish any missed work the next evening. Generally, I use the Family Medical Leave Act option to take sick or annual leave time for this purpose. FMLA is very valuable to me."

—Kathryn, mom of an eighteen-year-old with cerebral palsy

Chapter 23

Know Your Legal Rights at Work

As the parent of a child with disabilities, you have certain protections under the law. Depending on your circumstances, you may have a legal right to take time off from work to care for your child (under the Family Medical Leave Act, stronger state laws, or under employment laws in Canada). Moreover, thanks to the Americans with Disabilities Act, no employer (or potential employer) may discriminate against you because of your child's disability. (In Canada, this protection varies according to provincial Human Rights Codes.)

Hopefully, your employer is aware of and sensitive to your rights. If you're especially lucky, you work for a company that takes care of its employees beyond what's legally required—either because it values families, or because unionized employees have a collective bargaining agreement. But no matter what your employment situation, knowing your legal rights and responsibilities is essential.

The Family Medical Leave Act (FMLA)

Since the introduction of the Family Medical Leave Act (FMLA) in 1993, your chances of getting leave to care for your child with special needs have improved. The FMLA applies to all public agencies including state, local, and federal employers; and local education agencies (schools); and to private sector businesses with fifty or more employees.

Just under half of all private-sector employees are covered by FMLA, according to a 2000 Department of Labor survey. While very few parents we surveyed mentioned using the policy, those who did were grateful for it. One mom depended on FMLA to attend therapies and doctor's appointments when her son was young; another mom used it to extend her maternity leave by several weeks.

FMLA protects parents against job loss should they have to take time off to care for a child with a serious health condition that requires hospitalization or routine treatment by a health professional (such as a physician, physical therapist, speech therapist, nurse, psychologist, etc.). This includes leave for supervised therapy required by chronic conditions such as autism, developmental disabilities, or mental health disorders, as well as long-term physical illnesses. The law requires that group health benefits be maintained during the leave. (FMLA also covers maternity leave, adoption/foster care placement leave, and leave related to your own, your spouse's, or your parent's health conditions.)

Under FMLA, you are entitled to up to twelve weeks *unpaid* leave during any twelve month period. Leave can be taken in one long stretch or in short stints; e.g., a few hours one day, or two days in a row. A reduced work schedule is also permitted; e.g., taking one afternoon off per week or working shortened days for several weeks.

Short, unplanned leaves to attend to your child's physical or psychological needs also qualify—providing your child requires professional care. For example, if your child is under the care of a psychologist for his anxiety disorder, and he has a panic attack at school, you're covered for those hours away. However, your employer can ask you to use your vacation time and sick leave before using your FMLA allotment. So find out how your time away is being administrated. For your time away to be counted as FMLA leave, you must tell your employer within two business days of learning of your need to take leave.

Unfortunately, the FMLA doesn't stipulate that you must be paid for your time off. Although two-thirds of those who took leave in the 2000 Department of Labor study did receive some pay, more than half of those taking leave worried about not having enough money to pay their bills. Besides losing salary, you also must pay your portion of health benefits to maintain coverage while you're off. This may explain why many of our surveyed moms weren't taking advantage of FMLA.

Additionally, you can't collect unemployment insurance while on leave to care for sick family members. And, if you take frequent short leaves, such as one day or afternoon each week, your employer has the option of reassigning you to another "reasonable" position (with equal salary and benefits).

There are other conditions for FMLA leave—you must have been with your employer for at least a year and worked at least 1,250 hours in the last twelve months. So if you are a new or part-time employee, you may be ineligible. And if you work for a small company (under fifty employees) you may not get leave because your employer isn't required to comply. But many do anyway—so be sure to check.

Never assume your company implements FMLA, just because the law exists. If your company is covered by the FMLA, they're required to post a notice at your workplace that explains rights and responsibilities under the Act. However, the 2000 Department of Labor survey found that 15 percent of employers required to provide leave under FMLA didn't know it applied to them. And 41 percent of all employees were completely unaware of the Act. So it may be up to you to learn about FMLA and to educate your employer as well. For help, consult the Wrightslaw advocacy group for parents of children with special needs (see Resources).

If you do take FMLA leave, your employer must provide written documentation informing you of your rights, obligations, and the potential consequences of failing to meet these obligations. If you're missing documentation, ask for it. To protect yourself when asking for FMLA, use the checklist in "Communicating FMLA Leave."

Additional Family Leave Laws

Don't overlook state and other leave plans. Your company may also be covered under a state policy, collective bargaining agreement, or em-

Communicating FMLA Leave

Ensure all communication is in writing, including your requests and confirmations, and keep in a file. If you request leave verbally, follow up with a letter outlining your situation and leave request and ask for a reply. If you request FMLA leave, specify it by name. Printed business letters are preferable to email—but if you do use email, keep printed copies of everything.

In your letter, emphasize the seriousness of your child's disorder. The FMLA only covers "serious health conditions." Minor illnesses or conditions do not qualify.

Specify the duration of the leave—up to twelve weeks. If you asked for less than twelve weeks and later need more, follow up with a letter as soon as possible.

Make your request as far in advance as possible. The FMLA requires a thirty-day notice period, but that can be waived for emergencies. In your letter, specify if your situation is urgent.

Obtain documentation from your child's health care provider about your child's disability, in case your employer asks for it. Any health care provider that treats your child can complete the form. So, if you're on a waiting list to see a specialist, have your family doctor, psychologist, social worker, or other professional fill it out. If your employer requests this documentation, you must deliver it within a "reasonable" time frame. (Depending on leave circumstances, "reasonable" means two to fifteen business days, unless circumstances make that impractical.) For full details, contact the Department of Labor.

Frequently communicate with your manager and/or human resources personnel about your plans to return to work. Confirm all conversations in writing.

Adapted from *FMLA Leave Checklist* (www.wrightslaw.com)

ployer policy that is more generous. By law, an employer must abide by the most generous policy.

When an employee is entitled to leave under both federal and state law, the leave runs concurrently. For example, Wisconsin entitles a covered employee to take up to two weeks per year to care for a child, spouse, parent, or parent-in-law with a serious health condition. Suppose your child has a medical emergency that lasts twelve weeks. The first two weeks are covered by both laws, with the next twelve weeks of leave covered by FMLA. If you needed leave beyond the next ten weeks, any additional leave would be determined by your employer's leave policies.

Some states' plans include smaller employers or require fewer hours to qualify. If you worked for a forty-employee company in Oregon, for example, you wouldn't be entitled to any leave under FMLA, but you would be entitled to twelve weeks under the Oregon Family Leave Act, which covers employers of twenty-five or more.

Many states offer more generous leave to public sector employees. Almost all states offer these employees the option of using their own sick leave for family members; some allow employees to use sick leave donated by other employees or through sick leave pools.

Six states legally must allow private sector employees to use their paid sick leave for family members' medical needs (California, Connecticut, Hawaii, Minnesota, Washington, and Wisconsin).

States may also have maternity/paternity or adoption laws helpful to a parent with a newborn or newly placed adopted or foster child. Contact your state department of labor for further information on state policy. And talk to your human resource department or consult your employee handbook for information on your employer's benefits.

To view a detailed list of state family policies that may be helpful to families with special needs children, see Appendix 1.

Leave in Canada

In Canada, the federal government sets the employment standards for federal employees and industries that fall under federal jurisdiction (airlines, banks, shipping companies, railways, etc.). Otherwise, the province regulates employment matters.

Most provinces mandate some form of family-related leave, as well as up to a year of combined maternity and parental leave (including adoption). Your employer continues to pay into your health plan. If you worked enough hours in the past year, your maternity/paternal leave may be partially paid by unemployment insurance.

While maternity/paternity leaves are more substantial than in the U.S., *family leave* is not guaranteed across Canada. Each province varies in what you are allowed to use leave for, such as caring for a critically ill child or dealing with a family crisis.

Recently-passed federal legislation mandates up to eight weeks of "compassionate care leave" to care for "critically ill" family members of employees of the federal government or companies under federal jurisdiction. "Critically ill," under this law, is defined as having a significant risk of death within the next twenty-six weeks. All provinces except British Columbia, Alberta, and the Northwest Territories have followed suite with similar legislation for public and private sector employees. The leave may be partially paid by unemployment insurance compassionate care benefits. Most provinces cover emergencies to care for family members not critically ill under separate legislation. For details, see Appendix 2.

For more information about employment standards in your province, look up "Labour" in the government pages of your phone book to find contact numbers.

Even if you qualify for government-mandated family leave, you should explore other options first. Companies in either country may have leave policies through their own benefit plan or collective bargaining agreement that are more beneficial than government mandated ones.

The Americans with Disabilities Act

Under the 1990 Americans with Disabilities Act (ADA), employers can't fire you because you have a child with special needs. Nor can they refuse to hire or offer you other employment opportunities such as promotions or transfers. You are protected from this form of "discrimination by association" if your workplace has fifteen employees or more. Your employer may not refuse you health insurance because of your child's medical needs, even if those needs may increase their costs. You are entitled to the same health insurance choices as any other employee.

However, a parent of a child with a disability is not entitled to any work accommodations under the ADA. So, if you miss work regularly to tend to your child, and you have exceeded FMLA and any other leave you are entitled to, you may face demotion or dismissal.

Canadian Laws. Canada has no federal legislation comparable in scope to the ADA, although Ontario has an Accessibility for Ontarians with Disabilities Act (AODA) designed to remove barriers for individuals with disabilities in the public and private sector. Even the Canada Human Rights Act (which only covers employees of the federal government or industries under federal jurisdiction) does not protect you from being discriminated against because of your child's disability. However, some provincial Human Rights Acts are more enlightened. Contact your provincial Human Rights Commission.

When All Else Fails—Taking Legal Action

If you believe your employer has violated the provisions of the FMLA, contact The Wage and Hour Division of the U.S. Department of Labor's Employment Standards Administration (look under Government—Labor in the phone book). They will investigate the complaint and attempt to resolve it. If they can't, they may take your employer to court. Alternatively, you may file a lawsuit yourself. For FMLA violations, you can file suit up to two years after the violation, or three years if the violation was "willful" (i.e., if the company knew its actions violated the FMLA).

If the court determines you were wronged, you may be awarded back pay (e.g., any wages and other benefits you lost because your employer didn't allow you to return to your old job or a comparable one). Or, if applicable, the court may rule that you must be offered employment, reinstatement, or promotion. If you stayed on your job and were wrongfully denied FMLA, the court may award you expenses; for example, your employer may have to reimburse you the cost of a caregiver, equivalent to up to twelve weeks of your wages or salary with interest. Compensation is typically doubled unless your employer can prove it acted in good faith. You could also recover your legal costs.

If you have been fired and you suspect your employer discriminated against you because you have a child with a disability (prohibited by the ADA), you can file a charge of discrimination with the nearest office of the Equal Employment Opportunity Commission (EEOC).

Remember, your employer is not obligated to make accommodations (other than those required by FMLA or state law), so if you were fired because you didn't fulfill work responsibilities, you won't have a case.

You can also file a civil suit against your employer. If you're alleging discrimination under the ADA, your case must be investigated by EEOC before you can sue. You may file a lawsuit within ninety days after receiving a notice of a "right to sue" from EEOC. According to statistics from the Department of Labor and the Employment Opportunity Commission, about 90 percent of complaints filed under the FMLA or ADA are resolved without court action.

For Canadian readers, contact your provincial Ministry of Labour or Human Rights Commission to find out how to pursue work- or disability-related complaints.

Filing a legal claim should be a last resort, since most problems can be resolved by talking openly with your employer. Most companies want to obey laws and avoid legal hassles. Likely your problem is the result of an oversight, misunderstanding, or lack of legal knowledge. Before you take any action, contact an employment lawyer for advice. The lawyer may suggest that you write a brief summary about what has gone wrong and your recommendation for resolving the problem. The lawyer could also help you request a letter of apology from your employer or a recommendation letter that could help you find work at a more supportive company. Evaluate what you hope to accomplish. A lawsuit will cost thousands in employment lawyer fees, a huge investment of time, and emotional stress.

For legal advice, request a list of lawyers in your area from the office of the National Employment Lawyers Association in San Francisco. In Canada, contact the Canadian Bar Association and ask for the lawyer referral service in your area.

Experience Talks

"Use every piece of legislation to your advantage. Read what you are entitled to and ask for what you want."

—Shirley, mother of a preschooler with Down syndrome,
who negotiated part-time police work

"Due to pregnancy complications and the birth of preemie twins,
I was out for six months. My company held my job for me and I was paid
for all but twelve weeks. In addition, I took off three weeks to take my
daughter to a CP clinic out of state and my company paid me for the full
time in addition to my normal vacation days."

—Virginia, accounting manager and mother of a toddler with cerebral palsy

Chapter 24

Build Workplace Support

Does this sound like your workplace? Or can you relate more to the less idyllic situations we've heard about. One auto production worker said, "My supervisor really finds my absences to be a pain. Everyday he tells he how lucky I am to be unionized." And a mother of a child with a congenital heart defect, who worked as an administrative assistant, was constantly chastised by her manager for "increasing our company insurance premiums." But, according to the women we interviewed, these types of negative interactions are the exception, not the rule.

So what seems to be the key to supportive workplaces? We asked Nora Spinks, president of Work-Life Harmony Enterprises, who has more than twenty years experience consulting with corporations, governments, and community organizations on work/life issues, around the world. "Even if a company has great policies, procedures, and benefits, it can be hard for you to manage with an unsupportive supervisor," she says. "And if a company has few policies in place, you could still manage well, if your supervisor is supportive."

Adds Spinks, "In a large company, you have formal routes to go for support, such as human resources, employee relations, or the union. Without that, it's often a matter of education." Managers may be unsupportive because they don't know how to manage any differently. They may be afraid of setting a precedent. So you may need, for example, to tell your supervisor about employee accommodations that have worked successfully in other departments.

So where do you start?

Do You Come Out of the Closet?

If your child has just been diagnosed with a disability, you're probably still in shock. It can feel overwhelming to share your news at work, and you may fear "telling" will risk your job security or violate your family's privacy. Whether to tell is a personal decision that should be guided by your comfort level and knowledge of your workplace. You need to consider your immediate need for formal supports like FMLA or flexible working conditions, your perceived value to the company, the past supportiveness of your manager, etc.

As a general rule, if your work performance is affected, it may be time to tell others in your workplace. Otherwise, managers may question your reliability and coworkers may begin resenting you when you have to take a lot of time off, make a lot of personal phone calls, turn down overtime assignments, or just show less enthusiasm or interest in your work. One teacher and mother told us "Some coworkers feel I've gotten preferential treatment. They don't say anything directly to me, but I can tell by their mannerisms toward me that something is bothering them."

To win coworkers and your boss over, you need to find ways to get your work done, no matter what. As Amy Joyce, "Life at Work" columnist for The Washington Post, says, "Work hard, make sure that work is complete, on time, and without mistakes." Sometimes, this may mean taking work home to complete during your "off" hours—the last thing you may feel like doing. But when you can't keep up with your normal routine, you need to demonstrate that you can still produce the necessary results.

In order to be able to do their jobs effectively, most moms we surveyed were open with their employers. Speak with your supervisor and coworkers before your job performance suffers. Then they can be part of the solution.

Getting Your Boss on Board

"Constantly calling in and making excuses eventually gets tiring, and your boss will lose respect for you," says Netta, a graphic artist and mom to a son with a brain tumor and hydrocephalus. "I held a meeting with my boss at the time and explained about my child's needs, and what I needed from him and my coworkers. I was very up front and honest, and he was understanding and willing to compromise."

Sounds straightforward. But approaching your boss can be intimidating, especially if he hasn't shown you much support in the past. We asked Nora Spinks at Work-Life Harmony Enterprises for advice: "Go with your gut instinct—never sell yourself short and never go into a situation where you're aggressive and demanding or shy and deceitful," she says. "Don't apologize and don't deny you have these family responsibilities. But emphasize how accommodations will enable you to give 110 percent to your job." You could say, for example, "In order for me to fulfill my job responsibilities and do my best for you—provide you with *maximum* value—I'll need the following kinds of supports in the workplace...."

Although you may feel isolated in your situation, remember that other employees are facing different challenges—ill spouses, elderly parents, etc. It's been estimated that, in any given company, 8.6 percent of employees are caring for children with special needs. That means if you work for a company with 2,000 employees, odds are that 175 have children who require extra care. While not all those employees will need accommodations, it's unlikely you'll be the first person to approach your employer about a family or personal issue.

"Increasingly, employers are becoming more understanding of the complexity and diversity of families," says Spinks. They're starting to recognize that accommodating employees' family situations results in business advantages such as improved recruitment and retention, and positive community relations.

When you request an alteration to your normal work schedule, always stress the supports you've arranged outside of the workplace. True, you may need flexibility so you can take your child to a coveted specialist whenever he can fit her in. But make sure your boss knows that you've arranged supports such as backup child or nursing care, supportive school staff, etc., to cover more routine situations.

To help ensure your manager becomes your ally, try these strategies:

Educate decision makers. If your supervisor seems unsure about your need for workplace supports, provide information about your child and her diagnosis. Sometimes it's easier to explain if you provide a pamphlet about your child's condition from your local disability association. If they don't have any or your child has a rare disorder, prepare a fact sheet yourself detailing symptoms, treatments, and long-term prognosis. Also consider meeting with the human resources manager. If your employers know about your child's specific health issues, they may consider your child's needs when negotiating health insurance contracts. They may also offer you services like child care referral or employee counseling. Request confidentiality in all your discussions if this is important to you.

Ask for what you need. The best approach is a professional and straightforward one. Be as specific as you can about your request. For example, if your child will need medical treatments and assessments during work hours, say so up front. Early on, it might be hard to predict your needs. Just give your manager a "heads up" to your situation and explain that you may require time off or may have to take phone calls from the doctor or school during work hours. If you are after a more permanent work accommodation such as flextime, telecommuting, or a change in hours, you'll need to prepare a written proposal (see Chapter 25).

Provide info on best practices. Organizations such as Family Voices, the Families and Work Institute, and the Roeher Institute (see Resources) do research on extraordinary parenting demands and the most effective ways for employers to accommodate them. The Roe-her Institute and Family Voices have guides for employers of parents with special needs children (see Related Reading). Material from an authoritative source—especially if it includes statistics on how family-friendly policies save companies money—may help convince your bosses that the flexibility you're requesting will actually allow you to be more productive.

Emphasize your commitment to the organization. Tell your boss that your job is very important to you, and you want to "make this work." It's important that your supervisors know that you're still dedicated to your career, despite your child's pressing needs. (Even if your career *doesn't* feel that important to you at the moment, if you need to keep your job, you need to show enthusiasm for it.) Stress that having some flexibility—such as permission to take calls—will allow you to relax and better focus on your work.

Explain how you will minimize any work disruptions and make up for lost time. If you'll need time off, have a plan worked out beforehand. If completing missed work involves coworkers, make sure they have already agreed to anything you propose.

Don't apologize. Needing to care for your child is not something you should feel guilty about—so never imply that it is. Try statements such as: "I realize that this may restrict my availability during the day for meetings on project X, but I can participate in conference calls and online discussions. I have arranged to discuss the project's progress with Jane Smith at the end of each day."

Enlist Coworker Support

Some coworkers may have limited understanding of your situation. While you can't force someone to be supportive, a little information can go a long way. Since coworkers may be hesitant to ask about your personal life, you'll have to take the initiative.

Speak individually to people you work most closely with. Deb Berman, a consultant for the Nonprofit Professionals Advisory Group, says building personal relationships with coworkers is essential. "There needs to be boundaries, though," she emphasizes. "Use common sense. People don't need to hear you going on about your problems, but you can go for a walk at lunch with a coworker and let them know your situation." If they show interest in your child's disability, provide coworkers with a pamphlet or fact sheet.

Explain why and when you'll need to be away—and be specific. "My son gets fitted for his leg brace today," or "I have to leave at 2:00 for a school placement meeting for my daughter." Coworkers are more likely to be sympathetic the next time they see you leave early and may even volunteer to cover some of your responsibilities.

Always thank coworkers when they help. You might offer to return the favor once your life settles down. For example, volunteer to take a Saturday shift when your coworker wants to visit his family. Or say you'll cover the phones, so your officemates can take a long lunch. Follow through, and you may find yourself with new work allies.

Don't expect miracles. Despite your attempts at education, moms say some coworkers may still be resentful when their work is affected (or even when it isn't. There will always be troublemakers who just seem to like complaining). Chelsea, whose child has cerebral palsy and multiple complications, says her fellow employees "all understood that my son was very sick, but they didn't like having to pick up the slack." Bottom line—do what it takes to get your work done, so your coworkers have no reason to resent you. Beyond that—don't waste your time worrying about ignorant people's opinions.

Fortunately, coworkers and bosses often rise to the occasion.

Get 'Em Involved—And Give Credit Where Due

Building a supportive workplace is an ongoing effort. One way is to involve your workplace with "the cause." Ask coworkers to participate in fundraisers related to your child's disability such as a bike-a-thon or a Bingo night. When coworkers take time to fundraise together, everyone benefits. Not only do they help kids, but they also enjoy camaraderie at the workplace.

Offer to contact the media if your company takes extraordinary initiative in fundraising. For example, Ken and Marie work for a pharmaceutical company. When coworkers organized a walkathon for spina bifida research, they raised several thousand dollars. Marie contacted the local newspaper, and the company enjoyed positive media exposure. Now the walkathon is a yearly event that is also covered by local television and radio. Sales reps point out that dozens of new customers learned about the company through the walkathon.

Reach Out to Others

"Everyone in my office has pitched in with my daughter," shares Sandra, mother to a child with Down syndrome. "We have worked as a team, and now she has an extended family. I have a great situation. My daughter is seen as an asset of the work place."

One of the greatest gifts we bring to our workplaces is empathy. By being open about our children, we encourage coworkers to share their own struggles. Amy is amazed at the number of people who share their concerns about their kids with her—before they'd consider "coming out" to anyone else. As the mothers of children with special needs, we have the power to humanize the workplace for all employees. By providing a listening ear, and sharing what we've learned, we provide comfort, caring, and connections to those in our work community.

Experience Talks

"If need be, I could get up and leave my work at a moment's notice. I truly believe that it was my honesty about my son in the beginning that made my employers that way."

—Grace, mother of a teen with Asperger syndrome

"Do an A+ job, believe in yourself, and communicate your needs honestly. I have not allowed my home life to impact my work while I am working. I have been an asset to the company based on my

daily performance. It makes a difference in the supportiveness of my employer."

> —Kelly, mother of a fourteen-year-old with developmental disabilities, who's been granted extended leave from her job

"I was twenty-six when Anya was born, starting a career with a major IT corporation. Since then I've held different positions. My work is very stressful but fulfilling as well. I have adjusted and flexed my schedule to meet specialists' appointments. I've tried midnights, afternoons, and traditional nine-to-five. For the past two years, I have been working at home three days a week. I have not "called in sick" for me OR my children since I've worked from home. I am able to get everything done."

—Marsha, IT project manager, whose daughter has Down syndrome

Chapter 25

Explore Flexible Work Options

Supportive managers and coworkers are vital, and if you only have to deal with an occasional crisis, they may be all you need. Unfortunately, though, when your child has a chronic disability, your need for flexibility and support at the office may become chronic as well. Many of us need long-lasting, ongoing accommodations, like Marsha (above), so we can earn a living.

Fortunately, flexible work options are no longer pie-in-the-sky dreams. According to the 2003 Benefits Survey Report by the Society of Human Resource Management, over half of the 584 companies surveyed offered flexible work arrangements: 55 percent offered flex time, 34 percent had telecommuting, 31 percent allowed compressed work weeks, and 22 percent offered job sharing. More than one-in-four full-time workers in the U.S. now have some flexibility in their start and end times at work, according to the Bureau of Labor.

One of the biggest barriers to flexible work is fear. People considering telecommuting, part-time work, or job sharing often worry about being "invisible" at work. They fear being passed over for promotions and being seen as undedicated. So even though many large companies have established programs to address work/family issues, few people take advantage of them. But the results of a 1998 Families and Work Institute study are reassuring. Although 40 percent of surveyed employees believed accommodations could affect their future position in the company, only 10 percent of employers believed this to be true. So, workers' fears may be unfounded.

Not all jobs lend themselves to flex-time, as several moms discovered. Connie, mother of three-year-old twin girls, was director of aquatics at a large recreation center. Both girls have special needs—Samantha requires tube feeding, and Kaylie is deaf. During her children's first year, Connie missed work hours weekly to attend medical appointments.

While Connie and her supervisor tried to implement flexible hours, both eventually agreed that it wouldn't work. As director, Connie needed to handle all situations, including emergencies that arose during programming hours. Since working fewer hours was her best option, Connie accepted a part-time job as assistant director, instead. Although her responsibilities and salary were reduced, so were her mothering difficulties.

Work like Connie's—involving client contact, specialized equipment, or reliance on others—is less flexible than employment in information technology, insurance, finance, and real estate.

Some jobs must be carried out during certain hours, so are inflexible. If you're a factory worker or bus driver, for example, your only choice may be to switch shifts, if possible. If you're a teacher, office receptionist, or customer service representative, job sharing or part-time work may be your only flexibility options.

Companies such as NationsBank successfully incorporate job sharing in their customer service department. Job sharing is also increasing in the field of education. For example, the Independent School District in Aldine, Texas offers job sharing to attract new teachers (all it takes is the approval of the principal for two teachers to share a classroom).

Many nurses also responded to our survey. The majority worked their shifts in evenings or weekends so they could care for their kids during the week.

The surveyed moms who enjoyed the most flexibility worked for nonprofit organizations, often in the disability field. These were typically jobs that the mothers sought after the birth of their children with special needs. With few exceptions, mothers described unlimited flexibility and supportive workplaces. One mom who works for a riding school for people with disabilities said, "This job believes family is first. Everyone that works for this agency has a child with a disability. All of us need the support of each other."

If you're lucky, you work for an employer that already has supportive policies in place: flex time, telecommuting, family leave policies, etc. More likely, you'll need well-honed research, communication, and negotiation skills to get what you need.

Devising a Plan to Get the Flexibility You Need

"I work full time, but have changed my work hours so that I can be home to help my child with homework," says Della, whose child has Tourette syndrome, ADHD, and learning disabilities. "My hours were 9 a.m. to 5:30 p.m., and I often worked overtime. Now I work from 6 a.m. to 3 p.m. and, if necessary, do overtime work after hours at home. I generally schedule appointments after work hours. Since my work day ends at 3 p.m., that's not too difficult."

Many mothers, like Della, are able to negotiate a better work arrangement for their family. The first step is to figure out just what it is you need.

STEP 1. ANALYZE YOUR SITUATION

What stresses you the most about your current work situation (as it relates to your child with special needs)? Is it:

☐ Workplace interruptions? (Having to field phone calls from teachers, miss work for your child's doctor's appointments, or drop everything to deal with frequent crises?)

- ☐ Exhaustion? (Trying to juggle all your home responsibilities on top of a full-time job?)
- ☐ Child care drop-off and pick-up hassles?
- ☐ Irregular or unpredictable work hours?
- ☐ Too much overtime?
- ☐ Excessive business travel?
- ☐ Other?

STEP 2. EXPLORE THE DIFFERENT OPTIONS AVAILABLE AT YOUR WORKPLACE

Meet with the human resources department to discuss your company's formal policies on flexible work. For example, is there a telecommuting policy already in place? Flextime? Meal-break flexibility?

Even if a formal plan isn't offered, working flexible hours is still a possibility. While 25 percent of employees say they can work flexible hours, only 10 percent are part of a formal flex plan (Bureau of Labor). That means plenty of others have negotiated arrangements with their managers. If you have coworkers who have informally arranged flex hours, take them to lunch and find out how they did it.

Here are some common flexible work options that moms told us help ease their stress. Consider whether any of these will meet the needs you checked off:

Flextime: Arrange your working day by shifting your arrival and departure times earlier or later. You may need to work during "core" hours such as 10:00 a.m. to 3:00 p.m. For example, by working 7:00 a.m. to 3:00 p.m., you may be able to better coordinate child care and home life with your spouse.

Adjusted Lunch Periods: Shorten or lengthen your lunch breaks as necessary. For example, you could skip lunch (eat at your desk) and leave work an hour earlier. Or take thirty minute lunches (instead of the allotted hour) on Monday through Thursday, and take a three hour lunch on Friday, when you'll take your child to his appointment.

Compressed Work Week: Work the same number of hours you normally would, but in fewer days. For example, work four ten-hour days each week. Or work nine-hour days, and take half a day off each week, or a full day off every other week. This clears two to four days per month for your child's appointments, school meetings, etc.

Shift Work: Work evenings, nights, or weekends, trading child care off with your spouse and freeing up time during the weekday for appointments and therapies. Try to arrange a steady shift, so you won't have difficulties of arranging therapies and child care around changing schedules.

Work at Home/Telecommute: If you do very independent work (writing, programming, etc.), perhaps you could work from home during convenient times (e.g., when your kids are at school or asleep). The term "telecommuting" (and, in the federal government, "Flexiplace") describes a more structured schedule, including fixed hours at home and at work for regular meetings.

Comp Time: Arrange that, when you have to take time off for your child's needs, you'll make up the time by working extra hours. Stay late the next evening. Or, work a Saturday or Sunday one day a month to clear a weekday. Of course, a formal comp time policy goes both ways—if your boss asks you to work extra hours, you'll be given future time off in lieu of overtime pay. It's not as lucrative as being paid time-and-a-half, but can be a lifesaver if you have a hectic schedule.

Are there other ways you can relieve your stress? Move into a lateral position that's less demanding, requires less overtime or travel? Reconsider accepting a promotion? Work reduced hours? These are tough choices but may be necessary (see Chapter 26 for information on part-time, switching jobs, and taking leave).

STEP 3. REALISTICALLY EVALUATE YOUR WORK OPTIONS

Analyze each option. Does it suit your needs? Can your job still be done adequately?

Let's look, for example, at working from home. Assess your job responsibilities. Which of your tasks could be done at home and which must be done on site? Could any of your job duties be done differently to facilitate your request, e.g., eliminating unnecessary tasks, or reassigning unrelated tasks to a coworker? What challenges would your arrangement raise for customers? Coworkers? People you supervise? Management? What could you do to ease these challenges?

Do you have the discipline and the space available to make it work? Could you deal with the social isolation?

Working compressed hours presents different challenges. The longer days can be tiring and can affect performance. If you're not a morning person, or your child keeps you up most of the night, a 6:00 a.m. to 4:30 p.m. work schedule may not be realistic. What happens when you're off? Will someone else need to cover for you for the hours or days you're not at work?

If you're lucky, there may already be a precedent set in your department for flexibility. If not, you may have to be the trailblazer. For example, if you work shifts and your company offers little flexibility, could you ask your employer and union to work together to review how shifts are allocated?

STEP 4. ANALYZE HOW DIFFERENT OPTIONS WOULD AFFECT YOUR FAMILY

Consider how a different work arrangement would affect your child care, therapies, and family supports. Make sure your proposed schedule would accommodate therapy and appointments with specialists. Changing to a ten-hour day, or working a late or weekend shift will present child care challenges, unless your partner or other family members are available. If a change in child care would be required, explore your options immediately (see Chapter 18). If you would need your partner to shift his work schedule or take on more caregiving responsibilities, you'd need to get his buy-in. Get family members, friends, and disability workers on board by discussing your options beforehand. The more support you have, the better your chances of success.

Be sure to think about how a work schedule change might affect your finances, and factor that into your decision. Would you face increased transportation or child care costs? If you were working a compressed schedule, would you start spending more money on carryout meals, because you'd have less time to cook?

Look at the emotional toll as well. Would you miss out on the emotional support of your coworkers if you started working at home? Would a compressed schedule mean you'd miss out on family meals, or helping your kids with their homework? Would evening and weekend shifts mean you'd never have time alone with your spouse? And would a flexible schedule truly make your load bearable? (If not, the next chapter will help you evaluate other options.)

STEP 5. PREPARE A WRITTEN PROPOSAL

If your company considers these requests frequently, it may already have a standard form for you to fill out. If it doesn't—or if you find the form doesn't cover everything that you'd like to include—you can write a proposal memo (see Appendix 3 for an example). Whatever format you choose, be sure to include the following:

> The specific work schedule change being requested
> How the plan will benefit the company (e.g., cost effectiveness, customer satisfaction, team efficiency)
> What makes the plan feasible (aspects of the job that make it amenable to your flex option, your personal characteristics that will make it a success, etc.)
> What is necessary to make the plan work (such as communication, management, technology)
> How your performance will be measured (output, review process)
> An understanding that the arrangement depends upon a successful trial period.

If your company lacks formal policies on flexible work, you need to be a pioneer! You must define a successful arrangement and explain how it will benefit your employer.

To help you prepare, tap into any resources available to you through work, such as human resources, employee relations, unions, or an ombudsman. In some companies, employees can access a resource and referral program to guide you through your request for flexibility.

A common mistake, according to Nora Spinks, president of Work-Life Harmony Enterprises and an expert on work/family balance, is for employees to write their proposals from their own perspectives—how *they* would benefit from, say, flextime. "Then they wonder why it was turned down!" Look at it this way: If you were writing a sales proposal, would you write about how you would benefit from the commission, or about how your customer would benefit from your product? Well, your proposal *is* a sales pitch, so you need to write it from that perspective.

To sell your employer, you must convince them that your proposal makes business sense:

Example: Starting work earlier in the morning would mean I'd have fewer interruptions from people and phones, resulting in more accurate work done in less time. An earlier schedule would also mean I could eliminate work disruptions by scheduling personal appointments after work hours.

Example: Working a compressed work week would mean I'd increase my efficiency, productivity, and availability for clients. With a longer work day, I'd be able to complete projects in one day, rather than having to restart them later in the week. I'd be available to talk to clients later in the day, which would be particularly convenient for those calling from the west coast. My compressed schedule would also mean I'd no longer have to leave work in the middle of the day to take my child to medical appointments—I could schedule them for my regular day off every other week.

Example: Working at home would reduce my commuting time and sick leave, and would minimize interruptions—all resulting in more usable work time and better efficiency. Because I find it easier to write in a quiet environment, my productivity would increase. My working at home would also free up a desk for contract staff.

It's also important to anticipate your supervisor's objections to your proposal. Then head her off by embedding the solutions to these objections within your proposal letter. For instance:

Anticipated Objection: If you work (early/late/at home,) your availability will be limited.
Preemptive Strike: List ways and times you could be reached, e.g., cell phone, email, telephone, pager. Emphasize that you'll be available during core hours, for regularly scheduled meetings, etc. Suggest alternative means of "being there," such as conference calls.

Anticipated Objection: If you aren't in the office it will be difficult to monitor your output.
Preemptive Strike: Suggest tracking tools and methods, e.g., time sheets, timelines, deadlines, progress reports, review periods.

Anticipated Objection: No one else here has flex hours (or telecommutes, etc.). If I do this for you, I'll have to do it for everyone else.

Preemptive Strike: Sell your supervisor on the business merits. She shouldn't view this as a personal favor, but as a sound business decision. If there are precedents in other departments, or other companies in the industry, give examples.

Suggest a trial period of one month so that your supervisor doesn't feel locked into the arrangement. This also gives you time to see what adjustments might be needed.

Step 6. Practice and Present

Take the initiative by speaking to your supervisor. "Don't wait until your performance appraisal," advises Spinks. Unsure about the opening? Spinks suggests saying something like "I feel like I could be making more of a contribution—and it might be because of the multiple demands on my time—I'd like to present a proposal to you with solutions."

Most managers will ask you to prepare the proposal for a later discussion. But just in case, have a preliminary proposal already prepared, so you can discuss the points right away if necessary.

Approach your supervisor at a time when she's usually the most relaxed—that way, if she wants to talk immediately, you have a better chance of success. If your supervisor is having a bad week and you can put off your proposal, consider doing so.

Use the form you've prepared as an outline for the meeting, which will enable you to present well-thought out ideas. Make two copies so that you and your supervisor can refer to it during the meeting. If you suspect she will be unsupportive, "cc" your request to her boss, and to human resources. That way, she's less likely of being dismissive, and later, you can't be accused of going over her head.

If you're nervous about making your request, role play with a family member or a friend, and practice responding to various reactions or objections. If you're uncomfortable, use a tape recorder or video recorder, then review your presentation to see where you could tweak it. Make sure you make good eye contact and that you're not speaking too quickly (a common problem when you're nervous).

Some key pointers for the meeting:

Start on a positive note. Break the ice with some brief office "small talk," a compliment, or a work-related observation.

Present your ideas in a business-like fashion. Sell your proposal on its business merits first, not on its advantages for you and your family. "Coming in a few hours earlier each morning will give me uninterrupted time to finish the previous day's paperwork," as opposed to "I'd like to start work two hours earlier in the morning so I can be at home to meet my daughter's school bus."

Do your homework. Be ready with your counter-objections and examples of successful work flexibility in the company, or in similar workplaces.

Emphasize your accomplishments and positive performance reviews. Also, reassure your supervisor that you are strongly committed to the company.

Don't react emotionally to a negative decision. Be polite and courteous. Don't jeopardize a possible second round of negotiations with an outburst.

Make sure you come out of the office with a general understanding of what's been discussed or agreed on. Verbalize your understanding—"So, you're willing to consider an earlier start time, but need to get approval from the department head." Better yet, provide a paper trail by following up with a memo or email thanking your supervisor for their time, and restating your understanding of any agreements. If asked to provide follow-up information, do so as soon as possible.

STEP 7. ASSESS AND REASSESS

Congratulations! Your request has been accepted. Once you revise your work schedule, ensure that everyone knows when, how, and where to reach you. Check in regularly with your supervisor. Are these adjustments working for you and for your employer? If not, you may need to adjust them or consider other options. Be pro-active by suggesting modifications yourself, rather than waiting for your supervisor to say "this isn't working."

If you failed to successfully negotiate flexible work, don't give up. Try our suggestions in the following section.

Going to Bat a Second Time

So, you planned carefully, presented powerfully, and you still were turned down. What now?

"Don't give up too fast," says Selena, a part-time optometrist and mom to a child with Down syndrome. "I negotiated for a longer leave after both my children were born. Both times they said no at first, but polite persistence wore them down." First analyze your company's objections, and then get ready for round two! Here are possible scenarios and action plans:

Have you asked for more than they're willing to give? Are your demands unrealistic? Can you scale down your request? Is the timing off? Perhaps your department has recently lost crucial staff. If so, try again in a few months.

Is your manager unsupportive? Would education on the issues help? Especially if this is the first request of this type, your manager may be overwhelmed. Spinks points out that "managers may be unsupportive because they are afraid of setting a precedent. Most people have empathy," she says, "but feel they must deny your request for accommodation, because they don't have the skills to implement it." She suggests finding examples where flex work has worked in other departments, so managers can mentor each other.

Is there a personality conflict? Are coworkers enjoying flexible work options that you've been denied? If so, take your case to human resources, your manager's boss, or your union. Or, apply to work in another department with a more supportive manager.

Is your organization traditional, resistant to change, and autocratic? Unless you're willing to change workplaces, you have to become the trailblazer. Hit 'em where it counts—on the company's bottom line. Research shows that workplaces with family friendly policies are more productive. Their employees have greater job satisfaction, improved performance, increased loyalty, and less turnover. To make your case, present hard data, such as that in "When Work Works: Workplace Flexibility Toolkit" from the Families and Work Institute (see Resources).

Take your proposal to the human resources department with a list of employment consultants that specialize in this area.

Personality conflict aside, managers reward employees who have a history of reliability and hard work. Many of the moms who wrote us about successful accommodations felt their work history was what solidified the deal. Do some soul searching on your own work habits. If you routinely were behind in your work tasks, were an uncooperative team member, or were perceived as unreliable, it's unlikely that your request will be successful. In that case, you may have to put off your flexibility request until you prove your worth and dedication to the company.

Even if you are a dedicated worker, the sad fact is that you still may not be valued by your employer. If you work in a field requiring highly specialized skills, like Selena, you'll be in a better bargaining position. But if you work for minimum wage in the service sector where you can be easily replaced, you have little bargaining leverage.

If you're unable to negotiate flexible work hours, it may be time to consider other options—taking regular unpaid leave (which you may be entitled to under the Family Medical Leave Act,) cutting back to part-time, requesting an extended leave of absence, or even quitting. The next chapter will explore the pros and cons of these different options.

Experience Talks

"I negotiated an earlier work schedule for myself. I was able to do so because of my experience and value to the agency, and because my boss is sympathetic to my son's special needs. My advice is:

1. *Work hard so that management considers you a valuable employee whom they do not want to lose.*
2. *Suck up! Ingratiate yourself with the people who make these decisions.*
3. *If you can't negotiate something for yourself, band together with other mothers and decide on a unified approach.*
4. *Change jobs."*

—Della, mother of a child with Tourette syndrome,
ADHD, and learning disabilities

"Over the past nine years, I have changed my hours from
full-time to four days a week, back to full-time, and, three years ago,
to twenty-five hours a week with Fridays off."

—Bonnie, mom of a nine-year-old with severe physical and developmental disabilities

Chapter 26

Cut Back, Take Off, or Call It Quits

Sometimes it seems that life with your kids is cyclical. In a good patch, your child is doing well at school and home, so you can adequately focus on work. But, all that can change in a phone call—"Your son ran off the property during lunch. He's out of control," says the principal. Or "She's having a severe asthma attack." Leaving a pile of unfinished work, you race to pick up your child. This painful scenario repeats several times in one month. During tough times, juggling parenting and work is especially challenging.

If you haven't been able to negotiate a flexible work schedule—or you have, but you're still struggling to meet your child's needs—it's time to look at your other options: taking frequent time off, switching to part-time, requesting a leave of absence, finding a less demanding job, or quitting entirely.

If your workplace has fifty or more employees, you may qualify under the Family Medical Leave Act for short, unplanned absences, a temporary reduction in hours, or a longer-term leave to attend to your child's physical or psychological needs. (In Canada, you may qualify under other legislation—see Chapter 23.) But whether you qualify under FMLA or not, if your parenting responsibilities are making it impossible to be successful at your job, you need to make a plan.

Take Frequent, *Short* Absences

If your child has behavioral or medical problems, you may frequently get called to pick her up from school or daycare. Telephone calls and appointments can also cut into your work day. Moms frequently worry that these interruptions hurt their reputations at work. Brenda, mother of two children who are medically fragile, recalls "I confided in a coworker that I was worried I'd lose my job because I spend so much time taking my kids to medical appointments. My friend reminded me that family comes first and I shouldn't feel guilty. I'm just not sure management feels the same way."

Not only is Brenda worried about her children's medical issues, but she's also adding to her anxiety by avoiding a conversation with her employer. (See Chapter 24.) Instead of worrying, be proactive. Start by finding out the policies and practices in your organization, advises Nora Spinks, president of Work-Life Harmony Enterprises. If you're in a large organization, you're probably not the only one facing this kind of challenge. But in a small organization, you might be the first, so you'll need to spend more time educating others in your workplace.

"Don't do this alone," stresses Spinks. "Reaching out for help is a positive thing." One of the best strategies, she says, is talking to other parents in similar situations. Network with them locally and online to find out how they make it work.

As for policies—about 50 percent of businesses allow occasional time off to care for mildly ill children without using vacation time or losing pay (Families and Work Institute 1998 Business Work Life Study). Presumably, the same would be true for caring for children with special needs. Ask your human resources department if they have a written policy on family leave. Smaller companies may have more informal guidelines.

While some workplaces are flexible about time away if you maintain your workload, others will expect you to use vacation or sick days. Some companies give "comp time," allowing you to make up the hours you miss at a later date. Most of the moms we surveyed used vacation days to care for their children. Policies may vary by department, and managers may apply the rules differently. Talk to your coworkers about their experiences. If your workplace is unionized, check your collective bargaining agreement for leave policies.

Here are some tactics for managing work interruptions.

Plan ahead. Emergencies aside, tell your employer and coworkers about appointments, hospital stays, or other work interruptions well ahead of time, so they can plan. If you anticipate a crisis—your child is not coping at school, for example—warn them. Just as you don't like to be caught unaware by a crisis, neither does your employer—nor the coworker who may have to pick up the slack.

Suggest solutions. If you can suggest ways to deal with pressing work situations—people who can fill in for you, work you can bring home, deadlines that can be pushed back, meetings you can participate in via speakerphone—discuss them now.

Work around your company's schedule. Obviously, it's best to try to schedule medical and school appointments for lunch hour or before or after work. When that's not possible, at least aim for your office's slow day or hours, when you'll be missed least. Avoid scheduling appointments during the time you'd most like to get away from the office, or when it will give you a long weekend—it will be noticed and you'll lose credibility.

Be reachable when you're away from the office. While you shouldn't have to answer coworkers' calls from the emergency room, it's not unreasonable to call back from your child's hospital room after a crisis has passed. Try to be available when possible. Work out a plan for your office to contact you (by email, voice-mail, etc.) during office hours.

Pitch in extra when you can. Whether it's helping a coworker meet a deadline, or volunteering to bring a project home on the weekend, you'll increase your value to the company while giving extra effort when you can.

Be prepared to deal with objections from your supervisor by researching eligibility requirements for leave beforehand.

Switch to Part-time

"I have tried all methods of employment: full-time, part-time, and staying at home only," recalls Ann Marie, part-time ballet teacher and mom to a twelve-year-old with Down syndrome. "Working full-time and part-time (over twenty hours per week) were both too stressful and I could not cope. Staying at home without working eroded my self-esteem and sent me to therapy. Now I believe I have found the perfect balance of part-time teaching less than twenty hours per week. I love children and find much reward in sharing my knowledge. This helps me to value myself and know that I am contributing to the world."

If full-time work, even with a flexible schedule, seems overwhelming—and you can afford the pay cut—consider cutting back to fewer than thirty-five hours a week. Some moms we surveyed regretted taking so long to ask for accommodations because they were timid.

Don't underestimate your value to the company. Even if you work for a seemingly rigid employer, you may be surprised at their response. When Rachelle's baby with Down syndrome was born, she worked as a financial systems specialist for a company with a reputation for being uncaring. Initially fearful to ask for reduced hours, she was thrilled when they agreed to her request. She became the first person in her agency to go on a part-time schedule. "They supported me through five years of part-time, rather than lose me as an employee," she says.

Unfortunately, not all jobs fit part-time hours. In your job, could you complete core tasks on a reduced schedule? Do you have tasks you could eliminate, share with another employee, or reassign to another person or department? Too often, when employees cut back to part-time hours, their bosses still expect them to produce the same amount of work they did before. As one mom told us: "Although I was putting in part-time hours, it felt like full-time pressure."

So make sure you and your employer come to terms with a job description you can both agree on—in writing.

With part-time work, benefits are typically pro-rated. But some part-time jobs—such as college or night school teaching—offer no benefits at all. Before accepting a part-time arrangement, ask if you'd still be eligible for bonuses, vacation time, holiday pay, sick leave, and pension. Would your part-time hours equal or exceed the 1,250 hours annually required for FMLA? Would there be any conditions as to whether/when you could return to full-time work?

To cut back to part-time, you'd need to be willing to make other compromises. As your visibility at the office declined, you might have fewer opportunities for promotion. Since you'd have less time to socialize with coworkers, you might need to work harder to maintain professional relationships.

Despite these downsides, many women like Rachelle consider the decrease in stress worth it.

Job Share

"I am fortunate to be able to job share with another very competent co-worker, making my decision to cut back on work hours even easier," says Charisse, dental hygienist and mom to a preschooler with autism and a seizure disorder. "I feel rejuvenated when I return to work after 3½ days away. My children come first—above anything else—and having the extra time for my son allows for a better quality of life for all those involved."

Too much work to be done in part-time hours? Like Charisse, you might want to consider sharing your workload and salary with another employee. For example, you work mornings, while your co-worker covers afternoons, and the two of you catch up over lunch. Or choose between Monday through Wednesday noon and Wednesday noon through Friday.

If management is concerned about communication and consistency, each partner could work three days a week, with one overlapping day (Wednesday, for example).

A great selling point for job sharing is that both members of the team are less likely to take sudden leave, as each can schedule appointments on days off. The plan is even more appealing to employers if both team members bring some flexibility to the arrangement. For example, if one person is sick for several days or goes on vacation, the partner covers for her (if possible) to minimize the work disruption.

If your job has "peak" and "valley" times, a job share plan could be designed for the workload flow. Schedules could overlap during busy periods or have gaps during slow periods. If your job involves dealing with people around the country or around the world, job sharing could allow you to extend the work day (earlier or later) for better coverage.

For success, you and your partner would need frequent communication and an excellent rapport. You might need to be available on your days off until you had an effective system of communication worked out. Some consultants suggest making a "pre-job share agreement" with your job-share partner that details your responsibilities to the company and each other. It should also specify what happens if one partner bows out.

While some companies and government agencies will recruit for job share positions (especially if they want to keep a current employee on board), many successful job sharers have found each other themselves, then proposed the partnership to their employers. This is a time when networking can really pay off. Is there another mom in your office who might like to cut back her hours? Or do you know another mom who quit working to care for her child, but is missing the stimulation of a challenging job and adult conversation? Just make sure any potential partner shares not just your desire for part-time hours, but your work ethic and capabilities as well.

If your company is unfamiliar with job sharing, offer successful examples from elsewhere. Search for "job share" on the Internet, and you'll find stories of administrative assistants, tenured university professors, physicians, even bank vice presidents who made job sharing work for them. Again, sell your supervisor on the business benefits in a well thought-out proposal.

There are, of course, a few downsides to job sharing. As with other part-time work, benefits for job share participants may be prorated. If you're used to working independently, sharing assignments can take some adjustment. No one else will ever do a job exactly the same way you would, and you'd have to accept that (which can be really tough for perfectionists). If one partner lets things slip—say because her child's going through a rough patch—the other may get extra work dumped on her. Or worse, she may get chewed out for late or shoddy work, when it wasn't her fault.

But if both partners are responsible, flexible, and communicate well, job sharing can be a great solution. You keep (or find) a job you love, while having lots of time available to see to your child's needs.

Switch to a Less Demanding Job

Sometimes, it's not different hours you need, but a different boss or a different job. For example, Audrey, an insurance claims manager and mother of a child with Tourette syndrome, transferred to another work group when her supervisor couldn't understand why she needed to work from home sometimes. Her new boss allows her more flexibility.

Could you switch to a job with more support, a more suitable schedule, or a reduced work load? Even if it meant taking a step backward, career-wise, it could be a temporary solution that would bring you relief. Bonnie, mom to two young children and a nine-year-old who is severely disabled, sought out a less demanding position when her home life became unmanageable. Her feelings are mixed, but for now she's content with her decision. "I feel that I am not challenged enough at work, but I look for my challenges elsewhere for now."

Even a less demanding job can teach you new skills, expand your social network, or place you in a department where promotion is more likely in the future.

Moving within a company is easier in many ways than moving to a new workplace. You keep your benefits, the familiar working environment, and social contacts. And the job search is less stressful. On the other hand, if you take a step downward, you may find it awkward reporting to bosses who were once your equals (or who once reported to you).

Ask coworkers, look at internal job postings, and talk to human resources about possible openings. If you are considering a new job outside the company, see the chapters in Part VII to aid you in your job shift.

Take an Extended Leave

When we're lurching from crisis to crisis with our kids, the world of work can seem remote, unimportant, and irrelevant. When Heather's daughter Robyn suffered a frightening neurological episode at age three, the whole family's lives were turned upside down. "For months, I gave little thought to my consulting company and my role in it. Until our life resumed some state of normalcy, our daughter was my only focus."

Sometimes, if your child is in crisis, she needs 100 percent of your attention. Your initial impulse might be to simply quit your job. But before you do that—especially if you work at a supportive company at a job you like—explore taking an extended leave of absence instead.

You may be entitled to up to twelve weeks of family leave per year under the FMLA (see Chapter 23). But don't assume, if your company is too small to meet the FMLA criteria, that it won't grant you the time off. One-in-three companies that aren't required to still do so, according to the U.S. Department of Labor. The majority of these companies continue your health benefits and guarantee your job will be there when you return. Ask your human resources representative what your company's leave program offers.

Some companies—even small ones—have family emergency policies that are *better* than FMLA, such as longer leave times and partial or full salary while you are off. One in five companies (of all sizes) offer paid leave for family emergencies (SHRM Foundation, 2003). While a large company may be limited by inflexible policies, a smaller one may make decisions on a case-by-case basis. If a smaller company values you, it may provide generous accommodations. Talk to your boss, who may have to discuss your situation with the owner before any decision is made.

QUESTIONS TO KEEP IN MIND

How would an extended leave affect your family financially?

Just thinking about the financial impact of an extended leave can be frightening. But by putting the figures down on paper, you'll see the actual cost (see the Extended Leave Worksheet on page 376).

List your monthly expenses. Many experts advise you to track your expenses for a month. But if you're considering a leave during a time of crisis, you probably don't have time to do that. Instead, pull out your bank statements for the last three months and average expenses over the three (making allowances for major one-time expenses).

Add in the cost of any employee health benefits you may need to pay out of pocket, or added expenses of staying at home (e.g., heating, air conditioning, other utility costs).

Subtract the expenses you'll save by not working, such as commuting costs, and lunches out. Would you save on child care? Check with your daycare provider about their payment policy if your child will not be attending for a while. Some daycare centers may demand payment in full to hold a spot, but others may make exceptions for extenuating circumstances—or may point you toward an emergency fund.

Now subtract any partial salary you expect to be paid, and any other monthly income, such as your spouse's pay, and you'll be left with the amount you have to cover. Think of ways you can cover the shortfall such as savings or a loan.

What would be the impact on your career?

The law protects employees against discrimination for taking an FMLA leave, and requires the employer to retain your job and position except in a very limited number of circumstances. If your company isn't covered by the FMLA, you only have your employer's assurance that your job will be waiting. And even if you reclaim your previous job, you might (wrongfully) be ignored at promotion time. Talk to your Human Resources department to find out their policy. Try to get assurances in writing.

Keep in mind, though, that if you stay on your job and your work suffers, your career could be adversely affected as well.

Would taking your time off on a reduced leave schedule better serve your purpose?

For instance, if your child goes through a crisis period, you might take six straight weeks of FMLA leave, and then take two days per week (to take her to doctors' appointments and therapies) for the next fifteen weeks. That will allow you to ease back into your work schedule, while being there for your child.

Would your workplace allow other employees to donate their leave to you? Or does your employer have a pooled bank of time you could tap into?

If so, that could substantially relieve your financial burden. Sharon, for example, needed an extended leave after the birth of Kyle who has Down syndrome. Her supervisor and coworkers donated enough paid time off at the end of her leave to allow her to remain home for four more weeks. Coworkers often generously donate their leave time if they know it will be well used. This is another important reason to be open with people at work.

If you take leave without pay, how will you handle phone calls and requests from work?

While you can't prevent phone calls, it may be possible to limit them by preparing your workplace for your departure. Tie up outstanding tasks or projects before you go. If someone is moving temporarily

Extended Leave Worksheet

MONTHLY EXPENSES

Regular Monthly Expenses $_____ (A)

Leave-Related Expenses

    Employee Health Benefits $_____

    Other $_____

Total Leave-Related Expenses $_____ (B)

Total Monthly Expenses (Add A + B) $_____ (C)

WORK-RELATED SAVINGS

Child Care $_____

Lunches $_____

Travel Costs
(bus fare, gas money, etc.) $_____

Dry Cleaning/Clothing $_____

Income Tax $_____

Other (e.g., carryout or
restaurant dinners,
office contributions) $_____

Total Work-Related Savings $_____ (D)

MONTHLY INCOME

Partial Monthly Salary, If Any $_____

Other Income, If Any
(Spouse's salary, alimony, etc.) $_____

Total Monthly Income $_____ (E)

Amount Available to Offset Expenses (Add D + E) $_____ (F)

Total Monthly Shortfall (Subtract C–F) $_____

into your job, try to make yourself available to help train that person. That way, they won't have to rely on you as much when you're gone.

Most workplaces are sensitive about calling you at home on leave. But sometimes, they may need to contact you to help them to complete an important project. To maintain your value to the company and show your good will, help them out if you're able. Says Amy Joyce, "Life at Work" columnist for the *Washington Post*, "The more you help out when you actually can, the better off you'll look—and the more willing a supervisor will be to let you take time off in the future." Plus, you may be less likely to be replaced (if legally allowed) before your return.

On the other hand, if you're dealing with a crisis at home and are unable to deal with the phone calls you're getting, be honest with your employer and coworkers. Try to let them know when you'll be able to contact them.

Negotiate Professionally and Positively

Once you know what accommodation you're going to request, set up a meeting with your manager. Prepare a proposal as outlined in Chapter 25. Remember to always include the business merits of your request, e.g., "I'm juggling a lot at home right now. If I take some leave to manage things at home, I can return ready to focus 110 percent on my job." Be polite and professional. If your manager seems inflexible, use your knowledge of company policies and government legislation. Try saying, for example, "I'm not sure if you've heard about the FMLA...." Perhaps your boss is unaware of your rights.

Present your request as a thoroughly researched business plan that benefits both you and your employer. Ideally, together you can come up with a workable solution.

Document Everything!

If your boss blocks your attempts to access leave, or discriminates against you for taking leave, you may have to take action. Contact an employment lawyer for advice and gather any supporting documents. By having a written record of all correspondence and agreements, you can prevent misunderstandings and protect your rights. Be sure to collect and keep the following:

> *Company policies*—employee handbooks, management memos, company notices, and any written information that suggests policies treat workers unfairly. Write down any statements made by supervisors about unwritten company policy, including the date of the conversation and who was present.

> *Personnel Information*—written statements by supervisors or personnel, performance reviews.

> *Correspondence*—all letters, memos, and emails pertaining to your leave. Keep dated notes of all conversations about your leave, and get your supervisor to sign off on them, if possible.

Calling It Quits

Not all mothers can negotiate the flexibility to remain in the workplace. Some are forced to quit when their children's needs make it impossible to keep their jobs. Thirty percent of parents of children with special health care needs report that they have had to cut back on work or stop working altogether in order to care for their children (2001 National Survey of Children with Special Health Care Needs). For moms of children with emotional and behavioral disorders, the numbers are even higher. Portland State University's Parent Employment Experiences Survey of 349 parents reported 48 percent had to quit work altogether at one time or another to care for their children.

Some moms, when they feel like they're doing neither their jobs nor their families justice, decide to opt out of the work world—at least temporarily. A woman who disliked her job to begin with, or who wanted to be a stay-at-home mom, may be happy to walk away (albeit unhappy to lose the paycheck). But for a woman who considers her career part of her identity, the decision can be gut-wrenching. Nevertheless, many women who love their jobs decide to quit in order to care for their children during needy times.

Unfortunately, quitting often comes with a cost. You may lose future pension and retirement savings. And if you eventually decide to re-enter the workforce, it will likely be at a lower level than in the past. You may also lose your health insurance (so make sure you're covered by your partner's insurance or another plan). Two federal laws may help you continue your existing insurance coverage or purchase new insurance. COBRA (the Consolidated Omnibus Budget Reconciliation Act) may help you extend your coverage for up to three years at group rates (although you'll probably have to pay both your own and the employer's portion of the premium). If you switch policies, HIPAA (the Health Insurance Portability & Accountability Act) can limit the time insurers can deny your child full coverage or prevent them charging higher rates based on pre-existing health conditions. Contact the U.S. Department of Labor for information about these programs (see Resources), or contact your state insurance department.

Yet, most women we surveyed who altered their career paths were satisfied with their choices. As Netta, mother of a child with a brain tumor and hydrocephalus, says, "I've had to rearrange my schedules— quit school, take time off without pay, and even quit a waitressing job because of my son's needs. It has taken me twelve years to finish my business degree, because I have had to withdraw so often when my son was sick. But, I have never been resentful of the sacrifices I have had to make. I think I am a better person for putting my career on the back burner and having my son and other children come first."

Fortunately, joblessness is rarely permanent. And work change sometimes leads to creative opportunities. Netta (once a graphics artist) recently purchased a hair salon and looks forward to the control self-employment offers. Other women we surveyed eventually started new careers using skills developed through managing services and advocating for their child. If you'd like to explore self-employment or a new career, turn to the chapters in Part VII.

Experience Talks

"Your constant presence [at the office] is not the only way to do your job. Your absence from the workplace to tend to your child's needs is a reality—work around it. Accept it, and others are more

likely to do so as well, especially if you can address workplace issues in other creative ways."

—Jordan, psychologist and mom to a nine-year-old with
Asperger's syndrome and a seizure disorder

"If your career is important to you, at least try to hang on to work on a part-time basis. It is worth waiting and looking for the right employer who can be flexible in meeting your family commitments."

—Brenda, mom of two children who are medically fragile

"Look for employment opportunities that allow you to be content. Don't settle for a work situation that puts you at risk. Value yourself and know that in order to take care of others, you need to take care of yourself first. It might take some work up front to find this situation, but be persistent."

—Ann Marie, mother of a child with Down syndrome

PART VII

Redefining Your Work Life

"I always try to see the seasons of my life as just that...
seasons with a purpose."

—Sydney, mom of a daughter with Down syndrome

So...what season is your life in now? Are you scrambling to get early intervention and therapies going for your child? Are you sticking with a job that gives you a good income, so you can build a secure future for your child(ren)? Or do you have a child who is finally settled well in school, and now you're starting to feel unsettled yourself? No matter what your situation, it takes some soul searching and planning to determine what you'd like to change in your life in order to feel challenged, fulfilled, and purposeful.

Candace, for example, felt exhausted after years of arranging therapies and trying to get help for her son James with autism. But when he turned eleven, she realized that both of them needed a change. She longed to return to the interior design work she enjoyed. And James needed time to relax after a day in the classroom. Now, she's back at work, as her older son cares for his younger brother after school. As Candace says, "My son likes school [and] he's happy to hang out when he comes home. It's not that we've given up—but this is who he is. My work is important to me now."

Sometimes, when you're in a life situation that doesn't feel right, it can feel like you're stuck. So perhaps you're at home full-time, but would rather be working. Or perhaps you feel trapped in an unfulfilling job, when you'd rather have more time to care for your kids. Or you may be at the point where you want to change, restart, or reinvent your work life. Sometimes, it's helpful to realize, like Sydney (above), that your situation may serve a purpose for now, but it can change, if you want it to.

If you're like many women we surveyed, you may also find that through caring for your child with disabilities, you've started to change the way you think about yourself and your goals. Paige, a single mom of a six-year-old with multiple disabilities, says, "I used to define myself by my work (as a paramedic). I now have a broader, deeper sense of who I am, what I have to offer, and where I can serve myself, my family, and my community."

As the mother of a child with special needs—whether you're at home full-time or out in the workforce—odds are you've gained many skills you'd never anticipated. Your daily to-do list may include training home workers, attending medical appointments, and setting up "case conferences" about your children. When faced with non-existent services, you've probably written letters, attended meetings, and lobbied agencies. After learning to advocate, communicate, organize, and multi-task, you've likely developed strengths and skills far beyond what is required in typical parenting.

For many moms, these new abilities and sensibilities have, over time, translated into new careers, sometimes disability-related. Women we surveyed obtained disability-related work in:

> Education (teachers, teacher's aides, librarians, school administrators, tutors, trainers)
> Advocacy/Law (legal aides, mediators, educational consultants, lawyers, government workers, charitable grant writers)
> Social Work (case workers, social workers, parent advocates)
> Psychology (researchers, therapists)
> Therapeutic Arts—(music, art, and drama therapists—who previously worked as artists)
> Boards of Directors (for schools, government agencies, religious organizations)

We also heard from many moms who would like to change jobs or even careers. Most stay-at-home moms we surveyed said they eventually plan on returning to paid employment. Some shift in and out of the work force, depending on their families' needs. But even moms who plan to remain at home indefinitely should have a plan for what they'd do if they were suddenly forced to work again, as family situations can change through illness, death, divorce, or a spouse's job loss.

While some moms were unclear about the jobs they would seek, all knew what work conditions they needed. For example, mothers who had previously worked for inflexible organizations wanted employers with family-friendly policies. In order to ensure job flexibility, many hoped to start their own businesses—especially in services they couldn't find for themselves, such as inclusive child care.

Now, if you are lucky enough to already hold a job that's rewarding and meets your financial and flexibility needs, great! Hang onto it! Just remember to add the new skills you've developed to your resume.

If you're not so lucky, it's time to start planning—whether the time for change is now, or years down the line.

You can control your future economic well-being. In the following chapters, you'll learn how to determine what you want to do, how to remain employable, and how to nab the job you really want or create it with a home-based business.

"I've never even had a chance to think about working because of my son's high needs. I wouldn't even know where to start."

—Rhiannon, mother of a child with emotional and behavioral challenges

Chapter 27

Get Ready— Establishing Goals

If, like Rhiannon (above), you're not sure where to start, bring in the pros. Hiring a professional life/career coach or career counselor can help you examine your strengths, interests, goals, and work/life balance challenges. This might be the first step to determining if/when/how you want to resume paid employment.

Coaching can be expensive ($50 to $150 per hour), but most coaches offer a free thirty-minute phone call consultation. For low cost (or free) career counseling ask at your chamber of commerce, community college, adult education center, or small business center. (See Resources.) Search out online career self-assessment tools or read books such as *What Next?—The Complete Guide to Taking Control of Your Working Life* by Barbara Moses. (See Related Reading.)

While career coaches and books can help, you really need to ask yourself—What am I really good at? What do I care about? What environments allow me to shine?

It Begins with You

Before polishing off your resume or scanning the want ads, take a step back and look at who you are right now. Once you've determined your main interests, strengths, and priorities, you can make a plan to find work that fits.

Flexibility and convenience are important, of course. But you're much more likely to find your "ideal" job if you look for one that fits with your personality and interests. And ideally, you'd like to be exercising your key strengths. Start by putting your thoughts down on paper:

STEP 1. LIST YOUR PERSONAL ATTRIBUTES

Make three lists with the headings: "Interests," "Skills," and "Strengths/Personal Characteristics."

To help complete your lists, think of your past accomplishments, activities, and pastimes. Also, talk to your partner, friends, children, and/or co-workers to get their ideas.

Let's look at how one mom, Samantha, completed her lists:

Sample Lists for Samantha:
Interests
    Fitness
    Visual art and design
    Dance
    Music
    Children's development
    Literature
    Different learning styles
Skills
    Skiing
    Long distance running

Crafts
Photography
Writing
Teaching
Marketing
Cooking
Household management
Budgeting
Computer skills (word processing, spreadsheet, Internet)
Creating brochures
Strengths/Personal Characteristics
Optimistic
Courageous
Good leader
Spiritual
Funny (good sense of humor)
Energetic
Accepting
Creative
Flexible
Extraverted—thrives on contact with people

STEP 2. BRAINSTORM

Look at your lists from Step 1, and decide which of the different attributes are the most important to you. Then brainstorm different kinds of work that might allow you to use those interests, skills, and strengths.

Sample Brainstorm for Samantha:
Strongest Interests: Fitness, music, marketing
Most Developed Skills: Teaching, marketing and promotion, writing
Strengths and Personal Characteristics She'd Most Like to Use in her Work: Leadership skills, extraversion, and people skills/sociability
Possible jobs:
Fitness instructor at the YMCA or a private fitness facility
Personal trainer (self-employed)
Freelance writer for fitness and health magazines
Dance and fitness instructor for children

Step 3. Explore Your Options

Now you should have a few ideas. You may be ready to settle on a line of work, but take time to explore a variety of ideas before setting a goal. Then you can determine a course of action that will allow you to meet this goal.

Find examples of people doing similar work in the community. Identify the "KSAs" (Knowledge, Skills, and Attitudes) that enable them to be successful at their job, advises Roberta Neault, a career management specialist in British Columbia, Canada. Then, see how your own KSAs compare, and set some personal and professional goals based on that gap.

Samantha, for example, will take fitness instructor certification training at her local YMCA. She also invited a self-employed personal trainer to lunch for an "informational interview"—to find out what the job is really like. After her meeting, she realized that she doesn't know much about running a small business. So, if she decides she truly wants to be a private personal trainer, she'll take classes on running a small business.

Keeping your own unique preferences in mind you may decide to:
> Take a course or join a club to explore whether your interest might lead to future work
> Upgrade your skills to return to a previous job
> Take a college course to prepare yourself for a new career
> Switch to a new job in same field
> Change your field of work
> Start a business
> Volunteer in an area of interest to gain skills and see if it's a good fit
> Work part-time to update previous skills (in a field of work that suited you well)
> Other _____

Devise Your Game Plan

Once you've determined a course of action, you also should consider your financial reality. For example, if you've been at home for years, do you need a second income to fund a house for your child when he grows up? When do you (and or your partner) hope to retire? Meet with a financial planner to help determine what income you need in order to meet your long-term goals.

While starting a new career doesn't happen overnight, even small steps will help you achieve your professional goal. Take a look at Eve. Before having children, Eve enjoyed her work as a computer consultant. When her first son was born with cerebral palsy and developmental delays twelve years ago, she quit her job and never returned. Sometimes, just coping with her son's behaviors and trying to get help consumes all her time and energy. But even during these stressful periods, Eve does volunteer work to keep herself employable. She even sits on the board of a disability association. With her strong advocacy, communication, and organizational skills, she's well known in the community.

Recently, Eve volunteered in her son's school helping students with reading difficulties. "I have no background in teaching, but I really enjoy this," she says. Now she's investigating a community college course so she can work as a teaching assistant in the future.

Like Eve, there is much you can start to do right now to help you transition back into the workforce or start your own business.

Upgrade Your Skills through Courses

Taking a course or seminar develops your skills and also looks great on a resume (so keep a record of any workshops, networking groups, or training events that you attend, and file the handouts and references from them). Courses can help you pursue or test out a different career, acquire new ways to care for your child, or learn just for the joy of it. Consider these options:

UNIVERSITY/COLLEGE COURSES

In our surveys, many women were retraining to enter a new field of work. Some chose professions like therapy or teaching so they could put their life experience to work. Others chose professions based on flexibility and stress level. Fortunately, many colleges and universities offer evening and part-time courses so that mature students with families can participate.

Another popular option is distance education, where you take a course online, on television, or by correspondence. With distance education, you can finish your high school education or earn a university/college degree at the undergraduate or graduate level. In some cases, you may be able to earn credits for prior work/life experience. Just make sure the program you pick is on the up-and-up.

FINANCING YOUR EDUCATION

Wondering how you'll pay for classes or a degree? There may be funding available to you, but it can take some work to track it down.

Start by narrowing down the programs and colleges that interest you, so that you know which scholarships to aim for. Scholarships are typically offered on the basis of a particular background (e.g., religion, ethnicity, or experience), or a particular field of study (such as life sciences). If you have interests and experience in several categories, you may be able to apply for various ones. Also, look around your own community, since large companies may offer scholarships for local residents.

Scholarships, grants, and tuition waiver programs are often available in fields with employee shortages—particularly health care and education. For example, if your school district is having trouble filling special education teacher vacancies, it may offer to fund the cost of getting the appropriate degree and certification—as long as you agree to work for the local public schools for a set number of years. For other scholarship sources, check your library, local newspapers, schools or colleges, and the chamber of commerce.

The Business and Professional Women's Association has scholarships specifically for disadvantaged U.S. women who want to further their education in order to advance in their careers or to re-enter the workforce. (See Resources.) Many colleges and universities offer their own scholarships specifically for mature women. Search individual institutions' websites for details.

If you already have a bachelors degree, and are tempted by graduate school, see whether the program you're interested in has any research grants. Depending on the field, you may find that tuition waivers and stipends are available. Contact the academic department, or the professor listed as the "principle investigator" on a given study, to see if funding is available.

If you're dreaming of changing careers but are daunted by the retraining required, keep the long term view. Even if you take one course a year, you will eventually reach your goal. Justine, previously a medical assistant, is studying part-time to become a nurse. Since her husband is in the Navy, the base provides child care for her infant son (with Down syndrome) two hours a day, twice a week. "I figure by the time our son is in school full-time, I will be able to get my career started again," she says.

Start your scholarship search early, since filling out applications and writing essays are time consuming.

SHORT-TERM WORKSHOPS AND CLASSES

"But I don't have the time/child care/money/energy...."

Getting out for a course seems impossible when you can't remember when you last had a full night's sleep. Or if you can't find anyone you trust to care for your child. In that case, choose one important workshop far in advance, write it on your calendar, and make it happen. If money is an issue, budget for the workshop over a few months. Cut back on an everyday luxury (such as coffees or lunches out) and put it towards your Workshop Fund.

Fortunately, you needn't enroll in college or university to reap the benefits of continuing education.

Check out these sources for ideas in your own community:

> Local college catalogs ("non-credit" classes)
> Recreation and parks departments
> The "adult learning" or "extended learning" division of your school system
> Local newspapers' "calendar" listings
> Stores that specialize in your area of interest
> The local chamber of commerce or Women's Commission
> Public library and community bulletin boards for flyers and brochures
> The Internet

So which class should you choose? You could try an introductory class aimed at your new career, or check out what's new and exciting in your old one. Workshops in business communications—including writing, listening, and presentation skills—can help you advocate for your child and present yourself professionally in a job search.

But don't eliminate classes that simply intrigue you or sound fun. In addition to providing a new hobby, these activities could spark a new career interest. Most importantly, community involvement widens your circle of contacts; this network helps you if/when you look for work.

Skills Training

Upgrading your computer skills is always a good bet for any field of work. Also consider apprenticeships or training courses in high demand skills such as welding, plumbing, mechanics, etc., if these are areas of interest. Some offer scholarships to encourage women in the trades. Contact your local community college.

Disability-Related Training and Workshops

Join your local parent group and disability organization. Besides information and networking, groups often provide low-cost or free training for parents. Attending workshops in teaching strategies, behavior management, health care, etc., helps you parent effectively and also provides you with marketable skills. For example, parents who have been trained in one-to-one teaching sometimes work with other families to help them set up their own home therapy programs.

Join a Club

To explore an interest or learn a skill, investigate joining a club. Often, membership is free or minimal, and entitles you to workshops, meetings, events, and group activities. Examples of clubs include book discussions, hiking, birding, astronomy, folkdance, woodworking, choirs, etc. Heather, for example, has been a member of a mother-daughter book club for five years. "Besides being an activity I share with the girls, it has sparked an interest in young adult fiction and given me a discerning eye for good fiction," she says. She's also made contact with writers and publishers who are useful for her writing career. To find local clubs, see the recreation and parks brochures, ask at your library, and check local community bulletin boards.

Explore Interests through Casual Work

Short-term, temporary, or freelance work helps you explore new careers, keep your resume current, and establish professional contacts. Amy held several casual jobs when her daughter was young. She was trained as a teacher, but wanted work that didn't require a major time commitment, "so I taught a college business communications class one night per week and parent/child classes two mornings. Eventually, both jobs indirectly led to my present profession—home-based freelance writing. By teaching business communications, I honed my writing skills. And by running parent/child programs, I gained expertise to write articles for parenting magazines. Like others, I didn't take these jobs in order to establish a new career. I just wanted to maintain my professional identity."

Some women work occasional shifts to keep the door open at their previous workplaces. Others take temp jobs to earn extra money or get a parenting break. While few of these jobs lead directly to full-time employment, they can help you develop and maintain skills. Also, they prevent large unemployment gaps on your resume. Most importantly, they allow you to explore interests which may lead to a new career.

Casual jobs also provide good networking opportunities. Meredith, whose child has autism, earns a stipend chairing an autism research group. While it doesn't pay her bills, it keeps her abreast of autism research. She also has earned the respect of researchers. If she wants, this "small" job could be her ticket to graduate school or work as a research assistant.

If you hear about a job opportunity, consider whether it would help you achieve your long term goals. If you'd like to return to your previous profession, occasionally working a few hours in your field can give you an edge. Mothers we surveyed worked sporadically as substitute teachers, nurses, paramedics, bookkeepers, and, of course, "consultants."

To find work in your previous field, reconnect with your former employer. If your old boss can't offer casual work, she may know of another department or company that can. If you belong to a professional association, network with members and check association job listings. Also, call your contacts and check newspaper ads. If you're looking for a specific job, find a person working in that field and ask to meet with her. She may have advice or may even offer some short-term work. Or, you may find a way in by offering to volunteer—read on.

Volunteering

Volunteering can lead to interesting paid work. Lakeisha, who is trained as a social worker, volunteered on an agency committee advocating for services for children with developmental disabilities. When a part-time job came open, the agency asked Lakeisha to apply. Now, she works part-time at a job she loves.

Despite their busy lives, many mothers we surveyed volunteer; some while working part- or even full-time. Women told us they teach Sunday school, help in classrooms, attend PTA meetings, serve on boards, act as advocates, write newsletters, counsel breastfeeding mothers, lead girl scout troops, rehabilitate wildlife, and more.

Volunteering is appealing because it helps meet many needs. It provides a break from parenting, strengthens your social network, and increases your sense of competence. If you volunteer in areas related to your child's disability, your own family can benefit. Sometimes we volunteer to help our own children, and wind up staying on to give back to the community. Only later do we realize that our volunteer work was also valuable professional development.

Volunteering can help you to:

Keep your skills (and resume) fresh. Amy volunteers on her daughter's school council one evening per month. "By facilitating some meetings, I use my teaching/training skills that I now seldom use as a writer. For example, I try out team building exercises (that previously I used while teaching college) with school council members."

Master new professional skills. As Theresa, mother of two children with special needs, says, "Volunteering got me involved in projects I would never have dreamed of. I discovered skills I didn't know I had. I became part of a committee on special education that I later ended up chairing. I wrote resource guides, and put together workshops and conferences. I developed a passion for writing that led to several items being published. I met with a congressman and discovered that lobbying was the greatest and most fulfilling feeling of all! Later I was offered the job of putting together and running a respite program."

Explore new areas of interest. Katherine, mother of four, volunteers one morning a week, visiting residents at a senior's home. "I'm testing this out," she says. "If I decide I want to work in this field, I'll take a gerontology course part-time at university."

Develop contacts that may help in the future. Heather's support group writes and publishes a resource guide. "When updating information, I've contacted dozens of staff from various agencies. If I was job searching, I'd start with these contacts who already know my skills."

One final word of advice on volunteering: If you've been out of the workforce for many years, it may feel daunting to apply for volunteer jobs. Start small. For example, volunteer to make phone calls or stuff envelopes to promote a fundraising event of your parent group. Volunteering needn't be all or nothing. Some positions will only require you to show up and pitch in for a couple hours. Others, like with paid employment, may ask you to submit your resume and references, get a police check, attend orientations, and go through an interview.

WHERE TO VOLUNTEER

Schools, churches/synagogues/temples, museums, galleries, animal welfare agencies, libraries, recreational centers, youth groups, community theaters, hospitals, senior centers, social service agencies, arts groups, and more all use volunteers. Find out about volunteer information nights, often held in mid- to large-sized communities. Check whether your town or county offers a database of volunteer opportunities (possibly online). Or visit your public library or information center. See Resources for websites to help you get started.

Courses, retraining, and volunteering are great ways to utilize your strengths, keep your skills fresh, and move toward your long-term goals. Now, if you'd like to return to the workforce, change jobs, or start your own business, the following chapters will tell you how.

Experience Talks

"Look through a community booklet and find something that interests you. You commit to however much time you have. If a club or class for your interest isn't there, start it yourself!"
—Lise, mother of a child who is deaf and has fetal alcohol syndrome

"I spend my time researching, advocating for, and teaching my autistic son. I volunteer on parent committees and plan to work part-time as an ABA instructor therapist in the near future."
—Melissa, mother of an eleven-year-old with autism

*"Ideally I will continue to work part-time, but will move
from teaching assistant to working as an early intervention specialist
with other special needs families."*

—Brenda, mom of two children who are medically fragile

Chapter 28

Get Set—Changing Your Work Situation

If you're working already, like Brenda (above), you may be ready for a job change that makes better use of your interests and skills. If you've been at home, you may decide that you're ready to search for a new, rewarding career. Perhaps your child care barriers have lessened somewhat, if your child has reached a point where you can rely on siblings, peer helpers, or after-school programs.

Or perhaps the financial matters are driving your decision. Maybe you're tired of living frugally on one income alone. Or, if your current paycheck is not enough, you may need to look for a better paying job.

If it seems likely that your child will need lifetime financial (and perhaps hands-on) support, you may be realizing how imperative it is to start planning now. If you're an at-home mom, one income may not be enough. Earning a second income to accumulate savings may suddenly seem crucial.

Financial pressures also increase tremendously if your family situation changes. Women we surveyed whose marriages had broken up typically needed to rejoin the workforce, start their own business, or find higher paying work.

In married couples, a change in your partner's work can affect your ability to earn a living. For example, if your husband's job flexibility increases, he may become more available at home. This may in turn free up more of your hours, allowing you to work, pursue a job change, or start your own business.

Before considering re-entering the workforce or changing jobs, make sure it won't jeopardize any of your existing supports. Would you lose SSI, Medicaid, or employer-sponsored health insurance? Do you receive other means-related disability supports that may be affected? If the answer to any of these is "yes," you'll need to calculate whether the change would actually put more money in your pocket, and whether you'd lose benefits that couldn't be easily replaced.

Finances aside, it just may feel like the time is right to resume or change your work. You've worked hard for your family and now feel eager to pursue a professional challenge. Take the steps below to help you re-enter or adjust your work life to better meet your needs.

Prepare the Home Front

"When I sought employment after two years of being at home, I went to my family and asked them for their support," says Dale, mother of a seven-year-old with autism. "I explained exactly what was involved in the work I was looking for and that I needed to do this for myself. This was going to be hard on me and them. I was going to need additional help with chores—everyone would have to help out."

Many mothers we surveyed complained that they shoulder all the responsibility for the house and kids, on top of working a full-time job. Don't let this happen to you! Supermom is a myth. Even the job hunt itself takes a lot of time, networking, and researching. If you try to search for a new job while maintaining all your usual family and job obligations, you're setting yourself up for failure. Instead, you and your family will have to make changes.

See Chapter 8 for strategies in delegating, sharing, and simplifying household and family tasks. And keep these two important facts in mind: (1) Teaching your children to help around the house (to the best of their abilities) *is a good thing*. It prepares them to live independently in the real world. And (2) they won't necessarily see it that way. So be prepared for griping—and don't let it make you feel guilty.

Get Supports in Place

Once your family is on board, investigate child care possibilities (see Chapters 18-20 for advice). If you have school-aged children, you'll still need occasional child care, even if you're regularly home after school. Your children will be home on holidays, school breaks, and sick days. If you're starting a home-based business, don't fool yourself into thinking you won't need child care—how do you think you could balance ledgers, write articles, or phone clients through a constant barrage of "Mom! Look at me!" If your business will be one with strict deadlines or client visits, you'll need not just a child care plan, but a backup plan as well (for days the school is closed or the nanny phones in sick). And if you plan on changing jobs, you may need alternate child care to fit a different schedule or location.

Present Yourself Effectively— The Stand-Out Resume

In order to land an interview, your resume must stand out. "A person will typically spend only one minute looking at your resume. They may have received 200 applicants, so you need to pop out as a very strong candidate," says Deb Berman, a consultant for Nonprofit Professionals Advisory Group. How do you do that? Write a fabulous one-page cover letter. Then tailor your resume to the job (yes, we know that's a pain, but employers expect it). And be sure you include specifics—accomplishments, awards, relevant training, where you attended school, the year you graduated, etc. Don't leave any of that information out.

Use Your Parenting and Volunteering Experience to Broaden Your Resume

But what do you do if you don't have any recent work experience other than working with your own child and volunteering? It can be daunting to create a resume if you've been out of the workforce for several years. Fortunately, the skills you've developed as a mother of a child with special needs are marketable and can be used to fill the time gap that would appear on your resume.

Below is a sample list of specialized activities you may carry out as a mother, volunteer, etc., that can be incorporated into a resume:

Implementing early intervention for an infant with developmental delays

Coordinating an intensive behavioral intervention program for a preschooler with behavioral challenges

Initiating and running parent support group meetings

Providing specialized medical care—such as catheterizing a child, bandaging and skin dressing, using oxygen equipment or feeding tubes, giving injections

Researching work/volunteer and living options alongside your teen with special needs

Recruiting, hiring, training, and supervising support workers

Spearheading a media campaign to raise disability awareness

Coordinating the delivery of food to 350 students during school pizza day

Coaching a team of ten-year-old soccer players

Map All Your Skills and Abilities on Paper

To clarify your strengths, it may be helpful to get them down on paper in a visual way, using a graphic organizer. Or if you prefer, use the list of skills you developed in Chapter 27 as a starting point.

1. Write your name in the center of a blank piece of paper and circle it. Then, around your name, make circles branching out from it showing the key areas of your life, such as family, volunteer work, paid work, hobbies, spiritual life, etc. For each area, make additional circles showing your experiences. For your

"Family" circle, write down any activities you usually do with different family members. Then note skills you've developed from those activities. See the Key Interests Map for Kara on page 405 for an example.

2. For each cluster of circles, write down the accomplish-ments and skills you have developed. For help making your list of accomplishments, use your day planner or calendar from the past few months. Underneath, write down the skills that enabled you to complete the task. These are the skills you can emphasize on your resume and in an interview.

   Even if you don't have much paid work experience to draw from, you still can describe the skills you've developed through parenting, community involvement, and volunteering. Let's look at how Kara's experience can translate into marketable skills:

Family Experience
Accomplishment: Wrote advocacy letters to government and delivered speeches at community forums.
Skills: Persuasive writing, public speaking, media relations, speech writing

Accomplishment: Implemented alternative teaching techniques for child with autism.
Skills: Research, teaching, task analysis

Accomplishment: Wrote and delivered presentations about children with autism and their families to parks and recreation departments, professional conferences, high schools, and universities.
Skills: Writing, public speaking, marketing and promotion, research

Interests and Hobbies
Accomplishment: Organized and facilitated reading groups about fiction books
Skills: Research, teaching, group facilitation, literature analysis

Accomplishments: Completed three continuing education courses in water color painting, oil painting, and printmaking; exhibited three paintings at juried community art festival.
Skills: Visual arts, networking, arts promotion

Accomplishment: Started and maintained a regular fitness program of aerobics classes, strength training, and core strength exercises through Pilates classes.
Skills: Determination, ability to follow through

Accomplishments: Organized rehearsal schedule for a ten-person choir. Sang and performed with choir at three Christmas fundraising concerts
Skills: Organization, promotion, performance techniques, singing, reading music

Volunteer Work
Accomplishments: (1) Facilitated and chaired meetings for a fifteen-person Parent-Teacher Association, (2) As education chair of local Arts Council, organized and facilitated meetings, arranged speakers, recruited members, delivered arts workshops
Skills: Leadership, public speaking, promotion, meeting facilitation, teaching

Paid Employment
Accomplishment: Designed and taught community college courses in writing, teaching, and public speaking
Skills: Teaching, curriculum design, public speaking, writing
Accomplishment: Wrote and published essays and non-fiction articles for magazines across North America
Skills: Writing, research, interviewing, marketing

Accomplishment: Researched, planned, and taught cooking classes, including low-fat and vegetarian cooking
Skills: Health and nutrition research, promotion and marketing, cooking, teaching

Key Interests Map for Kara

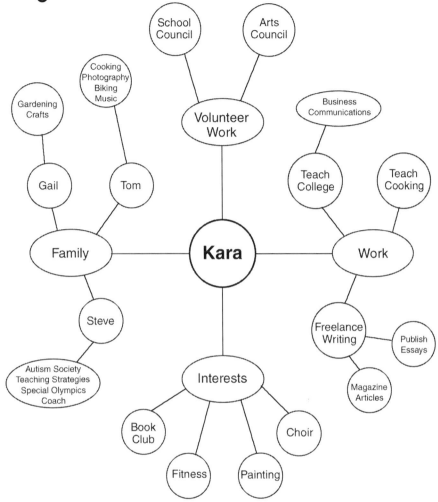

Resume Refreshers

Most public libraries and bookstores have at least a dozen books on how to write resumes. The most acceptable resume styles change rapidly so choose the most current book possible. One excellent guide is *202 Great Resumes* by Jay A. Block. In addition to tips and sample resumes, it includes how to write and post resumes online.

If you're changing careers or returning to the work force after a long break, avoid using a chronological resume, with a year-by-year employment description. Instead try a "functional" resume, in which you list your accomplishments by category. Each category has two to four accomplishments. Categories could include: Teaching, Advocacy, Public Relations, Staff Development, etc. After these categories include a brief listing of your titles, employer, and work in reverse chronological order.

Consult any resume book for samples of functional resumes and see the Sample Resume on the next page for ideas to get you started. We strongly recommend getting professional help creating your resume from your local career center, a professional resume writer, or a career coach.

If you've been an at-home mother for years, you have to account for that time on your resume. Rather than trying to hide the gap, simply write that you were a "full time parent or caregiver" during these years. And be sure to include the skills you've developed at home and by volunteering. You needn't specify whether or not you were paid for your work (use "Work History" rather than "Employment" as a resume heading, as not all of the work involves pay).

Especially if you have worked in various careers, you can create several versions of your resume, each emphasizing different skills you've developed. This is especially important if you have diverse experiences and are applying for work in different fields.

One mom, for example, works as an insurance salesperson and as a yoga teacher—so she would need a different resume, depending which job she's applying for. Some job hunter websites, such as CareerBuilder.com, allow you to create multiple versions of your resume online. If you're applying for a specific job at a company, take the time to highlight the skills in your resume that fit. And remember to keep your resume short—one to two pages, tops.

Some companies ask that you submit your resume by email. Check with the company to see if they prefer you send it as an attachment or in the body of your email message. They may request that you send a version in text format if they have a database of resumes they refer to when hiring. If your resume is in a word processing format, you may need to convert it to a plain text format by saving it as such in your word processing program. You may need to remove some formatting manually or insert formatting (such as tabs) to present it properly. Check online jobsites for the most up-to-date tips on formatting resumes for email. And, whatever you do, try emailing your resume to yourself, before you send it to a prospective employer. That will give you a chance to catch any formatting muck-ups before it hits the decision maker's desk.

SAMPLE RESUMÈ **MARIE JONES** SAMPLE RESUMÈ
4205 Somewhere Ave   Cool Place, California xxxxx   (xxx) xxx-xxxx
MarieJones@email.com

JOB OBJECTIVE: Educational assistant in elementary school special needs classroom

QUALIFICATIONS   8 years experience teaching and advocating for children with special needs.
A creative, dependable, and flexible educator with a record of success working with students who have autism, developmental disabilities, and behavioral challenges.
Educational Assistant certification

CORE STRENGTHS   Expertise in behavioral strategies, non-violent crisis intervention, sign language, and teaching techniques for children with autism
Advocacy and public speaking
Problem solving, leadership, and conflict resolution skills

EDUCATION/
PROFESSIONAL
DEVELOPMENT
Certificate in Intensive Behavioral Intervention, Smith Autism Institute, 2004
Educational Teaching Assistant Certification, Davis College, 1996
Bachelor of Arts, Social Sciences, Valley University, 1992

SELECTED ACCOMPLISHMENTS
Educational Program Development
Researched, devised, and taught a customized life skills and academic program to a kindergarten student with developmental disabilities.
Designed, coordinated, and monitored a year-long home treatment program for a preschooler with autism.
Hired, trained, and managed staff of three behavioral intervention specialists for intensive one-to-one home program.

Group Facilitation
Initiated, promoted, and facilitated a monthly support group for 25 parents of children with special needs.

Fundraising and Promotion
Revitalized fundraising committee for Parent Teacher Association at Wilson Elementary School. Supervised the planning and implementation of a fundraising art auction, generating over $5,000.
Spearheaded and marketed annual fundraising walk-a-thon for Community Living agency. Increased donations 25 percent over previous years. Supervised volunteers in arranging materials and activities for event. Wrote press releases, gave radio and television interviews.

Public Speaking
Created and presented 20 seminars on teaching strategies for children with autism to high school and university classes.
Received consistently high evaluations for seminar presentations.

WORK HISTORY   Silicon Valley Independent Living Center (2004 to Present)
Member, Board of Directors
Community Health Centre, San Jose (2003 to Present)
Coordinator, Parent Support Group
Pleasant School, San Jose (2002 to Present)
Chair, Fundraising Committee, Parent Teacher Association
Happy Students Elementary School, San Francisco, California (1997-2000)
Educational Assistant

Experience Talks

"My skills for work are stronger because of all the advocacy I have had to do for my children. I feel more confident dealing with support services and am able to share this information with the families I work with now."

—Brenda, mom of two children who are medically fragile (after a job switch from educational assistant to part-time early intervention worker)

"I found my latest job by word of mouth and I wasn't even looking."

—Carmelita, mother of a child with ADHD, sensory issues, and gross motor delays

Chapter 29

Go!
Finding and Landing
the Perfect Job

Some women, like Carmelita (above), land ideal jobs without conducting a formal job search. After maintaining their career contacts over the years, some just contact their previous employers. That was the case with Maggie, mom of a fourteen-month-old with Down syndrome:

"After having my baby, I decided to stay home. So I resigned. Then when I was ready to come back, I called and asked if they had any part-time evening work and they made room for me. I would advise other mothers to ask... ask... ask... for what you want and what you need. You'll be surprised at the positive response! I could not have asked for more support. They have given me everything I have needed to be a great mom and employee."

But for most people, it takes more effort to find work that meets your needs. And if you think the classified ads are the best place to start, think again.

Get the Word Out

"Networking is still the number one way to get a job," says Amy Joyce, career columnist for the *Washington Post*. That's because employers feel more comfortable hiring someone who they already know or who's been recommended to them by someone they trust.

Contacts led to an interesting job for Colleen, a single mother of two children with physical challenges. First, she narrowed down the kind of work she wanted—home-based, flexible, and computer-related. She told all her family and friends what she was looking for, and then volunteered to design a website for an acquaintance. He was so impressed with the site that he offered her a part-time job, doing computer work from her home.

"Contact everyone you know—even if you haven't spoken to them in years," advises Joyce. (See the box below for ideas.) "Explain

Networking Contacts for your Job Search

Friends
Friends of your spouse or partner
Former coworkers or supervisors
Former classmates and teachers
Your college alumni center
Association members (professional, alumni, or community associations)
Neighbors
Store owners
Church/synagogue members
Fitness buddies at the gym
Doctors, dentists, hairdressers, etc., etc.

your situation (as much as you are comfortable with) and ask if they have any advice for you." Offer to send your contacts copies of your resume, so they can pass it along if they come across others with job opportunities. Rather than calling, also consider sending out a brief email to friends with your request.

Career experts recommend making yourself a "transitional" business card as a networking tool. That way you don't have to walk around with a resume in your purse. On the card, include your name, phone, email, and a professional identifier such as "marketing specialist," "graphic designer," etc.

One of your contacts may also be able to hook you up with someone for an "informational interview," says Joyce. An informational interview is a brief meeting with a person who is working in a field you're interested in, who can give you an "insider's" view of the job and help you make additional contacts. (See the box "Getting the Lowdown" on the next page.)

In addition to speaking with family, friends, and acquaintances, contact people you know in disability organizations, community facilities, and schools. These places all need a variety of workers, including teachers, fundraisers, administrators, trades people, receptionists, and more. Perhaps you've volunteered on a committee or held a position on a board. Tell your contacts about your skills and that you are looking for employment. After all, you have an inside perspective on the agency, which can help you be an effective employee. Even if you don't want to work for the organization itself, use your contacts there. They may have friends or acquaintances who have job opportunities. If you belong to online forums or disability associations, also tell those members about your skills and job search.

Through her disability contacts, Elyse created her dream job. Although she previously worked in human resources, she quit because she found it hard to balance the job demands with caring for her son who has Down syndrome. When Elyse's son turned four, she contacted the disability agencies that had helped her family. Eventually, she landed an ideal job—working part-time at home as a regional coordinator for Families Together. Now, she supports other families of children with special needs and presents workshops at conferences.

To expand your circle of contacts, visit local business groups, advises Annette Richmond, founder of Career-Intelligence.com. To find out about groups and meetings, check the business calendar section of your local newspaper. Many communities have business groups

Getting the Lowdown— The Informational Interview

In an informational interview, you're not asking for a job, but for an insider's view of the field and, hopefully, some additional contacts.

The best way to land an informational interview is through networking. If one of your contacts can put you in touch with a friend or colleague in the field you're interested in, pick up the phone! Open with "My friend Sue Jones, in the finance department, suggested that I give you a call." Then ask if she'd be willing to meet with you for fifteen minutes to talk about her job and her workplace, since you'd like to re-enter (or change) your field of work. You can do the meeting by phone, in her office, or offer to take her for a quick lunch or coffee. This discussion gets you in the door, without the company feeling that you're applying for work. It also allows you to scout out the company for overall "feel" and evidence of family friendly policies.

At the meeting, talk briefly about your experience and the career options you're exploring. Then, ask specific questions about what the person enjoys most about the job, typical challenges, and essential skills. To subtly inquire about job possibilities, ask "Can you suggest anyone in the field I might talk with to find out about openings?" Follow up with a thank you note. And be sure to thank the contact person who originally introduced you, as well.

specifically designed for women to network. "Visit a few times," says Richmond. "If you decide to join, get involved. It's the best way to really get to know some people and to prove your worth."

Or try "cold calling" a headhunter who specializes in the field you're aiming for. Briefly describe your background, and if she thinks she can "sell" you to a client, she'll ask you to send in your resume.

What to Look For

Grace, mother of a teenager with Asperger syndrome, told us, "If I can't get away at a moment's notice to take care of a school issue or a 'meltdown,' then I can't consider taking the position." Before applying for any job, clarify which aspects of work are most important to you. Make a list, including: location, work hours, leave policies, insurance benefits, child care, supportive and interested workers/supervisors, work that matches your skills, etc. Like Grace, decide which work conditions are "must-haves" and which are "nice but not essential." This will help you set your priorities for the interview.

To avoid future hassles, check out workplaces before applying for a job there. If you have contacts at potential employers, ask them about the company's policies and whether employees typically take advantage of them. Ask to borrow a copy of their employee benefits information. If the company is unionized, ask how effective they've been in negotiating family friendly policies.

Consumer magazines often have articles on excellent employers. For example, *Working Mother, Fortune,* and *Canada Employment Weekly* all publish annual lists of the "best companies" to work for. City-specific publications, such as *Washingtonian,* often do the same with local companies. Of course, don't just accept a magazine's recommendation at face value. Companies that are trying to make it onto these lists know how to keep disgruntled employees away from reporters. But even if the specific companies listed aren't right for you, these articles will give you ideas for questions to ask in the interview.

Check each potential employer's website. Many include information for prospective employees about flexible or part-time hours and job sharing.

Landing an Interview

Eventually, after using all your strategies to hear about possible jobs, you'll target some that you want to apply for. Now, to get in the door, you'll need to write a cover letter (to accompany your resume) that makes you stand out in one page.

CRAFTING A COVER LETTER

One of the biggest mistakes that job applicants make, says Deb Berman, a consultant with Nonprofit Professionals Advisory Group, is talking about themselves in the cover letter, instead of about the organization. Do your homework by going online and finding out about an organization's past, present, and future goals. "Introduce yourself and describe why you're right for the job. Talk about what you know about the organization and how you're going to fill a gap that presently isn't being filled there."

Tell the employer how you heard about the job—e.g., in the newspaper, or on a specific job search website. If you have a connection in the company, be sure to mention that. For example, "Marie Star, on the board of directors, suggested that I apply, since my skills are a good fit for the role."

FOLLOWING UP

Once you've sent your resume and cover letter, you can wait and see if you're contacted for an interview. If you're feeling brave, follow up by calling and asking if they've reviewed applications yet. Very briefly describe your qualifications and ask if you can schedule an interview. If they haven't yet gone through applications, ask when they will be scheduling interviews.

If you can't speak directly to the manager, leave a brief voice message or send a short email.

If you have a contact within that organization, ask if they could recommend you to the person who is hiring.

Conquering the Interview—Drawing on Your Advocacy Skills

Many job candidates dread the interview process, but there's no reason to. Any woman who's been able to calm a screaming child, negotiate with a special education department, and hammer a hospital into correcting its bill can certainly communicate well enough to shine in a job interview!

Sylvia, mother of two kids under thirteen (one with cerebral palsy), targeted a social service agency with family friendly policies when she applied for an administrative job. Although she hadn't held a paid job since her eldest was born, she had been active as a volunteer and as her son's advocate. She admits to being terrified before the interview. But she felt positive afterward: "It was a confidence booster to have an interview with four people and to be able to answer all their questions effectively."

As an advocate for your child, you've had to learn to think on your feet, to speak diplomatically, and to problem solve. Now you're just going to put those skills to work in a different context.

Sell employers on your ability to get the job done. One excellent interview strategy involves researching the company (see above), and trying to identify its major challenge or goal (as you did to prepare your cover letter). In your interview, present yourself as someone who can solve their problem and meet that goal. If possible, provide concrete suggestions. For example, Sonya once applied to a non-profit organization as a recreational program coordinator. In her research, she discovered their biggest problem was finding staff for summer programs. So, in her interview, she suggested how she would improve staff recruitment. The results? She got the job.

Here are a few extra tips to score big at your interview:

> Bring a few extra copies of your resume, in case the interviewer has lost yours or asks someone else to join her.
> Use your body language to expresses confidence, enthusiasm, and ability. That means good eye contact, a firm handshake, and a warm smile when you meet.
> After the interview, always send a brief thank you note to your interviewers within twenty-four hours.

COMMON INTERVIEW QUESTIONS

Before your interview, rehearse the answers to these questions that commonly arise. Better yet, do a mock interview with a friend or family member playing the prospective boss.

Q: Tell me about yourself.
A: Describe a few of your job or volunteer-related experiences and accomplishments that are most relevant.

Q: What are your strengths?
A: Be prepared to discuss three of your strengths that are most relevant to the job requirements. For each,

describe an accomplishment that clearly demonstrates that strength, e.g., "I'm very skilled at explaining and teaching highly technical concepts. At a recent conference, I taught a session on ____ and received the top rating (for teaching effectiveness) on all 100 feedback forms."

Q: What are your weaknesses?

A: Describe one *minor* weakness and state what you are doing to overcome it. For example, you could say your spelling skills are relatively weak, but you compensate by spell-checking your documents.

Q: Why do you want to work for us?

A: Make sure you've done your company research. State specifically what you like about the organization, its goals, and how your skills fit well.

Q: What specific accomplishments are you most proud of?

A: Discuss a few accomplishments that are most relevant to the job you're applying for. "Use language that spins your experience to emphasize your leadership skills, ability to juggle and handle multiple priorities, manage people and resources, fundraise, etc.," advises Nora Spinks, president of Work-Life Harmony Enterprises. Even if you've been at home with your child, use vibrant language to describe your accomplishments; try: "spearheaded," "launched," "developed," and "researched."

Q: Where do you see yourself five or ten years from now?

A: Describe how your job within the company might progress. Stress how the company will benefit from your progress.

Usually interviewers proceed from these fairly straightforward questions to more situational ones. For example: "Describe a time when you successfully managed an emergency at the workplace." Or they may ask you to describe what you'd do in various situations at work. For example, if you're applying to be a teacher's assistant: "What would you do if the child you were working with constantly disrupted the classroom, and the teacher was upset?" So, to prepare, think of likely situations that would occur in that job, and rehearse your answers.

QUESTIONS FOR YOUR INTERVIEWER

At the end, most interviewers will ask if you have any questions. Ask a question that shows you have researched the company and have a keen interest in it. Or ask your interviewer what she most appreciates about the company.

Also be clear about the requirements of the job. Ask your interviewer to describe a typical work day for a person in this position. Find out if you would need to travel regularly or occasionally. If so, how much advance notice would you receive? Does the company provide any financial child care assistance for times you must travel? Are overtime, evening, weekend, or erratic hours usual for this job?

Always end by expressing your interest in the position, and ask what the next step in the interview process will be.

Many companies offer a tour of their facility at a first or later interview (ask if they don't offer). Walking through the halls gives you a sense of how family-friendly a place is. For example, do employees display family photos on their desks? On bulletin boards, do you see notices about parent support groups or company events that include families? Are there flyers about employee fitness/wellness classes offered during the day? In the lunchroom, are people eating alone or in groups? Can you see yourself fitting in here?

When to Raise the Sticky Questions

Only you can decide how much to divulge about your family situation. The Americans with Disabilities Act says employers may not ask if you or any family members have a disability. But some employers may ask personal questions because they aren't even aware of what is legal.

You need to be clear about if and when you want to disclose your situation. One mom who has interviewed job candidates in her position as a human resources specialist says to be cautious in interviews. She explains she was trained to ask "round-about" questions to uncover personal issues during an interview. If a prospective employee mentioned certain situations (including a child with extra needs), she was instructed to cut an interview short. On the other hand, a company using these interview practices would likely be a poor fit for you anyhow.

In your interview, don't lead off with your family situation, advises Spinks. To open the discussion, you could ask what kind of community involvement the organization has. You may find out, for example, that the CEO is on the board of the Independent Living Center because she has a child with special needs. So, you may be able to open up a dialogue with less fear, says Spinks.

You Have a Job Offer—Now Negotiate for What You Need

Flexibility—like salary—is a condition of your employment, typically negotiated towards the *end* of the hiring process—when you are offered the job. You have the most clout negotiating at this point, since the company is eager to hire you. In this final negotiating phase, this may be the time to disclose your family situation. "Honesty is a good position to start off with," says Spinks. "The more information you have about your precise needs, the better." So, you could say, for example, "I have a child with special needs, and, on average, once every two months I'll need to leave at noon to attend a specialist appointment." At the same time, stress that you have supports in place to ensure you can do excellent work. If you've promoted yourself well through the interview process, your terms are more likely to be accepted.

At this point, request everything on your "must-have" list. This might be flexible hours to attend appointments, or part-time or home-based work some days. After that, negotiate for as much as you think the employer will agree to. By now, from doing your research, you should have a "gut" feeling for company practices on flexible issues. Use that to decide how much to ask for. Remember that you can always negotiate more once you've proven yourself. See Chapter 25 for more advice.

Before you accept any job, you need to know about employee benefits. Ask to talk to someone from human resources, if you didn't during the interview process.

Even if you don't get the job, the interview is valuable. Sylvia, the mother we profiled earlier in this section, didn't get the first job she interviewed for. But going through the interview process increased her confidence and gave her goals to work toward. "They were impressed by all of my accomplishments—even though they weren't for pay," she says. The confidence and interview practice paid off. Several months later, she landed an administrative job for a social service agency. Best of all, she negotiated part-time hours that enable her to be home with her kids before and after school.

Accepting a Job

Congratulations—you've been offered a job—perhaps several! First closely evaluate the workplace's stand on family issues. Based on your tour and talks with the supervisor and other employees, do you have a good feel for the work atmosphere? Unless you have worked at the company in the past or know an employee, you'll need to trust your gut. Did the interviewer respond favorably to your questions about flexibility? Or, did she seem uncomfortable when discussing those issues? Even if you don't need flexibility now, you may need it in the future.

Before accepting a job, also know the workplace policies on:

> *Insurance.* How does the employer insurance plan compare to your existing insurance coverage (if you had coverage under a government program like Medicaid, you may find it lacking). Is it managed care? If so, do the primary care providers/specialists meet your needs? If not, can you go outside the plan? Will it cost? Does your plan include both medical and dental? Does it cover the services you need? Are there maximums or exemptions for pre-existing conditions? What are the deductibles or co-payments? How long does it take to get reimbursed? Some companies offer cafeteria-style (choice of) benefits. If yours is one, be prepared to assess your families' medical needs for at least a year. Call agents from the insurance plan directly, if the human resources person cannot answer all your questions.

> *Leave Policies.* Know what will happen if you must leave work in the middle of the day for a family emergency. Will the company overlook it, allow you to make the time up, or will they dock you pay? When absent for a day or longer to care for your child, must you use sick time or vacation days? Are there extended leave policies? What about protection under the FMLA?

Child care. Do employees have access to on-site child care, sick care or backup care, or support for summer arrangements? Does your employer have a dependent care assistance plan or other child care subsidies?

When you're fully aware of all job requirements and benefits, you can accept the position with confidence. And you can be comfortable that your finances, insurance, and child care plans all fit well with your new job.

Experience Talks

"As a parent representative, I do home visits, hold support groups, and acquire information regarding disabilities and services for parents of children with special needs. I also hold SibShops for the siblings. This is the most fulfilling job I have ever had—only acquired it as a result of my child."

—Raquel, mother of a child with traumatic brain injury

"Find a sympathetic employer or an organization (government or private) that is known for being supportive of working parents. A daycare center on the premises is a good indicator that the organization cares about working parents. Network with women's organizations and other working parents to find out which employers have flexible policies."

—Suki, mom to a child with Tourette syndrome, anxiety, and learning disabilities

"I've used the knowledge from having a child with special needs to start a business that sells unique gifts for healthcare professionals and educators. I find this comforting because I'm helping other parents to recognize these great people. In some ways, being the mom of a special-needs child is my identity. When I'm at a disability conference as an exhibitor, I feel that I am with my peers. There is a camaraderie when you are with people who go through the same things you do."

—Thea, mother of a young adult with multiple disabilities

Chapter 30

Be Your Own Boss— Starting a Home-Based Business

For some women, starting a home-based business offers endless benefits. We heard from many parents like Thea (above), who created a business based on experiences with their own children. While few originally intended to be entrepreneurs, their businesses evolved naturally from their lives.

While most self-employed women we surveyed worked from home, others owned their own clinics (doctors, psychologists, speech-language pathologists, etc.). Some worked in the service industry, e.g., owning a hair salon or a nursing agency.

Home-based businesses are more common for several reasons. Since flexibility is such a huge priority for mothers, home-based work is the top choice. If you have to leave work in the middle of the day, you aren't closing down a storefront. If you need to attend appointments with your child, you can complete work in the evening or on the weekend. Your start-up costs are minimized, since you don't have to rent space. Plus, many home-based businesses allow you to test out an idea on a part-time basis without major outlays of cash. And with today's technology—computers, email, faxes, etc.—working from home is much more feasible than in years past.

Some moms told us they started home businesses to develop or maintain their skills while earning extra money. Rather than starting businesses from scratch, some work as home-based sales reps (independent contractors) for various companies. For example, Iris, a mother of four (triplets with health problems and a child with Down syndrome), sells educational children's toys. This business was a natural for her, since she previously had worked as an early childhood educator. "I get to make my own schedule of when and how much I work," she says. "My children all benefit from playing with the toys—many of them are perfect for children with special needs."

Owning their own businesses also gives some moms a better sense of job security. Even at family-friendly workplaces, many women told us they felt their jobs were precarious. Morgan, mother to a child with cerebral palsy, felt tenuous in her position with a healthcare agency. While she did negotiate flextime and telecommuting, she always felt uneasy taking time off to take her child to appointments. And, she felt she was being passed over for promotions. Eventually, Morgan "fulfilled a dream" and became a partner in her own nursing agency, which she runs from home.

Of course, one of the main benefits to working at home is having more time with your kids—and some moms even involve their kids in their businesses. Glenda started a business making and selling handmade gourmet chocolates with her teenage daughter, Bridget, who has Down syndrome. As a preteen, Bridget learned to make chocolates alongside her mom on weekends and in the summer. On Saturdays the two of them sold the treats at their farmer's market.

Small businesses like this have exciting possibilities for the future. While Glenda started the business so that her daughter could take it over in adulthood, it has evolved. Bridget, now a young adult, prefers to work and volunteer at child care centers. So, Glenda is changing direction by making the business a charitable organization with a board of directors. Now she is investigating grants and training other adults with developmental disabilities to work as candy-makers in her business. She hopes to expand her company to a storefront, which would create even more employment opportunities. What started out as a dream for Glenda's child has wound up being a satisfying business enterprise and charitable project for herself.

Some of the home-based businesses owned by the women we surveyed include:

> Home-based child care—Inclusive child care to benefit their own children and other families'
> Freelance writing, editing, and graphic arts
> Computer-based services, including word processing and web design
> Freelance health services such as reflexology, massage therapy, and nursing care
> Speech, occupational, and physical therapy
> Consulting related to the moms' previous professions such as bookkeeping and tutoring
> Disability-related products or services. For example, one mother of a child with autism sells symbol boards, picture schedules, and other visual supports.
> Direct sales of products such as Tupperware, Mary Kay Cosmetics, and Discovery Toys

Questions to Ask Yourself If You're Considering a Home-Based Business

Wondering if you've got what it takes to start your own business? Research shows that women who are persistent, adaptable, optimistic, stubborn, resilient, and curious tend to succeed in a home-based business. If these characteristics describe you, it's hardly surprising. As mothers of children with disabilities, we try to be optimistic about the future. We stubbornly advocate for services and adapt as our children's needs change. Most of all, we're resilient—mainly, because we have to be.

Now that you see how well-suited you are, you may want to jump right in. But starting a business is no easy task.

First, ask yourself:

1. HOW MUCH TIME AND ENERGY DO I REALLY HAVE TO COMMIT TO A BUSINESS?

Despite the allure of job flexibility, don't underestimate the time and energy required to make your business a success. We interviewed Professor Donna Lero, co-director of the Centre for Families, Work, and Well-Being at the University of Guelph in Ontario, Canada. She observes that often mothers of kids with special needs leave employment to start businesses. But you need to be cautious, she says: "Think carefully about whether you have the energy and stamina to do it, and if you can have ebbs and flows in your involvement. For example, if you have a store, it needs to be covered. If you're working from home, you have to figure out realistically when you can work. It doesn't solve the child care dilemma. You'll still need child care."

2. CAN I AFFORD TO START A BUSINESS?

Expect a new business to start slowly, since most lose money the first year or first few years. But if your business requires little equipment or inventory, your expenses may be minimal. For example, if you already have a computer, you could start a word processing, writing, editing, or web design business from your home with minimal cost. Be realistic about what your business will earn. To calculate your expenses and projected earnings, work through a business plan and budget. You can find sample plans in books from the library or on Internet sites. The Small Business Administration offers many resources online, including sample detailed plans for various businesses. Your local community college or women's council may even offer short, non-credit courses in creating business plans.

Carefully consider your supports. Do you have a partner with a stable salary and benefits who can provide your primary income? Do you have regular child care in place, or will that be an added cost?

If you lack personal savings to start a business, look into pursuing alternative sources such as banks, government loans, family members, partners, etc. Many government programs have grants specifically to help women start businesses. Contact your state's Office of

Economic Development or Department of Commerce, or your county commission for women. In Canada, contact your nearest Canada Business Service Centre. (See Resources for ideas.)

Victoria, single mother to a teen with Asperger syndrome, was having a rough time at work. "My son's concerns and the constant phone calls from school made it difficult to maintain my full-time job. My sanity was definitely at risk." Eventually, Victoria took a stress leave and learned that her job was eliminated during her absence. But she used her severance pay to retrain as a massage therapist. Then she obtained a grant to start her business through a provincial government self-employment benefit program.

Like Victoria, it's wise to start small with a business that doesn't require you to outlay a lot of money to buy product. Consider a business that enables you to control your workload by limiting the number of clients or assignments you take on. Also, look for work that can be done in short spurts, depending on the needs of your child.

3. How will it affect my health insurance?

If you have a partner who gets excellent health insurance through his employer, you don't have to worry about covering your child's needs. But without such support, self-employment may not be the best solution. Nell, single mom of a twelve-year-old son with Duchenne's muscular dystrophy, has worked in the technical writing industry for fifteen years. Her financial pressures are intense, as insurance only partially covers the adaptations her son needs for home and school. As her son's degenerative disability progresses, she would like to work as a consultant from home, so she can care for him. But, she can't afford to lose what limited insurance she has.

Similarly, if your child or family receives SSI, Medicaid, or other subsidies tied to low income, check whether your self-employment income would jeopardize these supports. If so, factor into your decision the cost (and quality) of substitute health insurance.

If you do need health insurance, consider buying it through a group plan. Contact your local chamber of commerce, trade, and professional associations to see if they have access to discounted health insurance. The National Association for the Self-Employed, for example, offers a group health plan to members.

4. AM I SUITED TO WORKING AT HOME?

Take an honest look at your own personality. If you dislike working in isolation and get distracted easily, home-based work may not suit you. To test the waters, do some homework. Meet with other moms (with kids with special needs) who work from home and ask them how they manage their day, their work life, and their sense of isolation. With this realistic peek at the at-home work world, you may decide to take the plunge.

This may require some compromises. Brittany, mom of a teen with mental health issues, and previously a writer, started a home-based consulting company providing seminars about parenting high needs children. She says she'd much prefer to work in an office "to interact with people who have more 'normal' lives." If money wasn't tight, she'd hire a live-in child care provider so she could work in an office. "I always feel better when I get away," she says. But her home business allows her to work fewer hours and to earn more money than she did previously.

Women who get distracted easily may find working from home challenging. We heard from women who, like their children, have symptoms of ADHD. As a result, they feel overwhelmed by the lack of structure and distractions of home.

On the other hand, some moms who share the same diagnosis as their child (such as Asperger syndrome, learning disabilities, or physical challenges) may find that a home business enables them to earn an income without the pressures of social interaction or problems with accessibility. Such was the case with Lynne, who used personal contacts to find home-based work as a web designer. She says, "I found out a few years ago that I am autistic as well (diagnosed with Asperger syndrome). I realized that I should be an at-home mum because I wouldn't have survived the outer business world."

Still keen to start your own business? Read about the potential pitfalls that experienced home-based working moms described below.

Common Pitfalls of Self-Employment for Moms Like Us

Some days, working from home is idyllic. But not always. Amy remembers days that were more like this one: "After Talia walked home with me from school, she was frantic to play computer games. My magazine article would be due by the end of the day. I'd lock myself in my office and try to concentrate as Talia banged on the door sobbing, "Computer! Computer! Computer!"

Let's look at some typical challenges.

BLURRING OF HOME AND WORK LIFE

It can be stressful to wear several hats at home—that of breadearner/homemaker/mother/advocate. Studies show that women working part-time are the *most stressed*, because they are shouldering a full load of housework and child care in addition to their paid work. Image is also a problem. If your family members don't see you as having a "real" job, they may be less likely to pitch in and do their share of the household duties.

Brittany says she has little time to devote to her business. Since her son has high needs, she must complete all errands, housework, advocacy, fitness, etc., during the day while he is at school. "We still have a crisis lifestyle, which requires constant vigilance except during school hours," she says. Like in Brittany's household, your day can disappear as you make phone calls, attend appointments, and complete your child's paperwork.

Every day, a mom with a home-based business needs to prioritize. Do you call your client or do you call your child's speech therapist? Do you finish that business report by deadline, or do you keep your commitment to volunteer in the classroom? Don't think owning your own business means you'll no longer feel torn.

Try these solutions:

Make your office a room where you can close the door.

Plan your work hours for each day and try to stick to them. For example, if you know you're taking your child to appointments during the day, plan to work from 7:00 p.m. to 10:00 p.m. that night, when your partner can watch the kids.

Limit your interruptions by getting a separate phone line or email for business. Or use your answering machine or Caller ID feature to screen calls.

*Make family pitch in on household chores. (*See Chapter 8 for tips.)

Consider renting or borrowing a space (even in a neighboring house) where you can work without distractions.

Whenever possible, use email (after work hours) to manage your child's needs, rather than tying up your day with phone calls.

Hire out the tasks that you find time consuming, you procrastinate on, or aren't good at.

Consider taking a business partner so that one of you is always available, despite any crises with your children.

MAINTAINING A PROFESSIONAL IMAGE

"Downfalls (of a home business) include the difficulty of setting up and working to get clients to respect you as a legitimate business," says Amy Joyce. It's hard to be taken seriously if your kids answer your phone calls, or if you seldom take the time to answer emails and attract new customers.

Try these solutions to boost your business' image:

Create promotional materials. Even if money is tight, you can still create simple business cards (on your own computer or at an office supply store,) a promotional flyer, and basic website. Offer to exchange services with a friend who has skills to make a website for you. Once you have more available funds, a graphic designer or marketing person can help you create an effective brochure and business card.

Join professional associations. Most communities have small business associations that meet regularly to network and exchange ideas. Attend, connect with other small business owners, and give out your card and brochure.

Talk to everyone. Just like when you're job searching, tell absolutely everyone you know about your business and what you can do for them. Get your contacts to help you spread the word.

Despite the challenges, building a home-based business may do wonders for your learning, self-esteem, enjoyment, social life, and employability. It can also provide valuable work experience if you should decide to take an outside job in the future. However, it may not pay your bills immediately. So, if your goal is to earn a substantial full-time salary, you may have to be patient. Expect to work long hours, at least until your business is established. For further support, see the box "Online Resources for Starting Your Home-Based Business."

Ten Home-Based Businesses with Low Start-up Costs

Here are a few ideas to get you started. All these home-based businesses have low overhead costs. But check with your local small business administration, Chamber of Commerce, or county/town clerk (under "licenses and permits" in the government pages of your phone book) to see if you need a license, insurance, or bonding to legally operate in your area.

1. **Freelance writer, editor, or web designer.** If you used to work in print or web publishing, contact your former employers and offer to take on contract work from home. Get a business card and send out a letter describing your services to all your contacts. As a sideline, you could teach other small business owners how to design their own websites, newsletters, or business reports. To update your skills, take a few courses in web design or teach yourself from books or online resources.

2. **Direct sales representative.** Selling for companies such as Discovery Toys, Tupperware, or Mary Kay Cosmetics offers flexibility, incentive programs, and the possibility of financial success. Typically you

can buy a sample kit of products for under $100. You can combine socializing with earning income. For example, if you're selling toys, invite your mother's support group. Or operate a table at a disability group fundraiser and offer to donate a percentage of your sales. Some companies that are members of the Direct Selling Association may have health insurance programs that you can access.

3. **Pet services and treats.** If you enjoy animals, you could start a dog walking or pet sitting service, where you take care of animals in their home while the owners are away. Also popular are home-baked nutritious dog treats that can be packaged attractively and sold at craft sales or farmer's markets.

4. **Crafts person.** If you have an artistic streak, try making beaded jewelry, hand-painted clothing, photography nature cards, etc., at home. Contact your local arts council, chamber of commerce, and other artists to find out about art shows, festivals, and markets where you can sell your work.

5. **Catering, cooking classes, and food preparation.** Are you an expert in preparing healthy, gourmet, or ethnic foods? Run a business where you offer a unique kind of dinner party. At a client's home, you show guests how to prepare a meal, and then they have a chance to enjoy it together. Or cook and deliver healthy homemade meals that families can store in their freezer.

6. **Tutoring.** You may have gained expertise in alternative teaching techniques through helping your own child. Develop a tutoring resume and brochure to leave at local schools. Tutor children either at their home, your own home, or the local library.

7. **Cleaning service.** If you have excellent organizational skills, you could hire and manage a team of

home cleaners. Find ways to increase your competitive advantage. For example, can you leave fresh cut flowers or a container of freshly made soup at the homes where you clean? Or can you leave out a "report card" at homes, for people to give you feedback and request that certain parts of their house be cleaned?

8. **Sewing and alteration.** If you're handy with your sewing machine, this could be ideal flexible work. It's also a great way to make use of your special needs contacts. For example, could you adapt clothing (add Velcro, etc.) for people who are unable to fasten snaps and do up zippers?

9. **Small business support.** From your home computer, be a "virtual assistant" for a small business, handling scheduling, billing, or business letter writing.

10. **Computer consulting.** If you have good technical skills, help clients purchase, set up, and effectively use computers at home or in their business.

Online Resources for Starting your Home-Based Business

www.myownbusiness.com is a non-profit site for entrepreneurs. It offers a free twelve-session course (online) that takes you from brainstorming business ideas, to finances, to all aspects of starting and running your own business.

Home-Based Working Moms (www.hbwm.com) is a professional association and online community of women. Membership includes access to a database of Work At Home jobs including jobs such as computer work, bookkeeping, writing, graphic design, etc.

The Federal Trade Commission's Business Opportunities website (www.ftc.gov/bizopps) offers practical advice about avoiding common "work from home" scams. Or call 1-877-382-4357.

Experience Talks

"Freedom of schedule, freedom of choice for projects, ability to mesh my son's needs with my work, ability to be at school whenever I am needed or perceive a need, ability to network with professionals in a field I need information about . . . the list [of benefits] is endless."
—Josephine, self-employed dietitian and mom of a child who is non-verbal

"The upside is the flexibility, but the downside is if I don't work, I don't get paid. The time my business needs is generally evenings and weekends, which are my precious family time. I never seem to get away from work, since some of my clients give me work to take home."
—Polly, part-time accountant, and mother to a child with a chromosome disorder

PART VIII

Transformations

From Struggle
to Strength

"At some point you realize you are luckier than other women,
because unlike the mothers of the perfect little toddlers, you know
what miracles really are. You meet people you never would have met be-
cause disability affects all classes and crosses all boundaries.
After a while, you view life with a disabled child as invigorating—
there's never going to be a dull moment with your child."

—Aileen, mom to a ten-year-old with autism and a nine-year-old
with ADHD and speech and learning disabilities

When you're struggling with your child's behaviors, making endless phone calls for help, or watching your child endure medical procedures, life can feel overwhelming. But as you move through the difficult times, you also discover personal strengths, valuable skills, and a new life perspective.

Of course, life with a child who has special needs can be hard. Some women we surveyed said they felt exhausted rather than "enriched" by their mothering experience. All of us at times feel depressed, cynical, and isolated, like Fiona (whose child is deaf): "I feel different from all of my friends and it gets me down a lot of the time." In addition to feeling isolated, some moms said they have lost faith in the goodness of people. "I think (special needs mothering) has hardened me," confesses Rose. "I have to fight for everything my son deserves." Meg, mother of a child with Duchenne muscular dystrophy, has similar feelings. She finds the constant stares of people to be rude, uncaring, and unnerving.

Grace, the mother of a teen with Asperger syndrome, says she is now cynical about people. "They seem to want to believe the worst about a child (they're spoiled, undisciplined, overindulged, etc.) before realizing that there may be a legitimate reason for their behavior." Penny, mother of a child with autism, sadly relates that "I always thought that Western Society believed in the value of humans first. But it's direct personal economic gain that's the driving force—and true giving and support comes from a very few (and often mutually desperate) people."

Yet even women like Penny, who are disheartened, also cite positive changes. All say they have a broader and deeper perspective about people. Specifically, they have new respect and understanding for people with disabilities. As Luisa admits, "I used to be afraid of (people with disabilities) and I can't even remember why!" Says another, "There are many wonderful people in the special needs world and many of them are indeed the special needs people themselves."

Some mothers take something positive from even the most anguishing experiences. Margo watched her daughter endure and survive five open heart surgeries. "I know that I am a stronger person," she says. "I just think back to those times when things get tough, and I'm able to draw strength."

All in all, mothers say their attitude towards life has been transformed. When daily living is difficult, we learn to take one day at a time and to worry less about the future. When adapting to the slower pace of our children, we learn to be patient and to appreciate the moment. When going out in public is challenging, we learn not to care what other people think. And we learn not to sweat the small stuff, mainly because we're dealing with such incredibly big stuff!

Lives Transformed

In the past, researchers assumed that families were devastated by the "hardships" imposed by living with a child with disabilities. More recent research, however, verifies what we've found ourselves—that we grow, change, and benefit over time. Researchers Kate Scorgie (Azuza Pacific University) and Dick Sobsey (University of Alberta) looked at how parents manage life successfully when a child has a disability. They found that parents described three kinds of powerful transformations:

Personal. Over 90 percent of respondents agreed with statements such as "I have learned to speak out," and "I am more compassionate."

Relationships. Approximately 90 percent of respondents agreed that their life experiences brought wonderful people into their lives. More than 80 percent agreed that they have made a difference in the lives of others.

Perspective. Over 80 percent said they now have a more authentic view of success and of what is important in life. Many also expressed an increased appreciation for life. Over 60 percent agreed with the statement "I celebrate life more now."

Our own surveys turned up equally inspiring results. We asked, "Has mothering a child with special needs changed you? If so, in what way?" Of all questions we posed, this one generated the most enthusiastic and detailed responses.

COMPASSION, STRENGTH, AND DEPTH OF CHARACTER

Most of our respondents described positive changes in their personalities. Comments like the following from Sky, a mother of a child with global developmental delays, are typical: "My entire life has changed for the better. I have become a more compassionate, understanding, and loving person. I have more empathy for others. My outlook on life is more positive. I have developed better communication skills and have learned many augmentative skills. I am now a much more patient person."

Like Sky, almost all mothers describe themselves as more patient than they used to be. "I have often felt that my daughter was given to me to help me find the meaning of patience," says Judith.

DEEPENED SELF-AWARENESS AND INSIGHTS

Sometimes through our children we learn more about ourselves. It's not uncommon for parents of children with autism, learning disabilities, ADHD, anxiety, or other disabilities to discover they also have the disorder themselves. Or more commonly—share aspects of the disorder. As Heather learned more about Asperger syndrome, she found many of its characteristics in herself and other parents of children with autism spectrum disorders—passionate interests, social anxieties, security in routine, rigid thinking, etc. "Parents in our support group often jokingly refer to themselves as 'lesser variants,'" a term used by researchers to describe a more subtle form of a condition. The realization that we share some traits with our children helps us better understand and support each other—and to realize that everyone has a different set of strengths and challenges, whether or not they have disabilities.

A Myriad of New Strengths and Skills

All the women we surveyed say they acquired new skills and capabilities by caring for their child. With new skills comes confidence and optimism. When we can master a feeding tube, complex bandaging, or complicated therapies, we know we can tackle anything. Says Daphna, "I am wicked at multi-tasking, organizing, and getting the job at hand done. I have completed a Masters of Social Work with a child screaming in my ear and climbing on my back when I'm writing an essay on the computer and trying to filter through the pile of research papers."

Abby describes her can-do attitude: "I have become more optimistic than I would otherwise. I tend to focus on the positives and work from there, rather than getting hung up on the negatives and barriers. I have learned to set my goals and then figure out how to get there."

Grace also has found new strengths: "I have a lot more problem-solving skills than I ever would have expected. You learn to do enormous things with very little in the way of resources, money, or options. You learn to "dig" in new places to solve a problem."

Increased Confidence to Take on Challenges

As we fight every day for our children, we develop the ability to speak out and to be heard. Shyness is a luxury we cannot afford. Victoria recalls that "I was always a quiet person who went my own way. I let others rant and rave over things and made do with what I had to. I have had to reinvent myself. I have learned to stick up for my son and to keep pushing when we needed something."

Once they have advocated for their own children, many women use their power to push for social change in their own communities. Jeanette, for example, was told her son with Down syndrome wasn't entitled to speech therapy as he "wouldn't benefit from it." Appalled, she contacted the media and lobbied politicians. Fifteen months later, her son—and all other children with Down syndrome in her community—were offered speech therapy.

New Ways to Work and Contribute to the World

It feels good to know that you make a difference in the lives of others. With effective advocating skills and a keen awareness of social issues, some women pursue new work (volunteer or paid) in the disability field. Aileen writes about her new career: "I'm now very involved in the disabled community. I've written books on disability resources, advocated, and chaired two different groups. It's been thrilling to visit the local congressman to talk about IDEA revisions. With my new passion for lobbying and writing, I feel I have a whole new lease on my life. I never would have imagined this. Along the way, I have met such interesting people and have learned to use so many new skills."

INSIGHTS THAT ADD MEANING AND SKILLS TO PREVIOUS PROFESSIONS

Other moms find their life experience enriches the professional work they've always done. Having faced difficult life situations at home, we become excellent problem solvers at work. Our children also give us a crash course in empathy and understanding—important qualities for working with others. Jaya, who works as an insurance agent for the government, says, "I find my experience with my child and service providers has made me a more compassionate and understanding individual. This helps when you work with the public in the environment where patience and understanding is needed."

Even women who already worked in disability-related professions found themselves changed. Tessa, for example, had worked in the disability field for more than a decade, but "having a child (age sixteen months) with a special health care need has brought the issues I have fought for all of my professional life into sharp focus. I now have a glimpse of the struggles faced by families and am awed and humbled."

DIVERSE CONNECTIONS AND FRIENDSHIPS

By caring for our children, we gain not only confidence and skills, but also new contacts. Our children usher some amazing people into our lives. Most parents of kids with special needs say their networks of friends have increased greatly over time. And parents say these friendships are at a deeper level than they have experienced before.

All of us recognize an immediate bond when we meet another "special" mom. Dora describes her friendship with women from her Down syndrome support group as a "bond that goes far beyond the norm." Penny says she's met many "extra mile people," who give beyond what is required. "These are life savers and inspirational people—people you can genuinely and safely love."

We also have much to offer other friends with "typical" children. Beverley, whose adult daughter requires total care, says, "I've learned how to cope with many difficult times because I have 'been there.' So I can be empathetic and share my strength and support with my friends as they face their own challenges."

TRANSFORMED LIFE PRIORITIES AND PATHS

Our parenting experiences help us to evaluate our priorities. Eneid told us, "I am constantly reminded what is most important in life. My special-needs daughter keeps me grounded and focused and continually helps me to keep life in perspective."

For Antoinette, having a child with special needs meant a shift in her view of work: "Because of my son, it's now less important to me to 'climb the corporate ladder,' and more important to live a balanced life." For Betty, mother of a child with cerebral palsy, it meant putting her personal challenges in perspective. "Taking an exam is nothing compared to having a very sick child in ICU or learning he may never learn to walk," she says.

A RENEWED APPRECIATION OF LIFE

While some moms must face ongoing grief in their lives, special needs mothers can also experience incredible joy in everyday things that other parents fail to appreciate. As Cora says, "You don't take anything—no matter how small it may seem—for granted." At a time when most parents are complaining about chasing their toddler, she is savoring her four-year-old's first steps.

Sometimes the happiest moments are when we shut out the world and just appreciate our own families. Jane describes the joy of a family vacation: "We spent a few days together in a hotel and it was amazing. The kids jumped on the bed, got naked, laughed, and went swimming. There were no rules, no obstacles that we usually face in trying to fit our autistic boy into the everyday world."

A SENSE OF SPIRITUALITY AND FAITH

Some women say their child with special needs also helps them to develop their faith or deepen their sense of spirituality. Feeling that there is a larger purpose in having a child with special needs gives them solace and meaning.

Several women told us they take comfort in the fact that their pre-child life experiences prepared them for special needs mothering. As one mom phrased it, "Destiny prepared me to have a child with special needs." As a young adult, Amy ran recreational and respite programs for adults and children with disabilities. "Many of the individuals I worked with had autism. Destiny? Synchronicity? A coincidence? Who knows? But this life experience enriched my ability to mother and to understand my own daughter with autism."

LOVE WITHOUT LIMITS OR CONDITIONS

Raising our kids, appreciating their uniqueness, and developing close connections with them deepens our understanding of unconditional love. And tough times really test us. When Jane's son's behaviors were out of control, she said, "I've never felt such anger and such love for my son at the same time." Each woman we interviewed stressed that she loves her child beyond limits, no matter what. Beatrice told us, "Before I adopted my daughter, I didn't think I would be able to parent a special needs child. I feel like my heart has been stretched to include her special needs, and that all my skills have been put in her service. I now know the value of each life, no matter how fragmentary or diminished."

Some children teach us that we don't need words or even gestures to communicate. We are thrilled and touched to find ways of connecting with our kids. Rachel, mother of a teen who is non-verbal with Angelman syndrome, says, "I really enjoy being drawn into her own little world. I am fiercely protective of her. I think that my heart has opened so much by mothering her."

Over time, we find the balance between trying to "cure" our children and just enjoying them. As Rosita emphasized, "Life is precious—and what is considered 'normal' to the rest of the world doesn't bother me anymore. I wouldn't change anything about my son. I love him exactly the way he is."

A FULL AND BALANCED LIFE

As we watch our children grow and change, we experience a sense of fulfillment and accomplishment. We celebrate how our own love, efforts, and tenacity help our children to flourish. "I was the one who made her the best that she can be," says Nina. Even mothers forced to give up fulfilling jobs described the strength and satisfaction they've gained from their "special" mothering role. Jocelyn says her daughter has tested her to her limits, "and yet somehow, I am very satisfied with my life, with my accomplishments with her, the decisions I've made."

As Kayla, mother of five, including a young adult with Rett syndrome, explained, "My daughter has shaped me to be a humble human. I can see the beauty in little things that so many of us take for granted. I learned to listen and read body language. I learned patience, love, and good humor. I learned to really live."

The Journey From Struggle to Strength

After surveying 500 mothers and combing through mounds of research, we can say with confidence: Special needs mothering adds growth, change, richness, and meaning to your life. Of course, when coping with a particularly tough day, you may yearn for a more mundane (and less enriching) mothering experience! When we spoke to one exhausted mother, she told us, "I've just come back from the hospital from my son's sixty-fourth brain shunt revision." Some days you've just got to get through.

It helps to keep a long-term perspective. In time you will emerge stronger, wiser, and more compassionate from your mothering experience. Only so much is under your control. You can't always change the course of your child's condition or disability. You can't necessarily find the cure, therapy, or education that will improve your child. But there is much you can do to maintain the quality of your own life and that of your loved ones.

Make time to keep yourself strong—mentally, spiritually, socially, and physically. Keep trying new experiences and meeting new people. If you are in the workforce, talk openly with coworkers and management to make them aware of your strengths and your family needs. Each of us can transform the workplace one company and organization at a time. If you're at home, maintain skills and contacts so that you can support yourself financially, should you need to.

Enjoy time with people you love. Cherish and enjoy your partner, your children, and your friends. Celebrate the unique connection you have with your child with special needs. But try not to let your family life revolve solely around that child's needs.

Stay optimistic. As we know, and recent research proves, optimism is related to better physical and mental health. Balance out planning for the future with living one day at a time. Seek out and enjoy activities, people, and experiences that give you joy. Fortified with love, happiness, and optimism, you will survive and thrive during the tough times.

Most of all, remember that you are not alone in this mothering journey. Ask for the help, caring, and services you need. And reach out to others to share your own well-earned strength, wisdom, compassion, and love of life. We wish you well.

—Amy and Heather

"They say that life is a journey, not a destination—
disability just makes my journey more interesting."

—Theresa, mom of two children with special needs

Appendix 1: State Leave Policies
(as of December 2005)

Note: Only states with policies that expand on FMLA coverage for care of "seriously ill" family members (see Chapter 23) or provide leave for school/daycare activities are listed. Sick leave policies are only noted for employees of private companies (every state but Louisiana allows public sector employees to use sick time for family members and about a third allow employees to donate unused leave to other employees directly or through a "pool"). Requirements listed are for *unpaid* leave, unless otherwise noted. Employees of education agencies are often subject to separate provisions.

Check with your state labor office and/or your human resources department for full details.

Alaska requires employers with twenty-one employees or more to offer family leave coverage. This must include up to eighteen weeks of family leave in any twenty-four month period, as well as eighteen weeks for a birth or adoption in a twelve month period. Public sector employers must provide the same.

California's Paid Family Leave Plan provides six weeks of partially-paid benefits to a worker caring for an ill family member, newborn, or adopted child. (The worker must have paid into State Disability Insurance.) Employees may also take twelve weeks family leave *after* maternity leave, instead of concurrently. All workers may use up to half of their annual sick leave to care for a sick family member. Employees (of businesses with 25 employees or more) are also entitled to forty hours of leave per year (no more than eight hours in any month) to participate in children's school or daycare activities. Employees may use vacation, personal leave, or compensatory time off.

Colorado state employees are entitled to thirteen weeks of family leave to care for a seriously ill family member.

Connecticut requires employees work 1,000 hours (vs. 1,250 under FMLA) during a twelve-month period to qualify for twelve weeks of family and medical leave. State provisions stipulate that all private sector employers of seventy-five or more must provide up to sixteen weeks of family leave in any twenty-four month period. Public sector employers are obligated to provide up to twenty-four weeks. All employers must allow up to two weeks of sick leave to be used for care of ill family members.

District of Columbia employees who have worked at least one year without a break of service and at least 1,000 hours during the last twelve months are entitled to up to sixteen weeks per twenty-four-month period to care for a family member (applies to employers of twenty employees or more). Employees may use paid family, vacation, personal, or compensatory leave. They may also use paid leave donated by another employee or from an employer leave pool under certain conditions. Employees are entitled to twenty-four hours per year leave for school activities.

Florida state employees (those classified as 'Career Service') are entitled to six months of leave for a serious family illness. Accrued sick leave or other leave may be used.

Hawaii employees in companies of 100 or more can use up to ten days of sick leave per year to care for ill family members.

Illinois employers with fifty or more employees must grant up to eight hours of "school leave" per school year (no more than four hours in one day) if school meetings/activities can't be scheduled during non-working hours. School leave can only be used after all accrued leave time except sick and disability is exhausted.

Louisiana employers of twenty or more must allow up to sixteen hours leave during any twelve-month period to attend daycare or school activities that can't be rescheduled during non-working hours. An employee is allowed to substitute accrued vacation or other paid leave time.

Maine employees in companies of fifteen or more are entitled to ten weeks consecutive family leave every twenty-four months. Employees may use any type of paid leave provided by their employer.

Massachusetts employers with fifty or more employees are required to offer them twenty-four hours of leave during any twelve month period to participate in their children's school activities or to accompany their children (or elderly family members) to routine medical appointments. An employee is allowed to substitute accrued paid vacation, personal leave, or medical and sick leave.

Minnesota employers with twenty-one or more employees must allow sixteen hours of leave per year to parents so they can attend daycare or school conferences and activities. Employees may use accrued paid vacation time or other appropriate paid leave. Employees may also use sick leave to care for family members.

Nevada employers may not fire (or threaten to fire) an employee who takes time off to attend a meeting requested by her child's school or who is notified during work of a school emergency concerning her child.

New Jersey requires an employee have worked 1,000 hours (vs. 1,250 under FMLA) during a twelve month period to qualify for twelve weeks of family leave in any twenty-four month period.

North Carolina employers are required to offer up to four hours leave per year to parents so that they may attend school or daycare activities.

Oregon extends family leave requirements to businesses with twenty-five employees or more. Leave is extended to care for a sick child who does not have a serious health condition but requires home care. Parents who have taken twelve weeks of family leave to care for a newborn can take up to twelve additional weeks to care for a child who is suffering from an illness, injury, or condition that is not a serious health condition but requires home care.

Rhode Island public sector employers of thirty or more must offer thirteen weeks of family leave in any twenty-four month period. Private sector employers of fifty or more are obligated to the same. Parents who have been employed for twelve consecutive months are entitled to ten hours of "school involvement leave" per year. Employees may use accrued paid vacation or other appropriate leave.

Vermont requires companies of fifteen or more to allow employees to take twelve weeks leave to care for seriously ill family members. It also allows four hours leave in thirty-day periods for medical appointments and school activities (not to exceed twenty-four hours in a twelve-month period). Leave may be used for medical emergencies, routine appointments, and school activities. Employees may use up to six weeks of accrued sick, vacation, or other paid leave.

Washington employees who work at least thirty-five hours a week (for employers of 100 or more) may take twelve weeks family leave in addition to maternity leave, instead of concurrently. Washington gives all employees the right to use their sick leave or other paid leave to care for a sick family member.

West Virginia public sector employees are eligible for twelve weeks unpaid parental leave to care for a child with a serious health condition. All annual leave must be exhausted before the parental leave begins.

Wisconsin employees of companies with at least fifty workers, who have worked at least one year without a break in service and at least 1,000 hours (vs. 1,250 under FMLA) during the last twelve months, are entitled to two weeks leave to care for a seriously ill family member. Wisconsin employees may use any type of paid or unpaid leave provided by their employer.

Appendix 2: Provincial (Canadian) Leave Policies
(as of December 2005)

Federal employees and employees working in industries under federal jurisdiction are covered under the Canada Labour Code. These employees are entitled to "compassionate care *leave*"—up to eight weeks unpaid leave to provide care or support to a family member if a qualified medical practitioner issues a certificate stating that the family member has a serious medical condition with a significant risk of death within twenty-six weeks. They may receive partial salary, however, through unemployment insurance "compassionate care *benefits*" (a two-week unpaid waiting period and six weeks of payments).

These same unemployment insurance compassionate care benefits are available to all workers (private and public sector) in provinces or territories that mandate job-protected compassionate care leave (i.e., all except British Columbia, Alberta, or the Northwest Territories).

Provinces and territories that require compassionate leave (and/ or other types of leave that might be of use to employees with special needs children) are included below. None require employers to pay their workers for the mandated time off.

British Columbia employees get five job-protected "family responsibility" days per year to attend to the care, health, or education of a family member.

Manitoba requires employers to offer eight weeks of compassionate care leave (to care for dying family members) to employees who have worked for them for at least thirty days.

New Brunswick employees are entitled to three job-protected "family responsibility days" per year related to the health, care, or education of a family member. It also provides eight weeks compassionate care leave to care for dying family members.

Newfoundland/Labrador employers must offer workers who have been with them at least thirty days: (a) seven job-protected sick/

family responsibility days per year to care for their own health or the health or education of a family member, and (b) eight weeks compassionate care leave to care for dying family members.

Nunavut employees are entitled to eight weeks compassionate care leave to care for dying family members.

Nova Scotia guarantees employees three days per year of job-protected sick leave that can be used to care for ill family members and for medical or dental appointments. Employees who have worked for their employer at least three months also are entitled to eight weeks compassionate care leave to care for dying family members.

Ontario companies of fifty or more must offer their employees ten days per year of job-protected emergency leave for death, illness, injury, medical emergency, or urgent matters relating to the employee or family members. All Ontario workers are entitled to eight weeks "family medical leave" (compassionate care leave) to care for dying family members. In certain circumstances, an employee would be entitled to take a second eight-week leave if the family member was still gravely ill at the end of the twenty-six-week "at-risk" period.

Prince Edward Island guarantees employees (after six months of continuous service) up to three days of job-protected leave during a twelve-month period to meet immediate and extended family responsibilities. Employees are also entitled to eight weeks of compassionate care leave to care for dying family members.

Quebec workers are entitled to ten days per year of job-protected "family obligated leave" related to the health, custody, or education of a family member. An employee who has been with an employer for at least three months is also entitled to twelve weeks leave to stay with a family member because of a serious illness or accident (this includes compassionate care leave). If a minor child's condition is life-threatening, leave can be extended to 104 weeks.

Saskatchewan workers are entitled to up to twelve weeks of job-protected leave in a year to care for a seriously ill or injured family member. This is extended to sixteen weeks if the employee is receiving (or serving the waiting period for) the federal unemployment insurance compassionate care benefit. Workers not receiving the compassionate care benefit must have been employed by their employer for at least thirteen weeks to be eligible for family leave. If the illness or injury of the family member is not serious, the employee is entitled to twelve days in a calendar year.

Yukon employees are entitled to eight weeks of compassionate care leave to care for dying family members.

Appendix 3: Sample Flexibility Proposal Memo

(Note: When you write your own memo, be sure to include the elements pointed out in this sample and discussed in Chapter 25.)

BACKGROUND

Karen works weekdays 9:00 to 5:30 as a technical writer for an aerospace plant. Karen's husband Murray doesn't start work until 9:30, but often must work late into the evening. They have two school-age children. Their youngest, Helen, has cerebral palsy.

Karen would like to work flextime, so that she can be home with her daughters after school. That would allow her to schedule more therapy appointments for Helen, as well as help the girls with their homework. It would also save the family significant babysitting costs.

She will request a 6:00 a.m. to 2:30 p.m. workday.

PROPOSAL MEMO

    To: John Doe
  From: Karen MacDonald
    Re: Request for Flextime
  Date: May 17, 2006

{specific work schedule change requested}

As a team member of HI-Tech's Technical Writing Division for six years, I'd like to propose changing my work hours to 6:00 a.m. to 2:30 p.m., instead of 9:00 to 5:30.

{how the plan will benefit the company}

I believe that, with this earlier schedule, I would be able to improve my written output by at least a third. As I'm sure you know, writing and editing requires a great deal of solitary concentration. Although I enjoy the camaraderie of our open-concept office, I am frequently disrupted by nearby phone calls and discussions. With the earlier schedule, I would have several hours to work without distraction before most of my coworkers arrive each day.

An earlier schedule would also allow me to schedule my daughter's medical appointments after work, meaning I'd be able to take significantly less time off, yet still see to her needs.

{what makes the plan feasible}

I feel that my work record as a reliable, self-directed, and self-disciplined employee makes me an ideal candidate for flextime work.

Since I rarely interact directly with customers, customer service should not be compromised. Should an urgent matter arise after I'd left work for the day, I would still be accessible by cell phone.

My meetings with engineers can be easily rescheduled to take place before 2:30. I could still arrange to work a later schedule on days when my presence would be critical in the late afternoon—for example, if a client requested a 3:00 meeting.

{what is necessary to make the plan work}

To ensure success, I propose we meet weekly in the first month to review the arrangement. I would continue to report on my progress in weekly department meetings.

{how performance will be measured}

We can use the timelines currently in our product schedule to track my projects and measure productivity.

{an understanding that arrangement depends on a successful trial period}

I would like to discuss this proposal with you further to address any potential concerns you might have. I understand that you are responsible for the success of this department and must determine whether this plan works for our team as a whole. I suggest a trial period of one month, after which the arrangement could be assessed and revised, if necessary. I understand that if the plan is not working, I might be required to return to my original schedule.

Appendix 4: Checklist for Child Care Re: Special Needs

☐ Is the center or home secure? A child who bolts can race out the door in an instant. If you require extra locking devices at home, you'll also need them there.

☐ Will the caregiver install what is necessary to keep your child safe?

☐ Is the space open and free of hazards? Children using wheelchairs or walkers or who have coordination difficulties should be able to move comfortably and safely.

☐ Is the yard fenced and hazard free?

☐ Do they have specialists who can work with your child?

☐ If not, are they receptive to you bringing in your own?

☐ Is there space for the specialists to work with your child?

☐ Does the caregiver or staff have experience in special needs (especially your child's disability)?

☐ Will they agree to further training if required?

☐ Do they provide disability awareness training for other children in their care (e.g., through instruction, activities, books)?

☐ If you're looking at a center, are they willing to place your child with his peer group (instead of keeping him with younger children because he isn't walking or isn't toilet trained)?

☐ Is there a quiet place a child can go if he becomes over-stimulated?

☐ Do the personnel seem interested in your child's strengths, abilities, or interests—not just his disability?

☐ Does the center or caregiver expect you to provide any equipment or pay extra fees related to your child's disability? (Under the ADA, they cannot charge your child a higher tuition; however, they are not required to pay for one-on-one care.) If so, what must you pay for?

☐ Will the same caregiver be in charge of your child for an extended basis (as opposed to caregivers rotating)?

☐ Is the group size small?

☐ Is the center or caregiver educated on their obligations under the ADA?

☐ Are they willing to make necessary changes to policy and procedures, programs, and staff training?

☐ Will they remove barriers or provide adaptive equipment for your child?

☐ Do they have a way to communicate with parents about daily activities and progress?

Appendix 5: Sample Caregiver/ Support Worker Interview Questions

(This example is for interviewing a support worker for a child with autism. The job would involve providing care, recreation, life skills training, and one-on-one teaching, as well as taking the child on community outings. Adjust appropriately for your own child's special needs.)

1. Describe your previous work (paid or volunteer). What did you enjoy the most about it? What was the most challenging? What work was most related to working with kids with special needs?

2. Do you have CPR and first aid certification? If not, would you be willing to take a course to get certified? May we run a background/police records check?

3. What do you know about autism spectrum disorders and child development? Why do you think that children with autism spectrum disorders have behavioral difficulties?

4. What training would you be willing to undertake to make sure that you could work successfully with our daughter (e.g., attend courses, meet with the child's therapists and resource teacher, read books, etc.)?

5. What strengths would you bring to this position? What other skills do you have that you could bring to working with our child (e.g., swimming, gymnastics, music, teaching skills, crafts, etc.)?

6. What areas are you working on (weaknesses)?

7. Can you give an example of when you taught a child (with special needs) a new skill? How did you do it?

8. Can you give an example of a time when a child was showing some rather challenging behavior? What did you do and how was the situation resolved?

9. What would you do if my daughter...? (Present a challenging situation that may arise in your home.)

10. Have you ever had to develop learning activities based upon a goal that had been developed for a child? What kinds of activities did you do?

11. Do you have access to toys and materials to work with my child, or do you need me to provide them?

12. If you were in the park, what ideas do you have for helping my child to interact with other children?

13. What are your plans for the future? What field do you want to work in?

14. If you were to have one concern about taking this job what would it be? (If the candidate says, "I'm concerned I won't be able to do this," that's a red flag.)

15. When are you available? Do you have use of a car? Do you have adequate car insurance to cover transporting my child?

16. Can you provide me with some references—preferably supervisors from past jobs where you worked with children (especially those with special needs)?

17. Do you have any questions?

RESOURCES

Insure Kids Now—See Federal Government Resources

ADVOCACY, FINANCIAL, AND LEGAL RESOURCES

Advocis, The Financial Advisors Association
of Canada
350 Bloor Street East, 2nd Floor
Toronto, ON M4W 3W8
CANADA
416-444-5251 or 800-563-5822
www.advocis.ca
Provides information on how to choose an advisor and a "Find-an-Advisor" service.

Americans with Disabilities Act Homepage—
See Federal Government Resources

Judge David L. Bazelon Center for Mental
Health Law
1101 15th Street NW, Suite 1212
Washington, DC 20005
202-467-5730
www.bazelon.org
Publishes state-by-state list of advocacy groups.

The Canadian Bar Association
500 - 865 Carling Avenue
Ottawa, ON K1S 5S8
CANADA
613-237-2925 or 613-237-1988 or 800-267-8860
www.cba.org
Provides links to lawyer referral services throughout Canada.

Canadian Life and Health Insurance Assoc.
1 Queen Street East, Suite 1700
Toronto, ON M5C 2X9
CANADA
416-777-2221 or 800-268-8099
www.clhia.ca
Provides information about insurance industry practices, Canadian life and health insurance companies, and their products.

The Foundation Center
79 Fifth Avenue/16th Street
New York, NY 10003-3076
212-620-4230 or 800-424-9836
www.fdncenter.org
Has links to organizations providing grant money to individuals with disabilities. Also offers monthly subscription to online "Foundation Grants to Individuals" database (for fee).

National Association of Personal Financial
Advisors
3250 North Arlington Heights Road, Suite 109
Arlington Heights, IL 60004
800-366-2732
www.napfa.org
Provides questions to ask a financial planner and a "Find-a-Planner" service.

National Employment Lawyers Association
44 Montgomery Street, Suite 2080
San Francisco, CA 94104
415-296-7629
www.nela.org
Provides a locator for employment lawyers.

National Technical Assistance Alliance for
Parent Centers
PACER Center
8161 Normandale Boulevard
Minneapolis, MN 55437-1044
952-838-9000 or 888-248-0822
www.taalliance.org
100+ Parent Training and Information Centers (PTIs) and Community Parent Resource Centers (CPRCs) provide training and information to help families of children with disabilities (to age 22) advocate for appropriate education and services, resolve disputes with schools and agencies, and locate community services.

Organization of Protection and Advocacy
(P&A) Systems and Client Assistance
Programs (CAP)
National Disability Rights Network
900 Second Street NE, Suite 211
Washington, DC 20002
202-408-9514
www.napas.org
Provides federally-mandated legal representation and advocacy services to those with disabilities.

Partnership for Prescription Assistance
888-477-2669
www.pparx.org
Directs people to over 475 public and private patient assistance programs.

SNAP Special Needs Advocate for Parents
11835 W. Olympic Boulevard, Suite 465
Los Angeles, CA 90064
310-479-3755 or 888-310-9889
www.snapinfo.org
*Provides information on and support for
advocacy, life planning, insurance, etc.*

The Time Dollar Institute
5505 39th Street NW
Washington, DC 20015
www.timedollar.org
*Helps communities start a barter system for
services.*

Wrightslaw Special Education Law and
   Advocacy
P. O. Box 1008
Deltaville, VA 23043
804-257-0857
www.wrightslaw.com
*Provides legal and advocacy advice to parents
about special education, including a state-by-
state directory of resources.*

Assistive Technology

Alliance for Technology Access
1304 Southpoint Boulevard, Suite 240
Petaluma, CA 94954
707-778-3011
www.ataccess.org
*Network includes resource centers across
the US to help families obtain necessary
assistive technology.*

The Rehabilitation Engineering and Assistive
   Technology Society of North America
(RESNA)
1700 N. Moore St., Suite 1540
Arlington, VA 22209-1903
703-524-6686
www.resna.org/AFTAP
*Has a contact list of state financing programs
for assistive technology.*

Child Care and Respite Care

Aboriginal Head Start—See Federal
Government Resources (Canada)

ARCH National Respite Network
Chapel Hill Training-Outreach Project, Inc.
800 Eastowne Drive, Suite 105
Chapel Hill, NC 27514
919-490-5577
www.respitelocator.org
*National respite locator service and national
coalition that advocates for respite services.*

Au Pair Program—See Federal Government
Resources

BANANAS Inc.
Northern Alameda County's Child Care
   Resource & Referral Service
5232 Claremont Avenue
Oakland, CA 94618
510-658-7353
www.BANANASinc.org
*Offers pamphlets about child care such
as "Parent-Created Child Care—Shares,"
"Choosing Child Care for A Child With
Special Needs," and "How Do I Care for a
Child With Special Needs?"*

Canadian Live-In Caregiver Program—See
Federal Government Resources (Canada)

Child Care Aware
3101 Wilson Boulevard, Suite 350
Arlington, VA 22201
800-424-2246
www.childcareaware.org
*Provides publications about child care (some
specific to special needs) and a directory to
Child Care Resource and Referral Centers
across the U.S.*

Child & Family Canada
www.cfc-efc.ca
*Provides publications (some on special
needs) and links to Canadian child care
organizations.*

Head Start—See Federal Government
Resources

National Association for Sick Child Daycare
1716 5th Avenue North
Birmingham, AL 35203
205-324-8447
www.nascd.com
*Contact by phone to find a sick child daycare
in your area.*

Model Programs

These innovative solutions to lack of appropriate child care are examples of programs that may work in your community. To find out more about how these programs were developed, contact the organizations.

The Arc of Montgomery County
11600 Nebel Street
Rockville, MD 20852-2554
301-984-5777
www.arcmontmd.org
Arc's "After All" (after-school) integrated program for pre-teens and teens with disabilities was developed in collaboration with the Boys and Girls Club.

Easter Seals Southern California
1801 E. Edinger Avenue, Suite 190
Santa Ana, CA 92705
714-834-1111
www.essc.org
Offers recreational after-school programs for children with disabilities using public school sites and community settings.

Kids Included Together
10505 Sorrento Valley Road, 2nd Floor
San Diego, CA 92121
858-320-2050
www.kitonline.org
A partnership between a non-profit technology organization and this community agency provides after-school computer classes for teens with disabilities in San Diego.

COMMUNITY FELLOWSHIP/ SUPPORT GROUPS

Best Buddies
100 Southeast Second Street, Suite 2200
Miami, FL 33131
305-374-2233 or 800-89-BUDDY (800-892-8339)
www.bestbuddies.org
Provides opportunities for friendship between high school/college students and youths/ adults with intellectual disabilities.

Best Buddies Canada
2333 Dundas Street West, Suite 404
Toronto, ON M6R 3A6
CANADA
416-531-0003 or 888-779-061
www.bestbuddies.ca
See Best Buddies.

Big Brothers Big Sisters
230 North 13th Street
Philadelphia, PA 19107
215-567-7000
www.bbbsa.org
Matches caring adults with children ages 5 to 18 for one-to-one relationships.

Big Brothers Big Sisters of Canada
3228 South Service Road, Suite 113E
Burlington ON L7N 3H8
CANADA
905-639-0461 or 800-263-9133
www.bigbrothersbigsisters.ca
See Big Brothers Big Sisters.

The Family Village
Waisman Center
University of Wisconsin-Madison
1500 Highland Avenue
Madison, WI 53705-2280
www.familyvillage.wisc.edu
Provides resources to help parents and religious institutions integrate those with disabilities.

Parents Without Partners, Inc.
1650 South Dixie Highway, Suite 510
Boca Raton, FL 33432
561-391-8833
www.parentswithoutpartners.org
Offers education, support, and social activities (family and adult) for single parents.

Sibling Support Project of the Arc of the
   United States
6512 23rd Ave NW, #213
Seattle WA 98117
206-297-6368
www.thearc.org/siblingsupport
Provides information and training to start your own sibling support group.

Special Olympics—See Health and Fitness Organizations

Online Support Groups

The websites below offer online forums that provide support for parents of children with various disabilities. (Note: Many websites related to specific disabilities offer online forums as well.)

AOL (www.groups.aol.com) (in Canada: www.groups.aol.ca)

Google (www.google.com) (in Canada: www.google.ca) [Select Groups]

iVillage (www.ivillage.com) [Select Message Boards/Parenting and Pregnancy]

MSN (www.msn.com) [Select People/Groups and Chat] (in Canada: www.msn.sympatico. ca) [Select Connect/People and Chat]

Today's Parent Magazine (www.todaysparent. com) [Select Talk Forums]

Yahoo (www.yahoogroups.com) (in Canada: www.yahoogroups.ca)

DISABILITY ORGANIZATIONS

The Arc of the United States
1010 Wayne Avenue, Suite 650
Silver Spring, MD 20910
301-565-3842
www.thearc.org
Chapters across the U.S. offer information, support, and advocacy for people with developmental disabilities (and their families).

Canadian Abilities Foundation
340 College Street, Suite 401
Toronto, ON M5T 3A9
CANADA
416-923-1885
www.abilities.ca
Provides links to disability organizations in Canada and throughout the world, as well as information/message boards about disability issues.

Canadian Association for Community Living
Kinsmen Building, York University
4700 Keele Street
Toronto, ON M3J 1P3
CANADA
416-661-9611
www.cacl.ca
Provides links to provincial and territorial Associations for Community Living (offering information, support, and advocacy to those with intellectual disabilities and their families).

Easter Seals Disability Services
230 West Monroe Street, Suite 1800
Chicago, IL 60606
312-726-6200 or 800-221-6827
www.easterseals.com
450 centers across the country offer a variety of services to help people with disabilities address life's challenges and achieve personal goals.

Easter Seals Canada
90 Eglinton Avenue East, Suite 208
Toronto, ON M4P 2Y3
416-932-8382
www.easterseals.ca
See Easter Seals Disability Services.

Family Voices, Inc.
2340 Alamo SE, Suite 102
Albuquerque, NM 87106
505-872-4774 or 888-835-5669
www.familyvoices.org
Offers information, support, advocacy, and workplace information for families of children with special health care needs. Many publications available to download free.

National Alliance for the Mentally Ill (NAMI)
2107 Wilson Boulevard, Suite 300
Arlington, VA 22201-3042
703-524-7600
www.nami.org
Offers interactive "Special Needs Estate Planning Guidance System," as well as resources on mental illness.

National Dissemination Center for Children
   with Disabilities
P.O. Box 1492
Washington, DC 20013
800-695-0285
www.nichcy.org
Vast online clearinghouse provides information and links on all matters related to childhood disabilities, including resources, laws, research, and more.

Roeher Institute
Kinsmen Building York University
4700 Keele Street
Toronto, ON M3J 1P3
CANADA
416-661-9611 or 800-856-2207
www.roeher.ca
Does policy research and publishes materials related to disability.

EMPLOYMENT RESOURCES

Canada Business Service Centres/
Government Services for Entrepreneurs—
See Federal Government Services (Canada)

Direct Selling Association
1667 K Street NW, Suite 1100
Washington, DC 20006
202-452-8866
www.dsa.org
*Provides information about the direct selling
industry. Also offers a group health plan to
members.*

Families and Work Institute
267 Fifth Avenue, Floor 2
New York, NY 10016
212-465-2044
www.familiesandwork.org
*Its "When Work Works: Workplace Flexibility
Toolkit" helps employees make a case for
flexibility.*

International Coach Federation
2365 Harrodsburg Road, Suite A325
Lexington, KY 40504
888-423-3131 or 859-219-3580
www.coachfederation.com
*Offers a referral service to locate career
coaches by state or province.*

National Association for the Self-Employed
P.O. Box 612067
DFW Airport
Dallas, TX 75261-2067
800-232-6273
www.nase.org
*Provides resources for the self-employed and
micro-businesses (up to ten employees). Also
offers a group health plan to members.*

Office of Women's Business Ownership—See
Federal Government Resources

Professional Association of Resume Writers
   and Career Coaches PARW/CC
1388 Brightwaters Boulevard, N.E.
St. Petersburg, FL 33704
727-821-2274 or 800-822-7279
www.parw.com
*Provides links to certified resume writers,
employment interview specialists, and career
coaches across the U.S. and Canada.*

Small Business Administration—See Federal
Government Resources

FEDERAL GOVERNMENT RESOURCES

United States

FirstGov.gov
www.firstgov.gov
800-FED-INFO (800-333-4636)
*The official U.S. gateway to all government
information.*

Americans with Disabilities Act Home Page
U.S. Department of Justice
950 Pennsylvania Avenue NW
Civil Rights Division
Disability Rights Section NYAV
Washington, DC 20530
800-514-0301
www.ada.gov
*Provides extensive information about the
Americans with Disabilities Act.*

Au Pair Program
U.S. Department of State
Public Communication Division:
PA/PL, Rm. 2206
U.S. Department of State
2201 C Street NW
Washington, D.C. 20520
202-647-6575 or 202-647-4000
www.state.gov [search for "Au Pair program"
under Subject Index]
*Has information on au pair and Educare
programs, including a list of sponsoring
organizations.*

Centers for Medicare and Medicaid Services
7500 Security Boulevard
Baltimore, MD 21244
410-786-3000 or 877-267-3000
www.cms.hhs.gov
*Information on Medicare and Medicaid
benefit programs.*

DisabilityInfo.gov
www.disabilityinfo.gov
*Contains links to information for people with
disabilities, their families, employers, service
providers, and interested community members.*

Department of Housing and Urban
Development (HUD)
451 7th Street S.W.
Washington, DC 20202-708-1112
800-569-4287 (Housing Counseling Line)
www.hud.gov/groups/disabilities.cfm
*Provides information about programs that may
help you finance the purchase of a new home or
improve accessibility of your current home.*

Department of Labor
200 Constitution Avenue NW
Washington, DC 20210
866-4-USA-DOL (866-487-2365)
www.dol.gov
*Provides information on employment rights,
the Family Medical Leave Act, HIPAA,
COBRA, and more.*

Head Start Information and Publication Center
U. S. Department of Health & Human Services
Agency for Children & Families
1133 15th Street NW, Suite 450
Washington, DC 20005
202-737-1030 or 866-763-6481
www.headstartinfo.org
*Federal clearinghouse provides general
information about Head Start programs and
a search tool to find the program nearest you.*

Insure Kids Now
The U.S. Department of Health and Human
Services
200 Independence Avenue, SW
Washington, D.C. 20201
877-KIDS-NOW
www.insurekidsnow.gov
*Hotline and online information about your
state's health policies.*

Office of Women's Business Ownership
Small Business Administration
409 Third Street SW, Sixth Floor
Washington, DC 20416
202-205-6673
www.onlinewbc.gov
*Links to over 100 educational resource centers
designed to assist women in starting and
growing small businesses.*

Small Business Administration
409 Third Street SW
Washington, DC 20416
800-U-ASK-SBA (800-827-5722)
www.sba.gov
*Provides information on all aspects of small
business, including sample business plans
and links to state resources.*

Social Security Administration
Office of Public Inquiries
Windsor Park Building
6401 Security Boulevard
Baltimore, MD 21235
800-772-1213
www.ssa.gov
*Information on Social Security retirement
and disability programs and SSI
(Supplemental Security Income).*

Canada

Aboriginal Head Start
Division of Childhood and Adolescence
Public Health Agency of Canada
Tunney's Pasture, Address Locator: 1909C2
Ottawa, ON K1A 1B4
CANADA
800-O-Canada (800-622-6232)
www.phac-aspc.gc.ca (use the A-Z index)
*Provides general information about the
Canada-funded early childhood development
program for First Nations, Inuit, and Métis
children and their families.*

CanadaBenefits.ca
www.canadabenefits.ca
800-O-Canada (800-622-6232)
*Government of Canada Internet gateway to
government-wide information about benefit
programs and services for individuals,
including those with disabilities.*

Canada Business Service Centres—
Government Services for Entrepreneurs
(Call or see website for nearest location)
888-576-4444
www.cbsc.org
*Provides a single point of access for federal
and provincial/territorial government
services, programs, and regulatory
requirements for business.*

Canadian Human Rights Commission
344 Slater Street, 8th Floor
Ottawa, ON K1A 1E1
CANADA
613-995-1151 or 888-214-1090
www.chrc-ccdp.ca
Administers the Canadian Human Rights
Act and the Employment Equity Act,
and ensures that the principles of equal
opportunity and non-discrimination are
followed in all areas of federal jurisdiction.
Also provides links to provincial and
territorial human rights agencies.

Canadian Live-In Caregiver Program
Citizen & Immigration Canada
Administration Branch
300-300 Slater (Jean Edmonds North Tower) St.
Ottawa, ON K1A 1L1
and
Department of Human Resources and
   Skills Development
5 Charles St. S
Gananoque, ON K7G 1V9
800-O-Canada (800-622-6232)
www.cic.gc.ca or www.servicecanada.gc.ca
(search for "live-in caregiver")
Program brings qualified caregivers from
other countries to fill openings for live-in
care of children, elderly, and people with
disabilities.

Service Canada
Public Works and Government Services
Ottawa, ON K1A 0S5
CANADA
800-O-Canada (800-622-6232)
www.servicecanada.gc.ca
Helps people find government services in
person, by phone, or over the Internet.

FUTURE PLANNING RESOURCES

The Arc of the United States—See Disability
Organizations

Disabled and Alone
Life Services for the Handicapped, Inc.
61 Broadway, Suite 510
New York, NY 10006
212-532-6740 or 800-995-0066
www.disabledandalone.org
Assists member families across the U.S. with
future planning.

National Alliance for the Mentally Ill
(NAMI)—See Disability Organizations

PLAN
3665 Kingsway, Suite 260
Vancouver, BC V5R 5W2
CANADA
604-439-9566
www.plan.ca
Members are entitled to assistance with life
planning and creating personal networks
for their family member with a disability.
Links to PLAN affiliates across Canada and
Washington state.

The "Special Needs" Planning Group (SNPG)
70 Ivy Crescent
Stouffville, ON L4A 5A9
CANADA
905-640-8285
www.specialneedsplanning.ca
Assists parents in Ontario with life planning
for their family member with a disability.

Tennessee Microboard Association
615-907-1724
www.tnmicroboards.org
Website includes information on person-
centered planning and how to form a
microboard.

Vela Microboard Association
100 - 17564 - 56A Avenue
Surrey, BC V3S 1G3
CANADA
604-575-2588
www.microboard.org
Has information on person-centered planning
and how to create a microboard.

HEALTH AND FITNESS ORGANIZATIONS

America on the Move
The Partnership to Promote Healthy Eating
and Active Living
44 School Street, Suite 325
Boston, MA 02108
800-807-0077
www.americaonthemove.org
Has information and support about
healthy eating and fitness. Can register as
an individual or group to work towards
achieving health goals.

American Trails
P.O. Box 491797
Redding, CA 96049-1797
530-547-2060
www.AmericanTrails.org
State-by-state list of trails and greenways, groups, hiking agencies, and advocates.

American Volkssport Association
1001 Pat Booker Road, Suite 101
Universal City, TX 78148
210-659-2112 or 800-830-WALK (800-830-9255)
www.ava.org
Offers organized hikes and special family walking events in all states.

Special Olympics
1133 19th Street NW
Washington, DC 20036
202-628-3630
www.specialolympics.org
Provides opportunities for sports training and competition to children and adults with intellectual disabilities.

Special Olympics Canada
60 St. Clair Avenue East, Suite 700
Toronto, ON M4T 1N5
CANADA
416-927-9050
www.specialolympics.ca
See Special Olympics.

Trails Canada
5480 Canotek Road, Unit #16
Gloucester, ON K1J 9H6
CANADA
613-748-1800 or 888-822-2848
www.trailscanada.com
Lists walking trails by province and territory.

The World Laughter Tour, Inc.
1159 South Creekway Ct.
Gahanna, OH 43230
614-855-4733 or 800-NOW-LAFF
www.worldlaughtertour.com
Lists laughter clubs in the U.S. and Canada.

HEALTH PROFESSIONALS

The following organizations provide health/ mental health information and help you locate a professional in your area through a "locator" feature online or by phone.

American Academy of Sleep Medicine
One Westbrook Corporate Center, Suite 920
Westchester, IL 60154
708-492-0930
www.aasmnet.org
Has a listing of sleep clinics in each state.

American Association for Marriage and
  Family Therapists
112 South Alfred Street
Alexandria, VA 22314
703-838-9808
www.aamft.org
Lists therapists in the U.S. and Canada by city and state or province.

American Association of Naturopath
Physicians
4435 Wisconsin Ave NW, Suite 403
Washington, DC 20016
202-237-8150 or 866-538-2267
www.naturopathic.org

American Dietetic Association
120 South Riverside Plaza, Suite 2000
Chicago, IL 60606-6995
800-877-1600
www.eatright.org

American Medical Association
515 N. State Street
Chicago, IL 60610
800-621-8335
www.ama-assn.org

American Psychiatric Association
1000 Wilson Boulevard, Suite 1825
Arlington, VA 22209-3901
703-907-7300 or 1-888-35-PSYCH
(800-357-7924)
www.healthyminds.org

American Psychological Association
750 First Street NE
Washington, DC 20002-4242
202-336-5500 or 800-374-2721
www.helpcenter.org

Canadian Association of Naturopathic
  Doctors
1255 Sheppard Avenue E.
Toronto, ON M2K1E2
CANADA
416-496-8633 or 800-551-4381
www.naturopathicassoc.ca

Canadian Association of Social Workers
383 Parkdale Avenue, Suite 402
Ottawa, ON K1Y 4R4
CANADA
613-729-6668
www.casw-acts.ca [Look under Social Work
in Canada.]
*Has no finder service itself, but will refer you
to provincial/territorial associations of social
workers that do.*

Canadian Registry of Health Providers in
   Psychology
368 Dalhousie Street, Suite 300
Ottawa, ON K1N 7G3
613-562-0900
www.crhspp.ca

Canadian Sleep Society
Hôpital du Sacré-Cœur de Montréal
Centre de Recherche, 3K
5400, boul. Gouin ouest
Montréal, QC H4J 1C4
CANADA
www.css.to
Has a listing of sleep clinics across Canada.

Colleges of Physicians and Surgeons
[Canada]
To find the provincial/territorial regulatory
college, contact:
The College of Family Physicians of Canada
2630 Skymark Avenue
Mississauga, ON L4W 5A4
CANADA
905-629-0900 or 800-387-6197
www.cfpc.ca
*Look under Links/Provincial Colleges of
Physicians and Surgeons. Many colleges have
a "find a physician" feature.*

Dietitians of Canada
480 University Avenue, Suite 604
Toronto, ON M5G 1V2
CANADA
416-596-0857
www.dieticians.ca

National Association of Social Workers
750 First Street NE, Suite 700
Washington, DC 20002-4241
202-408-8600
www.socialworkers.org (Look under Quick
Links/Find a Clinical Social Worker.)

National Register of Health Service Providers
in Psychology
1120 G St NW, Suite 330
Washington, DC 20005
202-783-7663
www.nationalregister.org

HOUSING/INDEPENDENT LIVING

Canadian Association of Independent Living
   Centres
170 Laurier Avenue West, Suite 1104
Ottawa, ON K1P 5V5
CANADA
613-563-2581
www.cailc.ca
*Provides services and advocacy for people
with all kinds of disabilities. Lists Canadian
Independent Living Centres.*

The Federal National Mortgage Association
   (Fannie Mae)
3900 Wisconsin Avenue NW
Washington, DC 20016
800-7FANNIE (800-732-6643)
www.fanniemae.com
*HomeChoice mortgage loan program helps low
and moderate income people with disabilities
finance their own homes. Call for information
on participating coalitions in your area.*

Independent Living Research Utilization (ILRU)
2323 S. Shepherd, Suite 1000
Houston, TX 77019
713-520-0232
*Provides links to Statewide Independent
Living Councils (SILCs) and Centers for
Independent Living (CILs) in the U.S.,
Canada, and beyond.*

Residential Rehabilitation Assistance
Program for Persons with Disabilities (RRAP-
Disabilities)
Canada Mortgage and Housing Corporation
700 Montreal Road
Ottawa, ON K1A 0P7
CANADA
613-748-2000 or 800 668-2642
www.cmhc-schl.gc.ca
*Offers assistance for homeowners and
landlords to improve accessibility for persons
with disabilities.*

Social Security Administration—See Federal
Government Resources

U.S. Department of Housing and Urban Development (HUD)—See Federal Government Resources

Model Programs

These "home-grown" solutions to lack of housing and transportation are examples of programs that may work in your community. To find out more about how these programs were developed, contact the organizations.

Mason County Transportation Authority
790 E. Johns Prairie Road
P.O. Box 1880
Shelton, WA 98584
360-426-9434 or 800-281-9434
www.masontransit.org
Collaboration among school districts, local transit companies, disability, and other social service organizations helps those with disabilities (as well as other community members) travel to work and school.

Rent to Own Program
Community Living Ontario
240 Duncan Mill Road, Suite 403
Toronto, ON M3B 1Z4
CANADA
416-447-4348
www.communitylivingontario.ca
This group of agencies and individuals across Ontario developed a plan for private investors to help people with disabilities become homeowners.

Share Equity Housing Project
Ottawa-Carleton Association for Person with Developmental Disabilities (OCAPDD)
200-250 City Centre Avenue
Ottawa, ON K1R 6K7
CANADA
613-569-8993
www.ocapdd.on.ca
Partnership between a developmental disabilities association and a Canadian federal housing agency aims to provide more housing for adults with disabilities.

ORGANIZATIONAL AIDS

Children's Hospital and Regional Medical Center
Center for Children with Special Needs
P.O. Box 5371
Seattle, WA 98105-0371
206-987-5325 or 866-987-2500
www.cshcn.org
Offers the "CARE Organizer" (forms to document your child's activities, therapies, medical bills, etc.) and the "CARE Notebook" (an expanding file folder to organize the forms).

Children's Medical Organizer (web-based)
Provided by Children's Hospitals and Clinics of Minnesota
www.childrenshc.org/cmo
Online (only) organizer to keep track of all your family's medical information, from immunization records to doctor's appointments.

The National Center of Medical Home Initiatives for Children with Special Needs
American Academy of Pediatrics
The National Center of Medical Home Initiatives
141 Northwest Point Blvd
Elk Grove Village, IL 60007
847-434-4000
www.medicalhomeinfo.org
Provides links to various types of organizers and health care notebooks. (Look under Tools/Resources.)

POST-SECONDARY EDUCATION RESOURCES

The Business and Professional Women's Association
1900 M Street NW, Suite 310
Washington, DC 20036
202-293-1100 or
800-525-3729 (scholarship hotline)
www.bpwusa.org
Offers scholarships for disadvantaged U.S. women who want to further their education in order to advance in their careers or to re-enter the workforce.

The HEATH Resource Center
George Washington University
Graduate School of Education and Human
  Development.
2121 K Street NW, Suite 220
Washington, DC 20037
202-973-0904 or 800-544-3284
www.heath.gwu.edu/index.htm
*National clearinghouse on postsecondary
education for individuals with disabilities.*

National Center on Secondary Education
  and Transition
Institute on Community Integration
University of Minnesota
6 Pattee Hall
150 Pillsbury Drive SE
Minneapolis, MN 55455
612-624-2097
www.ncset.org
*Coordinates national resources, offers
technical assistance, and disseminates
information related to secondary education
and transition for youth with disabilities.*

National Educational Association of Disabled
  Students (NEADS)
Room 426, Unicentre
Carleton University
Ottawa, ON K1S 5B6
CANADA
613-526-8008
www.neads.ca
*Provides financial aid directory, listings of
campus disability centres, campus disability
organizations, and transition programs for
Canadian college and university students
with disabilities/special needs.*

www.petersons.com
*Online database provides detailed,
searchable information on adult education,
colleges, universities, and scholarships in
North America.*

Thinkcollege.net
School and Community Projects
Institute for Community Inclusion at the
  University of Massachusetts
100 Morrissey Boulevard
Boston, MA 02125
617-287-4310
www.thinkcollege.net
*Has information and searchable database
on special college training, courses, and
assistance for young adults with disabilities.*

VOLUNTEER OPPORTUNITIES

ServiceLeader.org
RGK Center for Philanthropy and
  Community Service
LBJ School of Public Affairs
P.O. Box Y
Austin, TX 78713-8925
512-232-7062
www.serviceleader.org
*Website based out of University of Texas
provides information on all aspects of
volunteering, including links to local
opportunities.*

Volunteer Canada
330 Gilmour Street
Ottawa, ON K2P 2P6
CANADA
613-231-4371 or 800-670-0401
www.volunteer.ca
Provides links to over 200 volunteer centers.

VolunteerMatch
385 Grove Street
San Francisco, CA 94102
415-241-6872
www.volunteermatch.org
*Helps find volunteer opportunities according
to location and interests.*

RELATED READING

BOOKS

Cochran, Eva and Moncrieff Cochran. *Child Care That Works: A Parent's Guide to Finding Quality Child Care*. Beltsville, MD: Robins Lane Press, 2000.

Douglas, Ann and Elizabeth Lewin. *Family Finance: The Essential Guide for Parents*. Chicago, IL: Dearborn Trade, 2001.

Gill, Barbara. *Changed by a Child: Companion Notes for Parents of a Child with a Disability*. Pella, IA: Main Street Books, 1998.

Gover, Tzivia. *Mindful Moments for Stressful Days: Simple Ways to Find Meaning and Joy in Daily Life*. North Adams, MA: Storey Publishing, 2002.

Moses, Barbara. *What Next? Finding the Work That's Right for You*. New York: DK Publishing, 2006.

Moses, Barbara. *What Next? The Complete Guide to Taking Control of Your Working Life*. New York: DK Publishing, 2003.

Pearson, Liz and Marilyn Smith. *The Ultimate Eating Plan That Still Leaves Room for Chocolate*. North Vancouver, BC: Whitecap Books, 2002.

Peterson's. *Colleges for Students with Learning Disabilities or ADD*. Lawrenceville, NJ: Peterson's, 2003.

Schlachter, Gail A. and R. David Weber. *Financial Aid for the Disabled & Their Families, 2004-2006*. El Dorado Hills, CA: Reference Service Press, 2004.

Seligman, Martin E.P. *Authentic Happiness: Using the New Positive Psychology to Realize Your Potential for Lasting Fulfillment*. New York: Free Press, 2004.

Seligman, Martin E.P. *Learned Optimism: How to Change Your Mind and Your Life*. New York: Vintage, 2006.

OTHER MATERIALS (ALL MATERIALS ARE FREE, UNLESS NOTED WITH *)

Children with Special Needs and the Workplace: A Guide for Employers
Available from:
Family Voices, Inc.
2340 Alamo SE, Suite 102
Albuquerque NM 87106
505-872-4774 or 888-835-5669
www.familyvoices.org (Look under Info & Publications/Employment & Benefits.)

Commonly Asked Questions About Child Care Centers and the Americans with Disabilities Act
Available from:
US Department of Justice
950 Pennsylvania Avenue, NW
Civil Rights Division
Disability Rights Section - NYAV
Washington, DC 20530
800-514-0301
www.ada.gov

Employees Who Are Parents of Children of Disabilities*
Available from:
L'Institut Roeher Institute
Kinsmen Building, York University
4700 Keele Street
Toronto, ON M3J 1P3
CANADA
416-661-9611 or 800-856-2207
www.roeher.ca

A Family Handbook on Future Planning
Available from:
The Arc of the United States
1010 Wayne Avenue, Suite 650
Silver Spring, MD 20910
301-565-3842
www.thearc.org/futureplanning.html

Pooled Trust Programs for People with Disabilities
Available from:
The Arc of the United States
1010 Wayne Avenue, Suite 650
Silver Spring, MD 20910
301-565-3842
www.thearc.org/publications

Removing The Mystery—An Estate Planning Guide for Families of People With Disabilities*
Available from:
Ontario Federation for Cerebral Palsy
104-1630 Lawrence Avenue West
Toronto, ON M6L 1C5
CANADA
416-244-9686 877-244-9686 (Ontario only)
www.ofcp.on.ca (Look under Publications.)

This is Your Life! Creating Your Self-Directed Life Plan.
Available from:
UIC National Research & Training Center on Psychiatric Disability
University of Illinois at Chicago
104 South Michigan Avenue, Suite 900
Chicago, IL 60603
312-422-8180
www.psych.uic.edu/mhsrp (Look under Self-Determination Tools.)

*With Open Arms: Embracing a Bright Financial Future for You and Your Child with
Disabilities and Other Special Needs*
Available from:
Easter Seals
230 West Monroe Street, Suite 1800
Chicago, IL 60606
312-726-6200 or 800-221-6827
www.easterseals.com (Look under Resources/Support/Financial Solutions.)

Workplace Benefits for Families of Children with Special Needs: A Guide for Employees
Available from:
Family Voices, Inc.
2340 Alamo SE, Suite 102
Albuquerque NM 87106
505-872-4774 or 888-835-5669
www.familyvoices.org (Look under Info & Publications/Employment & Benefits.)

RESEARCH REFERENCES

PART I: WELCOME TO OUR WORLD—PARENTING WITH A DIFFERENCE (INTRO)

U.S. Department of Health and Human Services, Health Resources and Services Administration, Maternal and Child Health Bureau. "Prevalence of Children with Special Health Care Needs." *The National Survey of Children with Special Health Care Needs Chartbook 2001.* U.S. Department of Health and Human Services, 2004. http://mchb.hrsa.gov/chscn/pages/prevalence.htm

1. Getting the Most Out of Life
Diener, Ed and Martin E.P. Seligman. "Very Happy People." *Psychological Science* 13, no. 1 (2002): 81-4.

Families and Work Life Institute. *Generation and Gender in the Workplace—An Issue Brief.* Families and Work Life Institute, 2004. http://familiesandwork.org/eproducts/genandgender.pdf

Seligman, Martin E.P. *Authentic Happiness: Using the New Positive Psychology to Realize Your Potential for Lasting Fulfillment.* New York: Free Press, 2002.

Seltzer, Marsha Mailick, Jan S. Greenburg, Frank J. Floyd, and Jinkuk Hong. "Accommodative Coping and Well-Being of Midlife Parents of Children with Mental Health Problems or Developmental Disabilities." *American Journal of Orthopsychiatry* 74, no. 2 (2004): 187-195.

PART II: TAKING CARE OF YOURSELF

2. Put Yourself on the To-Do List
Ai, Amy L., Christopher Peterson, Steven F. Bolling, and Harold Koenig. "Private Prayer and Optimism in Middle-Aged and Older Patients Awaiting Cardiac Surgery." *The Gerontologist* 42, no. 1 (2002): 70-81.

Doolittle, Benjamin R. and Michael Farrell. "The Association Between Spirituality and Depression in an Urban Clinic." *Primary Care Companion to the Journal of Clinical Psychiatry* 6, no. 3 (2004): 114-18.

3. Ya Gotta Have Friends
Diener, Ed and Martin E.P. Seligman. "Very Happy People." *Psychological Science* 13, no. 1 (2002): 81-4.

Greenberg, Jan S., Marsha Mailick Seltzer, Marty Wyngaarden Krauss, and Hea-won Kim. "The Differential Effects of Social Support on the Psychological Well-Being of Aging Mothers of Adults With Mental Illness or Mental Retardation." *Family Relations* 46, no. 4 (1997): 383-94.

Law, Mary, Susanne King, Debra Stewart, and Gillian King. "The Perceived Effects of Parent-Led Support Groups for Parents of Children with Disabilities." *Physical & Occupational Therapy in Pediatrics: A Quarterly Journal of Developmental Therapy* 21, no. 2-3 (2002): 29-48.

4. Get Through the Day—Fuel up with Food
Benton D., Rebecca Griffiths, and Jurg Haller. "Thiamine Supplementation, Mood and Cognitive Functioning." *Psychopharmacology* 129, no. 1 (1997): 66-71.

Christensen, L. and L. Pettijohn. "Mood and Carbohydrate Cravings." *Appetite* 36, no. 2 (2001): 137-145.

Koh-Banerjee, Pauline, Mary Franz, Laura Sampson, Simin Liu, David R Jacobs Jr., Donna
Spiegelman, Walter Willett, and Eric Rimm. "Changes in Whole-Grain, Bran, and Cereal
Fiber Consumption in Relation to 8-Y Weight Gain Among Men." *The American Journal of
Clinical Nutrition* 80, no. 5 (2004): 1237-45.

Lansdowne, Allen T.G. and Stephen C. Provost. "Vitamin D3 Enhances Mood in Healthy
Subjects During Winter." *Psychopharmacology* 135, no. 4 (1998): 319-23.

Lloyd, Helen M., Michael W. Green, and Peter J. Rogers. "Mood and Cognitive Performance
Effects of Isocaloric Lunches Differing in Fat and Carbohydrate Content." *Physiology &
Behavior* 56, no. 1 (1994): 51-57.

Ma, Yunsheng, Elizabeth R. Bertone, Edward J. Stanek, George W. Reed, James R. Hebert,
Nancy L. Cohen, Philip A. Merriam, and Ira S. Ockene. "Association Between Eating
Patterns and Obesity in a Free-Living U.S. Adult Population." *American Journal of
Epidemiology* 158, no. 1 (2003): 85-92.

Smith, A.W., A. Baum, and R.R. Wing. "Stress and Weight Gain in Parents of Cancer Patients."
International Journal of Obesity 29, no. 2 (2005): 244-50.

Vinson, Joe A., Ligia Zubik, Pratima Bose, Najwa Samman, and John Proch. "Dried Fruits:
Excellent In Vitro and In Vivo Antioxidants." *Journal of the American College of Nutrition*
24, no. 1 (2005): 44-50.

Vitaliano, Peter P., Joan Russo, and James M. Scanlan. "Weight Changes in Caregivers of
Alzheimer's Care Recipients: Psychobehavioral Predictors." *Psychology and Aging* 11, no. 1
(1996): 155-163.

5. Stay Strong and Healthy—Get Physical

Guszkowska, M. "Effects of Exercise on Anxiety, Depression and Mood." *Psychiatria Polska* 38,
no. 4 (2004): 611-20.

Hansen, Cheryl J., Larry C. Stevens, and Richard J. Coast. "Exercise Duration and Mood
State: How Much is Enough to Feel Better?" *Health Psychology* 20, no. 4 (2001): 267-275.

Jakicic, J.M., R.R. Wing, B.A. Butler, and R.J. Robertson. "Prescribing Exercise in Multiple
Short Bouts Versus One Continuous Bout: Effects on Adherence, Cardiorespiratory Fitness,
and Weight Loss in Overweight Women." *International Journal of Obesity and Related
Metabolic Disorders* 19, no. 12 (1995): 893-901.

Lane, A.M. and D.J. Lovejoy. "The Effects of Exercise on Mood Changes: The Moderating Effect of
Depressed Mood." *The Journal of Sports Medicine and Physical Fitness* 41, no. 4 (2001): 539-45.

Maroulakis, Emmanuel, and Yannis Zervas. "Effects of Aerobic Exercise on Mood of Adult
Women." *Perceptual and Motor Skills* 76, no. 3, pt. 1 (1993): 795-801.

Roeher Institute. *Beyond the Limits: Mothers Caring for Children with Disabilities.* Roeher
Institute, 2000.

Schmidt, Daniel W., Craig J. Biwer, and Linda K. Kalscheuer. "Effects of Long Versus Short
Bout Exercise on Fitness and Weight Loss in Overweight Females." *Journal of the American
College of Nutrition* 20, no. 5 (2001): 494-501.

Waelde, Lynn C., Larry Thompson, and Dolores Gallagher-Thompson. "A Pilot Study of a Yoga
and Meditation Intervention for Dementia Caregiver Stress." *Journal of Clinical Psychology*
60, no. 6 (2004): 677-87.

6. Desperately Seeking Sleep

Benca, Ruth M. "Consequences of Insomnia and Its Therapies." *The Journal of Clinical Psychiatry* 62, Suppl. 10: (2001): 33-8.

National Sleep Foundation. *2005 Sleep in America Poll*. March 2005. http://www.sleepfoundation.org/_content/hottopics/2005_summary_of_findings.pdf

Spiegel, Karine, Esra Tasali, Plamen Penev, and Eve Van Cauter. "Brief Communication: Sleep Curtailment in Healthy Young Men is Associated with Decreased Leptin Levels, Elevated Ghrelin Levels, and Increased Hunger and Appetite." *Annals of Internal Medicine* 141, no. 11 (2004): 846-50.

The University of Chicago Hospitals. "Sleep Loss Boosts Appetite, May Encourage Weight Gain," news release, December 6, 2004. http://www.uchospitals.edu/news/2004/20041206-sleep.html

7. Fighting Your Inner Darkness—Anger, Anxiety, and Depression

Cox, Deborah L., Patricia Van Velsor, and Joseph F. Hulgus. "Who Me, Angry? Patterns of Anger Diversion in Women." *Health Care for Women International* 25, no. 9 (2004): 872-93.

Epel, Elissa S., Elizabeth H. Blackburn, Jue Lin, Firdaus S. Dhabhar, Nancy E. Adler, Jason D. Morrow, and Richard M. Cawthon. "Accelerated Telomere Shortening in Response to Life Stress." *Proceedings of the National Academy of Sciences of the United States of America* 101, no. 49 (2004): 17312-5.

Greenberg, Jan Steven, Marsha Mailick Seltzer, Marty Wyngaarden Krauss, Rita Jing-Ann Chou, and Jinkuk Hong. "The Effect of Quality of the Relationship Between Mothers and Adult Children with Schizophrenia, Autism, or Down Syndrome on Maternal Well-Being: The Mediating Role of Optimism." *American Journal of Orthopsychiatry* 74, no. 1 (2004): 14-25.

Olsson, M.B. and C.P. Hwang. "Depression in Mothers and Fathers of Children with Intellectual Disability." *Journal of Intellectual Disability Research* 45, part 6 (2001): 535-43.

Seltzer, Marsha Mailick, Jan S. Greenburg, Frank J. Floyd, and Jinkuk Hong. "Accommodative Coping and Well-Being of Midlife Parents of Children with Mental Health Problems or Developmental Disabilities." *American Journal of Orthopsychiatry* 74, no. 2 (2004): 187-195.

Seltzer, Marsha Mailick, Jan S. Greenberg, and Marty Wyngaarden Krauss. "A Comparison of Coping Strategies of Aging Mothers of Adults with Mental Illness or Mental Retardation." *Psychology and Aging* 10, no. 1 (1995): 64-75.

PART III: DAILY LIFE—REALITY CHECK

8. The Time Crunch

U.S. Department of Health and Human Services, Health Resources and Services Administration, Maternal and Child Health Bureau. "Impact on Families." *The National Survey of Children with Special Health Care Needs Chartbook 2001*. U.S. Department of Health and Human Services, 2004. http://mchb.hrsa.gov/chscn/pages/impact.htm

9. Find the Help You Need

Raffaele, Linda M. and Janet Hess. *An Analysis of Community-Based Services and Supports for Children and Young Adults with Special Needs in Hillsborough County*. Hillsborough Coalition for Children and Youth with Special Needs, 2004. http://www.childrensboard.org/pubs_reports/documents/SNeedsfinalcxd.pdf

10. Advocacy 101—Speaking Up for Your Child
Nachshen, Jennifer S. and John Jamieson. "Advocacy, Stress, and Quality of Life in Parents of Children with Developmental Disabilities." *Developmental Disabilities Bulletin* 28, no. 1 (2000): 39-55.

Perrin, Ellen C., Corinne Lewkowicz, and Martin H. Young. "Shared Vision: Concordance Among Fathers, Mothers, and Pediatricians about Unmet Needs of Children with Chronic Health Conditions." *Pediatrics* 105, no. 1 (2000): 277-285. http://pediatrics.aappublications.org/cgi/content/abstract/105/1/S2/277

Seltzer, Marsha Mailick and Marty Wyngaarden Krauss. "Lessons We Have Learned From Aging Families Who Have an Adult Son or Daughter with Mental Retardation." *Intraactions*. Waisman Center, University of Wisconsin-Madison. February 1997. http://www.waisman.wisc.edu/intraactions/ia-1997-feb.html

11. Take Charge of Your Finances
U.S. Department of Health and Human Services, Health Resources and Services Administration, Maternal and Child Health Bureau. "Impact on Families." *The National Survey of Children with Special Health Care Needs: Chartbook 2001*. U.S. Department of Health and Human Services, 2004. http://mchb.hrsa.gov/chscn/pages/impact.htm

12. Create a Positive Future
Waldrop, Judith and Sharon M. Stern. *Disability Status: 2000. Census 2000 Brief*. Pub. C2KBR-17, U.S. Census Bureau, March 2003. http://www.census.gov/prod/2003pubs/c2kbr-17.pdf

13. Legal and Financial Steps to Planning Ahead
MetLife Inc., MetDESK, MetLife's Division of Estate Planning for Special Kids, "The Torn Security Blanket: Children With Special Needs and the Planning Gap," news release, April 11, 2005. http://www.metlife.com./Applications/Corporate/WPS/CDA/PageGenerator/ 0,1674,P250%257ES650,00.html

PART IV: FAMILY TIES (INTRO)

Costigan, Catherine L., Frank J. Floyd, Kristina S.M. Harter, and Joseph C. McClintock. "Family Process and Adaptation to Children with Mental Retardation: Disruption and Resilience in Family Problem-Solving Interaction." *Journal of Family Psychology*. 11, no. 4 (1997): 515-529

Floyd, Frank J., Kristina S.M. Harter, and Catherine L. Costigan. "Family Problem Solving with Children Who Have Intellectual Disabilities." *American Journal on Mental Retardation*. 109, no. 6 (2004): 507-524.

14. Who's Minding the Marriage?
Kreider, Rose M. and Jason M. Fields. *Number, Timing, and Duration of Marriages and Divorces: 1996*. Current Population Reports, P70-80. U.S. Census Bureau, February 2002. http://www.census.gov/prod/2002pubs/p70-80.pdf

Raina, Parminder, Maureen O'Donnell, Peter Rosenbaum, Jamie Brehaut, Stephen D. Walter, Dianne Russell, Marilyn Swinton, Bin Zhu, and Ellen Wood. "The Health and Well-Being of Caregivers of Children With Cerebral Palsy." *Pediatrics* 11, no. 6 (2005): e626-36. http://pediatrics.aappublications.org/cgi/content/full/115/6/e626

Scorgie, Kate and Dick Sobsey. "Transformational Outcomes Associated with Parenting Children Who Have Disabilities." *Mental Retardation* 38, no. 3 (2000): 195-206.

Seltzer, Marsha Mailick, Jan S. Greenberg, Frank J. Floyd, Yvette Pettee, and Jinkuk Hong. "Life Course Impacts of Parenting a Child With a Disability." *American Journal on Mental Retardation* 106, no. 3 (2001): 265-286.

16. The Joy of Siblings

Fisman, Sandra, Lucille Wolf, Deborah Ellison, and Tom Freeman. "A Longitudinal Study of Siblings of Children With Chronic Disabilities." *The Canadian Journal of Psychiatry* 45, no. 4 (2000): 396-75. http://www.cpa-apc.org/Publications/Archives/CJP/2000/May/Chronic.asp

Mandleco, Barbara, Susanne Frost Olsen, Tina Dyches, and Elaine Marshall. "The Relationship Between Family and Sibling Functioning in Families Raising a Child with a Disability." *Journal of Family Nursing* 9, no. 4 (2003): 365-396.

Seltzer, Marsha Mailick, Jan S. Greenberg, Gael I. Orsmond, and Julie Lounds. "Life Course Studies of Siblings of Individuals with Developmental Disabilities." *Mental Retardation* 43, no. 5 (2005): 354-59.

Stoneman, Zolinda. "Siblings of Children with Disabilities: Research Themes." *Mental Retardation* 43, no. 5 (2005): 339-50.

PART V: OVERCOMING BARRIERS TO QUALITY CARE—CHILDHOOD THROUGH ADULTHOOD (INTRO)

Chase, Richard and Ellen Shelton. *Child Care for Children with Special Needs: Fundamental Facts from the Minnesota Child Care Survey.* Amherst H. Wilder Foundation, June 2002. http://www.wilder.org/reportsummary.0.html?&tx_ttnews[swords]=child%20care%20for%20 children%20with%20special%20needs&tx_ttnews[tt_news]=941&tx_ttnews[backPid]=311 &cHash=0a5a74b620.

Irwin, Sharon Hope and Donna S. Lero. *In Our Way: Child Care Barriers to Full Workforce Participation Experienced by Parents of Children with Special Needs—and Potential Remedies.* Wreck Cove, NS: Breton Books, 1997.

Rosenzweig, Julie M., Eileen M. Brennan, and A. Myrth Ogilvie. "Work-Family Fit: Voices of Parents of Children with Emotional and Behavioral Disorders." *Social Work* 47, no. 4 (2002): 415-424.

18. Figure Out What Type of Care You Need

Chase, Richard and Ellen Shelton. *Child Care for Children with Special Needs: Fundamental Facts from the Minnesota Child Care Survey.* Amherst H. Wilder Foundation, June 2002. http://www.wilder.org/reportsummary.0.html?&tx_ttnews[swords]=child%20care%20for%20 children%20with%20special%20needs&tx_ttnews[tt_news]=941&tx_ttnews[backPid]=311 &cHash=0a5a74b620.

Snyder, Kathleen, Timothy Dore, and Sarah Adelman. "Use of Relative Care by Working Parents." *Snapshots of America's Families* 3, no. 23. Urban Institute, April 2005. http://www.urban.org/UploadedPDF/311161_snapshots3_no23.pdf

Sonenstein, Freya L., Gary Gates, Stefanie R. Schmidt, and Natalya Bolshun, *Primary Care Arrangements of Employed Parents: Findings from the 1999 National Survey of America's Families.* Urban Institute, May 2002. http://www.urban.org/UploadedPDF/310487_OP59.pdf

United States Department of Labor, Bureau of Labor Statistics. "Workers on Flexible and Shift Schedules in 2004 Summary," news release, USDL 05-1198, July 1, 2005. http://www.bls.gov/news.release/flex.nr0.htm

20. The Hunt for Care
Wyn, Roberta, Victoria Ojeda, Usha Ranji, and Alina Salganicoff. "Women, Work, and Family Health: A Balancing Act." Issue Brief: An Update on Women's Health Policy. The Henry J. Kaiser Family Foundation, April 2003.
http://www.kff.org/womenshealth/loader.cfm?url=/commonspot/security/getfile.cfm&PageID=14293

22. Paying the Price for Quality Care
Geres, Kellie and Pat Cascio. *INA Nanny Salary and Benefits Survey 2003-2004 Part 1.* International Nanny Association, 2004. http://www.nanny.org/INA_Salary_Survey2.pdf

Schulman, Karen. *Issue Brief: The High Cost of Child Care Puts Quality Care Out of Reach for Many Families.* Children's Defense Fund, 2000.
http://www.childrensdefense.org/earlychildhood/childcare/highcost.pdf

PART VI: CAREER AND HOME—THE ULTIMATE JUGGLING ACT (INTRO)

Family Voices. "Family Impacts: A Fact Sheet on Findings." *The Family Partners Project: The Health Care Experiences of Families of Children with Special Health Care Needs.* 2000.
http://www.familyvoices.org/YourVoiceCounts/family-impacts.html

Home, Alice. "The Work that Never Ends: Employed Mothers of Children with Disabilities." *Journal of the Association for Research on Mothering* 6, no. 2 (2004): 37-47.

United States Department of Labor, Bureau of Labor Statistics. "Employment Characteristics of Families in 2004," news release, USDL 05-876, June 9, 2005.
http://www.bls.gov/news.release/pdf/famee.pdf

United States Department of Labor, Bureau of Labor Statistics. *Women in the Labor Force: A Databook.* Report 973, February 2004. http://www.bls.gov/cps/wlf-databook.pdf

23. Know Your Legal Rights at Work
Waldfogel, John. "Family and Medical Leave: Evidence from the 2000 Surveys." *Monthly Labor Review Online* 124, no. 9 (2001): 17-23. http://www.bls.gov/opub/mlr/2001/09/art2full.pdf

24. Build Workplace Support
Center for Child and Adolescent Health Policy, MassGeneral Hospital for Children. *Children with Special Needs and the Workplace: A Guide for Employers.* MassGeneral Hospital for Children, June 2004. http://www.massgeneral.org/MGHfc/pdf/EmployerGuide.pdf

25. Explore Flexible Work Options
Burke, Mary Elizabeth, Evren Esen, and Jessica Collison. "2003 Benefits Survey." SHRM Foundation, June 2003.
http://www.shrm.org/hrresources/surveys_published/2003%20Benefits%20Survey.pdf

Galinsky, Ellen and Bond, James T. "The 1998 Business Work-Life Study: Executive Summary." Families and Work Life Institute, 1998.
http://www.familiesandwork.org/summary/worklife.pdf

United States Department of Labor, Bureau of Labor Statistics. "Workers on Flexible and Shift Schedules in May 2004," news release, USDL 05-1198, July 1, 2005.
http://www.bls.gov/news.release/flex.nr0.htm

26. Cut Back, Take Off, or Call it Quits
Burke, Mary Elizabeth, Evren Esen, and Jessica Collison. "2003 Benefits Survey." SHRM Foundation, June 2003.
http://www.shrm.org/hrresources/surveys_published/2003%20Benefits%20Survey.pdf

Galinsky, Ellen and Bond, James T. "The 1998 Business Work-Life Study: Executive Summary." Families and Work Life Institute, 1998. http://www.familiesandwork.org/summary/worklife.pdf

Rosenzweig, Julie M., Eileen Brennan, Paul Koren, and Kitty Huffstutter. "Common Ground? Families, Employers and Education." Research & Training Center on Family Support and Children's Mental Health, Portland State University, 2004. http://www.rtc.pdx.edu/pgProjCommon.php

Waldfogel, John. "Family and Medical Leave: Evidence from the 2000 Surveys." *Monthly Labor Review Online* 124, no. 9 (2001): 17-23. http://www.bls.gov/opub/mlr/2001/09/art2full.pdf

U.S. Department of Health and Human Services, Health Resources and Services Administration, Maternal and Child Health Bureau. "Impact on Families." *The National Survey of Children with Special Health Care Needs Chartbook 2001*. U.S. Department of Health and Human Services, 2004. http://mchb.hrsa.gov/chscn/pages/impact.htm

PART VIII: TRANSFORMATIONS—FROM STRUGGLE TO STRENGTH

Scorgie, Kate and Dick Sobsey. "Transformational Outcomes Associated With Parenting Children Who Have Disabilities." *Mental Retardation* 38, no. 3 (2000): 195-206.

Appendix 1. State Leave Policies

Columbia University, Mailman School of Public Health, National Center for Children in Poverty. "Family and Medical Leave," National Center for Children in Poverty, July 2005. http://www.nccp.org/policy_index_29.html

National Partnership for Women & Families. *Expecting Better: A State-by-State Analysis of Parental Leave Programs*. National Partnership for Women & Families, June 2005. http://www.nationalpartnership.org/portals/p3/library/PaidLeave/ParentalLeaveReportMay05.pdf

National Partnership for Women & Families. *Get Well Soon: Americans Can't Afford to be Sick*. National Partnership for Women & Families, June 2004. http://www.nationalpartnership.org/portals/p3/library/PaidLeave/SickDays/GetWellSoon.pdf

National Conferences of State Legislatures. "State Family and Medical Leave Laws," January 2006. http://www.ncsl.org/programs/employ/fmlachart.htm

United States Department of Labor, Employment Standards Administration, Wage and Hour Division. "Federal vs. State Family and Medical Leave Laws," January 2006. http://www.dol.gov/esa/programs/whd/state/fmla

Appendix 2: Provincial (Canadian) Leave Policies

Government of Canada, Social Development Canada. "Annex B—Family Responsibility and Sick Leave Provisions in Employment Standards Legislation. *Addressing Work-Life Balance in Canada*, April 2005. http://www.sdc.gc.ca/asp/gateway.asp?hr=/en/lp/spila/wlb/awlbc/07annex_b.shtml&hs=wnc

Osborne, Katie, Naomi Margo, and Osborne Margo. *Analysis and Evaluation: Compassionate Care Benefit*. Health Council of Canada, December 2005. http://hcc-ccs.com/docs/Compassionate_Care_BenefitsEN.pdf

INDEX

Accommodations, 160-61, 320
Activities, family, 23
Acupuncture, 85
ADA
    childcare and, 275, 317, 324, 329
    employment and, 215, 344-45, 419
    higher education and, 214
ADHD, 27, 51, 172, 437
Adults with special needs
    coping styles of mothers, 106
    daytime programs for, 299-300, 305-06
    employment of, 215-17
    recreation for, 179
Advocacy
    advice for, 170-72
    at school, 177-79
    group, 182-85, 440
    hiring professional to do, 185-86
    importance of, 170
    in community, 173
    in medical settings, 174-76
    in religious setting, 181-82
    self, 172, 210
Aerobic exercise, 70
Affirmations, 36
Allergies, food, 65
Alliance for Technology Access, 165
America on the Move, 78
American Volksport Association, 78
Americans with Disabilities Act. See ADA
Angelman syndrome, 26, 153
Anger, 104-105, 171
Antidepressants, 116
Antioxidants, 57
Anxiety. See also Worries
    alternative treatments for, 118
    counseling for, 115
    exercise and, 70
    generalized anxiety disorder and, 99
    panic attack and, 99-100
    symptoms of, 99
    treatment for, 116-18
Appetite, changes in, 50
ARCH National Respite Network, 155
Asperger syndrome, 22, 24, 26, 40, 175, 178,
    238, 415, 427, 437, 439
Assertiveness, 117
Assistive Technology Act, 164
Au pairs, 284-87
Authentic Happiness, 11

Autism
    advocacy, 183, 187
    mothers' comments about, 7, 24, 40, 90,
        216, 317, 383, 437
    mothers of children with, 101, 108
    Omega 3s and, 51
Babysitting. *See* Child care
Balls, exercise, 73
Bartering, 200
Baskin, Amy, 25, 43, 428
Beans, 58-59
Behavior, children's
    as grounds for exclusion from programs, 180
    connection to parents' stress, 114
    disagreements about, 267, 268
    effects of on mother's mental health,
        101-102
    tantrums, 99
Berman, Deb, 351, 401, 415
Best Buddies, 162, 303
Beverages, 59
Binders
    for information about child, 144
    for medical information, 143, 176
    for school information, 142
Book exchange, 26
Book hike, 78
Brain injury, 101
Brothers and sisters. *See* Siblings
Calendars, 141
Camps, summer, 153, 166, 296-97, 304-305
Canada Human Rights Act, 345
Cancer, 50, 57
Care Notebook, 143
Care Organizer, 143
Career counseling, 387
Career interests and aptitudes, 387-92.
        See also Work
Cerebral palsy, 101, 118, 157, 266, 329
Changed by a Child, 260
Child care
    after-school programs and, 289-90
    assessing needs for, 278-79
    backup, 316-17
    barriers to, 275-76
    centers, 282-83
    checklists for, 457-60
    communicating with providers of, 322
    cost of, 327-28
    deciding on, 315-16

ensuring quality of, 311-12
evaluating, 313-15
financial assistance with, 328-30
for older people with disabilities, 276,
    299-300, 303-306
for sick children, 316
good relationships with providers of, 321-22
home providers of, 283-84
honesty about needs for, 319-20
inclusive, 279-80
involving husband in, 243-45, 287
in your home, 134-35
law related to, 275-76, 317, 320, 324
licensed, 311-12
locating, 308-10
medical care and, 321
mother's helpers and, 292-93
nannies/au pairs and, 284-87, 312, 327-28
problems with, 323-25
reasonable accommodations and, 320
relatives' roles in, 270-71, 280-81
respite care, 152-56
short-term, 250
siblings' roles in, 262-63
special needs related to, 329-30
special needs workers and, 290-92
tax deductions for, 330-32
therapy and, 329
training caregivers and, 321, 324
taking short breaks from, 21-23
unconventional solutions to, 302
while exercising, 76-77, 250
Child Find, 157
Childproofing, 93
Children with special needs. *See also*
    Behavior, children's
costs of raising, 190
exercising with, 77-78
lifting, 69, 72
positive effects of, on mothers, 438-44
sleep problems of, 90-94
tantrums and, 99
teaching life skills to, 134, 138, 207-10, 401
time spent caring for, 127
CHIP, 195
Chocolate, 53
Cholesterol, 58
Chores. *See* Housekeeping
Cleaning, 139
Clothing, reducing costs of, 198-99
Clubs, 394
Clutter, 146-47. *See also* Organization
COBRA, 379
Cognitive behavioral techniques, 108, 117
College
for mothers, 391-93

for students with special needs, 214-15, 229
Communication books, 322
Conferences, 192
Continuing education, 393
Control, lack of, 107, 108
Cooking, 63, 138-38
Cooking club, 61, 63
Coping
accommodative, 10, 106
styles of, 105-107
Counseling
finding, 118-19
professionals who provide, 115-16
reasons to seek, 114
stigma of, 114
Counselor in Training, 304
Crises, mental health, 119-20
Day care. *See* Child care
Death, thoughts of, 98, 101
Denial, 238, 267
Dependent Care Assistance Plans, 330
Depression. *See also* Mood
alternative treatments for, 118
anger and, 104
appetite changes and, 50
chronic, 104
counseling for, 114-15
distracting self from, 110-12
effects of on marriage, 115
effects of on sleep, 83
in children, 114, 256
incidence of, 101
Omega 3s and, 51
relationships and, 110
risk factors for, 107, 108
symptoms of, 101, 102-03
treatment for, 116-18
Dietitians, 55-56
Diets, 52-53. *See also* Food
Discrimination, at work, 345-46, 375, 377
Divorce
custody agreements and, 229
parents of children with disabilities and,
    235-36
Doctors, 174-76. *See also* Medical appointments
Documents, organizing, 142-45
Doing it all, 128, 400
Down syndrome
advocacy and, 440
childcare and, 323
grandparents of children with, 269
medical problems and, 375
mothers' comments about, 23, 41, 104,
    178, 186, 272, 275, 295, 353, 355, 370
optimism and, 108
Drowsiness. *See* Sleep

Dysthymia, 104
Early intervention, 157-58, 279, 293-94, 329
Eating. *See* Cooking; Foods
Ellis, Albert, 108
Emotions. *See also* Anger; Happiness; Worry
  mothers' descriptions of, 437-38
  professionals who can help with, 114-15
  siblings', 257
  styles of coping with, 105-107, 237-38
Employment. *See* Work
Employment rates
  of adults with disabilities, 215
  of mothers, 337
Endorphins, 49
Energy, lack of, 98
Engagement, in life, 11
Equipment, cutting costs on, 192-93
Errands, 260. *See also* Shopping
Estate planning
  guardianship, 227-28
  lack of, 221-22
  letter of intent, 223-24, 225-26
  trusts, 212, 224, 227
  wills, 222-23
e-therapists, 119
Exercise
  aerobic, 70
  avoiding before bed, 86
  benefits of, 68-71
  childcare during, 76-77, 250
  during everyday activities, 71
  easy ways to increase, 78-79
  getting started with, 73-74
  making time for, 69
  motivating self to do, 75-76
  relaxation, 85
  setting goals for, 71-73
  with children, 77-78
  with friends, 42-43
Expenses, household, 197-202
Expenses, special needs
  examples of, 189-90
  financial assistance for, 163-67, 190-91
  for child care, 278
  for home-based businesses, 426-27
  reducing, 191-95
  tax-deductible, 203
Extended family. *See* Grandparents and
  extended family
Extended school year programs, 297-98
Faith. *See* Religion
Families and Work Institute, 7
Family activities, 23. *See also* Fun; Recreation
Family Medical Leave Act, 340-41, 345,
  368, 371
Fatigue. *See* Sleep

Fawcett, Heather, 26, 56, 439
Fetal alcohol syndrome, 36
Financial assistance. *See also* Expenses
  for children's needs, 163-67, 190-91
  for college, 392-93
Financial planning, 203, 390-91
Fish, 51
Fitness, 34. *See also* Exercise
Flexible Spending Accounts, 194, 330
Flextime, 358
Floortime, 128
FMLA. *See* Family Medical Leave Act
Foods
  child's resistance to, 64-65
  craving, 53-54
  eating at bedtime, 86
  frequency of eating, 61
  healthy, 57-64
  iron rich, 52
  labels on, 60
  mood and, 50
  Omega-3s and, 50-51
  snacks, 53, 54, 55, 59, 61, 62
  stress and, 49-50
Fragile X syndrome, 175
Friends. *See also* Socializing
  depression and, 110
  exercising with, 74
  finding and keeping, 41-44, 441
  finding time for, 24
  happiness and, 39
  impediments to having, 39-41
  siblings', 259
Fruit, 57, 59-60
Fun
  impact of children on, 257
  planning for, 30-33, 148
Funding, sources of, 163-67
Future, planning for child's, 206-19, 263.
  See also Estate planning
Generalized anxiety disorder, 99
Gill, Barbara, 260
Goals, redefining, 383
Gover, Tzivia, 36, 87
Grandparents and extended family
  communicating with, 267-68
  educating, 268-69
  reactions of, 266-67
  requesting support from, 270-71
  serious conflicts with, 271-72
Guindon, Cheryl, 73
Happiness. *See also* Fun
  factors contributing to, 10, 39
  levels of, 10-12
  checklist for rating level of, 12-13
Head Start, 294-95

Health insurance. *See* Insurance, health
Health Insurance Portability &
    Accountability Act (HIPAA), 379
Health, mothers', 67
Hearing impairment, 238, 437
Help. *See* Respite care; Support
Hobbies, 27-29
Home, Alice, 338
Home-based businesses
    benefits of, 424-25
    deciding whether to start, 425-28
    examples of, 425, 426, 431-33
    employment of children in, 242-25
    isolation of, 24
    maintaining professional image and, 430-31
    online resources for, 433
    pitfalls of, 428-30
Homeopathy, 85
Home schooling, 106
Hopelessness, 97
Housekeeping
    delegating, 134-35
    paying for, 135-36
    reducing amount of, 129-34
    tips for making easier, 136-40
Housing
    modifications, 164
    options for adults with special needs, 211-12
Human Rights Codes, 339, 345
Humor, 112-13
Husbands
    helping learn about disability, 239
    parenting differences with, 241
    uneven role in parenting and, 241-45
Hydrocephalus, 113, 179, 379
IDEA, 157, 159, 215, 279
IEP, 159, 329
IFSP, 158, 329
Illnesses, 67
Inclusion, 279-80
Independence, skills for, 134, 138, 207-10
Insomnia, 83-87
Insurance, health
    assessing, 421
    dependent coverage and, 229
    employer's requirement to provide, 344
    for the self-employed, 427
    getting payments from, 176-77
    inadequate, 166
    keeping when quitting job, 379
    paperwork, 144
    programs and waivers, 195-97
Insurance, unemployment, 341
Interests, career, 388-89
Internet support groups, 46
Interpersonal therapy, 117

Interviews
    disclosing personal information at, 419-21
    informational, 414
    job, 415-20
Irritability. *See* Depression; Stress; Worries
Isolation, 25. *See also* Friends; Socializing;
    Support groups
Jobs. *See* Careers; Work
Joubert's syndrome, 22
Joyce, Amy, 348, 377, 412
Juice, 59
Kataria, Madan, 113
Katie Beckett waiver, 196
Laughter yoga, 113
Laundry, 138
Learned Optimism, 109
Learning disabilities, 51
Leave, from work, 340-44, 365, 373-77, 447-53
Lennox Gastaut syndrome, 41
Lero, Donna, 426
Letters
    cover, 416
    requesting job flexibility, 455-56
Life skills plan, 208-10
Lists, 111
Love, 10, 443. *See also* Marriage
Lunches, packing, 137
Marriage. *See also* Divorce; Husbands
    counseling, 245-46
    effects of depression on, 115
    effects of on mental health, 110
    keeping romance in, 249-52
    lack of couple's time and, 247-48
    parenting conflicts and, 238-45
Meals, 61-64. *See also* Cooking; Foods
Meaningfulness, of life, 11, 112, 442
Meat, 59
Medicaid
    Home and Community service waivers,
        196, 324
    "medically needy" coverage, 196
    waivers for respite care, 153
Medical appointments
    children's, 368
    mothers', 67-68
Medical problems, 55, 324, 368, 375, 438
Medication
    for mental health issues, 116-17
    paying for, 193
Meditation, 35, 70, 87, 92
Melatonin, 85
Mental health. *See also* Anxiety; Depression;
    Stress
    crises, 119-20
    disorders, 27
    professionals, 114-15, 118-19

Mercury, 51
Microboard, 218
Migraines, 56
Mindful Moments for Stressful Days, 36, 87
Mindfulness, 35, 112
Montfort, Helen, 142
Mood
    diet and, 50
    exercise and, 69, 70
Mothers, of children with special needs
    incidence of depression in, 101
    numbers employed, 337, 378
    single, 252-53
    transformation of, over time, 438-44
Mothers, stay-at-home. *See* Stay-at-home
    mothers
Muscular dystrophy, 40, 101, 119, 256, 267,
    427, 437
Nannies, 284-87
Napping, 84, 89
National Survey of Children with Special
    Health Care Needs, 3
Naturopaths, 56, 95
Networking, 412-14
Nonprofit organizations, working for, 357
Notebooks. *See* Binders
Nurses, 357
Nutrition information, 60. *See also* Foods
Nutritionists, 55-56
Obsessive-compulsive behaviors, 104
Occupational therapists, 95, 134
Oils, cooking, 58
Omega 3 fatty acids, 50-51, 58
Optimism, 108-109
Organization, personal
    calendars and, 141
    de-cluttering and, 146-47
    of documents, 142-45, 171-72
    weekly, 140-41
Organizations, community, 161-63. *See also*
    Support
Panic attacks, 99-100
Papers, organizing, 142-45
PASS, 163, 217
Pearson, Liz, 51, 53
Pedometers, 74
Peer buddies, 303
Peers, at daycare, 323
Person-centered planning, 217-19
Pessimism, 108
Peterson, Christopher, 10, 11, 108
Physical therapists, 95
Picky eaters, 65
Prayer, 35
Preschool, 158-60, 288-89, 329
Priorities, mothers', 7-9

Problem-solving, steps for, 107
Protection and Advocacy systems, 186
Psychiatrists, 115
Psychodynamic therapy, 118
Psychologists, 115
Psychology, positive, 10, 108-109
Psychotherapy, 117-18
Reasonable accommodations. *See*
    Accommodations
Recreational activities
    clubs, 394
    for children, 179-80, 295-96
    restrictions on, 257
Red tape, 152
References, caregivers', 315-16
Rehabilitation Act of 1973, 160-61, 214
Related services, 158
Relationships. *See also* Friends; Marriage
    counseling for problems with, 117
    effects of on happiness, 10
Relaxation exercise, 85-86
Religion
    as source of meaning and happiness, 12,
        442-43
    children with disabilities and, 181-82
    mental health and, 34
Rent-to-Own Network, 219
Research, participating in, 185, 194
Resilience, keys to, 233
RESNA, 164
Respite care, 152-56, 251, 292, 298-99
Resumes, 401-09
Rett syndrome, 6, 8, 106, 176, 191, 266, 444
Rosenbaum, Peter, 101, 236
Rosenzwieg, Julie, 275
Routine, family, 146
Satisfaction, with life, 11. *See also* Happiness
Schizophrenia, 101, 108
Schools. *See also* College; Special education
    advocating at, 177-79
    extended school year and, 297-98
    kindergarten and, 288-89
    post-secondary, 213-15
    transitioning from, 213
Scorgie, Kate, 236, 438
Section 504, 160-61, 214
Sedatives, 85
Self-confidence, 107
Self-employment. *See* Home-based businesses
Seligman, Martin, 11, 109
Share Equity Housing Project, 219
Shopping
    cost-saving measures and, 200-202
    grocery, 61, 63, 148
Siblings
    as caregivers, 262-63

emotions of, 257
finding peers for, 259
mothers' worries about, 256-57
ways to support, 258-62
Single mothers and romance, 252-53
Sleep
deficit, 87-88
determining amount needed, 82
effects of child on mother's, 88-89
effects of depression on, 83
effects of food on, 55
effects of inadequate, 81-82
improving child's 90-94
insomnia and, 83-87
studies, 94-95
Snacks, 53, 54, 55, 59, 61, 62. *See also* Foods
Sobsey, Dick, 236, 438
Socializing. *See* Friends; Relationships
Social workers, 115
Special education, 158-60
Spina bifida, 39, 113
Spinks, Nora, 348, 349, 361, 418
Spirituality, 34-35. *See also* Religion
SSRIs, 116
Stairs, 79
State Children's Health Insurance Program, 195
Stay-at-home mothers, 43-44
Stress. *See also* Anxiety; Depression; Worries
advocacy and, 187
as cause of premature aging, 114
at work, 357-58, 429
food cravings and, 49
steps for managing, 110-13
symptoms of too much, 17, 98
typical ways to handle, 97
Strength, 69
Suicide, considering, 98, 101, 102
Support
finding sources of, 152
groups, 44-46, 394
requesting from family, 270-71
Tai Chi, 69, 86
Tantrums, 99
Taxes, 203, 330-32
Teasing, 173
Telecommuting, 359
Telework, 164
Therapy. *See* Counseling; Early intervention; Psychotherapy
"Time burden," 127
Time Dollar Institute, 200
Time management
for sibling activities, 263
making plan for, 128-34
Toilet training, 323

Tourette syndrome, 27, 373
Tranquilizers, 116
Transportation, for adults with disabilities, 216, 219
Trusts. *See* Estate planning
Ultimate Healthy Eating Plan, The, 51
Vacations, 251, 261
Vitamins, 51-52
Volunteering, 129, 172, 322, 391, 395-97
Walking, 73, 74
Water, 59
Weekends, 147-49
Weight gain/loss, 50, 54, 61. *See also* Exercise; Foods
Whole grains, 57
Wills. *See* Estate planning
Wilson, Steve, 113
Work. *See also* Careers; Resumes
absences from, 368-69
accepting an offer of, 421-22
analyzing stresses at, 357-58
and statistics related to mothers, 337, 349, 378
at home, 423-34
being fired from, 345
benefits of, 338
developing skills for, 26
disclosing child's disability at, 348-51
discrimination, 345-46, 377
flexibility at, 355-66
husbands' long hours at, 242
interviewing for, 415-20
job sharing at, 371-72
laws related to, 340-45
leave from, 340-44, 365, 373-77
legal complaints about, 345-46
missing stimulation of, 25-27
negative experiences at, 347
negotiating for changes at, 361-64, 377
options for adults with special needs, 215-17
part-time, 370-71, 411, 429
quitting, 378-79
returning to, 27, 395, 399-401
searching for, 412-14
shift, 248, 287-88, 359
supervisors at, 348, 363
support from coworkers at, 351-53
switching to less demanding, 373, 442
telecommuting, 359
temporary, 394
upgrading skills for, 391-97
volunteering and, 395-97
Worries. 84, 87, 99. *See also* Anxiety; Stress
Writing, therapeutic, 111
Yoga, 69, 70

ACKNOWLEDGEMENTS

We want to express our thanks to the hundreds of women who openly shared their life experiences and expertise. Their collective wisdom brings heart, soul, and hope to the pages.

Thank you to the dozens of organizations and support groups that helped us find women to take part in our surveys, by posting requests on their websites, and in newsletters and magazines. We'd especially like to acknowledge the National Down Syndrome Society, United Cerebral Palsy, and Autism Society Ontario who embraced our project wholeheartedly, making room on their busy websites for our mothers' questionnaire.

We are grateful to our editor, Lisa Barrett Mann, for asking the hard questions and pushing us to deepen and expand the book. Thank you to Susan Stokes, Fran Marinaccio, and the team at Woodbine House who believe in families and the power of books to enrich their lives.

We are grateful to the social workers, doctors, psychologists, fitness and health professionals, organizational consultants, business experts, researchers, and graduate students who shared their expertise through interviews and by sending us key research studies.

Special thanks to Jack Kesselman and David Lapp for many hours of computer assistance.

We would like to thank the writers who offered encouragement and advice—especially Ann Douglas (for her mentoring in book proposal writing), Teresa Pitman, Julie Stauffer, and members of the Guelph Chapter of the Professional Writers Association of Canada.

Heather would like to thank her Asperger Syndrome parent support group and the Ottawa autism community for their continued interest and encouragement. She would especially like to thank her support group co-facilitator Heather Pierscianowski for cheerfully handling added work when deadlines were pressing. Heartfelt thanks to her family—to her children, Robyn and Karin, for putting up with her long hours in front of the computer. To her husband, Dave, for his advice and willingness to listen. And to her friends and extended family who frequently re-inspired her to see this project as something special during times when the scope of it felt overwhelming.

Amy would like to thank her friends for helping her escape her computer for everything from fitness classes to movies and knitting parties. She would like to acknowledge the support of Gerda MacLeod, a superb educator and family friend. Thanks to Marvin Baskin, Eliot and Hilary Baskin, and Rachelle Kesselman for their cheerleading. Most of all, she thanks her husband, Jack, and daughters Leah and Talia for encouragement, practical support, and endless inspiration.

ABOUT THE AUTHORS

Amy Baskin is a writer, teacher, and public speaker. She has a Master of Adult Education degree and a teaching degree in Special Education from the University of Toronto. She writes about parenting, women, education, and disability issues for magazines across North America. She lives with her husband and two daughters in Guelph, Ontario, Canada. Her youngest child has autism.

Heather Fawcett is a writer who is active in special-needs advocacy. She chairs an Asperger syndrome parent support group serving 400 family and professional members in her community. She has earned multiple B.A. degrees in English, Applied Studies, and Psychology from the University of Waterloo and Carleton University. A mother of two, she resides in Ottawa, Ontario, Canada with her husband and children. Her oldest daughter has Asperger syndrome.

45129958R00279

Made in the USA
Charleston, SC
16 August 2015